101 Labs for the Cisco CCNA Exam

Hands-on Practical Labs for the Cisco CCENT and CCNA Exam

Paul Browning (LLB Hons), CCNP, MCSE
Farai Tafa, dual CCIE

LEGAL NOTICE

The advice in this book is designed to assist you in reaching the required standard for the CCENT/ICND1 and CCNA exams. The labs are designed to illustrate various learning points and are not suggested configurations to apply to a production network. Please check all your configurations with a qualified Cisco professional. Many of the commands, including debugs and clearing the IP routing table, can cause serious performance issues on live networks.

About the Authors

Paul Browning

Paul is the author of CCNA Simplified, which is one of the industry's leading CCNA study guides. He used to work for Cisco TAC but left in 2002 to start his own Cisco training company in the UK. Paul has taught over 2,000 Cisco engineers with both his classroom courses and online Cisco training site, www.howtonetwork.com.

Paul lives in Australia with his wife and daughters.

Farai Tafa

Farai is a dual CCIE in both Routing and Switching and Service Provider. He currently works for one of the world's largest telecom companies as a network engineer. He has written workbooks for the CCNA, CCNP, and Cisco Security exams.

Farai lives in Washington, D.C., with his wife and daughter.

Table of Contents

Introduction to the 2nd Edition

It's hard to believe that I wrote the first edition of this book in 2009.

Back then, the CCNA exam was mostly theory with a couple of labs thrown in. Scroll forward eight years and the exam is mostly hands-on labs and practical questions with some theory thrown in.

A hands-on lab manual was needed because there was a huge gap in the market for a practical manual. Most CCNA books are very theory heavy with a few labs thrown in. My CCNA study manuals *Cisco CCNA Simplified* and *Cisco CCNA in 60 Days* addressed this problem by being very lab heavy. After feedback from my students, I felt that most people would need an extra boost of practical experience for the CCNA exam.

In the CCNA exam, you can expect to be tested on the following hands-on scenarios:

1. Configure a lab according to specifications.
2. Troubleshoot and resolve a broken network or technology (e.g., ACL not working).
3. Use `show` commands to determine an issue or configuration and answer questions.

It gets even harder when you realize that you are not familiar with the topology and IP addressing scheme, and you will see the clock counting down before your eyes. You will be working on a router or switch emulator that only runs a limited number of IOS commands so some of your shortcuts may not work, such as `sh ip int brie` instead of `show ip interface brief`.

The goal of this lab manual is to get your hands-on skills way past the level required for the CCNA exam so when it comes to exam day, you will find the lab scenarios a breeze. I've had many of my students finish their exam with 30 minutes to spare because they solved the scenarios so quickly! This is where you should aim to be.

The fact that you have this book in your hands means that you are studying for your CCNA or CCENT exam or perhaps just want to polish your hands-on Cisco skills. Whatever your reason, we admire you for putting the effort into improving your hands-on ability.

We have marked the labs as either ICND1, ICND2, CCNA, or CCENT, but please do double-check the syllabus before you take the exam. We have also rated each lab on a scale of 1 to 10 for difficulty and have given you timings so you will know when you are ready for the real thing.

Best of luck with your studies.

Paul Browning—CCNP
Farai Tafa—CCIE (RS & SP) 14811

HOW TO USE THIS BOOK

First, this book is designed to cement the theory you have read in your CCNA study guide. If you don't have a good-quality study guide at the moment, then we highly recommend one of our CCNA study guides—*CCNA Simplified* or *Cisco CCNA in 60 Days*—which you can purchase on Amazon in printed or Kindle format. *CCNA Simplified* is targeted at those who want to approach the exams at a leisurely pace, while *CCNA in 60 Days* is available to those who want to pass the exams quickly and need a well-defined structure to follow as opposed to working on their own study plan.

The goal is to dramatically improve your hands-on knowledge and speed. We don't have the space here to cover the theory at all, so please refer to your CCNA study guide to get a good understanding of the learning points behind each lab. Every lab is designed to cover a particular theory issue, such as configuration requirements of RIP passive interfaces. As the labs progress, common commands such as how to create VLANs or add IP addresses to interfaces will not be repeated. This not only saves space but after a couple of labs, you should really know how to do these commands. I am telling you this because I had a few complaints from readers about not spelling out how to add an IP address to an interface, but by the time you are configuring advanced access lists, you really should know how to do that without being prompted!

If you want to take the two-exam route, Section One of the book covers the ICND1 topics, while Section Two presents the ICND2 topics. Each lab is followed by a solution so you can check yours against ours. Please bear in mind that Cisco has some subjects listed in both the ICND1 and ICND2 sections, such as native VLANs. Cisco also reserves the right to ask questions on the exam that are not even in the syllabus. I'm mentioning this because I sometimes get an e-mail from an angry student blaming me for the fact that something came up on the exam that I didn't cover.

Cisco also inserts test questions into the exam that are not marked, so don't sweat too much if something out of the ordinary appears. I took a Cisco switching exam once and an EIGRP routing question appeared on the screen! Do your best to answer it and move on.

As you progress through the labs, you will be given less and less configuration commands to follow, and instead you will simply refer to steps from previous labs. This is to cement the learning for you as well as to save space and time. The ICND1 and ICND2 sections finish with challenge labs but with a running configuration instead of a full solution.

Look at the challenge and configure as much as you can without looking at the solution. After you finish, check your solution against ours. Sometimes there is more than one way to configure a particular technology, so don't kick yourself if your solution works but is different than ours.

Hands-on Options

The best solution is to have your own home lab featuring Cisco routers and switches that you can cable up. Cisco tests you on the 15.X IOS release and the 2960 model of switch. There are various companies selling kits on eBay so check those out. You can resell them after your exam.

GNS3 is a free router emulator. You can drag and drop routers and switches to easily create different topologies. You need to supply your own IOS and these are only legally available via Cisco, so this may prove a challenge to many students. Try it out for yourself though.

Router simulators are available from a small number of companies. These do not run Cisco IOS but a programmer has created a number of commands that you can try out. I do not recommend that you use these because they aren't able to create flexible topologies and they don't act in the same way actual devices do.

A few companies offer remote racks of live equipment. The number is fairly limited due to the costs of hosting the equipment, and of course somebody needs to physically attend to the site at times to recover it in some cases. Cisco offers a live lab solution, and there are two full racks available 24/7 to all members of **https://www.howtonetwork.com.**

The last and best option for most students is Packet Tracer, which is now a free download from Cisco. It's still an emulator but you can drag IP phones, routers, switches, and other devices to create fairly complex topologies. It acts in a very similar way to actual equipment but doesn't offer all of the available commands. It's good enough for the CCNA exam level but be aware that not all syllabus topics are supported, for example, extended VLANs.

If you do not like router output interrupting you as you configure the labs, then please add the `logging synchronous` command to the console 0 line as shown below:

```
Router#config t
Router(config)#line console 0
Router(config-line)#logging synchronous
```

A Note about Interfaces

We have configured all of these labs on either our own Cisco equipment or the live racks at https://www.howtonetwork.com. Our interfaces match the diagrams for each lab, but please note that your equipment may have different interface numbers depending on the model. If you plugged your WIC card into a different slot, it may be numbered 0/0, 0/1, 1/0, 0/0/1, and so on. The best way to find your interface number is to issue the `show ip interface brief` command, and then mark it on the diagram. Even better, draw your own network diagram.

We have done our best to prepare you for the real world of Cisco internetworking. To this end, we have abbreviated many of the commands. Nobody in the real world types `config terminal` to enter configuration mode on a router, but rather `conf t` usually. In the exam, you will be using a router simulator though, so please understand the full version of the command just in case the shortened version doesn't work.

Are You Exam Ready?

The labs here are designed to prepare you well beyond the exam level and, of course, give you a strong foundation for real-world Cisco internetworking. But they are just the beginning. Before you take the actual exam, ensure that you can complete all the labs without looking at the solutions. Then change up the IP addressing scheme, change the interface types (if applicable), and add more routers or switches. Read up on the `configuration` and `show` commands using Cisco IOS documentation.

You should be very familiar with all the ways that the technology can be broken, the relevant `show` command(s) to establish whether your theory is correct, and, of course, how to fix any issues and finally prove that the scenario is working with relevant `debug` or `show` commands, or even a packet sniffer.

The sign of a student who I know will pass the exam is having a real interest in unpacking how the protocol works using theory, labs, and practice exams. Once you can do this you can easily plan, configure, verify, and troubleshoot anything in the syllabus. In fact, as soon as you look at a topology, you will know which commands should be present and which routes should be in the table (for example) on which router.

Help—My Lab Isn't Working

A big part of being a network engineer is troubleshooting. Most of the mistakes you will make will result from mistyping stuff or misreading the instructions. It's okay because this is part of the learning process. Double-check your configurations and then the solution.

Please do bear in mind that different IOS versions support different commands. Packet Tracer doesn't support everything in the CCNA syllabus (such as extended VLANS) so no matter how hard you try, the commands just won't work. GNS3 isn't live equipment so the `clock rate` command won't work as it does on live equipment. The Telnet lines on most equipment go from 0 to 15, but on GNS3 it's 0 to 903. If you try to configure a local password on the Telnet lines before adding a password on GNS3, you will get 1,001 error messages like the ones below:

```
% Login disabled on line 999, until 'password' is set
% Login disabled on line 1000, until 'password' is set
% Login disabled on line 1001, until 'password' is set
```

If things aren't working for you the way you expect, then check your configurations. Check that the commands are supported on your platform (via the Cisco IOS feature set/platform tool) or just Google it. Try the lab out on PT and then GNS3, and if all else fails, get some time on live equipment if you can. Nothing beats it.

For most of the labs we used live equipment, so some of your options and outputs may differ. Some commands may not be available to you and some of our show runs may differ slightly because Cisco enables/disables features depending on the IOS release and platform. If you see some slight differences, don't let this trouble you too much, especially if you choose to use Packet Tracer, which offers a limited set of commands and debugs.

Leave the lab and come back to it later with a fresh pair of eyes. Get a colleague to check it over or post the issue on a forum as a last resort.

101 CCNA LABS VIDEO COURSE

After writing this book, I had a large number of requests for a video course with me explaining the scenario and talking students through the solutions. I eventually did this and have put it on Udemy. The course matches most of this book with a few changes here and there. You certainly don't need to use it but if you learn best by watching an instructor, then the link is below. I've added a coupon so that you can get access for $10, which covers the cost of the video production software and the weeks of work that went into creating it.

https://www.udemy.com/101-cisco-ccna-labs/

Enter the coupon code below at checkout and the price will drop to $10:

101CCNA

Or use the direct URL below:

https://www.udemy.com/101-cisco-ccna-labs/?couponCode=101CCNA

Once again, you don't need the video course because I've designed this book as a stand-alone product, but if you want some extra teaching and have 10 bucks to spare, then check it out. Over 5,000 students have used it at the time of writing this new edition. Please drop me a review if you like it.

You can also post questions and requests on that platform, and there is a certificate of completion.

ICND1: 100-105

1.0 Network Fundamentals

LAB 1: CONFIGURE, VERIFY, AND TROUBLESHOOT IPV4 ADDRESSES

Lab Objective:
The objective of this lab exercise is for you to learn and understand how to create and troubleshoot IPv4 addresses on Cisco routers.

Lab Purpose:
Configuring IPv4 addressing is one of your most fundamental tasks as a Cisco engineer. In the exam, you may also be asked to troubleshoot IPv4 addressing that has already been configured but incorrectly, so you need to know which show commands to use.

Certification Level:
This lab is suitable for CCENT certification exam preparation.

Lab Difficulty:
This lab has a difficulty rating of 2/10.

Readiness Assessment:
When you are ready for your certification exam, you should complete this lab in no more than 10 minutes.

Lab Topology:
Please use the following topology to complete this lab exercise:

INTERFACE	IP ADDRESS
Loopback10	10.10.10.3/25
Loopback20	10.20.20.3/28
Loopback30	10.30.30.3/29

Task 1:

Configure the hostnames on routers R1 and R3 as illustrated in the topology.

Task 2:

Configure R1 S0/0, which is a DCE, to provide a clock rate of 768 Kbps to R3 (unless you are using GNS3). Configure the IP addresses on the Serial interfaces of R1 and R3 as illustrated in the topology. Configure the Loopback interfaces specified in the diagram on R1 and R3.

Task 3:

Use the correct show commands to check:

1. The summary of all configured IP addresses;
2. The status of the interface (up/down or administratively down); and
3. The subnet mask applied to the interface.

LAB 1: CONFIGURATION AND VERIFICATION

Task 1:
```
Router#config t
Enter configuration commands, one per line.  End with CTRL/Z.
Router(config)#hostname R1

Router#config t
Enter configuration commands, one per line.  End with CTRL/Z.
Router(config)#hostname R3
R3(config)#
```

Task 2:
```
R1(config)#interface s0/0
R1(config-if)#ip add 172.16.1.1 255.255.255.192
R1(config-if)#no shut

R3(config)#interface s0/0
R3(config-if)#ip add 172.16.1.2 255.255.255.192
R3(config-if)#no shut
R3(config)#interface lo10
R3(config-if)#ip add 10.10.10.3 255.255.255.128
R3(config)#interface lo20
R3(config-if)#ip add 10.20.20.3 255.255.255.240
R3(config)#interface lo30
R3(config-if)#ip add 10.30.30.3 255.255.255.248
```

Task 3:
```
R3#show ip int brie
Interface       IP-Address   OK? Method Status                 Protocol
FastEthernet0/0 unassigned   YES unset  administratively down down
Serial0/0       172.16.1.2   YES manual up                     up
Loopback10      10.10.10.3   YES manual up                     up
Loopback20      10.20.20.3   YES manual up                     up
Loopback30      10.30.30.3   ES  manual up                     up

R3#show interface s0/0
Serial0/0 is up, line protocol is up
  Hardware is GT96K Serial
  Internet address is 172.16.1.2/26
  MTU 1500 bytes, BW 1544 Kbit/sec, DLY 20000 usec,
     reliability 255/255, txload 1/255, rxload 1/255
  Encapsulation HDLC, loopback not set
```

LAB 2: CONFIGURE, VERIFY, AND TROUBLESHOOT IPV6 ADDRESSES

Lab Objective:
The objective of this lab exercise is for you to learn and understand how to create and troubleshoot IPv6 addresses on Cisco routers.

Lab Purpose:
Configuring IPv6 addressing is one of your most fundamental tasks as a Cisco engineer. In the exam, you may also be asked to troubleshoot IPv6 addressing that has been incorrectly configured, so you need to know which show commands to use.

Certification Level:
This lab is suitable for CCENT certification exam preparation.

Lab Difficulty:
This lab has a difficulty rating of 2/10.

Readiness Assessment:
When you are ready for your certification exam, you should complete this lab in no more than 10 minutes.

Lab Topology:
Please use the following topology to complete this lab exercise:

Task 1:
Configure the hostnames on routers R1 and R3 as illustrated in the topology.

Task 2:
Configure R1 S0/0, which is a DCE, to provide a clock rate of 768 Kbps to R3 (unless you are using GNS3). Configure the IP addresses on the Serial interfaces of R1 and R3 as illustrated in the topology. Configure the Loopback interfaces specified in the diagram on R1 and R3.

Task 3:

Use the correct show commands to check:

1. The summary of all configured IPv6 addresses (note the need to specify IPv6 in the show commands);
2. The status of the interface (up/down or administratively down); and
3. The subnet mask applied to the interface.

LAB 2: CONFIGURATION AND VERIFICATION

Task 1:
```
Router#config t
Enter configuration commands, one per line.  End with CTRL/Z.
Router(config)#hostname R1
R1(config)#

Router#config t
Enter configuration commands, one per line.  End with CTRL/Z.
Router(config)#hostname R3
R3(config)#
```

Task 2:
```
R1(config)#ipv6 unicast-routing
R1(config)#interface s0/0
R1(config-if)#ipv6 add 2001:abcd:abcd::1/64
R1(config-if)#no shut

R3(config)#ipv6 unicast-routing
R3(config)#interface s0/0
R3(config-if)#ipv6 add 2001:abcd:abcd::2/64
R3(config-if)#no shut
R3(config)#interface lo0
R3(config-if)#ipv6 add 2001::5/64
```

Task 3:
```
R3#show ipv6 int brief
Serial0/0                      [up/up]
    FE80::C001:6FF:FEDB:0
    2001:ABCD:ABCD::2
FastEthernet0/1                [administratively down/down]
Loopback0                      [up/up]
    FE80::C001:6FF:FEDB:0
    2001::5

R3#show ipv6 interface s0/0
Serial0/0 is up, line protocol is up
  IPv6 is enabled, link-local address is FE80::C006:8FF:FE88:0
  No Virtual link-local address(es):
  Global unicast address(es):
    2001:ABCD:ABCD::2, subnet is 2001:ABCD:ABCD::/64
  Joined group address(es):
    FF02::1
    FF02::2
    FF02::1:FF00:2
    FF02::1:FF88:0
  MTU is 1500 bytes

  [Output Truncated]
```

LAB 3: IPV6 ADDRESS AUTOCONFIGURATION

Lab Objective:

The objective of this lab exercise is for you to learn and understand how to configure IPv6 addresses on Cisco routers using address autoconfiguration and EUI-64 addressing.

Lab Purpose:

Configuring IPv6 addressing is one of your most fundamental tasks as a Cisco engineer. In the exam, you may also be asked to configure an IPv6 address using Stateless Address Autoconfiguration (SLACC) as well as EUI-64 addressing.

Certification Level:

This lab is suitable for CCENT certification exam preparation.

Lab Difficulty:

This lab has a difficulty rating of 4/10.

Readiness Assessment:

When you are ready for your certification exam, you should complete this lab in no more than 10 minutes.

Lab Topology:

Please use the following topology to complete this lab exercise:

INTERFACE	IPv6 ADDRESS
L0	2001:aaaa:aaaa:aaaa/64 eui

Task 1:

Configure the hostnames on routers R1 and R3 as illustrated in the topology.

Task 2:

Configure the IP addresses on the Ethernet interfaces of R1 and R3 as illustrated in the topology. Configure the Loopback interfaces specified in the diagram on R3.

F0/0 on R3 will use SLACC to obtain the address prefix from R1. Loopback0 will use EUI-64 to complete the host portion of the address.

Task 3:
Use the correct show commands to check:

1. The summary of all configured IP addresses;
2. The status of the interface (up/down or administratively down); and
3. The subnet mask applied to the interface.

LAB 3: CONFIGURATION AND VERIFICATION

Task 1:

```
Router#config t
Enter configuration commands, one per line.  End with CTRL/Z.
Router(config)#hostname R1
R1(config)#

Router#config t
Enter configuration commands, one per line.  End with CTRL/Z.
Router(config)#hostname R3
R3(config)#
```

Task 2:

```
R1(config)#ipv6 unicast-routing
R1(config)#interface f0/0
R1(config-if)#ipv6 add 2001:abcd:abcd::1/64
R1(config-if)#no shut

R3(config)#ipv6 unicast-routing
R3(config)#interface f0/0
R3(config-if)#ipv6 add autoconfig
R3(config-if)#no shut
R3(config)#interface lo0
R3(config-if)# ipv6 address 2001:aaaa:aaaa:aaaa::/64 eui-64
```

Task 3:

```
R3#show ipv6 int f0/0
FastEthernet0/0 is up, line protocol is up
 IPv6 is enabled, link-local address is FE80::C004:8FF:FE04:0
  No Virtual link-local address(es):
  Global unicast address(es):
    2001:ABCD:ABCD:0:C004:8FF:FE04:0, subnet is 2001:ABCD:ABCD::/64
[EUI/CAL/PRE]
      valid lifetime 2591952 preferred lifetime 604752
  Joined group address(es):
    FF02::1
    FF02::2
    FF02::1:FF04:0

[Output Truncated]

R3#show ipv6 int lo0
Loopback0 is up, line protocol is up
  IPv6 is enabled, link-local address is FE80::C011:AFF:FE16:0
  No Virtual link-local address(es):
  Global unicast address(es):
    2001:AAAA:AAAA:AAAA:C011:AFF:FE16:0, subnet is
2001:AAAA:AAAA:AAAA::/64 [EUI]
```

```
Joined group address(es):
  FF02::1
  FF02::2
  FF02::1:FF16:0
```

LAB 4: ARP AND PROXY ARP

Lab Objective:
The objective of this lab exercise is for you to learn and understand how ARP and Proxy ARP is used by the router in order to encapsulate the packet before it is sent to a neighbor device.

Lab Purpose:
You must understand how ARP works in order to pass the CCNA exam. You could well be faced with an ARP-related issue to troubleshoot in the exam or in the real world.

Certification Level:
This lab is suitable for CCENT certification exam preparation.

Lab Difficulty:
This lab has a difficulty rating of 4/10.

Readiness Assessment:
When you are ready for your certification exam, you should complete this lab in no more than 10 minutes.

Lab Topology:
Please use the following topology to complete this lab exercise:

Task 1:
Configure the hostnames on routers R1, R2, and R3 as illustrated in the topology.

Task 2:
Configure the IP addresses on the Ethernet interfaces of R1, R2, and R3 as illustrated in the topology (.1 for R1 and .2 for R2, and then .1 and .2 between R2 and R3).

Add static routes so that R1 can ping the host address on R3 and R3 can return the ping. Then check the ARP cache on R1. A default route for all traffic to leave via the Ethernet interface will do.

Task 3:

Use the correct show commands to check:

1. The ARP cache on R1. What are the times for the learned addresses? Which will not timeout and how can you tell?
2. What is the entry for R3 and why is it the same as the R2 Ethernet interface?
3. What does the "–" in the ARP table mean?

Note that your MAC address entries may differ from mine.

LAB 4: CONFIGURATION AND VERIFICATION

Task 1:

```
Router#config t
Enter configuration commands, one per line.  End with CTRL/Z.
Router(config)#hostname R1
R1(config)#

Router#config t
Enter configuration commands, one per line.  End with CTRL/Z.
Router(config)#hostname R2
R2(config)#

Router#config t
Enter configuration commands, one per line.  End with CTRL/Z.
Router(config)#hostname R3
R3(config)#
```

Task 2:

```
R1(config)#int f0/0
R1(config-if)#ip add 10.0.0.1 255.0.0.0
R1(config-if)#no shut
R1(config-if)#ip route 0.0.0.0 0.0.0.0 f0/0


R2(config)#int f0/0
R2(config-if)#ip add 10.0.0.2 255.0.0.0
R2(config-if)#no shut

R2(config)#int f0/1
R2(config-if)#ip add 192.168.1.1 255.255.255.0
R2(config-if)#no shut

R3(config)#int f0/1
R3(config-if)#ip add 192.168.1.2 255.255.255.0
R3(config-if)#no shut
R3(config-if)#ip route 0.0.0.0 0.0.0.0 f0/1
```

Task 3:

```
R1#show arp
Protocol  Address          Age (min)  Hardware Addr   Type    Interface
Internet  10.0.0.1              -      c213.0a9a.0000  ARPA    F0/0
R1#
R1#ping 10.0.0.2

Type escape sequence to abort.
Sending 5, 100-byte ICMP Echos to 10.0.0.2, timeout is 2 seconds:
.!!!!
Success rate is 80 percent (4/5), round-trip min/avg/max = 16/21/24 ms
```

```
R1#
R1#
R1#show arp
Protocol  Address          Age (min)  Hardware Addr    Type    Interface
Internet  10.0.0.1               -     c213.0a9a.0000   ARPA    F0/0
Internet  10.0.0.2               0     c214.0a9a.0000   ARPA    F0/0
R1#ping   192.168.1.2

Type escape sequence to abort.
Sending 5, 100-byte ICMP Echos to 192.168.1.2, timeout is 2 seconds:
..!!!
Success rate is 60 percent (3/5), round-trip min/avg/max = 12/30/40 ms
R1#show arp
Protocol  Address          Age (min)  Hardware Addr    Type    Interface
Internet  10.0.0.1               -     c213.0a9a.0000   ARPA    F0/0
Internet  10.0.0.2               0     c214.0a9a.0000   ARPA    F0/0
Internet  192.168.1.2            0     c214.0a9a.0000   ARPA    F0/0

R3#show int f0/1
FastEthernet0/1 is up, line protocol is up
  Hardware is Gt96k FE, address is c215.0a9a.0001 (bia c215.0a9a.0001)
  Internet address is 192.168.1.2/24

R1#show arp
Protocol  Address          Age (min)  Hardware Addr    Type    Interface
Internet  10.0.0.1               -     c213.0a9a.0000   ARPA    F0/0
Internet  10.0.0.2               1     c214.0a9a.0000   ARPA    F0/0
Internet  192.168.1.2            0     c214.0a9a.0000   ARPA    F0/0
R1#
```

2.0 LAN Switching Fundamentals

LAB 5: CONFIGURING STANDARD VLANS ON CATALYST SWITCHES

Lab Objective:

The objective of this lab exercise is for you to learn and understand how to configure standard VLANs 1–1001 on Cisco Catalyst IOS Switches. In addition, you are also required to familiarize yourself with the commands available in Cisco IOS to validate and check your configurations.

Lab Purpose:

VLAN configuration is a fundamental skill. VLANs allow you to segment your network into multiple, smaller broadcast domains. As a Cisco engineer, as well as in the Cisco CCNA exam, you will be expected to know how to configure VLANs on Cisco switches.

Certification Level:

This lab is suitable for both CCENT and CCNA certification exam preparation.

Lab Difficulty:

This lab has a difficulty rating of 4/10.

Readiness Assessment:

When you are ready for your certification exam, you should complete this lab in no more than 10 minutes.

Lab Topology:

Please use the following topology to complete this lab exercise:

VLAN NUMBER	VLAN NAME	PORT
10	SALES	FastEthernet0/5
20	MANAGERS	FastEthernet0/6
30	ENGINEERS	FastEthernet0/7
40	SUPPORT	FastEthernet0/8

Task 1:

In preparation for VLAN configuration, configure a hostname on Sw1 as well as the VLANs depicted in the topology.

Task 2:

Configure ports FastEthernet0/5 to FastEthernet0/8 as access ports and assign them to the VLANs specified.

Task 3:

Verify your VLAN configuration using relevant show commands in Cisco IOS.

LAB 5: CONFIGURATION AND VERIFICATION

Task 1:

```
Switch#config t
Enter configuration commands, one per line.  End with CTRL/Z.
Switch(config)#hostname Sw1
Sw1(config)#vlan10
Sw1(config-vlan)#name SALES
Sw1(config-vlan)#exit
Sw1(config)#vlan20
Sw1(config-vlan)#name MANAGERS
Sw1(config-vlan)#exit
Sw1(config)#vlan30
Sw1(config-vlan)#name ENGINEERS
Sw1(config-vlan)#exit
Sw1(config)#vlan40
Sw1(config-vlan)#name SUPPORT
```

> **NOTE:** By default, Cisco switches are VTP servers so no configuration is necessary for server mode. Use the `show vtp status` command to look at the current VTP operating mode of the switch.

Task 2:

```
Sw1(config)#interface fastethernet0/5
Sw1(config-if)#switchport mode access
Sw1(config-if)#switchport access vlan10
Sw1(config-if)#exit
Sw1(config)#interface fastethernet0/6
Sw1(config-if)#switchport mode access
Sw1(config-if)#switchport access vlan20
Sw1(config-if)#exit
Sw1(config)#interface fastethernet0/7
Sw1(config-if)#switchport mode access
Sw1(config-if)#switchport access vlan30
Sw1(config-if)#exit
Sw1(config)#interface fastethernet0/8
Sw1(config-if)#switchport mode access
Sw1(config-if)#switchport access vlan40
```

Task 3:

```
Sw1#show vlan brief

VLAN Name                             Status    Ports
---- -------------------------------- --------- -------------------------------
1    default                          active    Fa0/1, Fa0/2, Fa0/3, Fa0/4
                                                Fa0/9, Fa0/10, Fa0/11, Fa0/12
                                                Fa0/13, Fa0/14, Fa0/15, Fa0/16
                                                Fa0/17, Fa0/18, Fa0/19, Fa0/20
```

```
                                      Fa0/21, Fa0/22, Fa0/23, Fa0/24
                                      Gi0/1, Gi0/2
10   SALES                  active    Fa0/5
20   MANAGERS               active    Fa0/6
30   ENGINEERS              active    Fa0/7
40   SUPPORT                active    Fa0/8
1002 fddi-default           active
1003 token-ring-default     active
1004 fddinet-default        active
1005 trnet-default          active
```

LAB 6: CONFIGURING VTP CLIENTS AND SERVERS ON CATALYST SWITCHES

Lab Objective:

The objective of this lab exercise is for you to learn and understand how to configure VTP server and client modes on Cisco Catalyst Switches. By default, all Cisco switches are VTP server devices.

Lab Purpose:

Configuring VTP client and server modes is a fundamental skill. VLANs are configured on VTP servers and VTP clients receive VLAN information from the VTP servers in the same VTP domain. VLAN sharing is possible by using a trunk between the switches. As a Cisco engineer, as well as in the Cisco CCNA exam, you will be expected to know how to configure VTP client and server modes.

Certification Level:

This lab is suitable for both CCENT and CCNA certification exam preparation.

Lab Difficulty:

This lab has a difficulty rating of 5/10.

Readiness Assessment:

When you are ready for your certification exam, you should complete this lab in no more than 15 minutes.

Lab Topology:

Please use the following topology to complete this lab exercise:

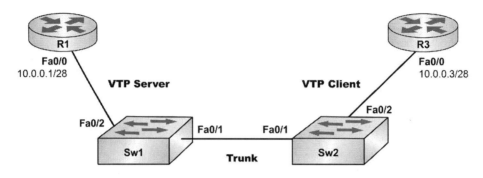

VLAN NUMBER	VLAN NAME	Sw1 & Sw2 INTERFACE
10	SALES	FastEthernet0/2
20	MANAGERS	

Task 1:

In preparation for VLAN configuration, configure a hostname on the switches and routers as depicted in the topology. Keep in mind that the default mode of operation of Cisco Catalyst Switches is VTP server mode. Remember to use a crossover cable between the switches.

Task 2:

Configure and verify Sw1 as a VTP server switch and configure Sw2 as a VTP client switch. Both switches should be in the VTP domain named CISCO.

Task 3:

Configure and verify FastEthernet0/1 between Sw1 and Sw2 as an 802.1Q trunk.

Task 4:

Configure and verify VLANs 10 and 20 on Sw1 with the names provided above. Assign FastEthernet0/2 on both Sw1 and Sw2 to VLAN10. This interface should be configured as an access port.

Task 5:

Configure R1 and R3 FastEthernet0/0 interfaces with the IP addresses 10.0.0.1/28 and 10.0.0.3/28, respectively. Test connectivity via your VLANs by pinging R1 from R3, and vice versa.

LAB 6: CONFIGURATION AND VERIFICATION

Task 1:

```
Switch#config t
Enter configuration commands, one per line.  End with CTRL/Z.
Switch(config)#hostname Sw1
Sw1(config)#

Switch#config t
Enter configuration commands, one per line.  End with CTRL/Z.
Switch(config)#hostname Sw2
Sw1(config)#

Router#config t
Enter configuration commands, one per line.  End with CTRL/Z.
Router(config)#hostname R1
R1(config)#

Router#config t
Enter configuration commands, one per line.  End with CTRL/Z.
Router(config)#hostname R3
R3(config)#
```

Task 2:

NOTE: By default, Cisco switches are VTP servers so no configuration is necessary for server mode on Sw1. This can be verified using the show vtp status command. However, you do need to configure the domain.

```
Sw1#config t
Enter configuration commands, one per line.  End with CTRL/Z.
Sw1(config)#vtp domain CISCO
Changing VTP domain name from Null to CISCO
Sw1(config)#

Sw2#config t
Enter configuration commands, one per line.  End with CTRL/Z.
Sw2(config)#vtp mode client
Setting device to VTP CLIENT mode.
Sw2(config)#vtp domain CISCO
Changing VTP domain name from Null to CISCO
Sw2(config)#end

Sw2#show vtp status
VTP Version                   : 2
Configuration Revision        : 0
Maximum VLANs supported locally : 250
Number of existing VLANs      : 5
VTP Operating Mode            : Client
```

```
VTP Domain Name             : CISCO
VTP Pruning Mode            : Enabled
VTP V2 Mode                 : Disabled
VTP Traps Generation        : Disabled
MD5 digest                  : 0x9D 0x1A 0x9D 0x16 0x9E 0xD1 0x38
0x59
Configuration last modified by 0.0.0.0 at 3-1-93 01:42:39
```

Task 3:

> **NOTE:** Some Cisco switches default to 802.1Q trunking so no explicit configuration is required. The 2960 Switch (used in the exam) is set to dynamic auto so you will have to set at least one side to trunk.

```
Sw1#show int f0/1 switchport
Name: Fa0/1
Switchport: Enabled
Administrative Mode: dynamic auto
Operational Mode: static access
Administrative Trunking Encapsulation: dot1q
Operational Trunking Encapsulation: native
Negotiation of Trunking: On
Sw1#config t
Enter configuration commands, one per line.  End with CTRL/Z.
Sw1(config)#interface fastethernet0/1
Sw1(config-if)#switchport mode trunk

Sw1#show interfaces trunk

Port        Mode         Encapsulation  Status       Native vlan
Fa0/1       on           802.1q         trunking     1

Port        Vlans allowed on trunk
Fa0/1       1-1005

Port        Vlans allowed and active in management domain
Fa0/1       1

Port        Vlans in spanning tree forwarding state and not pruned
Fa0/1       1
```

Task 4:

```
Sw1#config t
Enter configuration commands, one per line.  End with CTRL/Z.
Sw1(config)#vlan10
Sw1(config-vlan)#name SALES
Sw1(config-vlan)#exit
Sw1(config)#vlan20
Sw1(config-vlan)#name MANAGERS
Sw1(config-vlan)#exit
```

```
Sw1(config)#interface fastethernet0/2
Sw1(config-if)#switchport mode access
Sw1(config-if)#switchport access vlan10
Sw1(config-if)#end
Sw1#
Sw1#show vlan brief
```

```
VLAN Name                    Status     Ports
---- ---------------------- ---------  --------------------------------
1    default                active     Fa0/3, Fa0/4, Fa0/5, Fa0/6
                                        Fa0/7, Fa0/8, Fa0/9, Fa0/10
                                        Fa0/11, Fa0/12, Fa0/13, Fa0/14
                                        Fa0/15, Fa0/16, Fa0/17, Fa0/18
                                        Fa0/19, Fa0/20, Fa0/21, Fa0/22
                                        Fa0/23, Fa0/24, Gig0/1, Gig0/2

10   SALES                  active     Fa0/2
20   MANAGERS               active
1002 fddi-default           active
1003 token-ring-default     active
1004 fddinet-default        active
1005 trnet-default          active
Sw1#
```

```
Sw2#config t
Enter configuration commands, one per line.  End with CTRL/Z.
Sw2(config)#interface fastethernet0/2
Sw2(config-if)#switchport mode access
Sw2(config-if)#switchport access vlan10
Sw2(config-if)#end
Sw2#
Sw2#show vlan brief
```

```
VLAN Name                    Status     Ports
---- ---------------------- ---------  --------------------------------
1    default                active     Fa0/3, Fa0/4, Fa0/5, Fa0/6
                                        Fa0/7, Fa0/8, Fa0/9, Fa0/10
                                        Fa0/11, Fa0/12, Fa0/13, Fa0/14
                                        Fa0/15, Fa0/16, Fa0/17, Fa0/18
                                        Fa0/19, Fa0/20, Fa0/21, Fa0/22
                                        Fa0/23, Fa0/24, Gig0/1, Gig0/2

10   SALES                  active     Fa0/2
20   MANAGERS               active
1002 fddi-default           active
1003 token-ring-default     active
1004 fddinet-default        active
1005 trnet-default          active
```

Task 5:

```
R1#config t
Enter configuration commands, one per line.  End with CTRL/Z.
R1(config)#interface  fastethernet0/0
R1(config-if)#ip address 10.0.0.1 255.255.255.240
R1(config-if)#no shutdown
R1(config-if)#end
R1#


R3#config t
Enter configuration commands, one per line.  End with CTRL/Z.
R3(config)#interface  fastethernet0/0
R3(config-if)#ip address 10.0.0.3 255.255.255.240
R3(config-if)#no shutdown
R3(config-if)#end
R3#


R1#show ip interface brief
Interface       IP-Address      OK? Method Status      Protocol
FastEthernet0/0   10.0.0.1      YES manual up          up

R1#ping 10.0.0.3

Type escape sequence to abort.
Sending 5, 100-byte ICMP Echos to 10.0.0.3, timeout is 2 seconds:
.!!!!
Success rate is 80 percent (4/5), round-trip min/avg/max = 1/3/4 ms
```

NOTE: The first ping packet times out due to ARP resolution. Subsequent packets will be successful.

```
R3#show ip interface brief
Interface       IP-Address      OK? Method Status      Protocol
FastEthernet0/0   10.0.0.3      YES manual up          up

R3#ping 10.0.0.1

Type escape sequence to abort.
Sending 5, 100-byte ICMP Echos to 10.0.0.1, timeout is 2 seconds:
!!!!!
Success rate is 100 percent (5/5), round-trip min/avg/max = 1/3/4 ms
```

LAB 7: CONFIGURING VTP TRANSPARENT MODE

Lab Objective:

The objective of this lab exercise is for you to learn and understand how to configure VTP Transparent mode on Cisco Catalyst Switches. By default, all Cisco switches are VTP server devices.

Lab Purpose:

VTP Transparent mode configuration is a fundamental skill. VLANs configured on a switch in VTP Transparent mode are not automatically propagated to other switches within the same VTP domain as would be done by a VTP server. Switches configured in VTP Transparent mode use a trunk to forward traffic for configured VLANs to other switches. As a Cisco engineer, as well as in the Cisco CCNA exam, you will be expected to know how to configure VTP Transparent mode.

Certification Level:

This lab is suitable for both CCENT and CCNA certification exam preparation.

Lab Difficulty:

This lab has a difficulty rating of 5/10.

Readiness Assessment:

When you are ready for your certification exam, you should complete this lab in no more than 15 minutes.

Lab Topology:

Please use the following topology to complete this lab exercise:

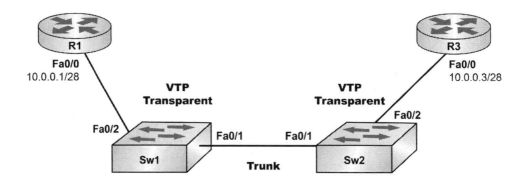

VLAN NUMBER	VLAN NAME	INTERFACE
2010	SALES	FastEthernet0/2
2030	MANAGEMENT	

VLAN NUMBER	VLAN NAME	INTERFACE
2010	SALES	FastEthernet0/2
2040	DIRECTORS	

Task 1:

In preparation for VLAN configuration, configure a hostname on switches 1 and 2 and routers 1 and 3 as illustrated in the topology.

Task 2:

Configure and verify Sw1 and Sw2 in VTP Transparent mode. Both switches should be in the VTP domain named CISCO. Remember that switches must be in the same VTP domain to share VLAN information via a trunk.

Task 3:

Configure and verify FastEthernet0/1 between Sw1 and Sw2 as an 802.1Q trunk.

Task 4:

Configure and verify VLANs 2010 and 2030 on Sw1 with the names provided above. Assign FastEthernet0/2 on Sw1 to VLAN2010 as an access port. Configure and verify VLANs 2010 and 2040 on Sw2 with the names provided above. Assign FastEthernet0/2 on Sw2 to VLAN2010 as an access port.

Task 5:

Configure R1 and R3 FastEthernet interfaces with the IP addresses 10.0.0.1/28 and 10.0.0.3/28, respectively. Test VLAN connectivity by pinging between R1 and R3.

LAB 7: CONFIGURATION AND VERIFICATION

Task 1:

```
Switch#config t
Enter configuration commands, one per line.  End with CTRL/Z.
Switch(config)#hostname Sw1
Sw1(config)#

Switch#config t
Enter configuration commands, one per line.  End with CTRL/Z.
Switch(config)#hostname Sw2
Sw1(config)#

Router#config t
Enter configuration commands, one per line.  End with CTRL/Z.
Router(config)#hostname R1
R1(config)#

Router#config t
Enter configuration commands, one per line.  End with CTRL/Z.
Router(config)#hostname R3
R3(config)#
```

Task 2:

```
Sw1#config t
Enter configuration commands, one per line.  End with CTRL/Z.
Sw1(config)#vtp mode transparent
Setting device to VTP TRANSPARENT mode.
Sw1(config)#end
Sw1#show vtp status
VTP Version                     : 2
Configuration Revision          : 2
Maximum VLANs supported locally : 250
Number of existing VLANs        : 5
VTP Operating Mode              : Transparent
VTP Domain Name                 : CISCO
VTP Pruning Mode                : Enabled
VTP V2 Mode                     : Disabled
VTP Traps Generation            : Disabled
MD5 digest                      : 0x9D 0x1A 0x9D 0x16 0x9E 0xD1 0x38
0x59
Configuration last modified by 10.1.1.3 at 3-1-93 01:42:39

Sw2#config t
Enter configuration commands, one per line.  End with CTRL/Z.
Sw2(config)#vtp mode transparent
Setting device to VTP TRANSPARENT mode.
Sw2(config)#end
Sw2#show vtp status
VTP Version                     : 2
```

```
Configuration Revision            : 2
Maximum VLANs supported locally   : 250
Number of existing VLANs          : 5
VTP Operating Mode                : Transparent
VTP Domain Name                   : CISCO
VTP Pruning Mode                  : Enabled
VTP V2 Mode                       : Disabled
VTP Traps Generation              : Disabled
MD5 digest                        : 0x9D 0x1A 0x9D 0x16 0x9E 0xD1 0x38
0x59
Configuration last modified by 10.1.1.3 at 3-1-93 01:42:45
```

Task 3:

> **NOTE:** Some Cisco switches default to 802.1Q trunking so no explicit configuration is required. This ISN'T the case for the 2960 Switch, which is used in the exam.

```
Sw1#config t
Enter configuration commands, one per line.  End with CTRL/Z.
Sw1(config)#interface fastethernet0/1
Sw1(config-if)#switchport mode trunk

Sw2#config t
Enter configuration commands, one per line.  End with CTRL/Z.
Sw2(config)#interface fastethernet0/1
Sw2(config-if)#switchport mode trunk
```

Task 4:

```
Sw1#config t
Enter configuration commands, one per line.  End with CTRL/Z.
Sw1(config)#vlan2010
Sw1(config-vlan)#name SALES
Sw1(config-vlan)#exit
Sw1(config)#vlan2030
Sw1(config-vlan)#name MANAGEMENT
Sw1(config-vlan)#exit
Sw1(config)#interface fastethernet0/2
Sw1(config-if)#switchport mode access
Sw1(config-if)#switchport access vlan 2010
Sw1(config-if)#end
Sw1#
Sw1#show vlan brief

VLAN Name                          Status    Ports
---- -------------------------- --------- -------------------------------
1    default                       active    Fa0/1, Fa0/3, Fa0/4
                                             Fa0/5, Fa0/6, Fa0/7, Fa0/8
                                             Fa0/9, Fa0/10, Fa0/11, Fa0/12
                                             Fa0/13, Fa0/14, Fa0/15, Fa0/16
                                             Fa0/17, Fa0/18, Fa0/19, Fa0/20
```

```
                                        Fa0/21, Fa0/22, Fa0/23, Fa0/24
                                        Gi0/1, Gi0/2
1002 fddi-default             active
1003 token-ring-default       active
1004 fddinet-default          active
1005 trnet-default            active
2010 SALES                    active      Fa0/2
2030 MANAGEMENT               active

Sw2#config t
Enter configuration commands, one per line.  End with CTRL/Z.
Sw2(config)#vlan2010
Sw2(config-vlan)#name SALES
Sw2(config-vlan)#exit
Sw2(config)#vlan2040
Sw2(config-vlan)#name DIRECTORS
Sw2(config-vlan)#exit
Sw2(config)#interface fastethernet0/2
Sw2(config-if)#switchport mode access
Sw2(config-if)#switchport access vlan2010
Sw2(config-if)#end
Sw2#
Sw2#show vlan brief

VLAN Name                     Status    Ports
---- ---------------------    --------- -------------------------------
1    default                  active    Fa0/1, Fa0/3, Fa0/4
                                        Fa0/5, Fa0/6, Fa0/7, Fa0/8
                                        Fa0/9, Fa0/10, Fa0/11, Fa0/12
                                        Fa0/13, Fa0/14, Fa0/15, Fa0/16
                                        Fa0/17, Fa0/18, Fa0/19, Fa0/20
                                        Fa0/21, Fa0/22, Fa0/23, Fa0/24
                                        Gi0/1, Gi0/2
1002 fddi-default             active
1003 token-ring-default       active
1004 fddinet-default          active
1005 trnet-default            active
2010 SALES                    active    Fa0/2
2040 DIRECTORS                active
```

NOTE: Default switches configured for VTP Transparent mode do not exchange VLAN information. You can see in the output above that VLAN2030 on Sw1 is not propagated to Sw2, and VLAN2040 on Sw2 is not propagated to Sw1. In Transparent mode, all VLANs must be manually configured on all switches.

Task 5:

```
R1#config t
Enter configuration commands, one per line.  End with CTRL/Z.
R1(config)#interface  fastethernet0/0
R1(config-if)#ip address 10.0.0.1 255.255.255.240
R1(config-if)#no shutdown
R1(config-if)#end

R3#config t
Enter configuration commands, one per line.  End with CTRL/Z.
R3(config)#interface  fastethernet0/0
R3(config-if)#ip address 10.0.0.3 255.255.255.240
R3(config-if)#no shutdown
R3(config-if)#end

R1#show ip interface brief
Interface       IP-Address    OK? Method Status          Protocol
FastEthernet0/0  10.0.0.1      YES manual up              up

R1#ping 10.0.0.3

Type escape sequence to abort.
Sending 5, 100-byte ICMP Echos to 10.0.0.3, timeout is 2 seconds:
.!!!!
Success rate is 80 percent (4/5), round-trip min/avg/max = 1/3/4 ms
```

NOTE: The first ping packet times out due to ARP resolution. Subsequent packets will be successful.

```
R3#show ip interface brief
Interface       IP-Address    OK? Method Status          Protocol
FastEthernet0/0  10.0.0.3      YES manual up              up

R3#ping 10.0.0.1

Type escape sequence to abort.
Sending 5, 100-byte ICMP Echos to 10.0.0.1, timeout is 2 seconds:
!!!!!
Success rate is 100 percent (5/5), round-trip min/avg/max = 1/3/4 ms
```

LAB 8: SECURING VTP DOMAINS

Lab Objective:
The objective of this lab exercise is for you to learn and understand how to secure VTP domains using Cisco Catalyst Switches. By default, VTP domains are not password-protected.

Lab Purpose:
Securing the VTP domain is a fundamental skill. When VTP domains are not configured with a password, rogue switches can be added to the network and disrupt service. As a Cisco engineer, as well as in the Cisco CCNA exam, you will be expected to know how to configure VTP passwords.

Certification Level:
This lab is suitable for both CCENT and CCNA certification exam preparation.

Lab Difficulty:
This lab has a difficulty rating of 4/10.

Readiness Assessment:
When you are ready for your certification exam, you should complete this lab in no more than 5 minutes.

Lab Topology:
Please use the following topology to complete this lab exercise:

VLAN NUMBER	VLAN NAME	PORT
10	SALES	FastEthernet0/5
20	MANAGERS	FastEthernet0/6
30	ENGINEERS	FastEthernet0/7
40	SUPPORT	FastEthernet0/8

Task 1:

In preparation for VLAN configuration, configure a hostname on Sw1 and Sw2 as depicted in the topology.

Task 2:

Configure and verify Sw1 as a VTP server switch and configure Sw2 as a VTP client switch. Both switches should be in the VTP domain named CISCO. Secure VTP messages with the VTP password CISCO.

Task 3:

Configure and verify FastEthernet0/1 between Sw1 and Sw2 as an 802.1Q trunk.

Task 4:

Configure and verify VLANs 10 to 40 on Sw1 with the names provided above. Validate that these VLANs are still propagated to Sw2 after VTP has been secured.

LAB 8: CONFIGURATION AND VERIFICATION

Task 1:

For reference information on configuring hostnames, please refer to the previous labs.

Task 2:

NOTE: By default, Cisco switches are VTP servers so no configuration is necessary for server mode on Sw1. This can be verified using the show vtp status command. However, you do need to configure the domain.

```
Sw1#config t
Enter configuration commands, one per line.  End with CTRL/Z.
Sw1(config)#vtp domain CISCO
Changing VTP domain name from Null to CISCO
Sw1(config)#vtp password CISCO
Setting device VLAN database password to CISCO
Sw1#show vtp status
VTP Version                   : 2
Configuration Revision        : 2
Maximum VLANs supported locally : 250
Number of existing VLANs      : 5
VTP Operating Mode            : Server
VTP Domain Name               : CISCO
VTP Pruning Mode              : Enabled
VTP V2 Mode                   : Disabled
VTP Traps Generation          : Disabled
MD5 digest                    : 0x00 0x7A 0x5E 0x47 0xF1 0xDD 0xB5 0x30

Sw2#config t
Enter configuration commands, one per line.  End with CTRL/Z.
Sw2(config)#vtp mode client
Setting device to VTP CLIENT mode.
Sw2(config)#vtp domain CISCO
Changing VTP domain name from Null to CISCO
Sw1(config)#vtp password CISCO
Setting device VLAN database password to CISCO
Sw2(config)#end
Sw2#show vtp status
VTP Version                   : 2
Configuration Revision        : 0
Maximum VLANs supported locally : 250
Number of existing VLANs      : 5
VTP Operating Mode            : Client
VTP Domain Name               : CISCO
VTP Pruning Mode              : Enabled
VTP V2 Mode                   : Disabled
VTP Traps Generation          : Disabled
MD5 digest                    : 0x9D 0x1A 0x9D 0x16 0x9E 0xD1 0x38 0x59
```

Task 3:

For reference information on configuring and verifying trunks, please refer to earlier labs.

Task 4:

For reference information on configuring and verifying VLANs, please refer to previous labs.

```
Sw2#show vlan brief

VLAN Name                         Status     Ports
---- ------------------------     ---------  ------------------------------
1    default                      active     Fa0/2, Fa0/3, Fa0/4, Fa0/5
                                             Fa0/6, Fa0/7, Fa0/8, Fa0/9
10   SALES                        active
20   MANAGERS                     active
30   ENGINEERS                    active
40   SUPPORT                      active
1002 fddi-default                 active
1003 token-ring-default           active
1004 fddinet-default              active
1005 trnet-default                active
```

NOTE: Make sure that the MD5 digest at the end of the output of the show vtp status command is the same when VTP passwords have been configured on switches within the same VTP domain.

LAB 9: CONFIGURING SWITCH ACCESS PORT SECURITY

Lab Objective:

The objective of this lab exercise is to configure basic switch security to prevent MAC address flooding on switchports. This is accomplished by limiting the number of MAC entries that are allowed to be learned on a port. By default, there is no limit on MAC addresses that can be learned on a port.

Lab Purpose:

Port security is a fundamental skill. A common Denial of Service technique used to cripple switched networks is MAC flooding. As a Cisco engineer, as well as in the Cisco CCNA exam, you will be expected to know how to configure port security to mitigate MAC flooding attacks.

Certification Level:

This lab is suitable for CCNA certification exam preparation.

Lab Difficulty:

This lab has a difficulty rating of 8/10.

Readiness Assessment:

When you are ready for your certification exam, you should complete this lab in no more than 15 minutes.

Lab Topology:

Please use the following topology to complete this lab exercise:

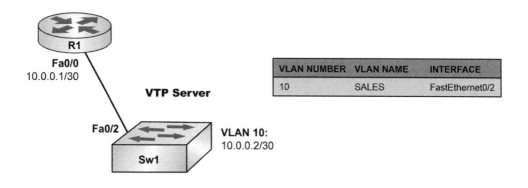

Task 1:

Configure hostnames on Sw1 and R1 as illustrated in the topology.

Task 2:

Create VLAN10 on Sw1 and assign port FastEthernet0/2 to this VLAN as an access port.

Task 3:

Configure IP address 10.0.0.1/30 on R1's FastEthernet0/0 interface and IP address 10.0.0.2/30 on Sw2's VLAN10 interface. Verify that R1 can ping Sw1, and vice versa.

Task 4:

Configure port security on port FastEthernet0/2 on Sw1 so that only one MAC address is allowed to be learned on that interface. In the event of port security configuration violations, where more than one MAC address is observed on that interface, the switch should shut the interface down. Verify your configuration with `port-security` commands in Cisco IOS.

LAB 9: CONFIGURATION AND VERIFICATION

Task 1:

For reference information on configuring hostnames, please refer to earlier labs.

Task 2:

For reference information on configuring VLANs, please refer to earlier labs. The port can't be dynamic if you intend to add port security. It must be manually set to trunk or access.

Task 3:

For reference information on configuring router IP interfaces, please refer to earlier labs.

```
Sw1(config)#int vlan10
%LINK-5-CHANGED: Interface Vlan10, changed state to up
Sw1(config-if)#ip add 10.0.0.2 255.255.255.252
Sw1(config-if)#no shut
Sw1(config-if)#end
Sw1#ping 10.0.0.1

Type escape sequence to abort.
Sending 5, 100-byte ICMP Echos to 10.0.0.1, timeout is 2 seconds:
.!!!!
Success rate is 80 percent (4/5), round-trip min/avg/max = 0/0/0 ms
```

Task 4:

```
Sw1#conf t
Enter configuration commands, one per line.  End with CTRL/Z.
Sw1(config)#interface fastethernet 0/2
Sw1(config-if)#switchport port-security
Sw1(config-if)#switchport port-security maximum 1
Sw1(config-if)#switchport port-security violation shutdown
Sw1(config-if)#end
Sw1#show port-security
Secure Port MaxSecureAddr CurrentAddr SecurityViolation Sec Action
            (Count)       (Count)       (Count)
-----------------------------------------------------------------------
Fa0/2            1             0             0              Shutdown
-----------------------------------------------------------------------
Total Addresses in System : 0
Max Addresses limit in System : 1024

[Output Truncated]
```

> **NOTE:** If you wanted to test your port security configuration, you could simply change the MAC address of FastEthernet0/0 on R1 to 000a.bc01.2300, and then you would see a port security violation. For example:

```
R1#conf t
Enter configuration commands, one per line.  End with CTRL/Z.
R1(config)#interface fastethernet0/0
R1(config-if)#mac-address 000a.bc01.2300
R1(config)#end
R1#

Sw1#show port-security
Secure Port MaxSecureAddr CurrentAddr SecurityViolation Sec Action
             (Count)        (Count)       (Count)
-----------------------------------------------------------------
Fa0/2           1              0             1              Shutdown
-----------------------------------------------------------------
Total Addresses in System : 0
Max Addresses limit in System : 1024

Sw1#show interfaces fastethernet 0/2
FastEthernet0/2 is down, line protocol is down (errdisabled)
```

As can be seen in the output above, the violation counter has incremented and the interface is now in an errdisabled mode, which basically means it has been shut down due to a port security violation. To bring this interface back up, you need to issue a `shutdown` command and then a `no shutdown` command under the interface.

LAB 10: CONFIGURING ADVANCED SWITCH ACCESS PORT SECURITY

Lab Objective:

The objective of this lab exercise is to ensure that learned MAC addresses on a secured port are retained in the switch's NVRAM in the event of a reboot. By default, secured MAC addresses are flushed during switch reboots.

Lab Purpose:

Retaining learned secure MAC addresses is an advanced skill. When a Cisco Catalyst Switch configured with port security reboots, learned secure MAC address entries are flushed and have to be relearned when the switch comes back up. As a Cisco engineer, understanding advanced features will give you the edge over your fellow CCNAs.

Certification Level:

This lab is suitable for CCENT and CCNA certification exam preparation.

Lab Difficulty:

This lab has a difficulty rating of 6/10.

Readiness Assessment:

When you are ready for your certification exam, you should complete this lab in no more than 15 minutes.

Lab Topology:

Please use the following topology to complete this lab exercise:

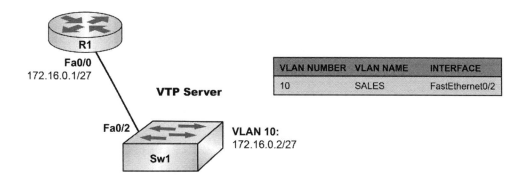

VLAN NUMBER	VLAN NAME	INTERFACE
10	SALES	FastEthernet0/2

Task 1:

Configure hostnames on Sw1 and R1 as illustrated in the topology.

Task 2:

Create VLAN10 on Sw1 and assign port FastEthernet0/2 to this VLAN as an access port.

Task 3:

Configure IP address 172.16.0.1/27 on R1's FastEthernet0/0 interface and IP address 172.16.0.2/27 on Sw2's VLAN10 interface. Verify that R1 can ping Sw1, and vice versa.

Task 4:

Configure port security on port FastEthernet0/2 on Sw1 so that any MAC addresses learned on that interface are written to the switch's NVRAM. The NVRAM is the startup configuration. Verify your configuration with `port-security` commands in Cisco IOS.

LAB 10: CONFIGURATION AND VERIFICATION

Task 1:

For reference information on configuring hostnames, please refer to earlier labs.

Task 2:

For reference information on configuring and verifying VLANs, please refer to earlier labs.

Task 3:

For reference information on configuring and verifying IP addresses, please refer to earlier labs.

Task 4:

```
Sw1#conf t
Enter configuration commands, one per line.  End with CTRL/Z.
Sw1(config)#interface fastethernet0/2
Sw1(config-if)#switchport port-security
Sw1(config-if)#switchport port-security mac-address sticky
Sw1(config-if)#end
Sw1#
Sw1#copy startup-config running-config
Destination filename [running-config]?
2167 bytes copied in 2.092 secs (1036 bytes/sec)
Sw1#
Sw1#show port-security
Secure Port MaxSecureAddr CurrentAddr SecurityViolation Sec Action
            (Count)        (Count)       (Count)
-------------------------------------------------------------------
Fa0/2          1              1             0             Shutdown
-------------------------------------------------------------------

Total Addresses in System : 1
Max Addresses limit in System : 1024

Sw1#show running-config interface fastethernet0/2
Building configuration...

Current configuration : 254 bytes
!
interface FastEthernet0/2
 switchport port-security
 switchport port-security mac-address sticky
 switchport port-security mac-address sticky 0004.c058.5fc0
end
```

NOTE: When configuring port security, by default the learned MAC addresses are flushed when the switch is reloaded. To prevent this and ensure that the switch preserves MAC addresses that are dynamically learned via port security, you need to configure sticky learning. This configuration, in conjunction with the `copy run start` command, saves the learned MAC addresses to NVRAM. This means that when the switch is rebooted, the MAC addresses learned are not lost. The switch adds the `switchport port-security mac-address sticky <mac-address>` command dynamically under the interface for every sticky dynamically learned MAC address. So if 100 MAC addresses are learned this way, the switch would add 100 of these statements after the `switchport port-security mac-address sticky` command that you issued under the interface. Be very careful because this can create a very large configuration file in the real world!

LAB 11: CONFIGURING ADVANCED STATIC SWITCH ACCESS PORT SECURITY

Lab Objective:
The objective of this lab exercise is for you to learn and understand how to configure static MAC entries for port security. By default, MAC entries are learned dynamically on a switchport.

Lab Purpose:
Static port security MAC entries are an advanced skill. Static MAC address entries are manually configured by the administrator. As a Cisco engineer, understanding advanced features will give you the edge over your fellow CCNAs.

Certification Level:
This lab is suitable for CCENT and CCNA certification exam preparation.

Lab Difficulty:
This lab has a difficulty rating of 8/10.

Readiness Assessment:
When you are ready for your certification exam, you should complete this lab in no more than 15 minutes.

Lab Topology:
Please use the following topology to complete this lab exercise:

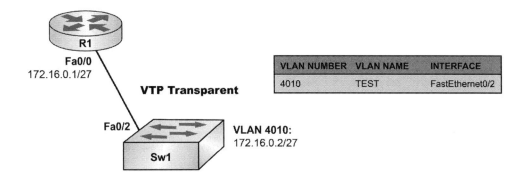

Task 1:

Configure hostnames on Sw1 and R1 as illustrated in the topology. Create VLAN10 on switch Sw1 and assign port FastEthernet0/2 to this VLAN as an access port.

Task 2:

Configure IP address 172.16.0.1/27 on R1's FastEthernet0/0 interface and IP address 172.16.0.2/27 on Sw2's VLAN10 interface. Verify that R1 can ping Sw1, and vice versa.

Task 3:

Configure port security on port FastEthernet0/5 on Sw1 for the following static MAC addresses:

  000a.1111.ab01
  000b.2222.cd01
  000c.3333.ef01
  000d.4444.ac01

The switch should restrict access to these ports for MAC addresses that are not known. Verify your configuration with `port-security` commands in Cisco IOS.

LAB 11: CONFIGURATION AND VERIFICATION

Task 1:

For reference information on configuring hostnames, please refer to earlier labs. For reference information on Transparent mode and extended VLANs, please refer to earlier labs.

Task 2:

For reference information on configuring IP interfaces, please refer to earlier labs.

Task 3:

```
Sw1#conf t
Enter configuration commands, one per line.  End with CTRL/Z.
Sw1(config)#interface fastethernet0/2
Sw1(config-if)#switchport port-security
Sw1(config-if)#switchport port-security maximum 4
Sw1(config-if)#switchport port-security mac-address 000a.1111.ab01
Sw1(config-if)#switchport port-security mac-address 000b.2222.cd01
Sw1(config-if)#switchport port-security mac-address 000c.3333.ef01
Sw1(config-if)#switchport port-security mac-address 000d.4444.ac01
Sw1(config-if)#end
Sw1#
Sw1#show port-security
Secure Port MaxSecureAddr CurrentAddr SecurityViolation  Sec Action
            (Count)        (Count)      (Count)
-------------------------------------------------------------------
Fa0/2          5              4             0            Shutdown
-------------------------------------------------------------------

Total Addresses in System : 5
Max Addresses limit in System : 1024

Sw1#show port-security interface fastethernet0/2
Port Security : Enabled
Port status : SecureUp
Violation mode : Shutdown
Maximum MAC Addresses : 4
Total MAC Addresses : 4
Configured MAC Addresses : 4
Sticky MAC Addresses : 0
Aging time : 0 mins
Aging type : Absolute
SecureStatic address aging : Disabled
Security Violation count : 0
```

NOTE: The requirements of this task seem pretty simple; however, a common mistake is often made by people who forget that by default, the maximum number of addresses that can be secured is one. Therefore, since you were given four MAC addresses, you need to increase the port security limit to four. Otherwise, if you did not add the `switchport port-security maximum 4` command, you would receive the following error when trying to add the second static MAC address for port security:

```
Sw1#conf t
Enter configuration commands, one per line.  End with CTRL/Z.
Sw1(config)#interface fastethernet0/2
Sw1(config-if)#switchport port-security
Sw1(config-if)#switchport port-security mac-address 000a.1111.ab01
Sw1(config-if)#switchport port-security mac-address 000b.2222.cd01
%Error: Cannot add secure address 000b.2222.cd01
%Error: Total secure addresses on interface reached its max limit of 1
%PSECURE: Internal Error in adding address
```

LAB 12: DISABLING AUTO-NEGOTIATION OF TRUNKING

Lab Objective:

The objective of this lab exercise is for you to learn and understand how to turn off the auto-negotiation of a trunk link.

Lab Purpose:

Switch interfaces are set to automatically attempt to create a trunk link when connected to another switch. You need to know how to disable this behavior. Note that this behavior varies depending on the switch model.

Certification Level:

This lab is suitable for the CCENT certification exam preparation.

Lab Difficulty:

This lab has a difficulty rating of 5/10.

Readiness Assessment:

When you are ready for your certification exam, you should complete this lab in no more than 15 minutes.

Lab Topology:

Please use the following topology to complete this lab exercise:

Task 1:

In preparation for the configuration, configure a hostname on Sw1 as well as Sw2.

Task 2:

Configure Sw1 so that auto-negotiation of trunking is disabled. Set the port to manually trunk.

Task 3:

Verify your configuration with the appropriate show commands.

LAB 12: CONFIGURATION AND VERIFICATION

Task 1:

For reference information on configuring hostnames, please refer to earlier labs.

Task 2:

```
Sw1#show interface fast0/1 switchport
Name: Fa0/1
Switchport: Enabled
Administrative Mode: dynamic auto
Operational Mode: down
Administrative Trunking Encapsulation: dot1q
Operational Trunking Encapsulation: native
Negotiation of Trunking: On
Access Mode VLAN: 1 (default)
Trunking Native Mode VLAN: 1 (default)

Sw1(config)#int fast0/1
Sw1(config-if)#switchport nonegotiate
Command rejected: Conflict between 'nonegotiate' and 'dynamic' status.
Sw1(config-if)#switchport mode trunk
Sw1(config-if)#switchport nonegotiate
Sw1(config-if)#end
```

Task 3:

NOTE: As you can see above, the interface cannot be left to dynamically become a trunk or access port if you want to disable auto-negotiation of trunking.

```
Sw1#show int fast0/1 switchport
Name: Fa0/1
Switchport: Enabled
Administrative Mode: trunk
Operational Mode: down
Administrative Trunking Encapsulation: dot1q
Operational Trunking Encapsulation: dot1q
Negotiation of Trunking: Off
Access Mode VLAN: 1 (default)
Trunking Native Mode VLAN: 1 (default)
Voice VLAN: none
```

LAB 13: SETTING SWITCHPORTS TO DYNAMIC

Lab Objective:
The objective of this lab exercise is for you to learn and understand how to set the auto-negotiation type on a trunk link.

Lab Purpose:
Switch interfaces are set to automatically attempt to create a trunk link when connected to another switch. You need to know how to set either dynamic desirable or dynamic auto.

Certification Level:
This lab is suitable for CCENT exam preparation.

Lab Difficulty:
This lab has a difficulty rating of 5/10.

Readiness Assessment:
When you are ready for your certification exam, you should complete this lab in no more than 10 minutes.

Lab Topology:
Please use the following topology to complete this lab exercise:

Task 1:
In preparation for the configuration, configure a hostname on Sw1 as well as Sw2.

Task 2:
Configure Sw1 so that auto-negotiation of trunking is set to dynamic auto.

Task 3:
Configure Sw2 so that auto-negotiation of trunking is set to dynamic desirable.

Task 4:
Verify your configurations with the appropriate show commands (illustrated in Task 3 below).

LAB 13: CONFIGURATION AND VERIFICATION

Task 1:

For reference information on configuring hostnames, please refer to earlier labs.

Task 2:

```
Sw1#show int fast0/1 switchport
Name: Fa0/1
Switchport: Enabled
Administrative Mode: dynamic auto
Operational Mode: static access
Administrative Trunking Encapsulation: dot1q
Operational Trunking Encapsulation: native
Negotiation of Trunking: On
Access Mode VLAN: 1 (default)
Trunking Native Mode VLAN: 1 (default)
```

The interface is actually already set to dynamic auto, which is the default setting for this model of switch (yours may vary). Let's put the command in anyway.

```
Sw1(config)#int fast0/1
Sw1(config-if)#switchport mode dynamic auto
```

Task 3:

> **NOTE:** You need to have at least one switch set to either trunk or dynamic desirable for a trunk link to form.

```
Sw2#show int fast0/1 sw
Name: Fa0/1
Switchport: Enabled
Administrative Mode: dynamic auto
Operational Mode: static access
Administrative Trunking Encapsulation: dot1q
Operational Trunking Encapsulation: native
Negotiation of Trunking: On
Access Mode VLAN: 1 (default)

Sw2#show interface trunk

Sw2(config)#int fast0/1
Sw2(config-if)#switchport mode dynamic desirable
Sw2(config-if)#end

Sw2#show int fast0/1 switchport
Name: Fa0/1
Switchport: Enabled
Administrative Mode: dynamic desirable
```

```
Operational Mode: trunk
Administrative Trunking Encapsulation: dot1q
Operational Trunking Encapsulation: dot1q
Negotiation of Trunking: On
Access Mode VLAN: 1 (default)
Trunking Native Mode VLAN: 1 (default)

Sw2#show interface trunk
Port        Mode        Encapsulation  Status       Native vlan
Fa0/1       desirable   n-802.1q       trunking     1
```

The n indicates that it negotiated the encapsulation type.

LAB 14: CONFIGURING A DEFAULT GATEWAY FOR ROUTERS AND SWITCHES

Lab Objective:

The objective of this lab exercise is to configure routers and switches to be able to communicate with remote networks. By default, devices can only communicate with locally-connected networks.

Lab Purpose:

Configuring a default gateway on routers and switches is a fundamental skill. Default gateways allow routers and switches to be reachable to and from remote subnets. As a Cisco engineer, as well as in the Cisco CCNA exam, you will be expected to know how to configure a router or switch default gateway.

Certification Level:

This lab is suitable for both CCENT and CCNA certification exam preparation.

Lab Difficulty:

This lab has a difficulty rating of 4/10.

Readiness Assessment:

When you are ready for your certification exam, you should complete this lab in no more than 10 minutes.

Lab Topology:

Please use the following topology to complete this lab exercise:

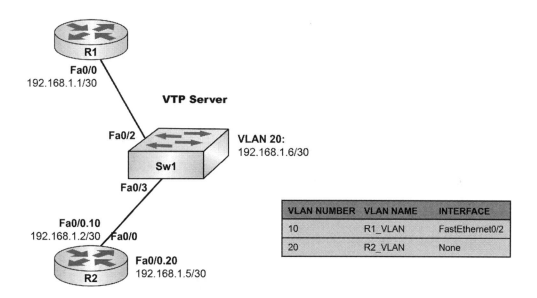

VLAN NUMBER	VLAN NAME	INTERFACE
10	R1_VLAN	FastEthernet0/2
20	R2_VLAN	None

Task 1:
Configure hostnames on Sw1, R1, and R2 as illustrated in the topology above.

Task 2:
Configure Sw1 as a VTP server and configure the VLANs as illustrated above. In addition, configure Sw1 interface FastEthernet0/3 as a trunk using 802.1Q encapsulation. Ensure that you place the correct switch interface into VLAN10.

Task 3:
Configure IP addressing on R1 and R2 and interface VLAN20 on Sw1 as illustrated above. In addition, configure a default gateway on Sw1 of 192.168.1.5 and a default route on R1 via FastEthernet0/0. Make VLAN20 the native VLAN on the router. Set the native VLAN on the switch trunk port to 20.

Task 4:
Verify your configuration by pinging from Sw1 to R1's FastEthernet0/0 address of 192.168.1.1.

LAB 14: CONFIGURATION AND VERIFICATION

Task 1:

For reference information on configuring hostnames, please refer to earlier labs.

Task 2:

For reference information on configuring and verifying VLANs and trunks, please refer to earlier labs.

Task 3:

```
R1#config t
Enter configuration commands, one per line.  End with CTRL/Z.
R1(config)#interface  fastethernet0/0
R1(config-if)#ip address 192.168.1.1 255.255.255.252
R1(config-if)#exit
R1(config)#ip route 0.0.0.0 0.0.0.0 fastethernet0/0
R1(config)#^Z
R1#
R1#show ip interface brief
Interface       IP-Address      OK? Method    Status     Protocol
FastEthernet0/0   192.168.1.1     YES manual    up         up

R2(config)#interface fastethernet0/0
R2(config-if)#description "Connected To Switch Trunk Fa0/3"
R2(config-if)#no shutdown
R2(config-if)#exit
R2(config)#interface fastethernet0/0.10
R2(config-subif)#description Subinterface For VLAN 10
R2(config-subif)#encapsulation dot1Q 10
R2(config-subif)#ip address 192.168.1.2 255.255.255.252
R2(config-subif)#exit
R2(config)#interface fastethernet 0/0.20
R2(config-subif)#description Subinterface For VLAN 20
R2(config-subif)#encapsulation dot1Q 20 native
R2(config-subif)#ip address 192.168.1.5 255.255.255.252
R2(config-subif)#end
R2#
R2#show ip interface brief
Interface       IP-Address      OK? Method    Status  Protocol
FastEthernet0/0   unassigned      YES manual    up      up
FastEthernet0/0.10  192.168.1.2   YES manual       up       up
FastEthernet0/0.20  192.168.1.5   YES manual    up      up

Sw1(config)#interface vlan1
Sw1(config-if)#shutdown
Sw1(config)#interface vlan20
Sw1(config-if)#ip address 192.168.1.6 255.255.255.252
Sw1(config-if)#no shutdown
```

```
Sw1(config-if)#int f0/3
Switch(config-if)#switchport trunk native vlan20
Sw1(config-if)#exit
Sw1(config)#ip default-gateway 192.168.1.5
Sw1(config)#^Z
Sw1#
Sw1#show ip interface brief
Interface   IP-Address     OK? Method Status                  Protocol
Vlan1       unassigned     YES NVRAM  administratively down   down
Vlan20      192.168.1.6    YES manual up                      up
Sw1#
Sw1#show ip redirects
Default gateway is 192.168.1.5

Host                Gateway          Last Use    Total Uses   Interface
ICMP redirect cache is empty
```

The `show ip redirects` **command won't work on Packet Tracer.**

Task 4:

```
Sw1#ping 192.168.1.1

Type escape sequence to abort.
Sending 5, 100-byte ICMP Echos to 192.168.1, timeout is 2 seconds:
..!!!
Success rate is 60 percent (3/5), round-trip min/avg/max = 1/3/4 ms
```

LAB 15: CISCO DISCOVERY PROTOCOL

Lab Objective:
The objective of this lab exercise is for you to learn and understand how to enable CDP and adjust CDP timers.

Lab Purpose:
Understanding CDP is a fundamental skill. CDP is a proprietary Cisco protocol that can be used for device discovery as well as internetwork troubleshooting. As a Cisco engineer, as well as in the Cisco CCNA exam, you will be expected to know how to enable and use CDP in internetwork discovery and troubleshooting.

Certification Level:
This lab is suitable for CCENT and CCNA certification exam preparation.

Lab Difficulty:
This lab has a difficulty rating of 5/10.

Readiness Assessment:
When you are ready for your certification exam, you should complete this lab in no more than 10 minutes.

Lab Topology:
Please use the following topology to complete this lab:

Task 1:
Configure hostnames on R1 and Sw1 as illustrated in the topology.

Task 2:
Configure an IP address of 172.29.100.1/24 on R1 F0/0.

Task 3:
Configure VLAN200 on Sw1 and name it CDP_VLAN. Configure interface VLAN200 on Sw1 and assign it the IP address 172.29.100.2/24. Assign port FastEthernet0/2 on Sw1 to this VLAN.

Task 4:

Enable CDP on R1 and Sw1 globally (it's already on by default but you can practice the command). Configure R1 and Sw1 to send CDP packets every 10 seconds. The timer command won't work on Packet Tracer so use live equipment or GNS3.

Task 5:

Use CDP to see detailed information about Sw1 from R1. Familiarize yourself with the information provided.

Task 6:

Now disable CDP on the router interface and disable CDP globally on the switch.

LAB 15: CONFIGURATION AND VERIFICATION

Task 1:

For reference information on configuring hostnames, please refer to earlier labs.

Task 2:
```
R1#conf t
Enter configuration commands, one per line.  End with CTRL/Z.
R1(config)#int fa0/0
R1(config-if)#ip address 172.29.100.1 255.255.255.0
R1(config-if)#no shut
R1(config-if)#^Z
R1#
```

Task 3:
```
Sw1#config t
Enter configuration commands, one per line.  End with CTRL/Z.
Sw1(config)#vlan200
Sw1(config-vlan)#name CDP_VLAN
Sw1(config-vlan)#exit
Sw1(config)#interface vlan1
Sw1(config-if)#shut
Sw1(config-if)#exit
Sw1(config)#int vlan200
Sw1(config-if)#no shut
Sw1(config-if)#ip address 172.29.100.2 255.255.255.0
Sw1(config-if)#exit
Sw1(config)#int f0/2
Sw1(config-if)#switchport mode access
Sw1(config-if)#switchport access vlan200
Sw1(config-if)#end
Sw1#ping 172.29.100.1

Type escape sequence to abort.
Sending 5, 100-byte ICMP Echos to 172.29.100.1, timeout is 2 seconds:
!!!!!
Success rate is 100 percent (5/5), round-trip min/avg/max = 1/203/1000
ms
Sw1#
```

Task 4:
```
R1#conf t
Enter configuration commands, one per line.  End with CTRL/Z.
R1(config)#cdp run
R1(config)#cdp timer 10
R1(config)#^Z
R1#show cdp interface fastethernet0/0
FastEthernet0/0 is up, line protocol is up
```

```
Encapsulation ARPA
Sending CDP packets every 10 seconds
Holdtime is 180 seconds

Sw1#conf t
Enter configuration commands, one per line.  End with CTRL/Z.
Sw1(config)#cdp run
Sw1(config)#cdp timer 10
Sw1(config)#end
Sw1#
Sw1#show cdp interface fastethernet0/2
FastEthernet0/2 is up, line protocol is up
  Encapsulation ARPA
  Sending CDP packets every 10 seconds
  Holdtime is 180 seconds
```

Task 5:

```
R1#show cdp neighbors detail
-------------------------
Device ID: Sw1
Entry address(es):
  IP address: 172.29.100.2
Platform: cisco WS-C2950G-24-EI,  Capabilities: Switch IGMP
Interface: FastEthernet0/0,  Port ID (outgoing port): FastEthernet0/2
Holdtime : 178 sec

Version :
Cisco Internetwork Operating System Software
IOS (tm) C2950 Software (C2950-I6Q4L2-M), Version 12.1(13)EA1, RELEASE
SOFTWARE (fc1)
Copyright (c) 1986-2003 by cisco Systems, Inc.
Compiled Tue 04-Mar-03 02:14 by yenanh

advertisement version: 2
Protocol Hello:  OUI=0x00000C, Protocol ID=0x0112; payload len=27, valu
e=00000000FFFFFFFF010221FF000000000000000DBD064100FF0000
VTP Management Domain: "CISCO"
Duplex: full
```

NOTE: The show cdp neighbors detail command provides detailed information about devices. This is a very useful troubleshooting command as you can find out the IP addresses (and more) of connected devices and access them remotely. Try this command on Sw1 and see the information you find out about on R1. Familiarize yourself with the contents of this command for both routers and switches.

Task 6:
```
R1#conf t
Enter configuration commands, one per line.  End with CTRL/Z.
R1(config)#int fa0/0
R1(config-if)#no cdp enable

Sw1(config)#no cdp run
```

NOTE: The CDP entries will still remain until they time out. You can clear the entries with the `clear cdp table` command, and then issue `show` commands to check that there are no entries. Knowing how to disable CDP is an important security task for the CCNA exam.

LAB 16: CONFIGURING LLDP

Lab Objective:

The objective of this lab exercise is for you to learn and understand how to enable the LLDP protocol on a Cisco Network.

Lab Purpose:

Configuring and applying the Link Layer Discovery Protocol (LLDP) allows network devices to discover other network devices directly connected to them. This is a fundamental skill that provides the same benefits that CDP does, but it's also compatible with non-Cisco equipment. As a Cisco engineer, as well as in the Cisco CCNA exam, you will be expected to know how to enable LLDP in your network.

Certification Level:

This lab is suitable for CCENT certification exam preparation.

Lab Difficulty:

This lab has a difficulty rating of 5/10.

Readiness Assessment:

When you are ready for your certification exam, you should complete this lab in no more than 20 minutes.

Lab Topology:

Please use the following topology to complete this lab exercise:

Task 1:

Configure the hostnames on R1 and R3 as illustrated in the topology.

Task 2:

Configure the IP addresses on the Ethernet interfaces of R1 and R3 as illustrated in the topology. There is no need to configure the Loopback interfaces for this lab.

Task 3:

Disable CDP globally on both routers and enable LLDP (it's disabled by default).

Task 4:

Make sure that both R1 and R3 have found each other via their Ethernet links using LLDP.

Task5:

Now disable one of the interfaces to prevent it from sending LLDP traffic.

LAB 16: CONFIGURATION AND VERIFICATION

Task 1:

For reference information on configuring hostnames, please refer to earlier labs.

Task 2:

For reference information on configuring IP addresses, please refer to earlier labs.

Task 3:

```
R1#config t
Enter configuration commands, one per line.  End with CTRL/Z.
R1(config)#no cdp run
R1(config)#lldp run
R1(config)#end
R1#
R3#conf t
Enter configuration commands, one per line.  End with CTRL/Z.
R3(config)#no cdp run
R1(config)#lldp run
R3(config)#end
R3#
```

Task 4:

```
R1#show lldp neighbors
Capability codes:
    (R) Router, (B) Bridge, (T) Telephone, (C) DOCSIS Cable Device
    (W) WLAN Access Point, (P) Repeater, (S) Station, (O) Other
Device ID          Local Intf    Hold-time  Capability     Port ID
R3                 Fa0/0         120        R              Fa0/0
Total entries displayed: 1


R3#show lldp neighbors
Capability codes:
    (R) Router, (B) Bridge, (T) Telephone, (C) DOCSIS Cable Device
    (W) WLAN Access Point, (P) Repeater, (S) Station, (O) Other
Device ID          Local Intf    Hold-time  Capability     Port ID
R1                 Fa0/0         120        R              Fa0/0
Total entries displayed: 1
```

Task 5:

```
Router(config-if)#no lldp transmit
```

LAB 17: CONFIGURING ERRDISABLE RECOVERY

Lab Objective:
The objective of this lab exercise is for you to learn and understand how the errdisable recovery feature works on a Layer 2 network. This lab will not work on Packet Tracer.

Lab Purpose:
Understanding how errdisable functionality works on a Layer 2 switch is a fundamental skill that will allow a network engineer to recover a port from the error-disable state. As a Cisco engineer, as well as in the Cisco CCNA exam, you will be expected to know how to recover any port in an error-disable state.

Certification Level:
This lab is suitable for CCENT certification exam preparation.

Lab Difficulty:
This lab has a difficulty rating of 5/10.

Readiness Assessment:
When you are ready for your certification exam, you should complete this lab in no more than 20 minutes.

Lab Topology:
Please use the following topology to complete this lab exercise:

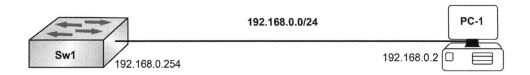

Task 1:
Configure the hostname on Sw1 as illustrated in the topology.

Task 2:
Create an SVI for VLAN1 on the switch and apply the respective IP address as illustrated in the topology (do the same thing with PC1).

Task 3:

Configure Sw1 port 0/1 with the following settings:

- Access-port mode
- Access-port VLAN1
- Switchport port-security enabled
- Switchport port-security maximum MACs of 1
- Switchport port-security violation mode shutdown

Task 4:

Remove PC1 and attach PC2 to the same port with a different IP address (192.168.10.2) and see how the port is shut down.

Task 5:

Configure the switch in such a way that any port being shut down by a security violation will recover automatically after 5 minutes. Check the status of the port where PC2 is connected after 5 minutes and make sure that the port is up and running. Issue a relevant show command.

LAB 17: CONFIGURATION AND VERIFICATION

Task 1:

For reference information on configuring hostnames, please refer to earlier labs.

Task 2:
```
SW1#conf t
Enter configuration commands, one per line.  End with CTRL/Z.
SW1(config)#interface vlan1
SW1(config-if)#ip address 192.168.0.254 255.255.255.0
SW1(config-if)#end
SW1#
```

Task 3:
```
SW1#conf t
Enter configuration commands, one per line.  End with CTRL/Z.
SW1(config)#interface gigabit0/1
SW1(config-if)#switchport mode access
SW1(config-if)#switchport access vlan1
SW1(config-if)#switchport port-security
SW1(config-if)#switchport port-security maximum 1
SW1(config-if)#switchport port-security violation-mode shutdown
SW1(config-if)#end
```

Task 4:
```
My-PC:~ admin$ ping 192.168.0.254
PING 192.168.0.1 (192.168.0.254): 56 data bytes
64 bytes from 192.168.0.254: icmp_seq=0 ttl=64 time=1.969 ms
64 bytes from 192.168.0.254: icmp_seq=1 ttl=64 time=1.986 ms
64 bytes from 192.168.0.254: icmp_seq=2 ttl=64 time=2.047 ms
64 bytes from 192.168.0.254: icmp_seq=3 ttl=64 time=3.192 ms
^C
--- 192.168.0.254 ping statistics ---
4 packets transmitted, 4 packets received, 0.0% packet loss
round-trip min/avg/max/stddev = 1.969/2.299/3.192/0.517 ms
```

After removing PC1 and adding a new PC (PC2), the port will be shut down because of a port-security violation (more than one MAC address is being learned over that Gigabit interface).

The following message will be seen at the switch CLI:

```
%PORT_SECURITY-2-PSECURE_VIOLATION: Security violation occurred, caused
by MAC address 001d.60b3.0aff on port FastEthernet0/1
```

If you go ahead and check the interface status, you will get the following:

```
Switch#show interface gigabit0/1
gigabitethernet0/1 is down, line protocol is down (err-disabled)
```

Task 5:
```
SW1#conf t
Enter configuration commands, one per line.  End with CTRL/Z.
SW1(config)#errdisable recovery cause psecure-violation
SW1(config)#errdisable recovery interval 300
SW1(config-if)#end
SW1#
```

After 5 minutes (300 seconds), you will see the following messages at the switch CLI:

```
%PM-4-ERR_RECOVER: Attempting to recover from psecure-violation
err-disable state on interface gigabit0/1
%LINK-3-UPDOWN: interface gigabit0/1, changed state to up
%LINEPROTO-5-UPDOWN: Line protocol on Interface FastEthernet0/13,
changed state to up
```

The new host is ready to be used, as the interface transitioned from shutdown (errdisabled) to up/up.

```
SW1#show errdisable recovery
ErrDisable Reason       Timer Status
----------------        -------------
Disabled udld
Disabled                bpduguard
Enabled                 security-violation
Disabled                channel-misconfig
Disabled                pagp-flap
Disabled                dtp-flap
Disabled                link-flap
Disabled                l2ptguard
Disabled                psecure-violation
Disabled                gbic-invalid
Disabled                dhcp-rate-limit
Disabled                mac-limit
Disabled                unicast-flood
Disabled                arp-inspection

Timer interval: 300 seconds
Interfaces that will be enabled at the next timeout:
Interface       Errdisable reason       Time left(sec)
---------       ------------------      -------------
Gig0/1          security-violation      300
```

3.0 Routing Fundamentals

LAB 18: CONFIGURING INTER-VLAN ROUTING (ROUTER ON A STICK)

Lab Objective:

The objective of this lab exercise is to configure a router to provide inter-VLAN communication. By default, hosts in one VLAN cannot communicate with hosts in another VLAN without a router routing between the two VLANs.

Lab Purpose:

Inter-VLAN routing configuration is a fundamental skill. Most networks typically have more than one VLAN, and the hosts in these VLANs are required to communicate with each other if the need arises. As a Cisco engineer, as well as in the Cisco CCNA exam, you will be expected to know how to configure inter-VLAN routing. In this example, you don't have a Layer 3 switch so you must use a router to route.

Certification Level:

This lab is suitable for CCNA certification exam preparation.

Lab Difficulty:

This lab has a difficulty rating of 9/10.

Readiness Assessment:

When you are ready for your certification exam, you should complete this lab in no more than 20 minutes.

Lab Topology:

Please use the following topology to complete this lab exercise:

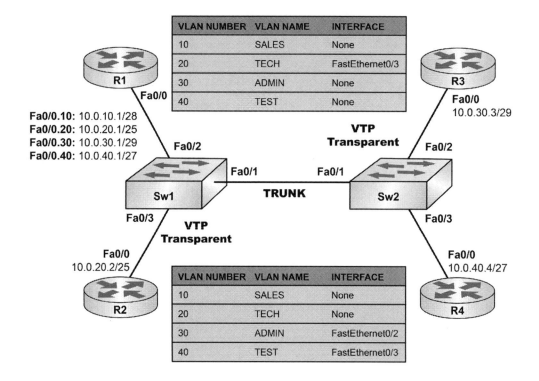

VLAN NUMBER	VLAN NAME	INTERFACE
10	SALES	None
20	TECH	FastEthernet0/3
30	ADMIN	None
40	TEST	None

Fa0/0
Fa0/0.10: 10.0.10.1/28
Fa0/0.20: 10.0.20.1/25
Fa0/0.30: 10.0.30.1/29
Fa0/0.40: 10.0.40.1/27

R1

R3
Fa0/0
10.0.30.3/29

VTP
Transparent

Fa0/2

Fa0/2

Fa0/1

TRUNK

Fa0/1

Sw1

Sw2

Fa0/3
VTP
Transparent

Fa0/3

Fa0/0
10.0.20.2/25

Fa0/0
10.0.40.4/27

R2

R4

VLAN NUMBER	VLAN NAME	INTERFACE
10	SALES	None
20	TECH	None
30	ADMIN	FastEthernet0/2
40	TEST	FastEthernet0/3

Task 1:

Configure a hostname on switches 1 and 2 and routers 1 through 4 as illustrated in the topology above.

Task 2:

Configure and verify Sw1 and Sw2 as VTP Transparent switches. Both switches should be in the VTP domain named CISCO. Secure VTP messages with the password CISCO.

Task 3:

Configure and verify FastEthernet0/1 between Sw1 and Sw2 as an 802.1Q trunk and configure VLANs as depicted in the topology above. Assign ports to depicted VLANs and configure Sw1 FastEthernet0/2 as a trunk. VLAN20 should have untagged Ethernet frames. Remember that on 802.1Q trunks, only the native VLAN is untagged.

Task 4:

Configure IP addresses on R2, R3, and R4 as illustrated in the diagram.

Task 5:

Configure subinterfaces off R1 FastEthernet0/0 in the corresponding VLANs in the diagram. Also, configure interface VLAN10 on Sw2 with the IP address 10.0.10.2/28.

Task 6:

Test network connectivity by pinging from R1 to routers R2, R3, and R4.

LAB 18: CONFIGURATION AND VERIFICATION

Task 1:

For reference information on configuring hostnames, please refer to earlier labs.

Task 2:

For reference information on configuring and verifying VTP, please refer to earlier labs.

Task 3:

```
Sw1#config t
Enter configuration commands, one per line.  End with CTRL/Z.
Sw1(config)#interface fastethernet0/1
Sw1(config-if)#switchport mode trunk
Sw1(config-if)#exit
Sw1(config)#vlan10
Sw1(config-vlan)#name SALES
Sw1(config-vlan)#exit
Sw1(config)#vlan20
Sw1(config-vlan)#name TECH
Sw1(config-vlan)#exit
Sw1(config)#vlan30
Sw1(config-vlan)#name ADMIN
Sw1(config-vlan)#exit
Sw1(config)#vlan40
Sw1(config-vlan)#name TEST
Sw1(config-vlan)#exit
Sw1(config)#interface fastethernet0/2
Sw1(config-if)#switchport mode trunk
Sw1(config-if)#switchport trunk native vlan20
Sw1(config-if)#exit
Sw1(config)#interface fastethernet0/3
Sw1(config-if)#switchport mode access
Sw1(config-if)#switchport access vlan20
Sw1(config-if)#end
Sw1#show interfaces trunk

Port       Mode        Encapsulation  Status     Native vlan
Fa0/1      on          802.1q         trunking   1
Fa0/2      on          802.1q         trunking   20

Port       Vlans allowed on trunk
Fa0/1      1-4094
Fa0/2      1-4094

Port       Vlans allowed and active in management domain
Fa0/1      1,10,20,30,40
Fa0/2      1,10,20,30,40
```

```
Port           Vlans in spanning tree forwarding state and not pruned
Fa0/1          1,20,30,40
Fa0/2          1,20,30,40

Sw2#config t
Enter configuration commands, one per line.  End with CTRL/Z.
Sw2(config)#interface fastethernet0/1
Sw2(config-if)#switchport mode trunk
Sw2(config-if)#exit
Sw2(config)#vlan10
Sw2(config-vlan)#name SALES
Sw2(config-vlan)#exit
Sw2(config)#vlan20
Sw2(config-vlan)#name TECH
Sw2(config-vlan)#exit
Sw2(config)#vlan30
Sw2(config-vlan)#name ADMIN
Sw2(config-vlan)#exit
Sw2(config)#vlan40
Sw2(config-vlan)#name TEST
Sw2(config-vlan)#exit
Sw2(config)#interface fastethernet0/2
Sw2(config-if)#switchport mode access
Sw2(config-if)#switchport access vlan30
Sw2(config-if)#exit
Sw2(config)#interface fastethernet0/3
Sw2(config-if)#switchport mode access
Sw2(config-if)#switchport access vlan40
Sw2(config-if)#^Z
Sw2#show interfaces trunk

Port           Mode         Encapsulation Status        Native vlan
Fa0/1          on           802.1q        trunking      1

Port           Vlans allowed on trunk
Fa0/1          1-4094

Port           Vlans allowed and active in management domain
Fa0/1          1,10,20,30,40

Port           Vlans in spanning tree forwarding state and not pruned
Fa0/1          1,20,30,40
```

Task 4:

For reference information on configuring IP interfaces, please refer to earlier labs.

Task 5:

```
R1#config t
Enter configuration commands, one per line.  End with CTRL/Z.
R1(config)#interface fastethernet0/0
R1(config-if)#description "Connected To Switch Trunk Fa0/2"
R1(config-if)#no shutdown
R1(config-if)#exit
R1(config)#interface fastethernet0/0.10
R1(config-subif)#description Subinterface For VLAN10
R1(config-subif)#encapsulation dot1Q 10
R1(config-subif)#ip address 10.0.10.1 255.255.255.240
R1(config-subif)#exit
R1(config)#interface fastethernet0/0.20
R1(config-subif)#description Subinterface For VLAN20
R1(config-subif)#encapsulation dot1Q 20 native
R1(config-subif)#ip address 10.0.20.1 255.255.255.128
R1(config-subif)#exit
R1(config)#interface fastethernet0/0.30
R1(config-subif)#description Subinterface For VLAN30
R1(config-subif)#ip address 10.0.30.1 255.255.255.248
R1(config-subif)#exit
R1(config)#interface fastethernet0/0.40
R1(config-subif)#description Subinterface For VLAN40
R1(config-subif)#encapsulation dot1Q 40
R1(config-subif)#ip address 10.0.40.1 255.255.255.224
R1(config-subif)#end
R1#show ip interface brief
Interface          IP-Address    OK?    Method    Status    Protocol
FastEthernet0/0    unassigned    YES    manual    up        up
FastEthernet0/0.10 10.0.10.1     YES    manual    up        up
FastEthernet0/0.20 10.0.20.1     YES    manual    up        up
FastEthernet0/0.30 10.0.30.1     YES    manual    up        up
FastEthernet0/0.40 10.0.40.1     YES    manual    up        up

Sw2(config)#interface vlan1
Sw2(config-if)#shutdown
Sw2(config)#interface vlan10
Sw2(config-if)#ip address 10.0.10.2 255.255.255.240
Sw2(config-if)#no shutdown
Sw2(config)#^Z
Sw2#show ip interface brief
Interface    IP-Address    OK? Method Status                    Protocol
Vlan1        unassigned    YES NVRAM  administratively down down
Vlan10       10.0.10.2     YES manual up                        up
Sw2#
```

Task 6:

```
R1#ping 10.0.10.2

Type escape sequence to abort.
Sending 5, 100-byte ICMP Echos to 10.0.10.2, timeout is 2 seconds:
.!!!!
Success rate is 80 percent (4/5), round-trip min/avg/max = 1/3/4 ms

R1#ping 10.0.20.2

Type escape sequence to abort.
Sending 5, 100-byte ICMP Echos to 10.0.20.2, timeout is 2 seconds:
.!!!!
Success rate is 80 percent (4/5), round-trip min/avg/max = 1/3/4 ms

R1#ping 10.0.30.3

Type escape sequence to abort.
Sending 5, 100-byte ICMP Echos to 10.0.30.3, timeout is 2 seconds:
.!!!!
Success rate is 80 percent (4/5), round-trip min/avg/max = 1/3/4 ms

R1#ping 10.0.40.4

Type escape sequence to abort.
Sending 5, 100-byte ICMP Echos to 10.0.40.4, timeout is 2 seconds:
.!!!!
Success rate is 80 percent (4/5), round-trip min/avg/max = 1/3/4 ms
```

NOTE: The first ping packet times out due to ARP resolution. Subsequent packets will be successful.

LAB 19: CONFIGURING AND ALLOWING INTER-VLAN ROUTING—SVI

Lab Objective:

The objective of this lab exercise is for you to learn and understand how to configure inter-VLAN routing using switched virtual interfaces (SVIs). This is technically in the ICND2 syllabus but inter-VLAN routing is also in the CCENT syllabus, so we'll cover it now.

Lab Purpose:

Understanding inter-VLAN routing and your configuration options is a vital skill for the exam and for administering live networks. You will need access to a Layer 3 switch for this lab, such as a 3560 (or use Packet Tracer).

Certification Level:

This lab is suitable for CCENT and ICND2 certification exam preparation.

Lab Difficulty:

This lab has a difficulty rating of 7/10.

Readiness Assessment:

When you are ready for your certification exam, you should complete this lab in no more than 15 minutes.

Lab Topology:

Please use the following topology to complete this lab exercise:

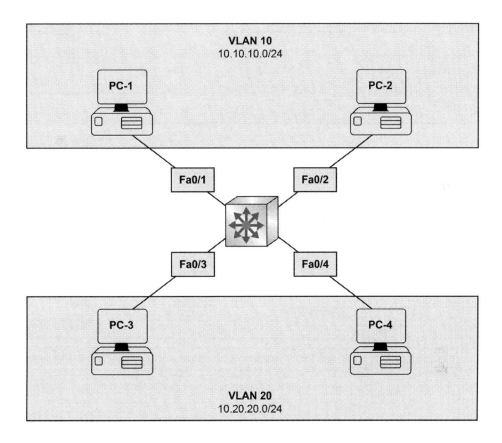

Task 1:

Configure the host IP addresses as well as VLANs 10 and 20 on the switch. Put the correct interfaces into the correct VLANs.

Task 2:

Configure SVIs on the switch for VLANs 10 and 20 of 10.10.10.1 and 10.20.20.1.

Task 3:

Verify your configuration with the correct show commands.

Task 4:

Enable IP routing on the switch. Then, test your configurations by pinging from a host in VLAN10 to a host in VLAN20.

LAB 19: CONFIGURATION AND VERIFICATION

Task 1:

For the hosts, you will need to manually add the IP addresses. Choose any addresses from the subnet but do not use the IPs required for the SVIs. Add the SVI IP address to the hosts as the default gateway. If your switch doesn't support the interface range facility, then configure each interface individually.

You may not be familiar with the switchport command because Layer 3 switches aren't covered in the theory part of the CCNA exam. This command specifies the interface to work as Layer 2 as opposed to an IP interface (as you would see on a router Ethernet port).

```
Switch(config)#vlan10
Switch(config-vlan)#name VLAN-10
Switch(config-vlan)#exit
Switch(config)#vlan20
Switch(config-vlan)#name VLAN-20
Switch(config-vlan)#exit
Switch(config)#interface range FastEthernet0/1-2
Switch(config-if-range)#switchport
Switch(config-if-range)#switchport mode access
Switch(config-if-range)#switchport access vlan10
Switch(config-if-range)#exit
Switch(config)#interface range FastEthernet0/3-4
Switch(config-if-range)#switchport
Switch(config-if-range)#switchport mode access
Switch(config-if-range)#switchport access vlan20
Switch(config-if-range)#exit
```

Task 2:

```
Switch(config)#interface vlan10
Switch(config-if)#description "SVI for VLAN 10"
Switch(config-if)#ip address 10.10.10.1 255.255.255.0
Switch(config-if)#no shutdown
Switch(config-if)#exit
Switch(config)#interface vlan20
Switch(config-if)#description "SVI for VLAN 10"
Switch(config-if)#ip address 10.20.20.1 255.255.255.0
Switch(config-if)#no shutdown
Switch(config-if)#exit
```

Task 3:

```
Switch#show vlan brief

VLAN Name                             Status     Ports
---- -------------------------- --------- -----------------------
1    default                    active     Fa0/5, Fa0/6, Fa0/7, Fa0/8
                                           Fa0/9, Fa0/10, Fa0/11, Fa0/12
                                           Fa0/13, Fa0/14, Fa0/15, Fa0/16
                                           Fa0/17, Fa0/18, Fa0/19, Fa0/20
                                           Fa0/21, Fa0/22, Fa0/23, Fa0/24
                                           Gig0/1, Gig0/2
10   VLAN0010                   active     Fa0/1, Fa0/2
20   VLAN0020                   active     Fa0/3, Fa0/4

[Output Truncated]

Switch#show interfaces vlan10
Vlan10 is up, line protocol is up
  Hardware is CPU Interface, address is 0004.9a53.b501 (bia 0004.9a53.
b501)
    Internet address is 10.10.10.1/24

[Output Truncated]

Switch#show ip interface brief
Interface        IP-Address   OK? Method Status                 Protocol
FastEthernet0/1  unassigned   YES unset  up                     up
FastEthernet0/2  unassigned   YES unset  up                     up
FastEthernet0/3  unassigned   YES unset  up                     up
FastEthernet0/4  unassigned   YES unset  up                     up
FastEthernet0/5  unassigned   YES unset  down                   down
Vlan1            unassigned   YES unset  administratively down  down
Vlan10           10.10.10.1   YES manual up                     up
Vlan20           10.20.20.1   YES manual up                     up

[Output Truncated]
```

Task 4:

```
Switch(config)#ip routing

PC#ping 10.20.20.2
```

LAB 20: CONFIGURING STATIC ROUTING VIA INTERFACES

Lab Objective:
The objective of this lab exercise is to configure static routes via Ethernet interfaces connected to a switch on two routers. This lab also goes through the validation of the configured static routes.

Lab Purpose:
Static route configuration is a fundamental skill. There are several methods to configure static routes on a Cisco router, and each way has its pros and cons. As a Cisco engineer, as well as in the Cisco CCNA exam, you will be expected to know how to configure static routes via any of the methods available in Cisco IOS.

Certification Level:
This lab is suitable for both CCENT and CCNA certification exam preparation.

Lab Difficulty:
This lab has a difficulty rating of 5/10.

Readiness Assessment:
When you are ready for your certification exam, you should complete this lab in no more than 15 minutes.

Lab Topology:

Please use the following topology to complete this lab exercise:

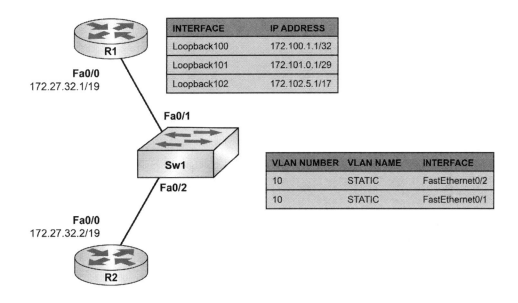

INTERFACE	IP ADDRESS
Loopback100	172.100.1.1/32
Loopback101	172.101.0.1/29
Loopback102	172.102.5.1/17

VLAN NUMBER	VLAN NAME	INTERFACE
10	STATIC	FastEthernet0/2
10	STATIC	FastEthernet0/1

Task 1:
Configure the hostnames on R1, R2, and Sw1 as illustrated in the topology.

Task 2:
Configure Sw1 as a VTP server and configure VLAN10 named STATIC. Assign ports FastEthernet0/1 and FastEthernet0/2 to this VLAN.

Task 3:
Configure IP addresses 172.27.32.1/19 and 172.27.32.2/19 on R1 and R2 Fa0/0 interfaces, respectively. In addition, configure the Loopback interfaces on R1 with the IP addresses listed in the topology.

Task 4:
Configure static routes via the FastEthernet0/0 interface on R2 to all the subnets configured on the Loopback addresses configured on R1. Verify your static route configuration with appropriate commands. Ping each Loopback interface configured on R1 from R2 to validate your static route configuration.

LAB 20: CONFIGURATION AND VERIFICATION

Task 1:

For reference information on configuring hostnames, please refer to earlier labs.

Task 2:

For reference information on configuring standard VLANs, please refer to earlier labs.

Task 3:

```
R1#conf t
Enter configuration commands, one per line.  End with CTRL/Z.
R1(config)#int fast0/0
R1(config-if)#ip address 172.27.32.1 255.255.224.0
R1(config-if)#no shutdown
R1(config-if)#end

R2#config t
Enter configuration commands, one per line.  End with CTRL/Z.
R2(config)#int fa0/0
R2(config-if)#ip add 172.27.32.2 255.255.224.0
R2(config-if)#no shu
R2(config-if)#^Z

R1#ping 172.27.32.2

Type escape sequence to abort.
Sending 5, 100-byte ICMP Echos to 172.27.32.2, timeout is 2 seconds:
.!!!!
Success rate is 80 percent (4/5), round-trip min/avg/max = 4/4/4 ms

R1#config t
Enter configuration commands, one per line.  End with CTRL/Z.
R1(config)#interface loopback100
R1(config-if)#ip address 172.100.1.1 255.255.255.255
R1(config-if)#exit
R1(config)#interface loopback101
R1(config-if)#ip address 172.101.0.1 255.255.255.248
R1(config-if)#exit
R1(config)#interface loopback102
R1(config-if)#ip address 172.102.5.1 255.255.128.0
R1(config-if)#^Z
R1#
R1#show ip interface brief
Interface       IP-Address      OK? Method Status          Protocol
FastEthernet0/0 172.27.32.1     YES manual up              up
Loopback100     172.100.1.1     YES manual up              up
Loopback101     172.101.0.1     YES manual up              up
Loopback102     172.102.5.1     YES manual up              up
```

NOTE: By default, Loopback interfaces will be enabled once you configure them. Therefore, there is no need to issue the `no shutdown` command when creating them.

Task 4:

```
R2#config t
Enter configuration commands, one per line.  End with CTRL/Z.
R2(config)#ip route 172.100.1.1 255.255.255.255 fastethernet0/0
R2(config)#ip route 172.101.0.0 255.255.255.248 fastethernet0/0
R2(config)#ip route 172.102.0.0 255.255.128.0 fastethernet0/0
R2(config)#end
R2#
R2#show ip route
Codes: C - connected, S - static, R - RIP, M - mobile, B—BGP,
       D - EIGRP, EX - EIGRP external, O - OSPF, IA - OSPF inter area,
       N1 - OSPF NSSA external type 1, N2 - OSPF NSSA external type 2,
       E1 - OSPF external type 1, E2 - OSPF external type 2,
       i - IS-IS, su - IS-IS summary, L1 - IS-IS level-1,
       L2 - IS-IS level-2, ia - IS-IS inter area,
       * - candidate default, U - per-user static route, o - ODR,
       P - periodic downloaded static route

Gateway of last resort is not set

     172.102.0.0/17 is subnetted, 1 subnets
S       172.102.0.0 is directly connected, FastEthernet0/0
     172.100.0.0/32 is subnetted, 1 subnets
S       172.100.1.1 is directly connected, FastEthernet0/0
     172.101.0.0/29 is subnetted, 1 subnets
S       172.101.0.0 is directly connected, FastEthernet0/0
     172.27.0.0/19 is subnetted, 1 subnets
C       172.27.32.0 is directly connected, FastEthernet0/0
```

NOTE: The `S` in front of the route indicates that this is a static route, as stated in the legend codes immediately following the `show ip route` command.

```
R2#sh ip route 172.100.1.1
Routing entry for 172.100.1.1/32
  Known via "static", distance 1, metric 0 (connected)
  Routing Descriptor Blocks:
  * directly connected, via FastEthernet0/0
      Route metric is 0, traffic share count is 1

R2#sh ip route 172.101.0.1
Routing entry for 172.101.0.0/29
  Known via "static", distance 1, metric 0 (connected)
  Routing Descriptor Blocks:
  * directly connected, via FastEthernet0/0
      Route metric is 0, traffic share count is 1
```

```
R2#sh ip route 172.102.5.1
Routing entry for 172.102.0.0/17
  Known via "static", distance 1, metric 0 (connected)
  Routing Descriptor Blocks:
  * directly connected, via FastEthernet0/0
      Route metric is 0, traffic share count is 1

R2#ping 172.100.1.1

Type escape sequence to abort.
Sending 5, 100-byte ICMP Echos to 172.100.1.1, timeout is 2 seconds:
.!!!!
Success rate is 80 percent (4/5), round-trip min/avg/max = 4/4/4 ms

R2#ping 172.101.0.1

Type escape sequence to abort.
Sending 5, 100-byte ICMP Echos to 172.101.0.1, timeout is 2 seconds:
.!!!!
Success rate is 80 percent (4/5), round-trip min/avg/max = 4/4/4 ms

R2#ping 172.102.5.1

Type escape sequence to abort.
Sending 5, 100-byte ICMP Echos to 172.102.5.1, timeout is 2 seconds:
.!!!!
Success rate is 80 percent (4/5), round-trip min/avg/max = 4/4/4 ms
```

NOTE: The first ping packet will always fail because of ARP resolution. Subsequent ping packets will pass.

LAB 21: CONFIGURING STATIC ROUTING VIA IP ADDRESSES

Lab Objective:
The objective of this lab exercise is to configure static routes via next hop IP addresses on interfaces connected to a switch on two routers. This lab also goes through the validation of the configured static routes.

Lab Purpose:
Static route configuration is a fundamental skill. There are several methods to configure static routes on a Cisco router, and each way has its pros and cons. As a Cisco engineer, as well as in the Cisco CCNA exam, you will be expected to know how to configure static routes via any of the methods available in Cisco IOS.

Certification Level:
This lab is suitable for both CCENT and CCNA certification exam preparation.

Lab Difficulty:
This lab has a difficulty rating of 5/10.

Readiness Assessment:
When you are ready for your certification exam, you should complete this lab in no more than 15 minutes.

Lab Topology:
Please use the following topology to complete this lab exercise:

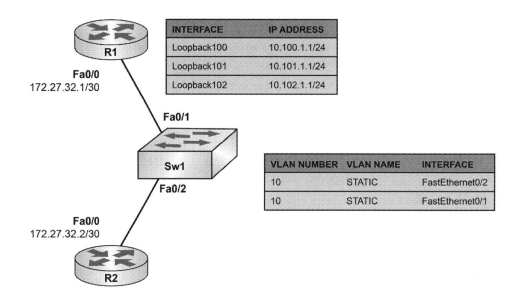

Task 1:
Configure the hostnames on R1, R2, and Sw1 as illustrated in the topology.

Task 2:
Configure Sw1 as a VTP sever and configure VLAN10 named STATIC. Assign ports FastEthernet0/1 and FastEthernet0/2 to this VLAN.

Task 3:
Configure IP addresses 172.27.32.1/30 and 172.27.32.2/30 on R1 and R2 Fa0/0 interfaces, respectively. In addition, configure the Loopback interfaces on R1 with the IP addresses in the topology.

Task 4:
Configure static routes via the next hop IP address of 172.27.32.2 on R2 to all the subnets configured on the Loopback addresses previously configured on R1. Verify your static route configuration. Ping each Loopback interface configured on R1 from R2 to validate your static route configuration.

LAB 21: CONFIGURATION AND VERIFICATION

Task 1:

For reference information on configuring hostnames, please refer to earlier labs.

Task 2:

For reference information on configuring standard VLANs, please refer to earlier labs.

Task 3:

```
R1#conf t
Enter configuration commands, one per line.  End with CTRL/Z.
R1(config)#int fast0/0
R1(config-if)#ip address 172.27.32.1 255.255.255.252
R1(config-if)#no shutdown
R1(config-if)#end

R2#config t
Enter configuration commands, one per line.  End with CTRL/Z.
R2(config)#int fa0/0
R2(config-if)#ip add 172.27.32.2 255.255.255.252
R2(config-if)#no shu
R2(config-if)#^Z

R1#ping 172.27.32.2

Type escape sequence to abort.
Sending 5, 100-byte ICMP Echos to 172.27.32.2, timeout is 2 seconds:
.!!!!
Success rate is 80 percent (4/5), round-trip min/avg/max = 4/4/4 ms

R1#config t
Enter configuration commands, one per line.  End with CTRL/Z.
R1(config)#int loop100
R1(config-if)#ip add 10.100.1.1 255.255.255.0
R1(config-if)#exit
R1(config)#int loop101
R1(config-if)#ip add 10.101.1.1 255.255.255.0
R1(config-if)#exit
R1(config)#int loop102
R1(config-if)#ip add 10.102.1.1 255.255.255.0
R1(config-if)#^Z
R1#
R1#sh ip int bri
Interface       IP-Address  OK? Method Status          Protocol
FastEthernet0/0 172.27.32.1 YES manual up              up
Loopback100     10.100.1.1  YES manual up              up
Loopback101     10.101.1.1  YES manual up              up
Loopback102     10.102.1.1  YES manual up              up
```

Task 4:

```
R2#conf t
Enter configuration commands, one per line.  End with CTRL/Z.
R2(config)#ip route 10.100.1.0 255.255.255.0 172.27.32.1
R2(config)#ip route 10.101.1.0 255.255.255.0 172.27.32.1
R2(config)#ip route 10.102.1.0 255.255.255.0 172.27.32.1
R2(config)#end
R2#

R2#show ip route
Codes: C - connected, S - static, R - RIP, M - mobile, B—BGP,
       D - EIGRP, EX - EIGRP external, O - OSPF, IA - OSPF inter area,
       N1 - OSPF NSSA external type 1, N2 - OSPF NSSA external type 2,
       E1 - OSPF external type 1, E2 - OSPF external type 2,
       i - IS-IS, su - IS-IS summary, L1 - IS-IS level-1,
       L2 - IS-IS level-2, ia - IS-IS inter area,
       * - candidate default, U - per-user static route, o - ODR,
       P - periodic downloaded static route

Gateway of last resort is not set

     172.27.0.0/30 is subnetted, 1 subnets
C       172.27.32.0 is directly connected, FastEthernet0/0
     10.0.0.0/24 is subnetted, 3 subnets
S       10.102.1.0 [1/0] via 172.27.32.1
S       10.101.1.0 [1/0] via 172.27.32.1
S       10.100.1.0 [1/0] via 172.27.32.1

R2#ping 10.100.1.1

Type escape sequence to abort.
Sending 5, 100-byte ICMP Echos to 10.100.1.1, timeout is 2 seconds:
!!!!!
Success rate is 100 percent (5/5), round-trip min/avg/max = 4/4/4 ms

R2#ping 10.101.1.1

Type escape sequence to abort.
Sending 5, 100-byte ICMP Echos to 10.101.1.1, timeout is 2 seconds:
!!!!!
Success rate is 100 percent (5/5), round-trip min/avg/max = 1/2/4 ms

R2#ping 10.102.1.1

Type escape sequence to abort.
Sending 5, 100-byte ICMP Echos to 10.102.1.1, timeout is 2 seconds:
!!!!!
Success rate is 100 percent (5/5), round-trip min/avg/max = 1/2/4 ms
```

NOTE: Notice the difference in this ping versus the one where you used an interface as the next hop for static routing. Because an IP address has been specified, there is no ARP timeout for the first packet since the next hop Layer 3 address has been specified.

LAB 22: CONFIGURING AND NAMING STATIC ROUTES

Lab Objective:
The objective of this lab exercise is to configure named static routes via next hop IP addresses on interfaces connected to a switch on two routers. This lab also goes through the validation of the configured static routes.

Lab Purpose:
Static route configuration is a fundamental skill. There are several methods to configure static routes on a Cisco router, and each way has its pros and cons. Naming the static routes allows you to easily identify what each static route is used for as you view the router configuration. As a Cisco engineer, as well as in the Cisco CCNA exam, you will be expected to know how to configure named static routes via any of the methods available in Cisco IOS.

Certification Level:
This lab is suitable for both CCENT and CCNA certification exam preparation.

Lab Difficulty:
This lab has a difficulty rating of 5/10.

Readiness Assessment:
When you are ready for your certification exam, you should complete this lab in no more than 15 minutes.

Lab Topology:
Please use the following topology to complete this lab exercise:

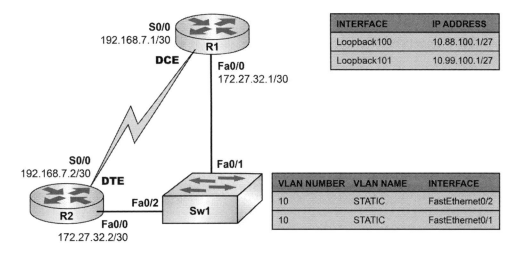

INTERFACE	IP ADDRESS
Loopback100	10.88.100.1/27
Loopback101	10.99.100.1/27

VLAN NUMBER	VLAN NAME	INTERFACE
10	STATIC	FastEthernet0/2
10	STATIC	FastEthernet0/1

Task 1:

Configure the hostnames on R1, R2, and Sw1 as illustrated in the topology.

Task 2:

Configure Sw2 as a VTP sever and configure VLAN10 named STATIC. Assign ports FastEthernet0/1 and FastEthernet0/2 to this VLAN. Configure the DCE interface Serial0/0 in R1 to provide clocking to R2 at a clock speed of 768 Kbps (not required if you are using GNS3).

Task 3:

Configure IP addresses 172.27.32.1/30 and 172.27.32.2/30 on R1 and R2 Fa0/0 interfaces, respectively. Configure IP addresses 192.168.7.1/30 and 192.168.7.2/30 on R1 and R2 S0/0 interfaces, respectively. In addition, configure the Loopback interfaces on R1 with the IP addresses in the topology.

Task 4:

Configure a static route named LAN-ROUTE on R2 via interface FastEthernet0/0 with a next hop IP address of 172.27.32.1 to the 10.88.100.1/27 subnet. Configure a static route named WAN-ROUTE on R2 via Serial0/0 with a next hop IP address of 192.168.7.1 to the 10.99.100.1/27 subnet. Verify your static route configuration.

Task 5:

Ping each Loopback interface configured on R1 from R2 to verify your static route configuration.

LAB 22: CONFIGURATION AND VERIFICATION

Task 1:

For reference information on configuring hostnames, please refer to earlier labs.

Task 2:

For reference information on configuring standard VLANs, please refer to earlier labs.

Task 3:

For reference information on configuring IP interfaces, please refer to earlier labs.

Task 4:

```
R2(config)#ip route 10.88.100.0 255.255.255.224 fa0/0 172.27.32.1 name
LAN-ROUTE
R2(config)#ip route 10.99.100.0 255.255.255.224 se0/0 192.168.7.1 name
WAN-ROUTE
R2(config)#end
R2#
R2#show ip route
Codes: C - connected, S - static, R - RIP, M - mobile, B—BGP,
       D - EIGRP, EX - EIGRP external, O - OSPF, IA - OSPF inter area,
       N1 - OSPF NSSA external type 1, N2 - OSPF NSSA external type 2,
       E1 - OSPF external type 1, E2 - OSPF external type 2,
       i - IS-IS, su - IS-IS summary, L1 - IS-IS level-1,
       L2 - IS-IS level-2, ia - IS-IS inter area,
       * - candidate default, U - per-user static route, o - ODR,
       P - periodic downloaded static route

Gateway of last resort is not set

     172.27.0.0/24 is subnetted, 1 subnets
C       172.27.32.0 is directly connected, FastEthernet0/0
     10.0.0.0/27 is subnetted, 2 subnets
S       10.88.100.0 [1/0] via 172.27.32.1, FastEthernet0/0
S       10.99.100.0 [1/0] via 192.168.7.1, Serial0/0
     192.168.7.0/30 is subnetted, 1 subnets
C       192.168.7.0 is directly connected, Serial0/0
```

NOTE: The names configured on the static routes do not show in the output of the show ip route command; however, they do show in the running configuration. Naming static routes allows you to easily identify what the configured static routes are being used for. This can be extremely helpful in a router where you have many static routes configured. You can simply issue the show run command and filter the output to include only statements that contain the word route as illustrated below:

```
R2#show running-config | include route
ip route 10.88.100.0 255.255.255.224 Ethernet0/0 172.27.32.1 name
LAN-ROUTE
ip route 10.99.100.0 255.255.255.224 Serial0/0 192.168.7.1 name
WAN-ROUTE
```

Task 5:

For reference information on how to ping, refer to earlier labs.

LAB 23: CONFIGURING DEFAULT STATIC ROUTES

Lab Objective:
The objective of this lab exercise is for you to learn and understand how to configure default static routes on Cisco IOS routers. By default, no default routes exist on Cisco IOS routers.

Lab Purpose:
Static default route configuration is a fundamental skill. Default routes are used to forward traffic to destinations where the router does not have a specific route to its routing table. They can also be used to forward all external traffic (such as Internet traffic) to an Internet Service Provider, for example. As a Cisco engineer, as well as in the Cisco CCNA exam, you will be expected to know how to configure static default routes.

Certification Level:
This lab is suitable for both CCENT and CCNA certification exam preparation.

Lab Difficulty:
This lab has a difficulty rating of 6/10.

Readiness Assessment:
When you are ready for your certification exam, you should complete this lab in no more than 10 minutes.

Lab Topology:
Please use the following topology to complete this lab exercise:

INTERFACE	IP ADDRESS
Loopback100	172.18.0.1/23
Loopback101	10.100.100.1/26
Loopback102	192.168.30.1/29

Task 1:
Configure the hostnames on routers R1 and R2 as illustrated in the topology.

Task 2:

Configure a back-to-back Serial connection between R1 and R2. Configure the DCE interface Serial0/0 in R1 to provide clocking to R2 at a clock speed of 256 Kbps. Ignore this if you are using GNS3.

Task 3:

Configure IP addresses 192.168.254.1/30 and 192.168.254.2/30 on R1 and R2 Serial0/0 interfaces, respectively. Configure the Loopback interfaces on R1 with the IP addresses illustrated in the topology.

Task 4:

Configure a static default route from R2 pointing to R1. Ping each Loopback interface configured on R1 from R2 to verify your static route configuration.

LAB 23: CONFIGURATION AND VERIFICATION

Task 1:

For reference information on configuring hostnames, please refer to earlier labs.

Task 2:

For reference information on configuring DCE interfaces, please refer to earlier labs.

Task 3:

```
R1#conf t
Enter configuration commands, one per line.  End with CTRL/Z.
R1(config)#int s0/0
R1(config-if)#ip add 192.168.254.1 255.255.255.252
R1(config-if)#exit
R1(config)#interface loop100
R1(config-if)#ip address 172.18.0.1 255.255.254.0
R1(config-if)#exit
R1(config)#interface loop101
R1(config-if)#ip add 10.100.100.1 255.255.255.192
R1(config-if)#exit
R1(config)#int loop102
R1(config-if)#ip address 192.168.30.1 255.255.255.248
R1(config-if)#^Z
R1#

R2#conf t
Enter configuration commands, one per line.  End with CTRL/Z.
R2(config)#int s0/0
R2(config-if)#ip add 192.168.254.2 255.255.255.252
R2(config-if)#end
R2#

R1#ping 192.168.254.2

Type escape sequence to abort.
Sending 5, 100-byte ICMP Echos to 192.168.254.2, timeout is 2 seconds:
!!!!!
Success rate is 100 percent (5/5), round-trip min/avg/max = 8/8/8 ms
```

Task 4:

```
R2#conf t
Enter configuration commands, one per line.  End with CTRL/Z.
R2(config)#ip route 0.0.0.0 0.0.0.0 serial0/0 192.168.254.1
R2(config)#end
R2#

R2#show ip route
Codes: C - connected, S - static, R - RIP, M - mobile, B—BGP,
```

```
         D - EIGRP, EX - EIGRP external, O - OSPF, IA - OSPF inter area,
         N1 - OSPF NSSA external type 1, N2 - OSPF NSSA external type 2,
         E1 - OSPF external type 1, E2 - OSPF external type 2,
         i - IS-IS, su - IS-IS summary, L1 - IS-IS level-1,
         L2 - IS-IS level-2, ia - IS-IS inter area,
         * - candidate default, U - per-user static route, o - ODR,
         P - periodic downloaded static route

Gateway of last resort is 192.168.254.1 to network 0.0.0.0

     192.168.254.0/30 is subnetted, 1 subnets
C        192.168.254.0 is directly connected, Serial0/0
     150.1.0.0/24 is subnetted, 1 subnets
C        150.1.1.0 is directly connected, FastEthernet0/0
S*   0.0.0.0/0 [1/0] via 192.168.254.1, Serial0/0

R2#ping 172.18.0.1

Type escape sequence to abort.
Sending 5, 100-byte ICMP Echos to 172.18.0.1, timeout is 2 seconds:
!!!!!
Success rate is 100 percent (5/5), round-trip min/avg/max = 8/12/32 ms

R2#ping 10.100.100.1

Type escape sequence to abort.
Sending 5, 100-byte ICMP Echos to 10.100.100.1, timeout is 2 seconds:
!!!!!
Success rate is 100 percent (5/5), round-trip min/avg/max = 8/8/8 ms

R2#ping 192.168.30.1

Type escape sequence to abort.
Sending 5, 100-byte ICMP Echos to 192.168.30.1, timeout is 2 seconds:
!!!!!
Success rate is 100 percent (5/5), round-trip min/avg/max = 4/7/8 ms
```

LAB 24: CONFIGURING IPV6 STATIC ROUTES

Lab Objective:
The objective of this lab exercise is for you to learn and understand how to manually configure static IPv6 routes.

Lab Purpose:
Manually configure IPv6 interface addressing, and then configure static routes so R1 can reach the addresses on the Loopbacks of R2.

Certification Level:
This lab is suitable for CCENT certification exam preparation.

Lab Difficulty:
This lab has a difficulty rating of 7/10.

Readiness Assessment:
When you are ready for your certification exam, you should complete this lab in no more than 10 minutes.

Lab Topology:
Please use the following topology to complete this lab exercise:

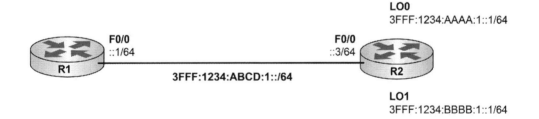

Task 1:
Configure the hostnames on routers R1 and R2 as illustrated in the topology.

Task 2:
Configure the IPv6 addresses on the FastEthernet interfaces of R1 and R2 as illustrated in the topology. Ping from R1 to R2. Also, using the relevant `show` commands, find the link-local IPv6 address and ping that.

Task 3:

Configure two static routes on R1 to allow traffic to reach the subnets connected to R2.

Task 4:

Ping across the link, and then use the relevant show commands to verify your configuration.

LAB 24: CONFIGURATION AND VERIFICATION

Task 1:

For reference information on configuring hostnames, please refer to earlier labs.

Task 2:

```
R1(config)#ipv6 unicast-routing
R1(config)#int f0/0
R1(config-if)#ipv6 add 3fff:1234:abcd:1::1/64
R1(config-if)#no shut
R1(config-if)#end
R1#show ipv6 interface brief
FastEthernet0/0            [up/up]
    FE80::C000:6FF:FEEC:0
    3FFF:1234:ABCD:1::1

R2(config)#ipv6 unicast-routing
R2(config)#int f0/0
R2(config-if)#ipv6 add 3fff:1234:abcd:1::3/64
R2(config-if)#no shut

R2#ping ipv6 3fff:1234:abcd:1::1

Type escape sequence to abort.
Sending 5, 100-byte ICMP Echos to 3FFF:1234:ABCD:1::1, timeout is 2
seconds:
!!!!!
Success rate is 100 percent (5/5), round-trip min/avg/max = 12/23/44 ms

R2#show ipv6 int f0/0
FastEthernet0/0 is up, line protocol is up
  IPv6 is enabled, link-local address is FE80::C001:8FF:FE52:0
No Virtual link-local address(es):
  Global unicast address(es):
    3FFF:1234:ABCD:1::3, subnet is 3FFF:1234:ABCD:1::/64

[Output Truncated]
```

NOTE: Because link-local IPv6 addresses are not held in the routing table, you need to specify an exit interface when issuing a ping.

```
R1#ping ipv6 FE80::C001:8FF:FE52:0
Output Interface: f0/0
% Invalid interface. Use full interface name without spaces (e.g.
Serial0/1)
Output Interface: fastethernet0/0
Type escape sequence to abort.
Sending 5, 100-byte ICMP Echos to FE80::C001:8FF:FE52:0, timeout is 2
seconds:
```

```
Packet sent with a source address of FE80::C000:8FF:FE52:0
!!!!!
Success rate is 100 percent (5/5), round-trip min/avg/max = 16/21/40 ms

R2(config-if)#interface Loopback0
R2(config-if)#ipv6 address 3FFF:1234:AAAA:1::1/64
R2(config-if)#interface Loopback1
R2(config-if)#ipv6 address 3FFF:1234:BBBB:1::1/64
```

Task 3:

```
R1(config)#ipv6 route 3FFF:1234:AAAA:1::/64 FastEthernet0/0
FE80::C001:8FF:FE52:0
R1(config)#ipv6 route 3FFF:1234:BBBB:1::/64 FastEthernet0/0
FE80::C001:8FF:FE52:0
```

Task 4:

```
R1#ping ipv6 3fff:1234:aaaa:1::1

Type escape sequence to abort.
Sending 5, 100-byte ICMP Echos to 3FFF:1234:AAAA:1::1, timeout is 2
seconds:
!!!!!
```

LAB 25: CONFIGURING IPV6 DEFAULT ROUTES

Lab Objective:
The objective of this lab exercise is for you to learn and understand how to manually configure static default IPv6 routes.

Lab Purpose:
Manually configure IPv6 interface addressing, and then configure a static default route so R1 can reach the addresses on the Loopbacks of R2.

Certification Level:
This lab is suitable for CCENT certification exam preparation.

Lab Difficulty:
This lab has a difficulty rating of 7/10.

Readiness Assessment:
When you are ready for your certification exam, you should complete this lab in no more than 10 minutes.

Lab Topology:
Please use the following topology to complete this lab exercise:

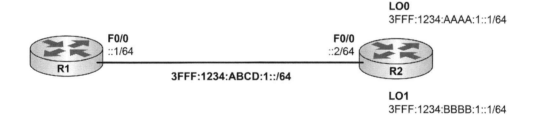

Task 1:
Configure the hostnames on routers R1 and R2 as illustrated in the topology.

Task 2:
Configure the IPv6 addresses on the FastEthernet interfaces of R1 and R2 as illustrated in the topology. Add the Loopback addresses to R2.

Task 3:

Configure a default static route on R1 to allow traffic to reach the subnets connected to R2.

Task 4:

Ping across the link, and then use relevant `show` commands to verify your configuration.

LAB 25: CONFIGURATION AND VERIFICATION

Task 1:

For reference information on configuring hostnames, please refer to earlier labs.

Task 2:
```
R1(config)#ipv6 unicast-routing
R1(config)#int f0/0
R1(config-if)#ipv6 add 3fff:1234:abcd:1::1/64
R1(config-if)#end
R1#

R2(config)#ipv6 unicast-routing
R2(config)#int f0/0
R2(config-if)#ipv6 add 3fff:1234:abcd:1::2/64
R2(config-if)#no shut
R2(config-if)#interface Loopback0
R2(config-if)#ipv6 address 3FFF:1234:AAAA:1::1/64
R2(config-if)#interface Loopback1
R2(config-if)#ipv6 address 3FFF:1234:BBBB:1::1/64

R2#show ipv6 int f0/0
FastEthernet0/0 is up, line protocol is up
  IPv6 is enabled, link-local address is FE80::C001:8FF:FE52:0
  No Virtual link-local address(es):
  Global unicast address(es):
    3FFF:1234:ABCD:1::2, subnet is 3FFF:1234:ABCD:1::/64
```

Task 3:
```
R1(config)#ipv6 route ::/0 f0/0 FE80::C001:8FF:FE52:0
```

Task 4:
```
R1#ping ipv6 3fff:1234:aaaa:1::1

Type escape sequence to abort.
Sending 5, 100-byte ICMP Echos to 3FFF:1234:AAAA:1::1, timeout is 2
seconds:
!!!!!
Success rate is 100 percent (5/5), round-trip min/avg/max = 12/19/24 ms

R1#ping ipv6 3fff:1234:bbbb:1::1

Type escape sequence to abort.
Sending 5, 100-byte ICMP Echos to 3FFF:1234:BBBB:1::1, timeout is 2
seconds:
!!!!!
Success rate is 100 percent (5/5), round-trip min/avg/max = 20/20/24 ms
```

```
R1#show ipv6 route
IPv6 Routing Table - 4 entries
Codes: C - Connected, L - Local, S - Static, R - RIP, B—BGP,
       U - Per-user Static route, M - MIPv6, I1 - ISIS L1,
       I2 - ISIS L2, IA - ISIS interarea, IS - ISIS summary,
       O - OSPF intra, OI - OSPF inter, OE1 - OSPF ext 1,
       OE2 - OSPF ext 2, ON1 - OSPF NSSA ext 1, ON2 - OSPF NSSA ext 2,
       D - EIGRP, EX - EIGRP external
S    ::/0 [1/0]
     via FE80::C001:8FF:FE52:0, FastEthernet0/0
C    3FFF:1234:ABCD:1::/64 [0/0]
     via ::, FastEthernet0/0
L    3FFF:1234:ABCD:1::1/128 [0/0]
     via ::, FastEthernet0/0
L    FF00::/8 [0/0]
     via ::, Null0
R1#
```

LAB 26: CONFIGURING IP FLOATING STATIC ROUTES

Lab Objective:
The objective of this lab exercise is for you to learn how to implement IP floating static route functionality on a Cisco router.

Lab Purpose:
Configuring a floating static route will allow your Cisco router to have a backup route to a destination in case the primary route fails. As a Cisco engineer, as well as in the Cisco CCNA exam, you will be expected to know how to implement IP floating static route functionality.

Certification Level:
This lab is suitable for CCENT certification exam preparation.

Lab Difficulty:
This lab has a difficulty rating of 6/10.

Readiness Assessment:
When you are ready for your certification exam, you should complete this lab in no more than 10 minutes.

Lab Topology:
Please use the following topology to complete this lab exercise:

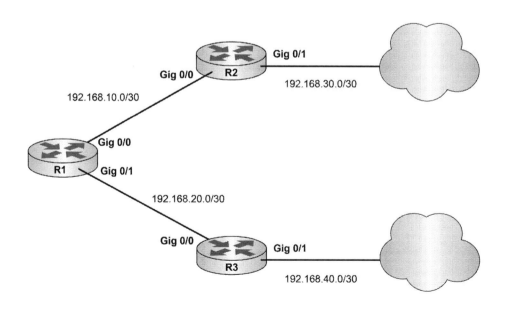

NOTE: Both R2 and R3 connect to the Internet, so R1 has two exit options to the Internet.

Task 1:
Configure the hostnames on R1, R2, and R3 as illustrated in the topology.

Task 2:
Configure the IP addresses on the Gig0/0 and Gig0/1 interfaces of R1, R2, and R3 as illustrated in the topology.

NOTE: R1 will always have the .1 IP in each of its Gig interfaces.

NOTE: R2 and R3 will have the .1 IP on the Gig0/1 interface.

Task 3:
Configure two default static routes on R1:

- The first one (primary one) will go to R2 with an administrative distance of 1.
- The secondary one will go to R3 with an administrative distance of 254.

Based on this, all traffic going to an unknown destination will be sent via R2.

Task 4:
Shut down the interface Gig0/0 of R1 and check via some `show` commands how the secondary route kicks in:

- `show ip route`
- `show ip interface brief`

Task 5:
Bring the interface Gig0/0 of R1 up again and check how it takes the primary role because of the lower administrative distance.

Run the same `show` commands and check the results.

LAB 26: CONFIGURATION AND VERIFICATION

Task 1:

For reference information on configuring hostnames, please refer to earlier labs.

Task 2:

```
R1#conf t
Enter configuration commands, one per line.  End with CTRL/Z.
R1(config)#int gig0/0
R1(config-if)#no shutdown
R1(config-if)#ip add 192.168.10.1 255.255.255.252
R1(config-if)#end
R1(config)#int gig0/1
R1(config-if)#no shutdown
R1(config-if)#ip add 192.168.20.1 255.255.255.252
R1(config-if)#end
R1#


R2(config)#int gig0/0
R2(config-if)#no shutdown
R2(config-if)#ip add 192.168.10.2 255.255.255.252
R2(config-if)#end
R2(config)#int gig0/1
R2(config-if)#no shutdown
R2(config-if)#ip add 192.168.30.1 255.255.255.252
R2(config-if)#end
R2#


R3(config)#int gig0/0
R3(config-if)#no shutdown
R3(config-if)#ip add 192.168.20.2 255.255.255.252
R3(config-if)#end
R3(config)#int gig0/1
R3(config-if)#no shutdown
R3(config-if)#ip add 192.168.40.1 255.255.255.252
R3(config-if)#end
R3#
```

Task 3:

```
R1#config t
Enter configuration commands, one per line.  End with CTRL/Z.
R1(config)#ip route 0.0.0.0 0.0.0.0 192.168.10.2
R1(config)#ip route 0.0.0.0 0.0.0.0 192.168.20.2 254
```

Task 4:

```
R1#config t
Enter configuration commands, one per line.  End with CTRL/Z.

R1(config)#int gig0/0
R1(config-if)#shutdown

R1#sh ip route
Codes: C - connected, S - static, R - RIP, M - mobile, B—BGP,
       D - EIGRP, EX - EIGRP external, O - OSPF, IA - OSPF inter area,
       N1 - OSPF NSSA external type 1, N2 - OSPF NSSA external type 2,
       E1 - OSPF external type 1, E2 - OSPF external type 2,
       i - IS-IS, su - IS-IS summary, L1 - IS-IS level-1,
       L2 - IS-IS level2, ia - IS-IS inter area,
       * - candidate default, U - per-user static, o - ODR,
       P - periodic downloaded static route

Gateway of last resort is 192.168.20.2 to network 0.0.0.0

192.168.20.0/24 is variably subnetted, 2 subnets, 2 masks
C 192.168.20.0/30 is directly connected, GigabitEthernet0/1
L 192.168.20.1/32 is directly connected, GigabitEthernet0/1
S* 0.0.0.0/0 [254/0] via 192.168.20.2

R1#sh ip int brief
Interface         IP-Address    OK? Method Status             Protocol
GigabitEthernet0/0 192.168.10.1 YES manual administratively down down
GigabitEthernet0/1 192.168.20.1 YES manual up                      up
```

Task 5:

```
R1#config t
Enter configuration commands, one per line.  End with CTRL/Z.
R1(config)#int gig0/0
R1(config-if)#no shutdown

R1#sh ip route
Codes: C - connected, S - static, R - RIP, M - mobile, B—BGP,
       D - EIGRP, EX - EIGRP external, O - OSPF, IA - OSPF inter area,
       N1 - OSPF NSSA external type 1, N2 - OSPF NSSA external type 2,
       E1 - OSPF external type 1, E2 - OSPF external type 2,
       i - IS-IS, su - IS-IS summary, L1 - IS-IS level-1,
       L2 - IS-IS level2, ia - IS-IS inter area,
       * - candidate default, U - per-user static,
       o - ODR, P - periodic downloaded static route

Gateway of last resort is 192.168.10.2 to network 0.0.0.0

    192.168.10.0/24 is variably subnetted, 2 subnets, 2 masks
C       192.168.10.0/30 is directly connected, GigabitEthernet0/0
L       192.168.10.1/32 is directly connected, GigabitEthernet0/0
```

```
     192.168.20.0/24 is variably subnetted, 2 subnets, 2 masks
C       192.168.20.0/30 is directly connected, GigabitEthernet0/1
L       192.168.20.1/32 is directly connected, GigabitEthernet0/1
S*   0.0.0.0/0 [1/0] via 192.168.10.2

R1#show ip int brief
Interface          IP-Address      OK? Method Status
Protocol
GigabitEthernet0/0  192.168.10.1  YES manual up              up
GigabitEthernet0/1  192.168.20.1  YES manual up              up
```

LAB 27: CONFIGURING RIP VERSION 2

Lab Objective:
The objective of this lab exercise is for you to learn and understand how to configure Routing Information Protocol version 2 on a Cisco IOS router.

Lab Purpose:
RIPv2 configuration is a fundamental skill. By default, when RIP is enabled on a Cisco router, both version 1 and version 2 updates are sent and received. Since RIPv1 is considered obsolete because of today's subnetted networks, it is imperative that you know how to enable RIPv2. As a Cisco engineer, as well as in the Cisco CCNA exam, you will be expected to know how to configure and verify RIPv2.

Certification Level:
This lab is suitable for both CCENT and CCNA certification exam preparation.

Lab Difficulty:
This lab has a difficulty rating of 5/10.

Readiness Assessment:
When you are ready for your certification exam, you should complete this lab in no more than 10 minutes.

Lab Topology:
Please use the following topology to complete this lab exercise:

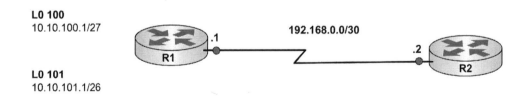

LO 100
10.10.100.1/27

192.168.0.0/30

.1

.2

R1

R2

LO 101
10.10.101.1/26

Task 1:
Configure the hostnames on routers R1 and R2 as illustrated in the topology.

Task 2:
Configure a back-to-back Serial connection between R1 and R2. Configure the DCE interface Serial0/0 in R2 to provide clocking to R1 at a clock speed of 2 Mbps (if this is the DCE end). Configure IP addresses 192.168.0.1/30 and 192.168.0.2/30 on R1 and R2

Serial0/0 interfaces, respectively. Configure the Loopback interfaces on R1 with the IP addresses illustrated in the topology.

Task 3:

Enable RIPv2 on R1 and configure RIPv2 routing for the Loopback interfaces and the Serial0/0 interface. Verify on either R1 or R2 that RIPv2 has been enabled using the appropriate commands.

LAB 27: CONFIGURATION AND VERIFICATION

Task 1:

For reference information on configuring hostnames, please refer to earlier labs.

Task 2:

```
R2#conf t
Enter configuration commands, one per line.  End with CTRL/Z.
R2(config)#int s0/0
R2(config-if)#clock rate 2000000
R2(config-if)#end
R2#
R2#sh controllers s0/0
Interface Serial0/0
Hardware is PowerQUICC MPC860
DCE V.35, clock rate 2000000

R1#conf t
Enter configuration commands, one per line.  End with CTRL/Z.
R1(config)#int s0/0
R1(config-if)#ip add 192.168.0.1 255.255.255.252
R1(config-if)#no shutdown
R1(config)#int loop100
R1(config-if)#ip add 10.10.100.1 255.255.255.224
R1(config-if)#exit
R1(config)#int loop101
R1(config-if)#ip add 10.10.101.1 255.255.255.192
R1(config-if)#end
R1#

R2#conf t
Enter configuration commands, one per line.  End with CTRL/Z.
R2(config)#int s0/0
R2(config-if)#ip address 192.168.0.2 255.255.255.252
R1(config-if)#no shutdown
R2(config-if)#end
R2#

R1#ping 192.168.0.2

Type escape sequence to abort.
Sending 5, 100-byte ICMP Echos to 192.168.0.2, timeout is 2 seconds:
!!!!!
Success rate is 100 percent (5/5), round-trip min/avg/max = 4/4/4 ms

R2#ping 192.168.0.1

Type escape sequence to abort.
Sending 5, 100-byte ICMP Echos to 192.168.0.1, timeout is 2 seconds:
```

```
!!!!!
Success rate is 100 percent (5/5), round-trip min/avg/max = 4/4/4 ms
```

Task 3:
```
R1#conf t
Enter configuration commands, one per line.  End with CTRL/Z.
R1(config)#router rip
R1(config-router)#version 2
R1(config-router)#network 10.0.0.0
R1(config-router)#network 192.168.0.0
R1(config-router)#end
R1#

R2#conf t
Enter configuration commands, one per line.  End with CTRL/Z.
R2(config)#router rip
R2(config-router)#version 2
R2(config-router)#network 192.168.0.0
R2(config-router)#end
R2#
```

NOTE: When configuring RIP routing, you must use the version 2 keyword under RIP configuration mode. By default, if RIP is enabled and this keyword is not issued, the Cisco IOS router will enable both RIPv1 and RIPv2. RIPv1 will be enabled for inbound and outbound routing updates, and RIPv2 will be enabled only for inbound routing updates. This is illustrated below for a router configured for RIP routing without the version 2 keyword:

```
R1#show ip protocols
Routing Protocol is "rip"
  Sending updates every 30 seconds, next due in 9 seconds
  Invalid after 180 seconds, hold down 180, flushed after 240
  Outgoing update filter list for all interfaces is not set
  Incoming update filter list for all interfaces is not set
  Redistributing: rip
  Default version control: send version 1, receive any version
    Interface          Send  Recv  Triggered RIP  Key-chain
    Serial0/0           1     1 2
```

The next thing to remember when enabling RIP is to always specify the network at its major classful boundary, regardless of the fact that it has been subnetted. For example, R1 has two Loopback interfaces: 10.10.100.1/27 and 10.10.101.1/26. Because these are part of the 10.0.0.0/8 subnet (which is a Class A address) the RIP network statement is configured using their major classful boundary and is configured as network 10.0.0.0 in RIP configuration mode.

```
R1#show ip protocols
Routing Protocol is "rip"
  Sending updates every 30 seconds, next due in 12 seconds
  Invalid after 180 seconds, hold down 180, flushed after 240
  Outgoing update filter list for all interfaces is not set
  Incoming update filter list for all interfaces is not set
  Redistributing: rip
  Default version control: send version 2, receive version 2
    Interface           Send  Recv  Triggered RIP  Key-chain
    Serial0/0           2     2
    Loopback100         2     2
    Loopback101         2     2
  Automatic network summarization is in effect
  Maximum path: 4
  Routing for Networks:
    10.0.0.0
    192.168.0.0
  Routing Information Sources:
    Gateway         Distance      Last Update
    192.168.0.2         120       00:02:47
  Distance: (default is 120)
```

LAB 28: RIPV2 AUTOMATIC SUMMARIZATION

Lab Objective:

The objective of this lab exercise is for you to learn and understand automatic network summarization using Routing Information Protocol version 2 on a Cisco IOS router. By default, when RIP routing is enabled on networks, it performs summarization at default network boundaries.

Lab Purpose:

RIPv2 configuration is a fundamental skill. By default, when RIP is enabled on a Cisco router, both version 1 and version 2 updates are sent and received. Since RIPv1 is considered obsolete because of today's subnetted networks, it is imperative that you know how to enable RIPv2. Also, because of the VLSM employed in today's networks, automatic summarization is a default feature that should not be used. As a Cisco engineer, as well as in the Cisco CCNA exam, you will be expected to know how to prevent automatic RIPv2 summarization.

Certification Level:

This lab is suitable for CCENT and CCNA certification exam preparation.

Lab Difficulty:

This lab has a difficulty rating of 6/10.

Readiness Assessment:

When you are ready for your certification exam, you should complete this lab in no more than 30 minutes.

Lab Topology:

Please use the following topology to complete this lab exercise:

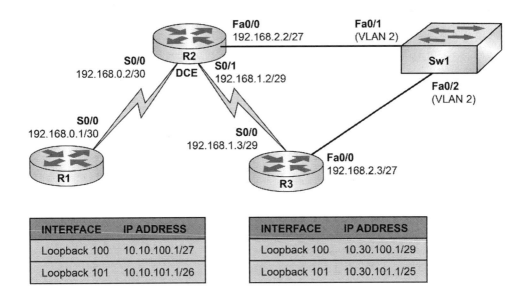

Task 1:

Configure the hostnames on R1, R2, R3, and Sw1 as illustrated in the topology.

Task 2:

Configure VLAN2 named RIPv2-VLAN on Sw2 and assign ports FastEthernet0/1 and FastEthernet0/2 to this VLAN as access ports. Configure FastEthernet0/0 in R2 with the IP address 192.168.2.2/27 and FastEthernet0/0 on R3 with the IP address 192.168.2.3/27. Verify your VLAN and interface configuration by using ping.

Task 3:

Configure a back-to-back Serial connection between R1 and R2. Configure the DCE interface Serial0/0 in R2 to provide clocking to R1 at a clock speed of 128 Kbps. Configure a back-to-back Serial connection between R2 and R3. Configure the DCE interface Serial0/1 in R2 to provide clocking to R3 at a clock speed of 128 Kbps. Configure the IP addresses between R1 and R2 Serial interfaces and R2 and R3 Serial interfaces as illustrated in the topology. Ping from R1 to R2, and vice versa, as well as from R2 to R3, and vice versa, to validate your configuration.

Task 4:
Configure both R1 and R3 with the Loopback interface specified in the topology.

Task 5:
Enable RIPv2 on R1, R2, and R3 for all subnets configured on the routers. Verify that RIPv2 has been enabled using the appropriate commands.

Task 6:
Look at the routing tables of R1, R2, and R3 and see if the 10.10.100.0/27 and 10.10.101.0/26 routes from R1 are present (check on R2 and R3), as well as if the 10.30.100.0/29 and 10.30.101.0/25 routes from R3 are present (check on R1 and R2). If you have configured the network as required, you will notice that you do not see these subnets, but instead only see a 10.0.0.0/8 subnet in the routing table.

Task 7:
Based on your studies, you know that RIPv2 performs automatic summarization at classful boundaries. Armed with this knowledge, disable this behavior on R1, R2, and R3. To reset the routing tables, issue the `clear ip route *` command on routers R1, R2, and R3.

Task 8:
Look at the routing tables of R2 and R3 and verify that the 10.10.100.0/27 and 10.10.101.0/26 routes from R1 are now present. Next, look at the routing table of R1 and R2 and verify that the 10.30.100.0/29 and 10.30.101.0/25 routes from R3 are now present.

LAB 28: CONFIGURATION AND VERIFICATION

Task 1:

For reference information on configuring hostnames, please refer to earlier labs.

Task 2:

For reference information on configuring and verifying VLANs and IP addresses, please refer to earlier labs.

Task 3:

For reference information on configuring and verifying VLANs and IP addresses, please refer to earlier labs.

Task 4:
```
R1#conf t
Enter configuration commands, one per line.  End with CTRL/Z.
R1(config)#int looop100
R1(config-if)#ip add 10.10.100.1 255.255.255.224
R1(config-if)#exit
R1(config)#int loop101
R1(config-if)#ip add 10.10.101.1 255.255.255.192
R1(config-if)#end
R1#

R3#conf t
Enter configuration commands, one per line.  End with CTRL/Z.
R3(config)#int loop100
R3(config-if)#ip add 10.30.100.1 255.255.255.248
R3(config-if)#exit
R3(config)#int loop101
R3(config-if)#ip add 10.30.101.1 255.255.255.128
R3(config-if)#^Z
R3#
```

Task 5:
```
R3#conf t
Enter configuration commands, one per line.  End with CTRL/Z.
R3(config)#router rip
R3(config-router)#ver 2
R3(config-router)#network 10.0.0.0
R3(config-router)#network 192.168.1.0
R3(config-router)#network 192.168.2.0
R3(config-router)#^Z
R3#

R3#show ip protocols
Routing Protocol is "rip"
```

```
    Sending updates every 30 seconds, next due in 12 seconds
    Invalid after 180 seconds, hold down 180, flushed after 240
    Outgoing update filter list for all interfaces is not set
    Incoming update filter list for all interfaces is not set
    Redistributing: rip
    Default version control: send version 2, receive version 2
       Interface            Send  Recv  Triggered RIP  Key-chain
       FastEthernet0/0        2     2
       Serial0/0             2     2
       Loopback100           2     2
       Loopback101           2     2
Automatic network summarization is in effect
    Maximum path: 4
    Routing for Networks:
       10.0.0.0
       192.168.1.0
       192.168.2.0
    Routing Information Sources:
       Gateway           Distance       Last Update
    Distance: (default is 120)

R2#conf t
Enter configuration commands, one per line.  End with CTRL/Z.
R2(config)#router rip
R2(config-router)#ver 2
R2(config-router)#net 192.168.0.0
R2(config-router)#net 192.168.1.0
R2(config-router)#net 192.168.2.0
R2(config-router)#end
R2#

R2#show ip prot
Routing Protocol is "rip"
    Sending updates every 30 seconds, next due in 3 seconds
    Invalid after 180 seconds, hold down 180, flushed after 240
    Outgoing update filter list for all interfaces is not set
    Incoming update filter list for all interfaces is not set
    Redistributing: rip
    Default version control: send version 2, receive version 2
       Interface            Send  Recv  Triggered RIP  Key-chain
       FastEthernet0/0        2     2
       Serial0/0             2     2
       Serial0/1             2     2

[Output Truncated]

R1#conf t
Enter configuration commands, one per line.  End with CTRL/Z.
R1(config)#router rip
R1(config-router)#net 10.0.0.0
R1(config-router)#net 192.168.0.0
```

```
R1(config-router)#end
R1#

R1#show ip protocols
Routing Protocol is "rip"
  Sending updates every 30 seconds, next due in 18 seconds
  Invalid after 180 seconds, hold down 180, flushed after 240
  Outgoing update filter list for all interfaces is not set
  Incoming update filter list for all interfaces is not set
  Redistributing: rip
  Default version control: send version 2, receive version 2
    Interface           Send  Recv  Triggered RIP  Key-chain
    Serial0/0           2     2
    Loopback100         2     2
    Loopback101         2     2

[Output Truncated]
```

Task 6:

```
R1#show ip route
Codes: C - connected, S - static, R - RIP, M - mobile, B—BGP,
       D - EIGRP, EX - EIGRP external, O - OSPF, IA - OSPF inter area,
       N1 - OSPF NSSA external type 1, N2 - OSPF NSSA external type 2,
       E1 - OSPF external type 1, E2 - OSPF external type 2,
       i - IS-IS, su - IS-IS summary, L1 - IS-IS level-1,
       L2 - IS-IS level-2, ia - IS-IS inter area,
       * - candidate default, U - per-user static route, o - ODR,
       P - periodic downloaded static route

Gateway of last resort is not set

     10.0.0.0/8 is variably subnetted, 2 subnets, 2 masks
C       10.10.100.0/27 is directly connected, Loopback100
C       10.10.101.0/26 is directly connected, Loopback101
     192.168.0.0/30 is subnetted, 1 subnets
C       192.168.0.0 is directly connected, Serial0/0
R    192.168.1.0/24 [120/1] via 192.168.0.2, 00:00:21, Serial0/0
R    192.168.2.0/24 [120/1] via 192.168.0.2, 00:00:21, Serial0/0

R2#show ip route
Codes: C - connected, S - static, R - RIP, M - mobile, B—BGP,
       D - EIGRP, EX - EIGRP external, O - OSPF, IA - OSPF inter area,
       N1 - OSPF NSSA external type 1, N2 - OSPF NSSA external type 2,
       E1 - OSPF external type 1, E2 - OSPF external type 2,
       i - IS-IS, su - IS-IS summary, L1 - IS-IS level-1,
       L2 - IS-IS level-2, ia - IS-IS inter area,
       * - candidate default, U - per-user static route, o - ODR,
       P - periodic downloaded static route

Gateway of last resort is not set
```

```
R    10.0.0.0/8 [120/1] via 192.168.0.1, 00:00:08, Serial0/0
                [120/1] via 192.168.1.3, 00:00:05, Serial0/1
                [120/1] via 192.168.2.3, 00:00:06, FastEthernet0/0
     192.168.0.0/30 is subnetted, 1 subnets
C       192.168.0.0 is directly connected, Serial0/0
     192.168.1.0/24 is variably subnetted, 2 subnets, 2 masks
C       192.168.1.0/29 is directly connected, Serial0/1
R       192.168.1.0/24 [120/1] via 192.168.2.3, 00:00:06,
FastEthernet0/0
     192.168.2.0/24 is variably subnetted, 2 subnets, 2 masks
C       192.168.2.0/27 is directly connected, FastEthernet0/0
R       192.168.2.0/24 [120/1] via 192.168.1.3, 00:00:06, Serial0/1

R3#show ip route
Codes: C - connected, S - static, R - RIP, M - mobile, B—BGP,
       D - EIGRP, EX - EIGRP external, O - OSPF, IA - OSPF inter area,
       N1 - OSPF NSSA external type 1, N2 - OSPF NSSA external type 2,
       E1 - OSPF external type 1, E2 - OSPF external type 2,
       i - IS-IS, su - IS-IS summary, L1 - IS-IS level-1,
       L2 - IS-IS level-2, ia - IS-IS inter area,
       * - candidate default, U - per-user static route, o - ODR,
       P - periodic downloaded static route

Gateway of last resort is not set

     10.0.0.0/8 is variably subnetted, 2 subnets, 2 masks
C       10.30.100.0/29 is directly connected, Loopback100
C       10.30.101.0/25 is directly connected, Loopback101
R    192.168.0.0/24 [120/1] via 192.168.1.2, 00:00:17, Serial0/0
                    [120/1] via 192.168.2.2, 00:00:08, FastEthernet0/0
     192.168.1.0/24 is variably subnetted, 2 subnets, 2 masks
C       192.168.1.0/29 is directly connected, Serial0/0
R       192.168.1.0/24 [120/1] via 192.168.2.2, 00:00:08,
FastEthernet0/0
     192.168.2.0/24 is variably subnetted, 2 subnets, 2 masks
C       192.168.2.0/27 is directly connected, FastEthernet0/0
R       192.168.2.0/24 [120/1] via 192.168.1.2, 00:00:17, Serial0/0
```

> **NOTE:** Pay attention to the routes marked R as these are RIP routes. The [120/1] that follows the subnet indicates [Administrative Distance/Metric]. By default, the administrative distance for RIP is 120. The metric for the route is based on the RIP metric—which is hop count. Therefore, a metric of 1 means that the route is 1 hop away, a metric of 2 means that the route is 2 hops away, and so forth. The largest value you will ever see for RIP is 15, since this is the maximum number of hops allowed in RIP. Make sure that you familiarize yourself with the codes for static, OSPF, EIGRP, and RIP routes for the CCNA certification exam.

Task 7:

```
R1#conf t
Enter configuration commands, one per line.  End with CTRL/Z.
R1(config)#router rip
R1(config-router)#no auto-summary
R1(config-router)#^Z
R1#
R1#cle ip rou *

R2#conf t
Enter configuration commands, one per line.  End with CTRL/Z.
R2(config)#router rip
R2(config-router)#no auto-summary
R2(config-router)#end
R2#
R2#cle ip ro *

R3#conf t
Enter configuration commands, one per line.  End with CTRL/Z.
R3(config)#router rip
R3(config-router)#no auto-summary
R3(config-router)#end
R3#
R3#clear ip route *
```

Task 8:

```
R1#show ip ro
Codes: C - connected, S - static, R - RIP, M - mobile, B—BGP,
       D - EIGRP, EX - EIGRP external, O - OSPF, IA - OSPF inter area,
       N1 - OSPF NSSA external type 1, N2 - OSPF NSSA external type 2,
       E1 - OSPF external type 1, E2 - OSPF external type 2,
       i - IS-IS, su - IS-IS summary, L1 - IS-IS level-1,
       L2 - IS-IS level-2, ia - IS-IS inter area,
       * - candidate default, U - per-user static route, o - ODR,
       P - periodic downloaded static route

Gateway of last resort is not set

     10.0.0.0/8 is variably subnetted, 5 subnets, 5 masks
R       10.0.0.0/8 [120/1] via 192.168.0.2, 00:01:16, Serial0/0
C       10.10.100.0/27 is directly connected, Loopback100
C       10.10.101.0/26 is directly connected, Loopback101
R       10.30.100.0/29 [120/2] via 192.168.0.2, 00:00:19, Serial0/0
R       10.30.101.0/25 [120/2] via 192.168.0.2, 00:00:19, Serial0/0
     192.168.0.0/30 is subnetted, 1 subnets
C       192.168.0.0 is directly connected, Serial0/0
     192.168.1.0/29 is subnetted, 1 subnets
R       192.168.1.0 [120/1] via 192.168.0.2, 00:00:19, Serial0/0
     192.168.2.0/27 is subnetted, 1 subnets
R       192.168.2.0 [120/1] via 192.168.0.2, 00:00:19, Serial0/0
```

```
R2#show ip route
Codes: C - connected, S - static, R - RIP, M - mobile, B—BGP,
       D - EIGRP, EX - EIGRP external, O - OSPF, IA - OSPF inter area,
       N1 - OSPF NSSA external type 1, N2 - OSPF NSSA external type 2,
       E1 - OSPF external type 1, E2 - OSPF external type 2,
       i - IS-IS, su - IS-IS summary, L1 - IS-IS level-1,
       L2 - IS-IS level-2, ia - IS-IS inter area,
       * - candidate default, U - per-user static route, o - ODR,
       P - periodic downloaded static route

Gateway of last resort is not set

     10.0.0.0/8 is variably subnetted, 4 subnets, 4 masks
R       10.10.100.0/27 [120/1] via 192.168.0.1, 00:00:11, Serial0/0
R       10.10.101.0/26 [120/1] via 192.168.0.1, 00:00:11, Serial0/0
R       10.30.100.0/29 [120/1] via 192.168.2.3, 00:00:11,
FastEthernet0/0
                       [120/1] via 192.168.1.3, 00:00:10, Serial0/1
R       10.30.101.0/25 [120/1] via 192.168.2.3, 00:00:11,
FastEthernet0/0
                       [120/1] via 192.168.1.3, 00:00:10, Serial0/1
     192.168.0.0/30 is subnetted, 1 subnets
C       192.168.0.0 is directly connected, Serial0/0
     192.168.1.0/29 is subnetted, 1 subnets
C       192.168.1.0 is directly connected, Serial0/1
     192.168.2.0/27 is subnetted, 1 subnets
C       192.168.2.0 is directly connected, FastEthernet0/0

R3#sh ip ro
Codes: C - connected, S - static, R - RIP, M - mobile, B—BGP,
       D - EIGRP, EX - EIGRP external, O - OSPF, IA - OSPF inter area,
       N1 - OSPF NSSA external type 1, N2 - OSPF NSSA external type 2,
       E1 - OSPF external type 1, E2 - OSPF external type 2,
       i - IS-IS, su - IS-IS summary, L1 - IS-IS level-1,
       L2 - IS-IS level-2, ia - IS-IS inter area,
       * - candidate default, U - per-user static route, o - ODR,
       P - periodic downloaded static route

Gateway of last resort is not set

     10.0.0.0/8 is variably subnetted, 5 subnets, 5 masks
R       10.0.0.0/8 [120/1] via 192.168.1.2, 00:02:25, Serial0/0
                   [120/1] via 192.168.2.2, 00:02:21, FastEthernet0/0
R       10.10.100.0/27 [120/2] via 192.168.2.2, 00:00:09,
FastEthernet0/0
                       [120/2] via 192.168.1.2, 00:00:08, Serial0/0
R       10.10.101.0/26 [120/2] via 192.168.2.2, 00:00:10,
FastEthernet0/0
                       [120/2] via 192.168.1.2, 00:00:08, Serial0/0
C       10.30.100.0/29 is directly connected, Loopback100
```

```
C       10.30.101.0/25 is directly connected, Loopback101
     192.168.0.0/24 is variably subnetted, 2 subnets, 2 masks
R       192.168.0.0/30 [120/1] via 192.168.2.2, 00:00:10,
FastEthernet0/0
                        [120/1] via 192.168.1.2, 00:00:08, Serial0/0
R       192.168.0.0/24 [120/1] via 192.168.2.2, 00:02:21,
FastEthernet0/0
                        [120/1] via 192.168.1.2, 00:02:25, Serial0/0
     192.168.1.0/29 is subnetted, 1 subnets
C       192.168.1.0 is directly connected, Serial0/0
     192.168.2.0/27 is subnetted, 1 subnets
C       192.168.2.0 is directly connected, FastEthernet0/0
```

LAB 29: DEBUGGING AND VERIFYING RIP VERSION 2 UPDATES

Lab Objective:
The objective of this lab exercise is for you to learn and understand how RIPv2 updates are sent. Unlike RIPv1, RIPv2 sends updates using multicast.

Lab Purpose:
RIPv2 update debugging is a fundamental skill. By default, RIPv2 sends updates via multicast. You can use debugging commands to troubleshoot network and routing problems. As a Cisco engineer, as well as in the Cisco CCNA exam, you will be expected to know how to verify RIPv2 updates using debugging commands.

Certification Level:
This lab is suitable for CCNA certification exam preparation.

Lab Difficulty:
This lab has a difficulty rating of 6/10.

Readiness Assessment:
When you are ready for your certification exam, you should complete this lab in no more than 10 minutes.

Lab Topology:
Please use the following topology to complete this lab exercise:

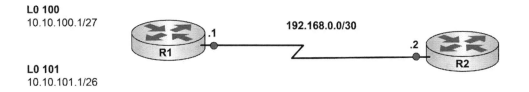

Task 1:
This lab will use only two routers. Configure the hostnames on routers R1 and R2 as illustrated in the topology.

Task 2:

Configure a back-to-back Serial connection between R1 and R2. Configure the DCE interface Serial0/0 in R2 to provide clocking to R1 at a clock speed of 2 Mbps.

Task 3:

Configure IP addresses 192.168.0.1/30 and 192.168.0.2/30 on R1 and R2 Serial0/0 interfaces, respectively. Configure the Loopback interfaces on R1 with the IP addresses illustrated in the topology.

Task 4:

Enable RIPv2 for the Serial0/0 interface on R2 and the Serial 0/0 and Loopback interfaces on R1.

Task 5:

Enable debugging on R1 and R2 and verify that RIPv2 updates are being sent out of all RIPv2-enabled networks. Keep in mind that by default, RIP sends updates every 30 seconds, so you will typically see updates within that timeframe. Familiarize yourself with the output of the debugs. Be sure to disable debugging when done.

LAB 29: CONFIGURATION AND VERIFICATION

Task 1:

For reference information on configuring hostnames, please refer to earlier labs.

Task 2:

For reference information on configuring DCE clocking, please refer to earlier labs.

Task 3:

For reference information on configuring IP addressing, please refer to earlier labs.

Task 4:

```
R2#conf t
Enter configuration commands, one per line.  End with CTRL/Z.
R2(config)#router rip
R2(config-router)#version 2
R2(config-router)#net 192.168.0.0
R2(config-router)#end
R2#

R1#conf t
Enter configuration commands, one per line.  End with CTRL/Z.
R1(config)#router rip
R1(config-router)#net 10.0.0.0
R1(config-router)#net 192.168.0.0
R1(config-router)#end
R1#
```

Task 5:

```
R1#debug ip rip events
RIP event debugging is on
*Mar  1 02:13:44.358: RIP: sending v2 update to 224.0.0.9 via
Loopback101 (10.10.101.1)
*Mar  1 02:13:44.358: RIP: Update contains 2 routes
*Mar  1 02:13:44.358: RIP: Update queued
*Mar  1 02:13:44.358: RIP: Update sent via Loopback101
*Mar  1 02:13:44.362: RIP: ignored v2 packet from 10.10.101.1 (sourced
from one of our addresses)
*Mar  1 02:13:46.189: RIP: sending v2 update to 224.0.0.9 via
Loopback100 (10.10.100.1)
*Mar  1 02:13:46.189: RIP: Update contains 2 routes
*Mar  1 02:13:46.189: RIP: Update queued
*Mar  1 02:13:46.189: RIP: Update sent via Loopback100
*Mar  1 02:13:46.193: RIP: ignored v2 packet from 10.10.100.1 (sourced
from one of our addresses)
*Mar  1 02:13:46.962: RIP: sending v2 update to 224.0.0.9 via Serial0/0
(192.168.0.1)
```

```
*Mar  1 02:13:46.962: RIP: Update contains 2 routes
*Mar  1 02:13:46.962: RIP: Update queued
*Mar  1 02:13:46.962: RIP: Update sent via Serial0/0
R1#undebug all
All possible debugging has been turned off

R2#debug ip rip events
RIP event debugging is on
*Mar  1 02:15:49.395: RIP: sending v2 update to 224.0.0.9 via Serial0/0
(192.168.0.2) - suppressing null update
*Mar  1 02:15:56.186: RIP: received v2 update from 192.168.0.1 on
Serial0/0
*Mar  1 02:15:56.186: RIP: Update contains 2 routes
*Mar  1 02:16:15.790: RIP: sending v2 update to 224.0.0.9 via Serial0/0
(192.168.0.2) - suppressing null update
*Mar  1 02:16:25.422: RIP: received v2 update from 192.168.0.1 on
Serial0/0
*Mar  1 02:16:25.422: RIP: Update contains 2 routes
R2#undebug ip rip events
RIP event debugging is off
```

NOTE: There are two other options available when it comes to debugging RIP:

```
R1#debug ip rip ?
  database  RIP database events
  events    RIP protocol events
  trigger   RIP trigger extension
  <cr>
```

Play around with these options and familiarize yourself with the information they print. Also, remember that debugging is very processor-intensive and can do more harm than good in a live network, so always make sure you disable debugging when you have captured the information you were looking for.

LAB 30: PASSIVE INTERFACES FOR RIPV2 UPDATES

Lab Objective:

The objective of this lab exercise is for you to learn and understand how to prevent RIPv2 from sending unnecessary updates by using passive interfaces.

Lab Purpose:

Preventing unnecessary RIPv2 updates using passive interfaces is a fundamental skill. By default, RIPv2 sends updates via multicast on all interfaces for which RIPv2 has been enabled. For example, it is not possible to ever have another device connected to a Loopback interface, so it is a waste of router processing power to have RIPv2 continuously sending updates to a Loopback interface. As a Cisco engineer, as well as in the Cisco CCNA exam, you will be expected to know how to prevent RIPv2 from sending unnecessary updates.

Certification Level:

This lab is suitable for CCNA certification exam preparation.

Lab Difficulty:

This lab has a difficulty rating of 6/10.

Readiness Assessment:

When you are ready for your certification exam, you should complete this lab in no more than 10 minutes.

Lab Topology:

Please use the following topology to complete this lab exercise:

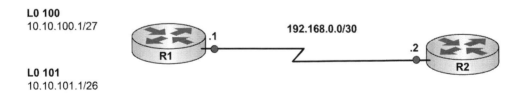

LO 100
10.10.100.1/27

LO 101
10.10.101.1/26

192.168.0.0/30

.1   R1   .2   R2

Task 1:

This lab will use only two routers. Configure the hostnames on routers R1 and R2 as illustrated in the topology.

Task 2:

Configure a back-to-back Serial connection between R1 and R2. Configure the DCE interface Serial0/0 in R2 to provide clocking to R1 at a clock speed of 2 Mbps.

Task 3:

Configure IP addresses 192.168.0.1/30 and 192.168.0.2/30 on R1 and R2 Serial0/0 interfaces, respectively. Configure the Loopback interfaces on R1 with the IP addresses illustrated in the topology. Enable RIPv2 for the Serial0/0 interface on R2 and R1 and attached Loopback subnets.

Task 4:

First, use the `show ip protocols` command to see the interfaces on which RIPv2 is sending updates. Next, enable debugging on R1 and verify that RIPv2 updates are being sent on all RIPv2-enabled interfaces. When you have verified this, disable debugging.

Task 5:

Prevent RIPv2 from sending updates on the Loopback interfaces. Verify your configuration by enabling debugging. Disable debugging when done.

LAB 30: CONFIGURATION AND VERIFICATION

Task 1:

For reference information on configuring hostnames, please refer to earlier labs.

Task 2:

For reference information on configuring DCE clocking, please refer to earlier labs.

Task 3:

For reference information on configuring Loopback interfaces and RIPv2, please refer to earlier labs.

Task 4:

```
R1#show ip protocols
Routing Protocol is "rip"
  Sending updates every 30 seconds, next due in 19 seconds
  Invalid after 180 seconds, hold down 180, flushed after 240
  Outgoing update filter list for all interfaces is not set
  Incoming update filter list for all interfaces is not set
  Redistributing: rip
  Default version control: send version 2, receive version 2
    Interface           Send  Recv  Triggered RIP  Key-chain
    Serial0/0           2     2
    Loopback100         2     2
    Loopback101         2     2

[Output Truncated]

R1#debug ip rip
RIP protocol debugging is on
*Mar  1 03:09:46.237: RIP: sending v2 update to 224.0.0.9 via Serial0/0
(192.168.0.1)
*Mar  1 03:09:46.237: RIP: build update entries
*Mar  1 03:09:46.237:   10.10.100.0/27 via 0.0.0.0, metric 1, tag 0
*Mar  1 03:09:46.237:   10.10.101.0/26 via 0.0.0.0, metric 1, tag 0
*Mar  1 03:09:53.248: RIP: sending v2 update to 224.0.0.9 via
Loopback101 (10.10.101.1)
*Mar  1 03:09:53.248: RIP: build update entries
*Mar  1 03:09:53.248:   10.10.100.0/27 via 0.0.0.0, metric 1, tag 0
*Mar  1 03:09:53.248:   192.168.0.0/30 via 0.0.0.0, metric 1, tag 0
*Mar  1 03:09:53.252: RIP: ignored v2 packet from 10.10.101.1 (sourced
from one of our addresses)
*Mar  1 03:10:09.070: RIP: sending v2 update to 224.0.0.9 via
Loopback100 (10.10.100.1)
*Mar  1 03:10:09.070: RIP: build update entries
*Mar  1 03:10:09.070:   10.10.101.0/26 via 0.0.0.0, metric 1, tag 0
*Mar  1 03:10:09.070:   192.168.0.0/30 via 0.0.0.0, metric 1, tag 0
```

```
*Mar  1 03:10:09.074: RIP: ignored v2 packet from 10.10.100.1 (sourced
from one of our addresses)
R1#
R1#undebug ip rip
RIP protocol debugging is off
```

> **NOTE:** Pay particular attention to the fact that RIPv2 is sending updates via the
> Loopback interfaces as illustrated below:

```
*Mar  1 03:09:53.248: RIP: sending v2 update to 224.0.0.9 via
Loopback101 (10.10.101.1)
*Mar  1 03:10:09.070: RIP: sending v2 update to 224.0.0.9 via
Loopback100 (10.10.100.1)
```

Loopback interfaces are logical interfaces that have the majority of the characteristics of physical interfaces. However, one important thing to remember is that no host can ever reside on a subnet configured for a Loopback interface. If you assign a Loopback interface as a /24 subnet mask, for example, you are simply wasting valuable IP address space. Given that no host can every reside on the same subnet as a Loopback interface, it is a waste of router resources to have a routing protocol send updates to a Loopback interface, as there will never be another router (or other device) that will ever respond back to these updates. Hence, when you configure Loopback interfaces, it is always considered best practice to disable routing protocols that can send updates to them using the passive-interface command as illustrated in Task 5 below:

Task 5:

```
R1#conf t
Enter configuration commands, one per line.  End with CTRL/Z.
R1(config)#router rip
R1(config-router)#passive-interface loopback100
R1(config-router)#passive-interface loopback101
R1(config-router)#end
R1#

R1#show ip protocols
Routing Protocol is "rip"
  Sending updates every 30 seconds, next due in 5 seconds
  Invalid after 180 seconds, hold down 180, flushed after 240
  Outgoing update filter list for all interfaces is not set
  Incoming update filter list for all interfaces is not set
  Redistributing: rip
  Default version control: send version 2, receive version 2
    Interface            Send  Recv  Triggered RIP  Key-chain
    Serial0/0            2     2
```

```
R1#debug ip rip
RIP protocol debugging is on
R1#
*Mar  1 03:20:02.355: RIP: sending v2 update to 224.0.0.9 via Serial0/0
(192.168.0.1)
*Mar  1 03:20:02.355: RIP: build update entries
*Mar  1 03:20:02.355:    10.10.100.0/27 via 0.0.0.0, metric 1, tag 0
*Mar  1 03:20:02.355:    10.10.101.0/26 via 0.0.0.0, metric 1, tag 0
R1#
*Mar  1 03:20:28.974: RIP: sending v2 update to 224.0.0.9 via Serial0/0
(192.168.0.1)
*Mar  1 03:20:28.974: RIP: build update entries
*Mar  1 03:20:28.974:    10.10.100.0/27 via 0.0.0.0, metric 1, tag 0
*Mar  1 03:20:28.974:    10.10.101.0/26 via 0.0.0.0, metric 1, tag 0
R1#undebug all
All possible debugging has been turned off
```

NOTE: Suppose you have a router with one Serial interface and 600 Loopback interfaces. Given such a scenario, issuing the passive-interface command for every one of those Loopback interfaces would take a great deal of time. Fortunately, Cisco recognized this and created the passive-interface default command in Cisco IOS. When this command is issued, all interfaces are configured as passive. In order to send updates on a particular interface, you would negate that interface as not being passive by issuing the no passive-interface command followed by the interface(s) you want to send routing protocol updates to. This is illustrated below:

```
R1#conf t
Enter configuration commands, one per line.  End with CTRL/Z.
R1(config)#router rip
R1(config-router)#passive-interface default
R1(config-router)#no passive-interface serial0/0
R1(config-router)#end
R1#
```

The configuration above makes all interfaces configured for RIP passive with the exception of interface Serial0/0. Make sure you remember this command, not only for the purposes of the CCNA exam but also for use in the real world.

LAB 31: RIPV2 SPLIT HORIZON

Lab Objective:
The objective of this lab exercise is for you to learn and understand the effects of split horizon in a typical hub-and-spoke topology.

Lab Purpose:
Configuring and troubleshooting split horizon is a fundamental skill. RIPv2 is a distance vector protocol, and as such uses split horizon to prevent routing loops. Split horizon mandates that RIPv2 will not send updates back out of the interface on which they were received. In newer versions of Cisco IOS software, split horizon is disabled by default for frame relay and SMDS. However, in the real world, you may encounter routers running older Cisco IOS software that do have split horizon enabled by default. It is for the preparation of such scenarios that you should be knowledgeable about split horizon. As a Cisco engineer, as well as in the Cisco CCNA exam, you will be expected to know how to address split horizon issues in RIPv2.

Certification Level:
This lab is suitable for CCNA certification exam preparation.

Lab Difficulty:
This lab has a difficulty rating of 8/10.

Readiness Assessment:
When you are ready for your certification exam, you should complete this lab in no more than 20 minutes.

> **IMPORTANT NOTE:** In order to configure frame relay between two routers in your lab, you will need THREE routers! The first two routers will be regular routers, and the third will need to be configured as a frame relay switch. This can be any Cisco router that has at least two Serial interfaces. Please refer to Appendix B: Cabling and Configuring a Frame Relay Switch for Three Routers for the appropriate configuration to issue on the frame relay switch.

Frame relay is no longer featured in the CCNA exam but we are using it here to demonstrate the split horizon issue. It's easier to set up without using the command line if you use Packet Tracer.

Lab Topology:

Please use the following topology to complete this lab exercise:

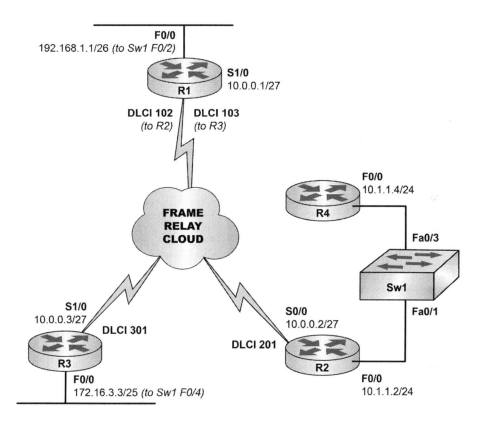

Task 1:

This lab will only be performed on routers R1, R2, and R3. Configure the hostnames on R1, R2, and R3 as illustrated in the topology.

Task 2:

Configure the switch in the topology with the hostname Sw1. Enable F0/1, F0/2, and F0/3 on Sw1 so that when you bring up the router interfaces connected to those switchports, they can come up.

Task 3:

Configure IP addresses on the Fa0/0 interfaces on R1, R2, and R3. Make sure that you enable these interfaces. Verify that the Fa0/0 interfaces on all three routers are up. We won't use R4 in this lab. Feel free to use Loopback interfaces instead if you wish.

Task 4:

Configure frame relay on R1, R2, and R3. Use the IP addresses in the topology for their respective Serial interfaces. Use the default frame relay encapsulation of Cisco.

Task 5:

Create a static frame relay map on each router for the other two routers. Verify your static frame relay maps. You can also use pings to test connectivity between the routers to double-check your frame relay mapping.

Task 6:

Enable RIPv2 on R1, R2, and R3 for all the subnets configured on those respective routers. Be sure to prevent RIPv2 from automatically summarizing at classful network boundaries on all routers.

Task 7:

Check your IP routing tables. If you have configured everything as required, you will be receiving all routes on all routers. You can also use pings to test connectivity between the routers to double-check your routing.

Task 8:

Generally, if you are working on a hub-and-spoke network running RIPv2 and the router is running a Cisco IOS image that has split horizon disabled by default, you do not want to enable that feature unless you have very good cause to do so. However, in order to better understand split horizon, enable this feature on the Serial interface of R1 and clear the IP routing tables of all three routers.

Having done so, check the routing table of R3 and you will see that the 10.1.1.0/24 route is no longer present. Next, check the routing table of R2 and you will see that the 172.16.3.0/25 route is no longer present. Finally, check the routing table of R1 and you will see both of these routes. Because split horizon has been enabled, R1 will not send updates out of the same interface it received them. Make sure that you understand split horizon.

LAB 31: CONFIGURATION AND VERIFICATION

Task 1:

For reference information on configuring hostnames, please refer to earlier labs.

Task 2:

```
Switch#config t
Enter configuration commands, one per line.  End with CTRL/Z.
Switch(config)#hostname Sw1
Sw1(config)#interface fastethernet0/1
Sw1(config-if)#no shutdown
Sw1(config-if)#exit
Sw1(config)#interface fastethernet0/3
Sw1(config-if)#no shutdown
Sw1(config-if)#end
Sw1#
```

Task 3:

```
R1#conf t
Enter configuration commands, one per line.  End with CTRL/Z.
R1(config)#int fa0/0
R1(config-if)#ip address 192.168.1.1 255.255.255.192
R1(config-if)#no shutdown
R1(config-if)#end

R2#conf t
Enter configuration commands, one per line.  End with CTRL/Z.
R2(config)#int fa0/0
R2(config-if)#ip add 10.1.1.2 255.255.255.0
R2(config-if)#no shut
R2(config-if)#end

R3#config term
Enter configuration commands, one per line.  End with CTRL/Z.
R3(config)#int fa0/0
R3(config-if)#ip address 172.16.3.3 255.255.255.128
R3(config-if)#no shutdown
R3(config-if)#end
```

Task 4:

```
R1#config t
Enter configuration commands, one per line.  End with CTRL/Z.
R1(config)#int s1/0
R1(config-if)#no shut
R1(config-if)#ip address 10.0.0.1 255.255.255.224
R1(config-if)#encapsulation frame-relay
R1(config-if)#end
R1#
```

```
R2#conf t
Enter configuration commands, one per line.  End with CTRL/Z.
R2(config)#int s0/0
R2(config-if)#no shut
R2(config-if)#encap frame-relay
R2(config-if)#ip address 10.0.0.2 255.255.255.224
R2(config-if)#^Z
R2#

R3#conf term
Enter configuration commands, one per line.  End with CTRL/Z.
R3(config)#int s1/0
R3(config-if)#ip address 10.0.0.3 255.255.255.224
R3(config-if)#encapsulation fram
R3(config-if)#no shut
R3(config-if)#end
R3#
```

Task 5:

```
R1#conf t
Enter configuration commands, one per line.  End with CTRL/Z.
R1(config)#int s1/0
R1(config-if)#frame-relay map ip 10.0.0.2 102 broadcast
R1(config-if)#frame-relay map ip 10.0.0.3 103 broadcast
R1(config-if)#end
R1#
R1#show frame-relay map
Serial1/0 (up): ip 10.0.0.2 dlci 102(0x66,0x1860), static,
               broadcast,
               CISCO, status defined, inactive
Serial1/0 (up): ip 10.0.0.3 dlci 103(0x67,0x1870), static,
               broadcast,
               CISCO, status defined, inactive

R2#config t
Enter configuration commands, one per line.  End with CTRL/Z.
R2(config)#int s0/0
R2(config-if)#frame-relay map ip 10.0.0.1 201 broadcast
R2(config-if)#frame-relay map ip 10.0.0.3 201 broadcast
R2(config-if)#end
R2#
R2#show frame-relay map
Serial0/0 (up): ip 10.0.0.1 dlci 201(0xC9,0x3090), static,
               broadcast,
               CISCO, status defined, active
Serial0/0 (up): ip 10.0.0.3 dlci 201(0xC9,0x3090), static,
               broadcast,
               CISCO, status defined, active
R3#conf ter
Enter configuration commands, one per line.  End with CTRL/Z.
```

```
R3(config)#int s1/0
R3(config-if)#frame-rel map ip 10.0.0.1 301 broad
R3(config-if)#frame-rel map ip 10.0.0.2 301 broad
R3(config-if)#^Z
R3#
R3#show frame-relay map
Serial1/0 (up): ip 10.0.0.1 dlci 301(0x12D,0x48D0), static,
               broadcast,
               CISCO, status defined, active
Serial1/0 (up): ip 10.0.0.2 dlci 301(0x12D,0x48D0), static,
               broadcast,
               CISCO, status defined, active
```

Task 6:

```
R1#config
Configuring from terminal, memory, or network [terminal]? term
Enter configuration commands, one per line.  End with CTRL/Z.
R1(config)#router rip
R1(config-router)#ver 2
R1(config-router)#no auto-summary
R1(config-router)#net 192.168.1.0
R1(config-router)#net 10.0.0.0
R1(config-router)#end
R1#

R2#conf t
Enter configuration commands, one per line.  End with CTRL/Z.
R2(config)#router rip
R2(config-router)#version 2
R2(config-router)#network 10.0.0.0
R2(config-router)#no auto-sum
R2(config-router)#^Z
R2#

R3#conf t
Enter configuration commands, one per line.  End with CTRL/Z.
R3(config)#router rip
R3(config-router)#ver 2
R3(config-router)#net 172.16.3.0
R3(config-router)#net 10.0.0.0
R3(config-router)#no auto-summary
R3(config-router)#end
R3#
```

Task 7:

```
R1#sh ip route rip
     172.16.0.0/25 is subnetted, 1 subnets
R       172.16.3.0 [120/1] via 10.0.0.3, 00:00:18, Serial1/0
     10.0.0.0/8 is variably subnetted, 2 subnets, 2 masks
R       10.1.1.0/24 [120/1] via 10.0.0.2, 00:00:07, Serial1/0
```

```
R2#show ip route rip
     172.16.0.0/25 is subnetted, 1 subnets
R       172.16.3.0 [120/2] via 10.0.0.3, 00:00:11, Serial0/0
     192.168.1.0/26 is subnetted, 1 subnets
R       192.168.1.0 [120/1] via 10.0.0.1, 00:00:11, Serial0/0

R3#show ip route rip
     10.0.0.0/8 is variably subnetted, 2 subnets, 2 masks
R       10.1.1.0/24 [120/2] via 10.0.0.2, 00:00:00, Serial1/0
     192.168.1.0/26 is subnetted, 1 subnets
R       192.168.1.0 [120/1] via 10.0.0.1, 00:00:00, Serial1/0
```

Task 8:
```
R1#conf t
Enter configuration commands, one per line.  End with CTRL/Z.
R1(config)#int s1/0
R1(config-if)#ip split-horizon
R1(config-if)#end
R1#
R1#clear ip route *
R1#
R1#show ip route rip
     172.16.0.0/25 is subnetted, 1 subnets
R       172.16.3.0 [120/1] via 10.0.0.3, 00:00:24, Serial1/0
     10.0.0.0/8 is variably subnetted, 2 subnets, 2 masks
R       10.1.1.0/24 [120/1] via 10.0.0.2, 00:00:09, Serial1/0

R2#clear ip route *
R2#
R2#show ip route rip
     192.168.1.0/26 is subnetted, 1 subnets
R       192.168.1.0 [120/1] via 10.0.0.1, 00:00:01, Serial0/0

R3#clear ip route *
R3#
R3#show ip route rip
     192.168.1.0/26 is subnetted, 1 subnets
R       192.168.1.0 [120/1] via 10.0.0.1, 00:00:03, Serial1/0
```

4.0 Infrastructure Services

LAB 32: CONFIGURING THE CISCO IOS DHCP SERVER

Lab Objective:

The objective of this lab exercise is for you to learn and understand how to configure the Cisco IOS DHCP server.

Lab Purpose:

Configuring the Cisco IOS DHCP server is a fundamental skill. DHCP (Dynamic Host Configuration Protocol) provides dynamic addressing information to hosts on a network. Typically, physical DHCP servers (such as Microsoft Windows servers) are used to provide addressing information to DHCP clients (which are devices that request configuration via DHCP). However, Cisco IOS routers can also be configured to act as DHCP servers and provide dynamic addressing to DHCP clients. As a Cisco engineer, as well as in the Cisco CCNA exam, you will be expected to know how to configure the Cisco IOS DHCP server.

Certification Level:

This lab is suitable for CCENT and CCNA certification exam preparation.

Lab Difficulty:

This lab has a difficulty rating of 7/10.

Readiness Assessment:

When you are ready for your certification exam, you should complete this lab in no more than 10 minutes.

> **IMPORTANT NOTE:** In order to test DHCP functionality, you will need a workstation DHCP client configured to receive IP addressing information via DHCP. If you do not have a DHCP client, feel free to substitute it with another Cisco IOS router configured as a DHCP client by using the `ip address dhcp` command on the interface connected to the DHCP router.

Lab Topology:

Please use the following topology to complete this lab exercise:

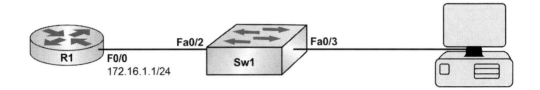

Task 1:

Configure the hostnames on R1 and Sw1 as illustrated in the topology.

Task 2:

Configure VLAN50 named DHCP_VLAN on Sw1. Assign the FastEthernet0/2 and FastEthernet0/3 interfaces on Sw1 to this VLAN. Ensure that the ports immediately transition to the Spanning Tree Forwarding state. This is actually an ICND2 requirement but I've slipped it in here (we'll do a PortFast lab in the ICND2 section).

Task 3:

Configure R1 as a Cisco IOS DHCP server with the following settings:

- DHCP pool name: CCNA-DHCP-POOL
- DHCP network: 172.16.1.0/24
- DNS server: 10.1.1.254
- WINS server: 10.2.2.254
- Default gateway: 172.16.1.1
- DNS domain: howtonetwork.net
- DHCP lease time: 5 days 30 minutes

Some of the options above are not available in Packet Tracer, so you may want to use GNS3.

Ensure that you exclude the IP address of the router interface from the DHCP pool.

Task 4:

Verify your DHCP configuration on the connected workstation (or other DHCP client) and verify that your Cisco IOS DHCP server is showing a leased DHCP address.

LAB 32: CONFIGURATION AND VERIFICATION

Task 1:

For reference information on configuring hostnames, please refer to earlier labs.

Task 2:

```
Sw1#config t
Enter configuration commands, one per line.  End with CTRL/Z.
Sw1(config)#vlan50
Sw1(config-vlan)#name DHCP_VLAN
Sw1(config-vlan)#exit
Sw1(config)#interface range fastethernet0/2–3
Sw1(config-if-range)#switchport mode access
Sw1(config-if-range switchport access vlan50
Sw1(config-if-range)#spanning-tree portfast
%Warning: portfast should only be enabled on ports connected to a
single host. Connecting hubs, concentrators, switches, bridges, etc...
to this interface when portfast is enabled, can cause temporary
bridging loops.
 Use with CAUTION

%Portfast will be configured in 2 interfaces due to the range command
 but will only have effect when the interfaces are in a non-trunking
mode.
Sw1(config-if-range)#no shutdown
Sw1(config-if-range)#end
Sw1#
```

Task 3:

```
R1#config t
Enter configuration commands, one per line.  End with CTRL/Z.
R1(config)#ip dhcp pool CCNA-DHCP-POOL
R1(dhcp-config)#network 172.16.1.0 255.255.255.0
R1(dhcp-config)#dns-server 10.1.1.254
R1(dhcp-config)#netbios-name-server 10.2.2.254
R1(dhcp-config)#default-router 172.16.1.1
R1(dhcp-config)#domain-name howtonetwork.net
R1(dhcp-config)#lease 5 0 30
R1(dhcp-config)#exit
R1(config)#ip dhcp excluded-address 172.16.1.1

R1#show ip dhcp pool CCNA-DHCP-POOL

Pool CCNA-DHCP-POOL :
Utilization mark (high/low) : 100 / 0
Subnet size (first/next) : 0 / 0
Total addresses : 254
Leased addresses : 0
Excluded addresses : 1
```

```
Pending event : none

1 subnet is currently in the pool
Current index IP address range Leased/Excluded/Total
172.16.1.1 172.16.1.1 - 172.16.1.254 0 / 1 / 254

Task 4:
I used another router as a DHCP client, as you can see below. If you
use a host, then configure it to obtain the IP address via DHCP.
Router(config)#int f0/0
Router(config-if)#ip address dhcp
Router(config-if)#no shut
%LINK-5-CHANGED: Interface FastEthernet0/0, changed state to up
%DHCP-6-ADDRESS_ASSIGN: Interface FastEthernet0/0 assigned DHCP address
172.16.1.2, mask 255.255.255.0, hostname Router3

Router#show ip dhcp binding
IP address    Client-ID/       Lease expiration          Type
              Hardware address
172.16.1.2    0060.47BC.7A01    --                       Automatic
```

The `ipconfig /all` command on a Windows-based workstation would show the following:

```
Ethernet adapter Local Area Connection 2:

        Connection-specific DNS Suffix  . : howtonetwork.net
        Description . . . . . . . . . . . : Broadcom NetXtreme 57xx Gigabit Cont
roller
        Physical Address. . . . . . . . . : 00-1D-09-D4-02-38
        Dhcp Enabled . . . . . . . . . .  : Yes
        Autoconfiguration Enabled . . . . : Yes
        IP Address . . . . . . . . . . .  : 172.16.1.2
        Subnet Mask . . . . . . . . . . . : 255.255.255.0
        Default Gateway . . . . . . . . . : 172.16.1.1
        DHCP Server . . . . . . . . . . . : 172.16.1.1
        DNS Servers . . . . . . . . . . . : 10.1.1.254
        Primary WINS Server . . . . . . . : 10.2.2.254
        Lease Obtained. . . . . . . . . . : Sunday, April 19, 2009 10:02:13 PM
        Lease Expires . . . . . . . . . . : Friday, April 24, 2009 10:32:13 PM

Ethernet adapter Local Area Connection:

        Media State . . . . . . . . . . . : Media disconnected
        Description . . . . . . . . . . . : Bluetooth Personal Area Network
        Physical Address. . . . . . . . . : 00-21-86-42-0A-8A

C:\>
```

NOTE: If you have configured another Cisco IOS device as a DHCP client to test your configuration, you should see the following output:

```
Router#show ip dhcp pool

Pool CCNA-DHCP-POOL :
 Utilization mark (high/low)    : 100 / 0
 Subnet size (first/next)       : 0 / 0
 Total addresses                : 254
 Leased addresses               : 1
 Excluded addresses             : 1
 Pending event                  : none

 1 subnet is currently in the pool
 Current index       IP address range           Leased/Excluded/Total
 172.16.1.1          172.16.1.1 - 172.16.1.254     1    / 1  / 254
```

LAB 33: TROUBLESHOOTING AND CONFIGURING DHCP (CLIENT-SERVER ROUTER-BASED)

Lab Objective:
The objective of this lab exercise is for you to learn how to implement DHCP in a Cisco router both as a DHCP server and a DHCP client.

Lab Purpose:
Configuring DHCP is a very important task for every network engineer, as this protocol is in charge of the assignment of IP addresses. In this lab, you will learn the steps required to both provide and learn an IP address via DHCP. As a Cisco engineer, as well as in the Cisco CCNA exam, you will be expected to know how to implement DHCP in your network.

Certification Level:
This lab is suitable for ICND1 certification exam preparation.

Lab Difficulty:
This lab has a difficulty rating of 6/10.

Readiness Assessment:
When you are ready for your certification exam, you should complete this lab in no more than 20 minutes.

Lab Topology:
Please use the following topology to complete this lab exercise:

NOTE: R1 will be the DHCP server and R2 will be configured as a DHCP client to obtain an IP address on its Gig0/0 interface.

Task 1:
Configure the hostnames on R1 and R2 as illustrated in the topology.

Task 2:

Configure the IP addresses on the Gig0/0 interface of R1 as illustrated in the topology.

NOTE: R2 will obtain the IP of its Gigabit interface via DHCP.

Task 3:

Configure a DHCP pool on R1 to provide an IP address to the different devices connected on its interface Gig0/0 with the following settings:

- DHCP pool name: Pool-1
- DHCP subnet: 192.168.10.0/24
- DHCP DNS server: 4.2.2.2
- DHCP default gateway: 192.168.10.1

NOTE: Make sure you exclude the 192.168.10.1 address from the DHCP pool.

Task 4:

Configure R2 interface Gig0/0 to obtain its IP address via DHCP.

Task 5:

Confirm the assignment of the IP address on both the DHCP client and DHCP server running the following commands:

On the DHCP server:

- `show ip dhcp pool` (to check the DHCP configuration)
- `show ip dhcp binding` (to check the database of IPs provided and the clients that have obtained each of those IPs)

On the DHCP client:

- `show ip interface brief` (to confirm that it gets an IP and it's obtained via DHCP)

Task 6:

Now break the lab in a few ways. Start from the beginning (reload the routers):

- Don't exclude the IP address.
- Miss off the `ip address dhcp` command on the host.
- Configure the wrong network range.
- Configure the correct network range but with the subnet of 255.255.255.252 (so you only have two host addresses).

LAB 33: CONFIGURATION AND VERIFICATION

Task 1:

For reference information on configuring hostnames, please refer to earlier labs.

Task 2:
```
R1#conf t
Enter configuration commands, one per line.  End with CTRL/Z.
R1(config)#int gig0/0
R1(config-if)#no shutdown
R1(config-if)#ip add 192.168.10.1 255.255.255.0
R1(config-if)#end
```

Task 3:
```
R1#config t
R1(config)#ip dhcp pool Pool-1
R1(dhcp-config)#network 192.168.10.0 255.255.255.0
R1(dhcp-config)#dns-server 4.2.2.2
R1(dhcp-config)#default-router 192.168.10.1
R1(dhcp-config)#exit
R1(config)#ip dhcp excluded-address 192.168.10.1
```

Task 4:
```
R2#config t
Enter configuration commands, one per line.  End with CTRL/Z.
R2(config)#int gig0/0
R2(config-if)#ip address dhcp
R2(config-if)#exit
```

Task 5:

On the server side:

```
R1#sh ip dhcp pool

Pool Pool-1 :
 Utilization mark (high/low)    : 100 / 0
 Subnet size (first/next)       : 0 / 0
 Total addresses                : 254
 Leased addresses               : 1
 Pending event                  : none
 1 subnet is currently in the pool :
 Current index      IP address range                      Leased addresses
 192.168.10.3       192.168.10.1 - 192.168.10.254     1

R1#sh ip dhcp binding
```

```
Bindings from all pools not associated with VRF:
IP address    Client-ID/           Lease expiration      Type
              Hardware address/
              User name
192.168.10.2  0063.6973.636f.2d63. Mar 02 2002 08:14 PM   Automatic
              3030.322e.3235.6362.
              2e30.3030.302d.4661.
              302f.30
```

On the client side:

```
R2#show ip interface brief
Interface          IP-Address      OK?  Method  Status    Protocol
FastEthernet0/0    192.168.10.2    YES  DHCP    up        up
```

LAB 34: DHCP RELAY

Lab Objective:
The objective of this lab exercise is for you to learn and understand how Cisco IOS routers forward DHCP requests to remote DHCP servers.

Lab Purpose:
Configuring Cisco IOS routers to forward DHCP requests to remote DHCP servers is a fundamental skill. In some cases, DHCP servers are located in a central location (such as the Headquarters) and DHCP requests from local clients need to be forwarded on to these servers. By default, Cisco IOS routers do not forward broadcast traffic. Therefore (because DHCP requests are broadcast packets), configuration is required on the Cisco IOS devices to forward these broadcasts to the DHCP servers. As a Cisco engineer, as well as in the Cisco CCNA exam, you will be expected to know how to configure Cisco IOS routers to forward DHCP requests to remote DHCP servers.

Certification Level:
This lab is suitable for CCENT and CCNA certification exam preparation.

Lab Difficulty:
This lab has a difficulty rating of 5/10.

Readiness Assessment:
When you are ready for your certification exam, you should complete this lab in no more than 10 minutes.

> **IMPORTANT NOTE:** In order to test DHCP functionality, you will need a workstation DHCP client configured to receive IP addressing information via DHCP. If you do not have a DHCP client, feel free to substitute it with another Cisco IOS router configured as a DHCP client as illustrated in the previous lab.

Lab Topology:

Please use the following topology to complete this lab exercise:

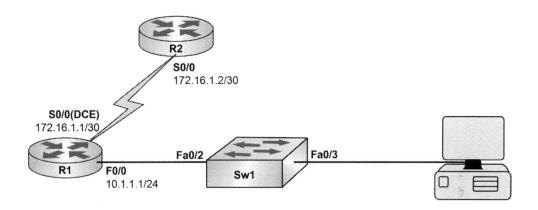

Task 1:

Configure the hostnames on R1, R2, and Sw1 as illustrated in the topology.

Task 2:

Configure R1 to provide clocking information for R2 at a speed of 256 Kbps. Configure the IP addresses on R1 and R2 S0/0 interface as illustrated in the topology.

Task 3:

Configure VLAN300 named DHCP_VLAN on Sw1. Assign the FastEthernet0/2 and FastEthernet0/3 interfaces on Sw1 to this VLAN. Ensure that the ports immediately transition to the Spanning Tree Forwarding state.

Task 4:

Configure R2 as a Cisco IOS DHCP server with the following settings:

- DHCP pool name: REMOTE-DHCP-POOL
- DHCP network: 10.1.1.0/24
- DNS server: 192.168.1.254
- WINS server: 172.30.1.254
- Default gateway: 10.1.1.1
- DHCP lease time: 8 days

You will need to add a static route to the 10 network on R2 because it will otherwise drop any traffic not listed in its routing table.

Task 5:

Configure R1 to forward DHCP requests from DHCP clients connected to F0/0 to R2 (the IOS DHCP server).

Task 6:

Verify your DHCP configuration on the connected workstation (or other DHCP client), and also verify that your Cisco IOS DHCP server is showing a leased DHCP address.

LAB 34: CONFIGURATION AND VERIFICATION

Task 1:

For reference information on configuring hostnames, please refer to earlier labs.

Task 2:

For reference information on configuring DCE clocking and IP addressing, please refer to earlier labs.

Task 3:

```
Sw1#config t
Enter configuration commands, one per line.  End with CTRL/Z.
Sw1(config)#vtp mode transparent
Setting device to VTP TRANSPARENT mode.
Sw1(config)#vlan300
Sw1(config-vlan)#name DHCP_VLAN
Sw1(config-vlan)#exit
Sw1(config)#interface range fastethernet0/2-3
Sw1(config-if-range)#switchport mode access
Sw1(config-if-range switchport access vlan300
Sw1(config-if-range)#spanning-tree portfast
%Warning: portfast should only be enabled on ports connected to a
single host. Connecting hubs, concentrators, switches, bridges, etc...
to this interface when portfast is enabled, can cause temporary
bridging loops.
 Use with CAUTION

%Portfast will be configured in 2 interfaces due to the range command
 but will only have effect when the interfaces are in a non-trunking
mode.
Sw1(config-if-range)#no shutdown
Sw1(config-if-range)#end
Sw1#
```

Task 4:

```
R2#config term
Enter configuration commands, one per line.  End with CRTL/Z.
R2(config)#ip dhcp pool REMOTE-DHCP-POOL
R2(dhcp-config)#network 10.1.1.0 /24
R2(dhcp-config)#dns-server 192.168.1.254
R2(dhcp-config)#netbios-name-server 172.30.1.254
R2(dhcp-config)#default-router 10.1.1.1
R2(dhcp-config)#lease 8
R2(dhcp-config)#exit
R2(config)#ip dhcp excluded-address 10.1.1.1
R2(config)#ip route 10.1.1.0 255.255.255.0 s0/0
R2(config)#exit
R2#
```

Task 5:

```
R1#conf t
Enter configuration commands, one per line.  End with CRTL/Z.
R1(config)#int fastethernet0/0
R1(config-if)#ip helper-address 172.16.1.2
R1(config-if)#end
R1#
```

> **NOTE:** The `ip helper-address` command is used to point an interface connected to a subnet with DHCP clients to a remote DHCP server. You can specify more than one DHCP server with this command; however, the first one configured will always be tried first.

Task 6:

```
R2#show ip dhcp pool REMOTE-DHCP-POOL

Pool REMOTE-DHCP-POOL :
 Utilization mark (high/low)    : 100 / 0
 Subnet size (first/next)       : 0 / 0
 Total addresses                : 254
 Leased addresses               : 1
 Pending event                  : none
 1 subnet is currently in the pool :
 Current index     IP address range                     Leased addresses
 10.1.1.3          10.1.1.1-10.1.1.254                   1

R2#show ip dhcp binding
Bindings from all pools not associated with VRF:
IP address        Client-ID/            Lease expiration        Type
                  Hardware address/
                  User name
10.1.1.2          0100.1d09.d402.38     Mar 09 2017 04:27 AM    Automatic
```

```
Ethernet adapter Local Area Connection 2:

        Connection-specific DNS Suffix  . :
        Description . . . . . . . . . . . : Broadcom NetXtreme 57xx Gigabit Cont
roller
        Physical Address. . . . . . . . . : 00-1D-09-D4-02-38
        Dhcp Enabled  . . . . . . . . . . : Yes
        Autoconfiguration Enabled . . . . : Yes
        IP Address  . . . . . . . . . . . : 10.1.1.2
        Subnet Mask . . . . . . . . . . . : 255.255.255.0
        Default Gateway . . . . . . . . . : 10.1.1.1
        DHCP Server . . . . . . . . . . . : 10.1.1.1
        DNS Servers . . . . . . . . . . . : 192.168.1.254
        Primary WINS Server . . . . . . . : 172.30.1.254
        Lease Obtained. . . . . . . . . . : Sunday, April 19, 2009 10:44:04 PM
        Lease Expires . . . . . . . . . . : Monday, April 27, 2009 10:44:04 PM

Ethernet adapter Local Area Connection:

        Media State . . . . . . . . . . . : Media disconnected
        Description . . . . . . . . . . . : Bluetooth Personal Area Network
        Physical Address. . . . . . . . . : 00-21-86-42-0A-8A

C:\>
```

NOTE: If you decided to use another Cisco IOS device as a DHCP client, you will need to add the command below to the FastEthernet interface:

```
R3(config-if)#ip address dhcp
R3(config-if)#no shut
R3(config-if)#end
*Mar  1 00:04:55.603: %LINK-3-UPDOWN: Interface FastEthernet0/0,
changed state to up
*Mar  1 00:04:56.603: %LINEPROTO-5-UPDOWN: Line protocol on Interface
FastEthernet0/0, changed state to up
*Mar  1 00:05:07.375: %DHCP-6-ADDRESS_ASSIGN: Interface FastEthernet0/0
assigned DHCP address 10.1.1.2, mask 255.255.255.0, hostname R3
```

You can check your DHCP configuration by issuing the `show dhcp server` command (if you are using a router as a host) as illustrated in the following output:

```
R4#show dhcp server
   DHCP server: ANY (255.255.255.255)
   Leases:   3
   Offers:   3      Requests: 3      Acks: 3      Naks: 0
   Declines: 0      Releases: 6      Bad:  0
   DNS0:   192.168.1.254,   DNS1:  0.0.0.0
   NBNS0:  172.30.1.254,    NBNS1: 0.0.0.0
   Subnet: 255.255.255.0   DNS Domain: howtonetwork.com
```

LAB 35: CONFIGURING A ROUTER AS AN NTP CLIENT

Lab Objective:
The objective of this lab exercise is for you to learn and understand how to configure the Cisco router to access the time from an NTP server.

Lab Purpose:
NTP is an important tool used by Cisco equipment to ensure that devices share a consistent time. It is also used to add accurate timestamps to debug messages.

Certification Level:
This lab is suitable for CCENT and CCNA certification exam preparation.

Lab Difficulty:
This lab has a difficulty rating of 5/10.

Readiness Assessment:
When you are ready for your certification exam, you should complete this lab in no more than 5 minutes.

> **IMPORTANT NOTE:** In order to test NTP, you will need to be connected to an actual NTP server that you probably will not have with a home lab or remote rack.

Lab Topology:
Please use the following topology to complete this lab exercise:

R1

Task 1:
Configure the hostname on router R1 as illustrated in the topology.

Task 2:
Set the clock manually to any time zone and time of your choice.

Task 3:
Configure R1 to access two NTP servers. Use any IP addresses you wish.

Task 4:
Verify your NTP configurations with the appropriate show commands.

LAB 35: CONFIGURATION AND VERIFICATION

Task 1:

For reference information on configuring hostnames, please refer to earlier labs.

Task 2:

```
R1#clock set 15:10:30 15 June 2014
R1#
*Jun 15 15:10:30.000: %SYS-6-CLOCKUPDATE: System clock has been updated
from 00:02:21 UTC Fri Mar 1 2002 to 15:10:30 UTC Sun Jun 15 2014,
configured from console by console.
R1#show clock
15:10:35.375 UTC Sun Jun 15 2014
```

Task 3:

Some of these commands won't work with Packet Tracer.

```
R1(config)#ntp server 10.1.1.1 prefer
R1(config)#ntp server 172.16.1.1
R1(config)#
R1(config)#end
```

Task 4:

```
R1#show ntp associations

address      ref clock      st  when  poll reach  delay  offset    disp
~10.1.1.1    0.0.0.0        16   -     64   0      0.0    0.00      16000.
~172.16.1.1  0.0.0.0        16   -     64   0      0.0    0.00      16000.
 * master (synced), # master (unsynced), + selected, - candidate, ~
configured

R1#show ntp status
Clock is unsynchronized, stratum 16, no reference clock
nominal freq is 250.0000 Hz, actual freq is 250.0000 Hz, precision is
2**18
reference time is 00000000.00000000 (00:00:00.000 UTC Mon Jan 1 1900)
clock offset is 0.0000 msec, root delay is 0.00 msec
root dispersion is 0.00 msec, peer dispersion is 0.00 msec
R1#
```

You can add another router and configure it as an NTP server with the command below:

```
R1(config)#ntp master ?
  <1-15>  Stratum number
  <cr>
```

LAB 36: CONFIGURING AND APPLYING STANDARD NUMBERED ACLS

Lab Objective:
The objective of this lab exercise is for you to learn and understand how to create and apply standard numbered access control lists (ACLs).

Lab Purpose:
Configuring and applying standard ACLs is a fundamental skill. Standard ACLs filter based on source address, and they should be applied as close to the destination as possible. As a Cisco engineer, as well as in the Cisco CCNA exam, you will be expected to know how to create and apply standard numbered ACLs.

Certification Level:
This lab is suitable for CCENT and CCNA certification exam preparation.

Lab Difficulty:
This lab has a difficulty rating of 7/10.

Readiness Assessment:
When you are ready for your certification exam, you should complete this lab in no more than 20 minutes.

Lab Topology:
Please use the following topology to complete this lab exercise:

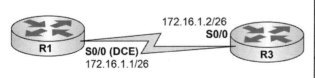

INTERFACE	IP ADDRESS
Loopback10	10.10.10.3/25
Loopback20	10.20.20.3/28
Loopback30	10.30.30.3/29

Task 1:
Configure the hostnames on routers R1 and R3 as illustrated in the topology.

Task 2:
Configure R1 S0/0, which is a DCE, to provide a clock rate of 768 Kbps to R3. Configure the IP addresses on the Serial interfaces of R1 and R3 as illustrated in the topology.

Configure a static default route on R1 pointing to R3 over the Serial connection between the two routers. Also, configure a static default route on R3 pointing to R1 via the Serial connection between the two routers. Configure the Loopback interfaces specified in the diagram on R1 and R3.

Task 3:

To test connectivity, ping R1 from R3 Serial0/0, Loopback10, Loopback20, and Loopback30 interfaces. To ping from the Loopback interfaces, use the `ping <ip_address> source <interface>` command.

Task 4:

On R1, create a standard numbered ACL to prevent inbound traffic from the Loopback20 subnet on R3, but explicitly allow all inbound traffic from Loopback10 and Loopback30 subnets on R3. Apply this ACL inbound on Serial0/0. Now try to ping R1 from R3 Serial0/0, Loopback10, Loopback20, and Loopback30 using the `ping <ip_address> source <interface>`. If you have configured this correctly, only Loopback10 and Loopback30 should still be able to ping.

LAB 36: CONFIGURATION AND VERIFICATION

Task 1:

For reference information on configuring hostnames, please refer to previous labs.

Task 2:

For reference information on configuring IP addresses, please refer to previous labs.

```
R1#config t
Enter configuration commands, one per line.  End with CTRL/Z.
R1(config)#ip route 0.0.0.0 0.0.0.0 serial0/0 172.16.1.2
R1(config-if)#end
R1#

R3#conf t
Enter configuration commands, one per line.  End with CTRL/Z.
R3(config)#ip route 0.0.0.0 0.0.0.0 serial0/0 172.16.1.1
R3(config)#int loop10
R3(config-if)#ip address 10.10.10.3 255.255.255.128
R3(config-if)#exit
R3(config)#int loop20
R3(config-if)#ip address 10.20.20.3 255.255.255.240
R3(config-if)#exit
R3(config)#int loop30
R3(config-if)#ip address 10.30.30.3 255.255.255.248
R3(config-if)#end
R3#
```

Task 3:

```
R3#ping 172.16.1.1

Type escape sequence to abort.
Sending 5, 100-byte ICMP Echos to 172.16.1.1, timeout is 2 seconds:
!!!!!
Success rate is 100 percent (5/5), round-trip min/avg/max = 4/5/8 ms

R3#ping 172.16.1.1 source loopback10

Type escape sequence to abort.
Sending 5, 100-byte ICMP Echos to 172.16.1.1, timeout is 2 seconds:
Packet sent with a source address of 10.10.10.3
!!!!!
Success rate is 100 percent (5/5), round-trip min/avg/max = 4/6/8 ms

R3#ping 172.16.1.1 source loopback20

Type escape sequence to abort.
Sending 5, 100-byte ICMP Echos to 172.16.1.1, timeout is 2 seconds:
```

```
Packet sent with a source address of 10.20.20.3
!!!!!
Success rate is 100 percent (5/5), round-trip min/avg/max = 4/4/8 ms

R3#ping 172.16.1.1 source loopback30

Type escape sequence to abort.
Sending 5, 100-byte ICMP Echos to 172.16.1.1, timeout is 2 seconds:
Packet sent with a source address of 10.30.30.3
!!!!!
Success rate is 100 percent (5/5), round-trip min/avg/max = 4/4/4 ms
```

Task 4:

```
R1#conf t
Enter configuration commands, one per line.  End with CTRL/Z.
R1(config)#access-list 10 remark "Permit From R3 Loopback10"
R1(config)#access-list 10 permit 10.10.10.0 0.0.0.127
R1(config)#access-list 10 remark "Deny From R3 Loopback20"
R1(config)#access-list 10 deny   10.20.20.0 0.0.0.15
R1(config)#access-list 10 remark "Permit From R3 Loopback30"
R1(config)#access-list 10 permit 10.30.30.0 0.0.0.7
R1(config)#int s0/0
R1(config-if)#ip access-group 10 in
R1(config)#end
R1#show ip access-lists
Standard IP access list 10
    10 permit 10.10.10.0, wildcard bits 0.0.0.127
    20 deny   10.20.20.0, wildcard bits 0.0.0.15
    30 permit 10.30.30.0, wildcard bits 0.0.0.7
```

> **NOTE:** The wildcard masks used in ACLs are configured in the same way as those for Enhanced Interior Gateway Routing Protocol (EIGRP) and OSPF. To determine the wildcard mask, you can simply subtract the network mask for the network on which you want to match with the ACL from the broadcast mask. This concept is illustrated in the subtraction table shown below:

Broadcast Mask	255	255	255	255
[minus] Subnet Mask	255	255	255	128
[equals] Wildcard Mask	0	0	0	127

In our example, the subnet mask of the 10.10.10.0/25 subnet is 255.255.255.128. If this is subtracted from the broadcast mask of 255.255.255.255, the result is 0.0.0.127, which is the wildcard mask we will use in the ACL match for this subnet. Using the same concept, the subnet mask of the 10.20.20.0/28 subnet is 255.255.255.240. If we used the table above to determine the wildcard mask, we would get the following:

Broadcast Mask	255	255	255	255
[minus] Subnet Mask	255	255	255	240
[equals] Wildcard Mask	0	0	0	15

And, finally, the subnet mask of the 10.30.30.0/29 subnet is 255.255.255.248. If we used the same table to get the wildcard mask, we would end up with the following:

Broadcast Mask	255	255	255	255
[minus] Subnet Mask	255	255	255	252
[equals] Wildcard Mask	0	0	0	7

It is extremely important to practice creating wildcards for ACLs. Take time out to practice these until you are extremely comfortable with them. ACLs are a very important part of the CCNA certification exam and in the real world.

While it is not mandatory, I prefer to use the access-list [number] remark [description] statement so that I know which ACL line is matching what. This will make it easier for you. You may or may not want to do so, but I feel that it is good practice to do so. Do whatever you feel comfortable doing.

```
R3#ping 172.16.1.1

Type escape sequence to abort.
Sending 5, 100-byte ICMP Echos to 172.16.1.1, timeout is 2 seconds:
U.U.U
Success rate is 0 percent (0/5)

R3#ping 172.16.1.1 source loopback10

Type escape sequence to abort.
Sending 5, 100-byte ICMP Echos to 172.16.1.1, timeout is 2 seconds:
Packet sent with a source address of 10.10.10.3
!!!!!
Success rate is 100 percent (5/5), round-trip min/avg/max = 4/4/4 ms

R3#ping 172.16.1.1 source loopback20

Type escape sequence to abort.
Sending 5, 100-byte ICMP Echos to 172.16.1.1, timeout is 2 seconds:
Packet sent with a source address of 10.20.20.3
U.U.U
Success rate is 0 percent (0/5)

R3#ping 172.16.1.1 source loopback30
```

```
Type escape sequence to abort.
Sending 5, 100-byte ICMP Echos to 172.16.1.1, timeout is 2 seconds:
Packet sent with a source address of 10.30.30.3
!!!!!
Success rate is 100 percent (5/5), round-trip min/avg/max = 4/4/4 ms
```

NOTE: Whenever you see a ping fail and the router shows U.U.U, it is typically because your ping request was administratively prohibited by an ACL on the other end.

The second lesson to be learned in this exercise is that even though the ACL configuration focused on R3 Loopback10, Loopback20, and Loopback30, because we did not explicitly allow the Serial0/0 subnet between R1 and R3, this is implicitly denied at the end of the ACL. Keep this in mind: if traffic is not explicitly permitted, it is implicitly denied. It is very important to understand this aspect in regard to access control lists. The explicitly configured statements show as matches against ACL entries, but implicit deny matches do not.

```
R1#show access-lists
Standard IP access list 10
    10 permit 10.10.10.0, wildcard bits 0.0.0.127 (15 matches)
    20 deny   10.20.20.0, wildcard bits 0.0.0.15 (11 matches)
    30 permit 10.30.30.0, wildcard bits 0.0.0.7 (15 matches)
```

Your output may differ from mine due to differences in IOS releases and platforms.

LAB 37: CONFIGURING AND APPLYING STANDARD NAMED ACLS

Lab Objective:
The objective of this lab exercise is for you to learn and understand how to create and apply standard named access control lists.

Lab Purpose:
Configuring and applying standard ACLs is a fundamental skill. Standard ACLs filter based on source address, and they should be applied as close to the destination as possible. As a Cisco engineer, as well as in the Cisco CCNA exam, you will be expected to know how to create and apply standard numbered ACLs.

Certification Level:
This lab is suitable for CCNA certification exam preparation.

Lab Difficulty:
This lab has a difficulty rating of 7/10.

Readiness Assessment:
When you are ready for your certification exam, you should complete this lab in no more than 20 minutes.

Lab Topology:
Please use the following topology to complete this lab exercise:

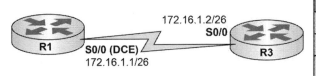

INTERFACE	IP ADDRESS
Loopback10	10.10.10.3/25
Loopback20	10.20.20.3/28
Loopback30	10.30.30.3/29

Task 1:
Configure the hostnames on routers R1 and R3 as illustrated in the topology.

Task 2:
Configure R1 S0/0, which is a DCE, to provide a clock rate of 768 Kbps to R3. Configure the IP addresses on the Serial interfaces of R1 and R3 as illustrated in the topology.

Configure a static default route on R1 pointing to R3 over the Serial connection between the two routers. Also, configure a static default route on R3 pointing to R1 via the Serial connection between the two routers. Configure the Loopback interfaces specified in the diagram on R3.

Task 3:

To test connectivity, ping R1 from R3 Serial0/0, Loopback10, Loopback20, and Loopback30 interfaces. To ping from the Loopback interfaces, use the `ping <ip_address> source <interface>` command.

Task 4:

On R1, create a standard named ACL to prevent inbound traffic from the Loopback10 and Loopback30 subnets on R3, but explicitly allow all inbound traffic from Serial0/0 and Loopback20 subnets on R3. This ACL should be named LOOPBACK-10-30-ACL. Apply this ACL inbound on Serial0/0. Now try to ping R1 from R3 Serial0/0, Loopback10, Loopback20, and Loopback30 using the `ping <ip_address> source <interface>` command. If you have configured this correctly, only the ping from Serial0/0 and Loopback20 will work.

LAB 37: CONFIGURATION AND VERIFICATION

Task 1:

For reference information on configuring hostnames, please refer to earlier labs.

Task 2:

For reference information on configuring IP addresses and static routes, please refer to earlier labs.

Task 3:

For reference information on pinging IP addresses, please refer to earlier labs.

Task 4:
```
R1#conf t
Enter configuration commands, one per line.  End with CTRL/Z.
R1(config)#ip access-list standard LOOPBACK-10-30-ACL
R1(config-std-nacl)#remark "Deny Traffic From R3 Loopback10"
R1(config-std-nacl)#deny 10.10.10.0 0.0.0.127
R1(config-std-nacl)#remark "Permit Traffic From R3 Loopback20"
R1(config-std-nacl)#permit 10.20.20.0 0.0.0.15
R1(config-std-nacl)#remark "Deny Traffic From R3 Loopback30"
R1(config-std-nacl)#deny 10.30.30.0 0.0.0.7
R1(config-std-nacl)#remark "Permit Traffic From Serial0/0 Subnet"
R1(config-std-nacl)#permit 172.16.1.0 0.0.0.63
R1(config-std-nacl)#exit
R1(config)#int s0/0
R1(config-if)#ip access-group LOOPBACK-10-30-ACL in
R1(config-if)#end
R1#

R3#ping 172.16.1.1

Type escape sequence to abort.
Sending 5, 100-byte ICMP Echos to 172.16.1.1, timeout is 2 seconds:
!!!!!
Success rate is 100 percent (5/5), round-trip min/avg/max = 4/4/4 ms

R3#ping 172.16.1.1 source loop10

Type escape sequence to abort.
Sending 5, 100-byte ICMP Echos to 172.16.1.1, timeout is 2 seconds:
Packet sent with a source address of 10.10.10.3
U.U.U
Success rate is 0 percent (0/5)

R3#ping 172.16.1.1 source loop20
```

```
Type escape sequence to abort.
Sending 5, 100-byte ICMP Echos to 172.16.1.1, timeout is 2 seconds:
Packet sent with a source address of 10.20.20.3
!!!!!
Success rate is 100 percent (5/5), round-trip min/avg/max = 4/4/8 ms

R3#ping 172.16.1.1 source loop30

Type escape sequence to abort.
Sending 5, 100-byte ICMP Echos to 172.16.1.1, timeout is 2 seconds:
Packet sent with a source address of 10.30.30.3
U.U.U
Success rate is 0 percent (0/5)
```

NOTE: Take note of the different syntax for creating a named ACL versus a numbered ACL. Named ACLs perform the same way as numbered ACLs but allow for easier identification of what the ACL is used for because they can be assigned a name. You can view named ACLs using the same commands as you would for numbered ACLs:

```
R1#show ip access-lists LOOPBACK-10-30-ACL
Standard IP access list LOOPBACK-10-30-ACL
    10 deny   10.10.10.0, wildcard bits 0.0.0.127 (11 matches)
    20 permit 10.20.20.0, wildcard bits 0.0.0.15 (15 matches)
    30 deny   10.30.30.0, wildcard bits 0.0.0.7 (11 matches)
    40 permit 172.16.1.0, wildcard bits 0.0.0.63 (15 matches)
```

To view ACLs applied to an interface, you can use either the show run interface <name> command or the show ip interface <name> command as illustrated below:

```
R1#show running-config interface serial 0/0
Building configuration...

Current configuration : 139 bytes
!
interface Serial0/0
 ip address 172.16.1.1 255.255.255.192
 ip access-group LOOPBACK-10-30-ACL in
 clock rate 768000
 no fair-queue
end

R1#show ip interface serial 0/0
Serial0/0 is up, line protocol is up
  Internet address is 172.16.1.1/26
  Broadcast address is 255.255.255.255
  Address determined by setup command
  MTU is 1500 bytes
  Helper address is not set
  Directed broadcast forwarding is disabled
  Outgoing access list is not set
  Inbound  access list is LOOPBACK-10-30-ACL
```

LAB 38: CONFIGURING AND APPLYING EXTENDED NUMBERED ACLS INBOUND

Lab Objective:
The objective of this lab exercise is for you to learn and understand how to create and apply extended numbered access control lists.

Lab Purpose:
Configuring and applying extended ACLs is a fundamental skill. Extended ACLs filter based on source and destination address, as well as Layer 4 protocols TCP (Transmission Control Protocol) and UDP (User Datagram Protocol). Extended ACLs should be applied as close to the source as possible. As a Cisco engineer, as well as in the Cisco CCNA exam, you will be expected to know how to create and apply extended numbered ACLs.

Certification Level:
This lab is suitable for CCENT and CCNA certification exam preparation.

Lab Difficulty:
This lab has a difficulty rating of 8/10.

Readiness Assessment:
When you are ready for your certification exam, you should complete this lab in no more than 20 minutes.

Lab Topology:
Please use the following topology to complete this lab exercise:

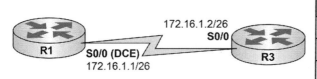

INTERFACE	IP ADDRESS
Loopback10	10.10.10.3/25
Loopback20	10.20.20.3/28
Loopback30	10.30.30.3/29

Task 1:
Configure the hostnames on routers R1 and R3 as illustrated in the topology.

Task 2:

Configure R1 S0/0, which is a DCE, to provide a clock rate of 768 Kbps to R3. Configure the IP addresses on the Serial interfaces of R1 and R3 as illustrated in the topology.

Task 3:

Configure a static default route on R1 pointing to R3 over the Serial connection between the two routers. Also, configure a static default route on R3 pointing to R1 via the Serial connection between the two routers. Configure the Loopback interfaces specified in the diagram on R1 and R3.

Task 4:

To test connectivity, ping R1 from R3 Serial0/0, Loopback10, Loopback20, and Loopback30 interfaces. To ping from the Loopback interfaces, use the `ping <ip_address> /source <interface>` command.

Task 5:

Configure both R1 and R3 to allow Telnet connections. The password CISCO should be used for Telnet access. Also, configure an enable secret of CISCO on both routers.

Task 6:

Configure a numbered extended ACL on R1 to allow Telnet from R3 Loopback10 and Loopback30 networks. Explicitly configure the extended ACL to deny Telnet from R3 Loopback20 but allow ping traffic from R3 Loopback20. When done, apply this ACL inbound on R1 Serial0/0 interface.

Telnet to R1 from R3 Loopback10, Loopback20, and Loopback30 interfaces using the `telnet <ip_address> /source-interface <name>` command. If your ACL has been configured correctly, Telnet should be allowed from Loopback10 and Loopback30 only.

Ping R1 from Loopback10, Loopback 20, and Loopback30 interfaces using the `ping <ip_address> /source <interface>` command. If your ACL has been configured correctly, ping should only work when you ping from R3 Loopback20.

LAB 38: CONFIGURATION AND VERIFICATION

Task 1:

For reference information on configuring hostnames, please refer to earlier labs.

Task 2:

For reference information on configuring clock rates and IP addresses, please refer to earlier labs.

Task 3:

For reference information on configuring static routes, please refer to earlier labs.

Task 4:

For reference information on pinging, please refer to earlier labs.

Task 5:
```
R1#conf t
Enter configuration commands, one per line.  End with CTRL/Z.
R1(config)#enable secret CISCO
R1(config)#line vty 0 4
R1(config-line)#password CISCO
R1(config-line)#login
R1(config-line)#end
R1#

R3#conf t
Enter configuration commands, one per line.  End with CTRL/Z.
R3(config)#enable secret CISCO
R3(config)#line vty 0 4
R3(config-line)#password CISCO
R3(config-line)#login
R3(config-line)#end
R3#
```

NOTE: GNS3 has more VTY lines so use the ? to establish how many you need to configure.

```
R1(config)#line vty 0 ?
  <1-903>  Last Line number
  <cr>
```

Task 6:
```
R1#conf t
Enter configuration commands, one per line.  End with CTRL/Z.
R1(config)#access-list 150 remark "Allow Telnet For R3 Loopback10"
```

```
R1(config)#access-list 150 permit tcp 10.10.10.0 0.0.0.127 any eq
telnet
R1(config)#access-list 150 remark "Deny Telnet For R3 Loopback20"
R1(config)#access-list 150 deny tcp 10.20.20.0 0.0.0.15 any eq telnet
R1(config)#access-list 150 remark "Allow Telnet For R3 Loopback30"
R1(config)#access-list 150 permit tcp 10.30.30.0 0.0.0.7 any eq telnet
R1(config)#access-list 150 remark "Allow PING For R3 Loopback20"
R1(config)#access-list 150 permit icmp 10.20.20.0 0.0.0.15 any echo
R1(config)#int s0/0
R1(config-if)#ip access-group 150 in
R1(config-if)#end
R1#
```

NOTE: Extended ACLs have the capability to match Layer 4 protocol information. This means that you must know your well-known TCP and UDP port numbers. Fortunately, instead of having TCP and UDP port numbers, Cisco IOS ACLs allow you to use keywords for common protocols. For example, you can use the keyword telnet instead of having to use port number 23 to configure an ACL to match Telnet traffic. However, if you do decide to use a port number, Cisco IOS automatically converts it to the common name as illustrated below:

```
R1#conf t
Enter configuration commands, one per line.  End with CRTL/Z.
R1(config)#access-list 100 permit tcp any any eq 23
R1(config)#access-list 100 permit tcp any any eq 80
R1(config)#access-list 100 permit tcp any any eq 179
R1(config)#access-list 100 permit udp any any eq 520
R1(config)#access-list 100 permit 88 any any
R1(config)#access-list 100 permit 89 any any
R1(config)#end
R1#
R1#show ip access-lists 100
Extended IP access list 100
    10 permit tcp any any eq telnet
    20 permit tcp any any eq www
    30 permit tcp any any eq bgp
    40 permit udp any any eq rip
    50 permit eigrp any any
    60 permit ospf any any
```

As can be seen, while we configured the ACL using port numbers, IOS converted it to common names.

Now test the ACL from the lab. To quit your Telnet access, hit the Control-Shift-6 key at the same time and then let go and press the X key. Don't hit the enter key right after or it will resume your Telnet session.

```
R3#telnet 172.16.1.1 /source-interface loopback10
Trying 172.16.1.1 ... Open

User Access Verification

Password:
R1#

R3#telnet 172.16.1.1 /source-interface loopback20
Trying 172.16.1.1 ...
% Destination unreachable; gateway or host down

R3#telnet 172.16.1.1 /source-interface loopback30
Trying 172.16.1.1 ... Open

User Access Verification

Password:
R1#

R3#ping 172.16.1.1 source loopback 20

Type escape sequence to abort.
Sending 5, 100-byte ICMP Echos to 172.16.1.1, timeout is 2 seconds:
Packet sent with a source address of 10.20.20.3
!!!!!
Success rate is 100 percent (5/5), round-trip min/avg/max = 4/5/8 ms
```

NOTE: When you see the message % Destination unreachable; gateway or host down when trying to telnet to a host, it is typically because there is an ACL preventing Telnet to this device. Based on our configuration, everything works, and if we looked at the ACL configured on R1, we would see matches against it as follows:

```
R1#show ip access-lists 150
Extended IP access list 150
    10 permit tcp 10.10.10.0 0.0.0.127 any eq telnet (66 matches)
    20 deny tcp 10.20.20.0 0.0.0.15 any eq telnet (3 matches)
    30 permit tcp 10.30.30.0 0.0.0.7 any eq telnet (465 matches)
    40 permit icmp 10.20.20.0 0.0.0.15 any echo (15 matches
```

LAB 39: CONFIGURING AND APPLYING EXTENDED NAMED ACLS INBOUND

Lab Objective:

The objective of this lab exercise is for you to learn and understand how to create and apply extended named access control lists.

Lab Purpose:

Configuring and applying extended ACLs is a fundamental skill. Extended ACLs filter based on source and destination address, as well as Layer 4 protocols TCP and UDP. Extended ACLs should be applied as close to the source as possible. As a Cisco engineer, as well as in the Cisco CCNA exam, you will be expected to know how to create and apply extended named ACLs.

Certification Level:

This lab is suitable for CCENT and CCNA certification exam preparation.

Lab Difficulty:

This lab has a difficulty rating of 8/10.

Readiness Assessment:

When you are ready for your certification exam, you should complete this lab in no more than 20 minutes.

Lab Topology:

Please use the following topology to complete this lab exercise:

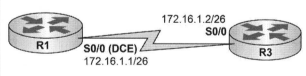

INTERFACE	IP ADDRESS
Loopback10	172.16.4.1/26
Loopback20	192.168.5.1/29
Loopback30	10.10.10.1/27

Task 1:

Configure the hostnames on routers R1 and R3 as illustrated in the topology.

Task 2:

Configure R1 S0/0, which is a DCE, to provide a clock rate of 768 Kbps to R3. Configure the IP addresses on the Serial interfaces of R1 and R3 as illustrated in the topology. Configure the Loopback interfaces on R1.

Task 3:

Configure RIPv2 on R1 and R3 for Serial0/0 on both routers and the 172.16.4.0/26 Loopback10 on R1. Configure EIGRP using AS 10 on R1 and R3 for Serial0/0 on both routers and the 192.168.5.0/29 Loopback20 on R1. Configure OSPF using process 10 and area 0 on R1 and R3 Serial0/0 on both routers and the 10.10.10.0/27 Loopback30 on R1. I know we haven't covered these yet but just copy my commands as we need to test the ACL.

Task 4:

Verify your configuration using the `show ip route` command on R3 to ensure that all three routes are seen via the different configured routing protocols. To test connectivity, ping the three Loopback interfaces on R1 from R3. These should all be reachable.

Task 5:

Configure a named extended ACL on R3 called ROUTING-ACL. This ACL should deny RIPv2, allow EIGRP, deny OSPF, and allow all other IP traffic. Apply this ACL inbound on R3 Serial0/0.

Task 6:

Issue the `clear ip route *` command followed by the `show ip route` command on R3 and look at the routing table again. If you have configured this ACL correctly, you should only have the EIGRP route in the routing table.

LAB 39: CONFIGURATION AND VERIFICATION

Task 1:

For reference information on configuring hostnames, please refer to earlier labs.

Task 2:

```
R1#conf t
Enter configuration commands, one per line.  End with CTRL/Z.
R1(config)#int s0/0
R1(config-if)#no shutdown
R1(config-if)#clock rate 768000
R1(config-if)#ip add 172.16.1.1 255.255.255.192
R1(config-if)#exit
R1(config)#int lo10
R1(config-if)#ip address 172.16.4.1 255.255.255.192
R1(config-if)#exit
R1(config)#int lo20
R1(config-if)#ip address 192.168.5.1 255.255.255.248
R1(config-if)#exit
R1(config)#int lo30
R1(config-if)#ip address 10.10.10.1 255.255.255.224
R1(config-if)#exit
R1#

R3#config term
Enter configuration commands, one per line.  End with CTRL/Z.
R3(config)#int s0/0
R3(config-if)#ip address 172.16.1.2 255.255.255.192
R3(config-if)#no shut
R3(config-if)#end
R3#
```

Task 3:

```
R1#conf t
Enter configuration commands, one per line.  End with CTRL/Z.
R1(config)#router rip
R1(config-router)#version 2
R1(config-router)#network 172.16.1.0
R1(config-router)#network 172.16.4.0
R1(config-router)#no auto-summary
R1(config-router)#exit
R1(config)#router eigrp 10
R1(config-router)#network 172.16.1.0 0.0.0.63
R1(config-router)#network 192.168.5.0
R1(config-router)#no auto-summary
R1(config-router)#exit
R1(config)#router ospf 10
R1(config-router)#network 172.16.1.0 0.0.0.63 area 0
R1(config-router)#network 10.10.10.0 0.0.0.31 area 0
R1(config-router)#end
R1#
```

```
R3#conf t
Enter configuration commands, one per line.  End with CTRL/Z.
R3(config)#router rip
R3(config-router)#ver 2
R3(config-router)#net 172.16.1.0
R3(config-router)#no auto-sum
R3(config-router)#exit
R3(config)#router eigrp 10
R3(config-router)#network 172.16.1.0
R3(config-router)#no auto-summary
*Mar  1 03:18:45.296: %DUAL-5-NBRCHANGE: IP-EIGRP(0) 10: Neighbor
172.16.1.1 (Serial0/0) is up: new adjacency
R3(config)#router ospf 10
R3(config-router)#network 172.16.1.0 0.0.0.63 area 0
R3(config-router)#end
*Mar  1 03:19:08.550: %OSPF-5-ADJCHG: Process 10, Nbr 192.168.5.1 on
Serial0/0 from LOADING to FULL, Loading Done
```

Task 4:

```
R3#show ip route
Codes: C - connected, S - static, R - RIP, M - mobile, B—BGP,
       D - EIGRP, EX - EIGRP external, O - OSPF, IA - OSPF inter area,
       N1 - OSPF NSSA external type 1, N2 - OSPF NSSA external type 2,
       E1 - OSPF external type 1, E2 - OSPF external type 2,
       i - IS-IS, su - IS-IS summary, L1 - IS-IS level-1,
       L2 - IS-IS level-2, ia - IS-IS inter area,
       * - candidate default, U - per-user static route, o - ODR,
       P - periodic downloaded static route

Gateway of last resort is not set

     172.16.0.0/26 is subnetted, 2 subnets
R       172.16.4.0 [120/1] via 172.16.1.1, 00:00:06, Serial0/0
C       172.16.1.0 is directly connected, Serial0/0
     192.168.5.0/29 is subnetted, 1 subnets
D       192.168.5.0 [90/2297856] via 172.16.1.1, 00:03:16, Serial0/0
     10.0.0.0/32 is subnetted, 1 subnets
O       10.10.10.1 [110/65] via 172.16.1.1, 00:07:53, Serial0/0

R3#ping 172.16.4.1

Type escape sequence to abort.
Sending 5, 100-byte ICMP Echos to 172.16.4.1, timeout is 2 seconds:
!!!!!
Success rate is 100 percent (5/5), round-trip min/avg/max = 4/6/16 ms

R3#ping 192.168.5.1

Type escape sequence to abort.
Sending 5, 100-byte ICMP Echos to 192.168.5.1, timeout is 2 seconds:
!!!!!
Success rate is 100 percent (5/5), round-trip min/avg/max = 4/4/8 ms
```

```
R3#ping 10.10.10.1

Type escape sequence to abort.
Sending 5, 100-byte ICMP Echos to 10.10.10.1, timeout is 2 seconds:
!!!!!
Success rate is 100 percent (5/5), round-trip min/avg/max = 4/4/8 ms
```

Task 5:

```
R3#conf t
Enter configuration commands, one per line.  End with CTRL/Z.
R3(config)#ip access-list extended ROUTING-ACL
R3(config-ext-nacl)#remark "Deny RIP (UDP Port 520)"
R3(config-ext-nacl)#deny udp any any eq 520
R3(config-ext-nacl)#remark "Permit EIGRP (IP Protocol 88)"

R3(config-ext-nacl)#permit 88 any any
R3(config-ext-nacl)#remark "Deny OSPF (IP Protocol 89)"
R3(config-ext-nacl)#deny 89 any any
R3(config-ext-nacl)#remark "Permit All Other IP Traffic"
R3(config-ext-nacl)#permit ip any any
R3(config-ext-nacl)#exit
R3(config)#int s0/0
R3(config-if)#ip access-group ROUTING-ACL in
R3(config-if)#^Z
R3#
```

> **NOTE:** Notice that I used the IP protocol numbers 88 and 89 for EIGRP and OSPF, respectively, instead of the keywords `eigrp` and `ospf`. Even though I did so, Cisco IOS converted these to their common names, which is what you will see when you issue the `show access-lists` command.

Task 6:

```
R3#clear ip route *
R3#show ip route
Codes: C - connected, S - static, R - RIP, M - mobile, B–BGP,
       D - EIGRP, EX - EIGRP external, O - OSPF, IA - OSPF inter area,
       N1 - OSPF NSSA external type 1, N2 - OSPF NSSA external type 2,
       E1 - OSPF external type 1, E2 - OSPF external type 2,
       i - IS-IS, su - IS-IS summary, L1 - IS-IS level-1,
       L2 - IS-IS level-2, ia - IS-IS inter area,
       * - candidate default, U - per-user static route, o - ODR,
       P - periodic downloaded static route

Gateway of last resort is not set

     172.16.0.0/26 is subnetted, 1 subnets
C       172.16.1.0 is directly connected, Serial0/0
     192.168.5.0/29 is subnetted, 1 subnets
D       192.168.5.0 [90/2297856] via 172.16.1.1, 00:00:03, Serial0/0
```

> **NOTE:** You may be wondering why the OSPF neighbor did not immediately go down when you applied the ACL inbound. This is because the adjacency is only removed when the OSPF dead timer expires. Therefore, after a few seconds, you should see the following message on your console:

```
*Mar  1 03:34:01.683: %OSPF-5-ADJCHG: Process 10, Nbr 192.168.5.1 on
Serial0/0 from FULL to DOWN, Neighbor Down: Dead timer expired
```

The reason we need to issue the `clear ip route *` command is because RIP routes only get removed from the routing tables after the timers expire. This will be a few minutes. Therefore, if you ever see a RIP route that is older than 30 seconds, RIP holddown timers have kicked in, as illustrated in the following output:

```
R3#show ip route
Codes: C - connected, S - static, R - RIP, M - mobile, B-BGP,
       D - EIGRP, EX - EIGRP external, O - OSPF, IA - OSPF inter area,
       N1 - OSPF NSSA external type 1, N2 - OSPF NSSA external type 2,
       E1 - OSPF external type 1, E2 - OSPF external type 2,
       i - IS-IS, su - IS-IS summary, L1 - IS-IS level-1,
       L2 - IS-IS level-2, ia - IS-IS inter area, * - candidate
default,
       U - per-user static route, o - ODR,
       P - periodic downloaded static route

Gateway of last resort is not set

     172.16.0.0/26 is subnetted, 2 subnets
R       172.16.4.0 [120/1] via 172.16.1.1, 00:03:05, Serial0/0
```

Based on the configuration tasks, we know that the ACL is working because we can ping R3 from R1 and the ACL on R3 shows matches for configured rules, as follows:

```
R1#ping 172.16.1.2

Type escape sequence to abort.
Sending 5, 100-byte ICMP Echos to 172.16.1.2, timeout is 2 seconds:
!!!!!
Success rate is 100 percent (5/5), round-trip min/avg/max = 4/4/8 ms

R3#show ip access-lists ROUTING-ACL
Extended IP access list ROUTING-ACL
    10 deny udp any any eq rip (80 matches)
    20 permit eigrp any any (453 matches)
    30 deny ospf any any (135 matches)
    40 permit ip any any (15 matches)
```

LAB 40: CONFIGURING AND APPLYING EXTENDED NUMBERED ACLS

Lab Objective:
The objective of this lab exercise is for you to learn and understand how to create and apply extended numbered access control lists.

Lab Purpose:
Configuring and applying extended ACLs is a fundamental skill. Extended ACLs filter based on source and destination address, as well as Layer 4 protocols TCP and UDP. Extended ACLs should be applied as close to the source as possible. As a Cisco engineer, as well as in the Cisco CCNA exam, you will be expected to know how to create and apply extended numbered ACLs.

Certification Level:
This lab is suitable for CCENT and CCNA certification exam preparation.

Lab Difficulty:
This lab has a difficulty rating of 8/10.

Readiness Assessment:
When you are ready for your certification exam, you should complete this lab in no more than 20 minutes.

Lab Topology:
Please use the following topology to complete this lab exercise:

INTERFACE	IP ADDRESS
Loopback10	172.16.4.1/26
Loopback20	172.17.5.1/29

INTERFACE	IP ADDRESS
Loopback10	10.10.10.3/25
Loopback20	10.20.20.3/28
Loopback30	10.30.30.3/29

Task 1:

Configure the hostnames on routers R1 and R3 as illustrated in the topology.

Task 2:

Configure R1 S0/0, which is a DCE, to provide a clock rate of 768 Kbps to R3. Configure the IP addresses on the Serial interfaces of R1 and R3 as illustrated in the topology.

Task 3:

Configure a static default route on R1 pointing to R3 over the Serial connection between the two routers. Also, configure a static default route on R3 pointing to R1 via the Serial connection between the two routers. Configure the Loopback interfaces specified in the diagram on R1 and R3.

Task 4:

To test connectivity, ping R1 from R3 Serial0/0, Loopback10, Loopback20, and Loopback30 interfaces. To ping from the Loopback interfaces, use the `ping <ip_address> /source <interface>` command.

Task 5:

Configure both R1 and R3 to allow Telnet connections. The password CISCO should be used for Telnet access.

Task 6:

Configure a numbered extended ACL on R3 to allow Telnet from R1 Loopback10 to R3 Loopback20 and Loopback30. Add another line to the extended ACL to only allow ping traffic from R1 Loopback20 to R3 Loopback10. Apply this ACL inbound on R3 Serial0/0.

To test your Telnet ACL configuration, telnet from R1 Loopback10 to R3 Loopback10, Loopback20, and Loopback30. If you have configured your ACL correctly, only Telnet sessions to Loopback20 and Loopback30 will work.

Task 7:

To test your ping ACL configuration, ping from R1 Loopback20 to R3 Loopback10, Loopback20, and Loopback30. If you have configured your ACL correctly, only pings from R1 Loopback10 to R3 Loopback20 should work. Use the `ping <ip_address> / source <interface>` command to send pings from the Loopback interfaces.

Feel free to try the lab again but blocking/permitting host addresses.

LAB 40: CONFIGURATION AND VERIFICATION

Task 1:

For reference information on configuring hostnames, please refer to earlier labs.

Task 2:

For reference information on configuring DCE clocking, please refer to earlier labs.

Task 3:

For reference information on configuring IP addressing and static routes, please refer to earlier labs.

Task 4:

For reference information on sourcing traffic from other interfaces, please refer to earlier labs.

Task 5:

For reference information on permitting Telnet, please refer to earlier labs.

Task 6:

```
R3#conf t
Enter configuration commands, one per line.  End with CTRL/Z.
R3(config)#access-list 180 remark "R1 Loop10->R3 Loop20"
R3(config)#access-list 180 per tcp 172.16.4.0 0.0.0.63 10.20.20.0
0.0.0.15 eq telnet
R3(config)#access-list 180 remark "R1 Loop10->R3 Loop30"
R3(config)#access-list 180 per tcp 172.16.4.0 0.0.0.63 10.30.30.0
0.0.0.7 eq telnet
R3(config)#access-list 180 per icmp 172.17.5.0 0.0.0.7 10.10.10.0
0.0.0.127 echo
R3(config)#access-list 180 per icmp 172.17.5.0 0.0.0.7 10.10.10.0
0.0.0.127 echo-reply
R3(config)#int s0/0
R3(config-if)#ip access-group 180 in
R3(config-if)#end
R3#

R1#telnet 10.10.10.3 /source-interface loopback10
Trying 10.10.10.3 ...
% Destination unreachable; gateway or host down

R1#telnet 10.20.20.3 /source-interface loopback10
Trying 10.20.20.3 ... Open

User Access Verification
```

```
Password:
R3#

R1#telnet 10.30.30.3 /source-interface loopback10
Trying 10.30.30.3 ... Open

User Access Verification
Password:
R3#
```

Task 7:

```
R1#ping 10.10.10.3 source loopback20

Type escape sequence to abort.
Sending 5, 100-byte ICMP Echos to 10.10.10.3, timeout is 2 seconds:
Packet sent with a source address of 172.17.5.1
!!!!!
Success rate is 100 percent (5/5), round-trip min/avg/max = 4/4/8 ms

R1#ping 10.20.20.3 source loopback20

Type escape sequence to abort.
Sending 5, 100-byte ICMP Echos to 10.20.20.3, timeout is 2 seconds:
Packet sent with a source address of 172.17.5.1
U.U.U
Success rate is 0 percent (0/5)

R1#ping 10.30.30.3 source loopback20

Type escape sequence to abort.
Sending 5, 100-byte ICMP Echos to 10.30.30.3, timeout is 2 seconds:
Packet sent with a source address of 172.17.5.1
U.U.U
Success rate is 0 percent (0/5)
```

LAB 41: RESTRICTING INBOUND TELNET ACCESS USING EXTENDED ACLS

Lab Objective:
The objective of this lab exercise is for you to learn and understand how to create and apply extended access control lists to restrict Telnet access to a router or switch.

Lab Purpose:
Configuring and applying extended ACLs to restrict Telnet access is a fundamental skill. Extended ACLs filter based on source and destination address, as well as Layer 4 protocols TCP and UDP. Extended ACLs should be applied as close to the source as possible. As a Cisco engineer, as well as in the Cisco CCNA exam, you will be expected to know how to restrict inbound Telnet traffic to the router or switch using ACLs.

Certification Level:
This lab is suitable for CCENT and CCNA certification exam preparation.

Lab Difficulty:
This lab has a difficulty rating of 8/10.

Readiness Assessment:
When you are ready for your certification exam, you should complete this lab in no more than 20 minutes.

Lab Topology:
Please use the following topology to complete this lab exercise:

INTERFACE	IP ADDRESS
Loopback10	10.10.10.3/25
Loopback20	10.20.20.3/28
Loopback30	10.30.30.3/29

Task 1:
Configure the hostnames on routers R1 and R3 as illustrated in the topology.

Task 2:

Configure R1 S0/0, which is a DCE, to provide a clock rate of 2 Mbps to R3. Configure the IP addresses on the Serial interfaces of R1 and R3 as illustrated in the topology.

Task 3:

Configure a static default route on R1 pointing to R3 over the Serial connection between the two routers. Next, configure the Loopback interfaces specified in the diagram on R3. Finally, configure R1 to allow Telnet sessions. Use the password CISCO for Telnet login.

Task 4:

To test connectivity, ping R1 from R3 Loopback10, Loopback20, and Loopback30 interfaces.

Task 5:

Create an extended named ACL called TELNET-IN on R1. This ACL should permit Telnet traffic from host 10.10.10.3 to any IP address on R1; deny Telnet from host 10.20.20.3 to any IP address on R1; permit Telnet from host 10.30.30.3 to any IP address on R1. Apply this ACL to the Telnet lines on R1 for inbound traffic.

Task 6:

To test your ACL configuration, telnet to R1 from R3 Loopback10, Loopback20, and Loopback30 interfaces using the `telnet <ip_address> /source-interface <interface>` command. If your ACL configuration is correct, only Telnet from R3 Loopback10 and Loopback20 should work. Verify matches against your ACL.

LAB 41: CONFIGURATION AND VERIFICATION

Task 1:

For reference information on configuring hostnames, please refer to earlier labs.

Task 2:

For reference information on configuring IP addresses and clock rates, please refer to earlier labs.

Task 3:

```
R1#config t
Enter configuration commands, one per line.  End with CTRL/Z.
R1(config)#ip route 0.0.0.0 0.0.0.0 serial0/0 172.16.1.2
R1(config)#line vty 0 4
R1(config-line)#password CISCO
R1(config-line)#login
R1(config-line)#end
R1#


R3#conf t
Enter configuration commands, one per line.  End with CTRL/Z.
R3(config)#int loop10
R3(config-if)#ip address 10.10.10.3 255.255.255.128
R3(config-if)#exit
R3(config)#int loop20
R3(config-if)#ip address 10.20.20.3 255.255.255.240
R3(config-if)#exit
R3(config)#int loop30
R3(config-if)#ip address 10.30.30.3 255.255.255.248
R3(config-if)#exit
R3(config)#line vty 0 4
R3(config-line)#password CISCO
R3(config-line)#login
R3(config-line)#end
R3#
```

Task 4:

```
R1#ping 10.10.10.3

Type escape sequence to abort.
Sending 5, 100-byte ICMP Echos to 10.10.10.3, timeout is 2 seconds:
!!!!!
Success rate is 100 percent (5/5), round-trip min/avg/max = 4/4/4 ms

R1#ping 10.20.20.3

Type escape sequence to abort.
Sending 5, 100-byte ICMP Echos to 10.20.20.3, timeout is 2 seconds:
```

```
!!!!!
Success rate is 100 percent (5/5), round-trip min/avg/max = 1/3/4 ms

R1#ping 10.30.30.3

Type escape sequence to abort.
Sending 5, 100-byte ICMP Echos to 10.30.30.3, timeout is 2 seconds:
!!!!!
Success rate is 100 percent (5/5), round-trip min/avg/max = 1/2/4 ms
```

Task 5:

```
R1#conf t
Enter configuration commands, one per line.  End with CNTL/Z.
R1(config)#ip access-list extended TELNET-IN
R1(config-ext-nacl)#remark "Permit Telnet From Host 10.10.10.3"
R1(config-ext-nacl)#permit tcp host 10.10.10.3 any eq 23
R1(config-ext-nacl)#remark "Deny Telnet From Host 10.20.20.3"
R1(config-ext-nacl)#deny tcp host 10.20.20.3 any eq 23
R1(config-ext-nacl)#remark "Permit Telnet From Host 10.30.30.3"
R1(config-ext-nacl)#permit tcp host 10.30.30.3 any eq 23
R1(config-ext-nacl)#exit
R1(config)#line vty 0 4
R1(config-line)#access-class TELNET-IN in
R1(config-line)#end
R1#
```

Of course, we would permit all other IP traffic normally in an ACL but we are just testing out the block Telnet feature for this example.

Task 6:

```
R3#telnet 172.16.1.1 /source-interface loopback10
Trying 172.16.1.1 ... Open

User Access Verification

Password:
R1#

R3#telnet 172.16.1.1 /source-interface loopback20
Trying 172.16.1.1 ...
% Connection refused by remote host

R3#telnet 172.16.1.1 /source-interface loopback30
Trying 172.16.1.1 ... Open

User Access Verification

Password:
R1#
```

> **NOTE:** The `access-class` command is used to apply ACLs to the router or switch VTY lines to prevent inbound Telnet and/or SSH sessions from reaching the device. This is not the same as using ACLs that are applied to interfaces to prevent Telnet and/or SSH sessions from reaching the device. Make a mental note of this.

Based on our example above, we can see matches to the ACL rules as follows:

```
R1#sh ip access-lists TELNET-IN
Extended IP access list TELNET-IN

    10 permit tcp host 10.10.10.3 any eq telnet (2 matches)
    20 deny tcp host 10.20.20.3 any eq telnet (1 match)
        30 permit tcp host 10.30.30.3 any eq telnet (2 matches)
```

LAB 42: DEBUGGING NETWORK TRAFFIC USING EXTENDED ACLS

Lab Objective:
The objective of this lab exercise is for you to learn and understand how to create extended access control lists to troubleshoot the network using the `debug ip packet` command.

Lab Purpose:
Limiting debugging to specific traffic types using ACLs is a fundamental skill. Extended ACLs can be configured to match source and destination address, as well as Layer 4 protocols TCP and UDP. Using extended ACLs, you can debug specific types of traffic to troubleshoot a network. As a Cisco engineer, as well as in the Cisco CCNA exam, you will be expected to know how to create and debug specific types of traffic using extended numbered ACLs.

Certification Level:
This lab is suitable for CCNA certification exam preparation.

Lab Difficulty:
This lab has a difficulty rating of 6/10.

Readiness Assessment:
When you are ready for your certification exam, you should complete this lab in no more than 5 minutes.

Lab Topology:
Please use the following topology to complete this lab exercise:

Task 1:
Configure the hostnames on routers R1 and R3 as illustrated in the topology.

Task 2:
Configure R1 S0/0, which is a DCE, to provide a clock rate of 768 Kbps to R3. Configure the IP addresses on the Serial interfaces of R1 and R3 as illustrated in the topology.

Task 3:

Configure an extended ACL on R1 to match and permit all ICMP traffic. Use ACL number 111.

Task 4:

Enable detailed debugging on R1 using the `debug ip packet 111 detail` command. This ACL specifies that we are only going to be limiting debugging to the traffic type specified in the ACL, which is ICMP.

Task 5:

Ping R2 from R1. You should see some detailed information printed on the console on R1 based on your debugging. When you are done, disable debugging on R1.

LAB 42: CONFIGURATION AND VERIFICATION

Task 1:

For reference information on configuring hostnames, please refer to earlier labs.

Task 2:

For reference information on configuring DCE clocking and IP addressing, please refer to earlier labs.

Task 3:
```
R1#conf t
Enter configuration commands, one per line.  End with CTRL/Z.
R1(config)#access-list 111 remark "Permit all ICMP traffic"
R1(config)#access-list 111 permit icmp any any
R1(config)#end
R1#
```

Task 4:
```
R1#debug ip packet 111 detail
IP packet debugging is on (detailed) for access list 111
R1#
```

Task 5:
```
R1#ping 172.16.1.2

Type escape sequence to abort.
Sending 5, 100-byte ICMP Echos to 172.16.1.2, timeout is 2 seconds:
!!!!!
Success rate is 100 percent (5/5), round-trip min/avg/max = 8/8/8 ms
R1#
*Mar  1 01:10:16.600: IP: tableid=0, s=172.16.1.1 (local), d=172.16.1.2
(Serial0/0), routed      via FIB
*Mar  1 01:10:16.600: IP: s=172.16.1.1 (local), d=172.16.1.2
(Serial0/0), len 100, sending
*Mar  1 01:10:16.604:     ICMP type=8, code=0
*Mar  1 01:10:16.608: IP: tableid=0, s=172.16.1.2 (Serial0/0),
d=172.16.1.1 (Serial0/0), routed via RIB
*Mar  1 01:10:16.608: IP: s=172.16.1.2 (Serial0/0), d=172.16.1.1
(Serial0/0), len 100, rcvd 3
*Mar  1 01:10:16.608:     ICMP type=0, code=0
*Mar  1 01:10:16.608: IP: tableid=0, s=172.16.1.1 (local), d=172.16.1.2
(Serial0/0), routed via FIB
*Mar  1 01:10:16.608: IP: s=172.16.1.1 (local), d=172.16.1.2
(Serial0/0), len 100, sending
*Mar  1 01:10:16.612:     ICMP type=8, code=0
*Mar  1 01:10:16.616: IP: tableid=0, s=172.16.1.2 (Serial0/0),
d=172.16.1.1 (Serial0/0), routed via RIB
```

```
*Mar  1 01:10:16.616: IP: s=172.16.1.2 (Serial0/0), d=172.16.1.1
(Serial0/0), len 100, rcvd 3
*Mar  1 01:10:16.616:    ICMP type=0, code=0
R1#undebug all
All possible debugging has been turned off
```

NOTE: Based on the ping, we can see that ICMP Type 8, Code 0 messages are being sent from R1 to R3 and ICMP Type 0, Code 0 messages are being sent from R3 to R1. You are required to know the different ICMP Types and Codes for the Cisco CCNA exam, so if you are not sure what these two codes are, now would be a good time to look them up. Make sure you commit the ICMP Types and Codes to memory.

LAB 43: ACL SEQUENCE NUMBERS

Lab Objective:
The objective of this lab exercise is for you to learn and understand how to use ACL sequence numbers to add and remove (edit) a live access list.

Lab Purpose:
With IOS 12.4 onward, Cisco IOS adds sequence numbers to ACL entries, allowing you to add additional lines where you want and remove those no longer necessary.

Certification Level:
This lab is suitable for CCENT certification exam preparation.

Lab Difficulty:
This lab has a difficulty rating of 6/10.

Readiness Assessment:
When you are ready for your certification exam, you should complete this lab in no more than 5 minutes.

Lab Topology:
Please use the following topology to complete this lab exercise:

Task 1:
Configure the hostname on router R1 as illustrated in the topology.

Task 2:
Add a standard named ACL with three lines of configuration. Use the relevant show command to display the lines.

Task 3:
Add an entry between entries 10 and 20. Remove line 30. Use the relevant show command to display the lines.

Task 4:
Resequence the ACL numbers to increment in 20s, starting from number 100. Use the relevant show command to display the lines.

LAB 43: CONFIGURATION AND VERIFICATION

Task 1:

For reference information on configuring hostnames, please refer to earlier labs.

Task 2:
```
R1(config)#ip access-list standard sequence
R1(config-std-nacl)#permit 172.16.1.1
R1(config-std-nacl)#permit 172.20.1.1
R1(config-std-nacl)#permit 192.168.1.1
R1(config-std-nacl)#
R1(config-std-nacl)#end

R1#show ip access-lists
Standard IP access list sequence
    30 permit 192.168.1.1
    20 permit 172.20.1.1
    10 permit 172.16.1.1
```

Task 3:
```
R1(config)#
R1(config)#ip access-list standard sequence
R1(config-std-nacl)#15 permit 10.1.1.1
R1(config-std-nacl)#no 30
R1(config-std-nacl)#end
R1#show ip access-lists
Standard IP access list sequence
    15 permit 10.1.1.1
    20 permit 172.20.1.1
    10 permit 172.16.1.1

R1#show ip access-lists
Standard IP access list sequence
    15 permit 10.1.1.1
    20 permit 172.20.1.1
    10 permit 172.16.1.1
```

Task 4:
```
R1(config)#ip access-list resequence sequence 100 20
R1(config)#do show ip access-lists
Standard IP access list sequence
    100 permit 10.1.1.1
    120 permit 172.20.1.1
    140 permit 172.16.1.1
```

LAB 44: LOGGING ACL MATCHES

Lab Objective:
The objective of this lab exercise is for you to learn and understand how to configure access control lists to log traffic that matches any particular entry within the configured ACL.

Lab Purpose:
Logging traffic based on ACL rule configuration is a fundamental skill. Both named and numbered standard and extended ACLs can be configured to log information on matches against their configured rules. This logging can be performed locally (on the router or switch) or remotely (to a SYSLOG server). As a Cisco engineer, as well as in the Cisco CCNA exam, you will be expected to know how to configure ACLs to log information against configured rules.

Certification Level:
This lab is suitable for CCNA certification exam preparation.

Lab Difficulty:
This lab has a difficulty rating of 6/10.

Readiness Assessment:
When you are ready for your certification exam, you should complete this lab in no more than 5 minutes.

Lab Topology:
Please use the following topology to complete this lab exercise:

Task 1:
Configure the hostnames on routers R1 and R3 as illustrated in the topology.

Task 2:
Configure R1 S0/0, which is a DCE, to provide a clock rate of 768 Kbps to R3. Configure the IP addresses on the Serial interfaces of R1 and R3 as illustrated in the topology.

Task 3:

Enable local logging on R3. The logging level should be for informational messages only.

Task 4:

Configure an extended named ACL on R3 to permit all Telnet and ICMP traffic types. This ACL should log when Telnet or ICMP traffic matches it. Configure this ACL with the name MyACL and apply it inbound on R3 Serial0/0.

Task 5:

Clear the logs on R3 using the `clear log` command. Ping R3 from R1 and check the log on R3 with the `show log` command. If you have configured the ACL correctly, you will have a log message about the ACL line permitting ICMP traffic to R3. Telnet to R3 from R1 and check the log on R3 with the `show log` command. If you have configured the ACL correctly, you will have a log message about the ACL line permitting Telnet traffic to R3.

LAB 44: CONFIGURATION AND VERIFICATION

Task 1:

For reference information on configuring hostnames, please refer to earlier labs.

Task 2:

For reference information on configuring DCE clocking, please refer to earlier labs.

Task 3:
```
R3#conf t
Enter configuration commands, one per line.  End with CTRL/Z.
R3(config)#logging on
R3(config)#logging buffered informational
R3(config)#end
R3#
```

> **NOTE:** When configuring logging, it is always good practice to enable logging with the `logging on` command. When logging messages to the buffer on the router, the options available are as follows:

```
R3#conf t
Configuring from terminal, memory, or network [terminal]?
Enter configuration commands, one per line.  End with CTRL/Z.
R3(config)#logging buffered ?
  <0-7>              Logging severity level
  <4096-2147483647>  Logging buffer size
  alerts             Immediate action needed           (severity=1)
  critical           Critical conditions               (severity=2)
  debugging          Debugging messages                (severity=7)
  emergencies        System is unusable                (severity=0)
  errors             Error conditions                  (severity=3)
  informational      Informational messages            (severity=6)
  notifications      Normal but significant conditions (severity=5)
  warnings           Warning conditions                (severity=4)
  xml                Enable logging in XML to XML logging buffer
  <cr>
```

If you specify a severity of 5 (Notifications), then the router or switch will log all messages up to and including that severity level. In other words, the device will log message levels 1 through 5, inclusive. To see debugging output, you must enable a severity of 7. When logging debugging messages, ensure that there is enough buffer space for these messages. Use the `logging buffered <4096-2147483647>` command to specify the buffer size.

Task 4:

```
R3#conf t
Enter configuration commands, one per line.  End with CTRL/Z.
R3(config)#ip access-list extended MyACL
R3(config-ext-nacl)#permit tcp any any eq telnet log
R3(config-ext-nacl)#permit icmp any any log
R3(config-ext-nacl)#exit
R3(config)#int s0/0
R3(config-if)#ip access-group MyACL in
R3(config-if)#end
R3#show ip access-lists
Extended IP access list MyACL
    10 permit tcp any any eq telnet log
    20 permit icmp any any log
```

Task 5:

For information on how to ping or telnet from Cisco routers, please see the earlier labs.
Ensure that you enable Telnet access.

```
R3#clear log
Clear logging buffer [confirm]
R3#
R3#show log
Syslog logging: enabled (0 messages dropped, 1 messages rate-limited, 0
flushes, 0 overruns, xml disabled)
    Console logging: disabled
    Monitor logging: level debugging, 0 messages logged, xml disabled
    Buffer logging: level informational, 6 messages logged, xml
disabled
    Logging Exception size (4096 bytes)
    Count and timestamp logging messages: disabled
    Trap logging: level informational, 35 message lines logged

Log Buffer (4096 bytes):

*Mar  1 01:29:00.370: %SEC-6-IPACCESSLOGDP: list MyACL permitted icmp
172.16.1.1 -> 172.16.1.2 (0/0), 1 packet
*Mar  1 01:29:54.771: %SEC-6-IPACCESSLOGP: list MyACL permitted tcp
172.16.1.1(17218) -> 172.16.1.2(23), 1 packet
*Mar  1 01:30:16.751: %SEC-6-IPACCESSLOGDP: list MyACL permitted icmp
172.16.1.1 -> 172.16.1.2 (8/0), 1 packet
*Mar  1 01:30:23.186: %SEC-6-IPACCESSLOGP: list MyACL permitted tcp
172.16.1.1(60418) -> 172.16.1.2(23), 1 packet
```

LAB 45: CONFIGURING STATIC NETWORK ADDRESS TRANSLATION

Lab Objective:
The objective of this lab exercise is for you to learn and understand how to configure static NAT.

Lab Purpose:
NAT configuration is a fundamental skill. Static NAT provides a one-to-one translation between a private IP address (RFC 1918) and a public IP address. Static NAT is typically used to provide access to private inside hosts from outside hosts or networks. When static NAT is configured, outside hosts or networks connect to devices on the inside using a public or external IP address. This hides the private IP addresses of hosts on the inside. As a Cisco engineer, as well as in the Cisco CCNA exam, you will be expected to know how to configure static NAT.

Certification Level:
This lab is suitable for CCENT and CCNA certification exam preparation.

Lab Difficulty:
This lab has a difficulty rating of 7/10.

Readiness Assessment:
When you are ready for your certification exam, you should complete this lab in no more than 10 minutes.

Lab Topology:
Please use the following topology to complete this lab exercise:

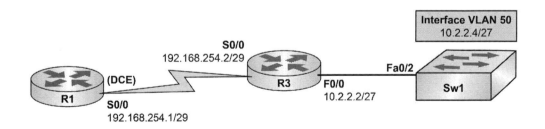

Task 1:

Configure the hostnames on R1, R3, and Sw1 as illustrated in the topology.

Task 2:

Configure R1 S0/0, which is a DCE, to provide a clock rate of 256 Kbps to R3. Configure the IP addresses on the Serial interfaces of R1 and R3 as illustrated in the topology.

Task 3:

Configure VLAN50 named NAT_VLAN on Sw1. Assign the FastEthernet0/2 interface on Sw1 to this VLAN. Also, configure Sw1 to allow Telnet access using the password CISCO.

Task 4:

Configure interface VLAN50 on Sw1 and assign it the IP address illustrated in the topology. The default gateway on Sw1 should be 10.2.2.2. Next, configure interface FastEthernet0/0 in R3 and assign it the IP address illustrated in the topology.

Task 5:

Test connectivity by pinging from R1 to R3 and pinging from R3 to Sw1. These should all be successful. However, since R1 does not know about the 10.2.2.0/27 subnet, Sw1 will not be able to ping R1. Verify this.

Task 6:

Configure R3 F0/0 as the inside NAT interface and S0/0 as the outside NAT interface. Next, create a static NAT statement on R3 mapping the inside address of 10.2.2.4 (Sw1 interface VLAN50) to the outside address of 192.168.254.4.

Task 7:

Ping from Sw1 to R1 and verify that the ping is successful. Next, telnet from R1 to 192.168.254.4 and verify that you are connected to Sw1 via the NAT configured on R3.

LAB 45: CONFIGURATION AND VERIFICATION

Task 1:

For reference information on configuring hostnames, please refer to earlier labs.

Task 2:

For reference information on configuring DCE clocking and IP addressing, please refer to earlier labs.

Task 3:

```
Sw1#conf t
Enter configuration commands, one per line.  End with CTRL/Z.
Sw1(config)#vlan50
Sw1(config-vlan)#name NAT_VLAN
Sw1(config-vlan)#exit
Sw1(config)#int f0/2
Sw1(config-if)#switchport mode access
Sw1(config-if)#switchport access vlan50
Sw1(config-if)#no shutdown
Sw1(config-if)#exit
Sw1(config)#line vty 0 15
Sw1(config-line)#password CISCO
Sw1(config-line)#login
Sw1(config-line)#end
Sw1#
Sw1#show vlan brief

VLAN Name                             Status    Ports
---- -------------------------------- --------- -------------------------------
1    default                          active    Fa0/1, Fa0/3, Fa0/4, Fa0/5
                                                Fa0/6, Fa0/7, Fa0/8, Fa0/9
                                                Fa0/10, Fa0/11, Fa0/12, Fa0/13
                                                Fa0/14, Fa0/15, Fa0/16, Fa0/17
                                                Fa0/18, Fa0/19, Fa0/20, Fa0/21
                                                Fa0/22, Fa0/23, Fa0/24, Gi0/1
                                                Gi0/2
50   NAT_VLAN                         active    Fa0/2

[Output Truncated]
```

Task 4:

```
Sw1#conf t
Enter configuration commands, one per line.  End with CTRL/Z.
Sw1(config)#int vlan1
Sw1(config-if)#shutdown
Sw1(config-if)#exit
Sw1(config)#int vlan50
Sw1(config-if)#no shutdown
```

```
Sw1(config-if)#ip address 10.2.2.4 255.255.255.224
Sw1(config-if)#exit
Sw1(config)#ip default-gateway 10.2.2.2
Sw1(config)#end
Sw1#

R3#conf t
Enter configuration commands, one per line.  End with CTRL/Z.
R3(config)#int fa0/0
R3(config-if)#no shutdown
R3(config-if)#ip address 10.2.2.2 255.255.255.224
R3(config-if)#end
R3#
```

Task 5:

```
R1#ping 192.168.254.2

Type escape sequence to abort.
Sending 5, 100-byte ICMP Echos to 192.168.254.2, timeout is 2 seconds:
!!!!!
Success rate is 100 percent (5/5), round-trip min/avg/max = 4/4/4 ms

R3#ping 192.168.254.1

Type escape sequence to abort.
Sending 5, 100-byte ICMP Echos to 192.168.254.1, timeout is 2 seconds:
!!!!!
Success rate is 100 percent (5/5), round-trip min/avg/max = 4/4/4 ms

R3#ping 10.2.2.4

Type escape sequence to abort.
Sending 5, 100-byte ICMP Echos to 10.2.2.4, timeout is 2 seconds:
..!!!
Success rate is 60 percent (3/5), round-trip min/avg/max = 1/3/4 ms

Sw1#ping 10.2.2.2

Type escape sequence to abort.
Sending 5, 100-byte ICMP Echos to 10.2.2.2, timeout is 2 seconds:
!!!!!
Success rate is 100 percent (5/5), round-trip min/avg/max = 4/4/8 ms

Sw1#ping 192.168.254.1

Type escape sequence to abort.
Sending 5, 100-byte ICMP Echos to 192.168.254.1, timeout is 2 seconds:
.....
Success rate is 0 percent (0/5)
```

Task 6:

```
R3#conf t
Enter configuration commands, one per line.  End with CTRL/Z.
R3(config)#int fa0/0
R3(config-if)#ip nat inside
R3(config-if)#exit
R3(config)#int s0/0
R3(config-if)#ip nat outside
R3(config-if)#exit
R3(config)#ip nat inside source static 10.2.2.4 192.168.254.4
R3(config)#end
R3#
R3#show ip nat translations
Pro Inside global    Inside local       Outside local      Outside
global
--- 192.168.254.4    10.2.2.4           ---                ---
```

Task 7:

```
Sw1#ping 192.168.254.1

Type escape sequence to abort.
Sending 5, 100-byte ICMP Echos to 192.168.254.1, timeout is 2 seconds:
!!!!!
Success rate is 100 percent (5/5), round-trip min/avg/max = 4/6/8 ms

R1#telnet 192.168.254.4
Trying 192.168.254.4 ... Open

User Access Verification

Password:
Sw1#
```

> **NOTE:** You can look at translation statistics using the show ip nat statistics command. If you are having issues with NAT, this command can show you the hits versus the misses, which indicates successful versus unsuccessful translations. Use those counters to troubleshoot Network Address Translation. If it isn't working, check that you added the NAT statements to the interfaces and the default gateway to the switch.

```
R3#show ip nat statistics
Total active translations: 1 (1 static, 0 dynamic; 0 extended)
Outside interfaces:
  Serial0/0
Inside interfaces:
  FastEthernet0/0
Hits: 53  Misses: 0
Expired translations: 0
Dynamic mappings:
```

Also keep in mind that because you configured static NAT, you will not see any dynamic NAT mappings or translation statistics until you configure dynamic NAT.

LAB 46: CONFIGURING DYNAMIC NETWORK ADDRESS TRANSLATION

Lab Objective:
The objective of this lab exercise is for you to learn and understand how to configure dynamic NAT using a pool of IP addresses for translation.

Lab Purpose:
NAT configuration is a fundamental skill. Dynamic NAT provides dynamic one-to-one translation between private IP addresses (RFC 1918) and public IP addresses. Dynamic NAT is typically used to provide inside private hosts with access to public or external networks without revealing the private IP addresses of the inside hosts. When dynamic NAT is used, hosts on the outside cannot access hosts on the inside. In other words, dynamic NAT works only when traffic is coming from hosts on the inside. As a Cisco engineer, as well as in the Cisco CCNA exam, you will be expected to know how to configure dynamic NAT.

Certification Level:
This lab is suitable for CCNA certification exam preparation.

Lab Difficulty:
This lab has a difficulty rating of 8/10.

Readiness Assessment:
When you are ready for your certification exam, you should complete this lab in no more than 10 minutes.

Lab Topology:
Please use the following topology to complete this lab exercise:

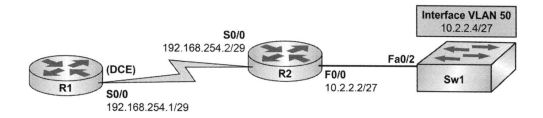

Task 1:

Configure the hostnames on R1, R2, and Sw1 as illustrated in the topology.

Task 2:

Configure R1 S0/0, which is a DCE, to provide a clock rate of 256 Kbps to R2. Configure the IP addresses on the Serial interfaces of R1 and R2 as illustrated in the topology.

Task 3:

Configure VLAN50 named NAT_VLAN on Sw1. Assign the FastEthernet0/2 interface on Sw1 to this VLAN. Also, configure R1 to allow Telnet access using the password CISCO.

Task 4:

Configure interface VLAN50 on Sw1 and assign it the IP address illustrated in the topology. The default gateway on Sw1 should be 10.2.2.2. Next, configure interface FastEthernet0/0 in R2 and assign it the IP address illustrated in the topology.

Task 5:

Test connectivity by pinging from R1 to R2 and pinging from R2 to Sw1. These should all be successful. However, since R1 does not know about the 10.2.2.0/27 subnet, Sw1 will not be able to ping R1, or vice versa.

Task 6:

Configure R3 F0/0 as the inside NAT interface and S0/0 as the outside NAT interface. Next, create an ACL to permit all IP traffic from the 10.2.2.0/27 subnet to any destination. You can use either a named or numbered ACL.

Task 7:

Create a NAT pool called Dynamic-NAT. The starting IP address in this pool should be 192.168.254.3 and the ending IP address should be 192.168.254.6. This should have the same prefix length as the Serial0/0 subnet.

Task 8:

Configure NAT to translate all addresses specified in the ACL pool you created in Task 7.

Task 9:

Ping R1 from Sw1. Next, ping R1 from the FastEthernet0/0 interface of R2 using the `ping <ip_address> source <interface>` command (it won't work on Packet Tracer). If you have configured your NAT translation correctly, the ping should be successful. Use the `show ip nat translations` command to verify your dynamic NAT translations.

LAB 46: CONFIGURATION AND VERIFICATION

Task 1:

For reference information on configuring hostnames, please refer to earlier labs.

Task 2:

For reference information on configuring DCE clocking and IP addresses, please refer to earlier labs.

Task 3:

For reference information on configuring VLANs, please refer to earlier labs.

Task 4:

For reference information on configuring Telnet, please refer to earlier labs.

Task 5:

For reference information on pinging, please refer to earlier labs.

Task 6:
```
R2#conf t
Enter configuration commands, one per line.  End with CTRL/Z.
R2(config)#int fa0/0
R2(config-if)#ip nat inside
R2(config-if)#exit
R2(config)#int s0/0
R2(config-if)#ip nat outside
R2(config-if)#exit
R2(config)#ip access-list extended NAT-ACL
R2(config-ext-nacl)#remark "Permit The 10.2.2.0/27 Subnet To Be NATd"
R2(config-ext-nacl)#permit ip 10.2.2.0 0.0.0.31 any
R2(config-ext-nacl)#end
R2#
```

Task 7:
```
R2#conf t
Enter configuration commands, one per line.  End with CTRL/Z.
R2(config)#ip nat pool Dynamic-NAT 192.168.254.3 192.168.254.6 prefix-
length 29
R2(config)#^Z
R2#
```

Task 8:
```
R2#config t
Enter configuration commands, one per line.  End with CTRL/Z.
R2(config)#ip nat inside source list NAT-ACL pool Dynamic-NAT
```

```
R2(config)#end
R2#
R2#show ip nat statistics
Total active translations: 0 (0 static, 0 dynamic; 0 extended)
Outside interfaces:
  Serial0/0
Inside interfaces:
  FastEthernet0/0
Hits: 53  Misses: 0
Expired translations: 0
Dynamic mappings:
-- Inside Source
[Id: 1] access-list NAT-ACL pool Dynamic-NAT refcount 0
 pool Dynamic-NAT: netmask 255.255.255.248
        start 192.168.254.3 end 192.168.254.6
        type generic, total addresses 4, allocated 0 (0%), misses 0
```

Task 9:

```
Sw1#ping 192.168.254.1

Type escape sequence to abort.
Sending 5, 100-byte ICMP Echos to 192.168.254.1, timeout is 2 seconds:
!!!!!
Success rate is 100 percent (5/5), round-trip min/avg/max = 4/6/8 ms

R2#ping 192.168.254.1 source fastethernet0/0

Type escape sequence to abort.
Sending 5, 100-byte ICMP Echos to 192.168.254.1, timeout is 2 seconds:
Packet sent with a source address of 10.2.2.2
!!!!!
Success rate is 100 percent (5/5), round-trip min/avg/max = 4/4/4 ms

R2#show ip nat translations
Pro Inside global     Inside local      Outside local       Outside
global
--- 192.168.254.3   10.2.2.4          ---                 ---
--- 192.168.254.4   10.2.2.2          ---                 ---

R2#show ip nat statistics
Total active translations: 2 (0 static, 2 dynamic; 0 extended)
Outside interfaces:
  Serial0/0
Inside interfaces:
  FastEthernet0/0
Hits: 91  Misses: 2
Expired translations: 0
Dynamic mappings:
-- Inside Source
[Id: 1] access-list NAT-ACL pool Dynamic-NAT refcount 2
```

```
pool Dynamic-NAT: netmask 255.255.255.248
      start 192.168.254.3 end 192.168.254.6
      type generic, total addresses 4, allocated 2 (50%), misses 0
```

NOTE: Now that you have dynamic NAT configured, and you have pinged R1 from the F0/0 interface of R2 as well as from Sw1, you can see two dynamic translations in the NAT table. The first is a translation of the inside address 10.2.2.4 to the outside address of 192.168.254.3, and the second is the translation of the inside address 10.2.2.2 to the outside address of 192.168.254.4. Because the NAT pool only has four total IP addresses allocated, you can see that half of the pool is in use as specified in the line `type generic, total addresses 4, allocated 2 (50%), misses 0`. Pay attention to the information printed by this command and commit it to memory.

LAB 47: CONFIGURING INTERFACE-BASED PORT ADDRESS TRANSLATION

Lab Objective:
The objective of this lab exercise is for you to learn and understand how to configure interface-based PAT.

Lab Purpose:
PAT configuration is a fundamental skill. PAT provides many-to-one translation using random port numbers. This means that multiple inside hosts can use the same outside address to communicate with external devices, while hiding their private IP addresses. Like dynamic NAT, PAT works in one direction only: from the inside to the outside. Interface-based PAT translates all private IP addresses to the outside interface on the router. As a Cisco engineer, as well as in the Cisco CCNA exam, you will be expected to know how to configure interface-based Port Address Translation.

Certification Level:
This lab is suitable for CCNA certification exam preparation.

Lab Difficulty:
This lab has a difficulty rating of 8/10.

Readiness Assessment:
When you are ready for your certification exam, you should complete this lab in no more than 10 minutes.

Lab Topology:
Please use the following topology to complete this lab exercise:

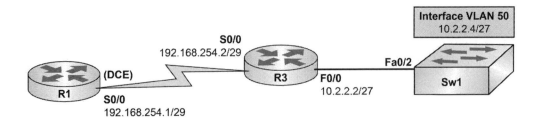

Task 1:
Configure the hostnames on R1, R3, and Sw1 as illustrated in the topology.

Task 2:
Configure R1 S0/0, which is a DCE, to provide a clock rate of 256 Kbps to R2. Configure the IP addresses on the Serial interfaces of R1 and R3 as illustrated in the topology.

Task 3:
Configure VLAN50 named NAT_VLAN on Sw1. Assign the FastEthernet0/2 interface on Sw1 to this VLAN. Also, configure R1 to allow Telnet access using the password CISCO.

Task 4:
Configure interface VLAN50 on Sw1 and assign it the IP address illustrated in the topology. The default gateway on Sw1 should be 10.2.2.2. Next, configure interface FastEthernet0/0 in R2 and assign it the IP address illustrated in the topology.

Task 5:
Test connectivity by pinging from R1 to R3 and pinging from R2 to Sw1. These should all be successful. However, since R1 does not know about the 10.2.2.0/27 subnet, Sw1 will not be able to ping R1, or vice versa.

Task 6:
Create an ACL to permit only ICMP and Telnet traffic from the 10.2.2.0/27 subnet to any destination. You can create either a named or numbered ACL to complete this task.

Task 7:
Configure R3 F0/0 as the inside interface for NAT and S0/0 as the outside interface for NAT. Next, configure PAT to translate all IP addresses specified in the ACL you configured in Task 6 to the S0/0 interface of R3.

Task 8:
Ping R1 from Sw1. Also, perform a telnet from Sw1 to R1. If you have configured interface-based PAT correctly, the ping and telnet should work. Check the NAT translation table on R3 using the `show ip nat translations` command.

LAB 47: CONFIGURATION AND VERIFICATION

Task 1:

For reference information on configuring hostnames, please refer to earlier labs.

Task 2:

For reference information on configuring DCE clocking and IP addresses, please refer to earlier labs.

Task 3:

For reference information on configuring VLANs and Telnet, please refer to earlier labs.

Task 4:

For reference information on configuring SVIs and default gateways, please refer to earlier labs.

Task 5:

For reference information on pinging, please refer to earlier labs.

Task 6:
```
R3#conf t
Enter configuration commands, one per line.  End with CTRL/Z.
R3(config)#access-list 140 remark "Permit ICMP Traffic For NAT"
R3(config)#access-list 140 permit icmp 10.2.2.0 0.0.0.31 any
R3(config)#access-list 140 permit tcp 10.2.2.0 0.0.0.31 any eq telnet
R3(config)#end
R3#
R3#show ip access-lists 140
Extended IP access list 140
    10 permit icmp 10.2.2.0 0.0.0.31 any
    20 permit tcp 10.2.2.0 0.0.0.31 any eq telnet
```

Task 7:
```
R3#conf t
Enter configuration commands, one per line.  End with CTRL/Z.
R3(config)#int fa0/0
R3(config-if)#ip nat inside
R3(config-if)#exit
R3(config)#int s0/0
R3(config-if)#ip nat outside
R3(config-if)#exit
R3(config)#ip nat inside source list 140 interface serial0/0 overload
R3(config)#end
R3#
```

> **NOTE:** Port Address Translation (or NAT Overload) is enabled with the `overload` keyword in the `ip nat inside source list` command. This allows the router to overload address translation to the specified interface or IP address. Do not forget to issue this keyword when configuring PAT. Otherwise, you will have created dynamic NAT and will run out of addresses after the very first translation.

Task 8:

Perform a ping, and then telnet from Sw1 and disconnect from the Telnet session.

```
Sw1#ping 192.168.254.1
Sw1#telnet 192.168.254.1

R3#show ip nat translations
Pro Inside global      Inside local    Outside local      Outside global
Tcp 192.168.254.2:11777 10.2.2.4:11777 192.168.254.1:23
192.168.254.1:23
icmp 192.168.254.2:4176 10.2.2.4:4176   192.168.254.1:4176
192.168.254.1:4176
icmp 192.168.254.2:4177 10.2.2.4:4177   192.168.254.1:4177
192.168.254.1:4177
icmp 192.168.254.2:4178 10.2.2.4:4178   192.168.254.1:4178
192.168.254.1:4178
icmp 192.168.254.2:4179 10.2.2.4:4179   192.168.254.1:4179
192.168.254.1:4179
icmp 192.168.254.2:4180 10.2.2.4:4180   192.168.254.1:4180
192.168.254.1:4180
```

> **NOTE:** Notice that there is only one translation for telnet but there are five translations for ping. This is because a dynamic translation is created for every ping packet sent. By default, Cisco routers and switches will send five ping packets. You can tell they are from the same `ping` because the port numbers are sequential.

Also, by using interface-based PAT, R1 will see all packets (ping and telnet) being sourced from the Serial0/0 interface of R3. If you enabled the `debug ip packet detail` command on R1, you would see the following for Telnet:

```
*Mar  1 01:07:45.127:     TCP src=23, dst=12289, seq=2994196370,
ack=125681435, win=4085 ACK PSH
*Mar  1 01:07:45.272: IP: tableid=0, s=192.168.254.2 (Serial0/0),
d=192.168.254.1 (Serial0/0), routed via RIB
```

In a similar manner, you would also see the following for pings from Sw1:

```
*Mar  1 01:08:40.907: IP: s=192.168.254.2 (Serial0/0), d=192.168.254.1
(Serial0/0), len 100, rcvd 3
*Mar  1 01:08:40.907:     ICMP type=8, code=0
```

```
*Mar  1 01:08:40.907: IP: tableid=0, s=192.168.254.1 (local),
d=192.168.254.2 (Serial0/0), routed via FIB
*Mar  1 01:08:40.907: IP: s=192.168.254.1 (local), d=192.168.254.2
(Serial0/0), len 100, sending
*Mar  1 01:08:40.907:      ICMP type=0, code=0


R#show ip nat statistics
Total active translations: 5 (0 static, 5 dynamic; 5 extended)
Outside interfaces:
  Serial0/0
Inside interfaces:
  FastEthernet0/0
Hits: 153  Misses: 23
Expired translations: 16
Dynamic mappings:
-- Inside Source
[Id: 3] access-list 140 interface Serial0/0 refcount 5
```

LAB 48: CONFIGURING POOL-BASED PORT ADDRESS TRANSLATION

Lab Objective:
The objective of this lab exercise is for you to learn and understand how to configure pool-based PAT.

Lab Purpose:
PAT configuration is a fundamental skill. PAT provides many-to-one translation using random port numbers. This means that multiple inside hosts can use the same outside address to communicate with external devices, while hiding their private IP addresses. Like dynamic NAT, PAT works in one direction only: from the inside to the outside. Pool-based PAT translates all private IP addresses to the outside interface on the router. As a Cisco engineer, as well as in the Cisco CCNA exam, you will be expected to know how to configure pool-based Port Address Translation.

Certification Level:
This lab is suitable for CCNA certification exam preparation.

Lab Difficulty:
This lab has a difficulty rating of 8/10.

Readiness Assessment:
When you are ready for your certification exam, you should complete this lab in no more than 10 minutes.

Lab Topology:
Please use the following topology to complete this lab exercise:

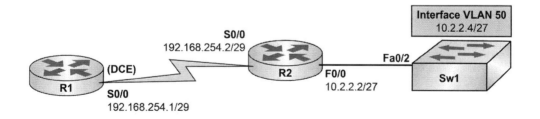

Task 1:
Configure the hostnames on R1, R2, and Sw1 as illustrated in the topology.

Task 2:
Configure R1 S0/0, which is a DCE, to provide a clock rate of 256 Kbps to R2. Configure the IP addresses on the Serial interfaces of R1 and R2 as illustrated in the topology.

Task 3:
Configure VLAN50, named NAT_VLAN, on Sw1. Assign the FastEthernet0/2 interface on Sw1 to this VLAN. Also, configure R1 to allow Telnet access using the password CISCO.

Task 4:
Configure interface VLAN50 on Sw1 and assign it the IP address illustrated in the topology. The default gateway on Sw1 should be 10.2.2.2. Next, configure interface FastEthernet0/0 on R2 and assign it the IP address illustrated in the topology.

Task 5:
Test connectivity by pinging from R1 to R2 and pinging from R2 to Sw1. These should all be successful. However, since R1 does not know about the 10.2.2.0/27 subnet, Sw1 will not be able to ping R1, or vice versa.

Task 6:
Create an ACL to permit all IP traffic from the 10.2.2.0/27 subnet to the 192.168.254.0/29 subnet. You can create either a named or numbered ACL to complete this task.

Task 7:
Configure R2 F0/0 as the inside interface for NAT and S0/0 as the outside interface for NAT. Next, configure a pool called PAT-POOL to be used for PAT translation. This pool should have both a single starting and ending IP address of 192.168.254.4. Use the same subnet mask as that of S0/0 for this pool.

Task 8:
Configure PAT on R2 to translate traffic specified in the ACL configured in Task 6 to the pool named PAT-POOL. Telnet from Sw1 to R1. If you have configured PAT correctly, this should work. The same applies for pings from Sw1 or the Fa0/0 interface of R2 to R1.

Task 9:
Check the NAT translation table on R2 using the `show ip nat translations` command.

LAB 48: CONFIGURATION AND VERIFICATION

Task 1:

For reference information on configuring hostnames, please refer to earlier labs.

Task 2:

For reference information on configuring DCE clocking and IP addressing, please refer to earlier labs.

Task 3:

For reference information on configuring and verifying VLANs and Telnet, please refer to earlier labs.

Task 4:

For reference information on configuring IP interfaces, please refer to earlier labs.

Task 5:

For reference information on configuring pinging, please refer to earlier labs.

Task 6:
```
R2#config t
Enter configuration commands, one per line.  End with CTRL/Z.
R2(config)#ip access-list extended NAT-ACL
R2(config-ext-nacl)#remark "NAT Traffic from 10.2.2.0/27 To
192.168.254.0/29"
R2(config-ext-nacl)#permit ip 10.2.2.0 0.0.0.31 192.168.254.0 0.0.0.7
R2(config-ext-nacl)#^Z
R2#
```

Task 7:
```
R2#conf t
Enter configuration commands, one per line.  End with CTRL/Z.
R2(config)#int fa0/0
R2(config-if)#ip nat inside
R2(config-if)#exit
R2(config)#int s0/0
R2(config-if)#ip nat outside
R2(config-if)#exit
R2(config)#ip nat pool PAT-POOL 192.168.254.4 192.168.254.4 netmask
255.255.255.240
R2(config)#end
R2#
```

Task 8:

```
R2#conf t
Enter configuration commands, one per line.  End with CTRL/Z.
R2(config)#ip nat inside source list NAT-ACL pool PAT-POOL overload
R2(config)#end
R2#
```

> **NOTE:** Again, do not forget to issue the `overload` keyword when configuring NAT overload/PAT.

```
Sw1#ping 192.168.254.1

Type escape sequence to abort.
Sending 5, 100-byte ICMP Echos to 192.168.254.1, timeout is 2 seconds:
!!!!!
Success rate is 100 percent (5/5), round-trip min/avg/max = 8/8/12 ms

Sw1#telnet 192.168.254.1
Trying 192.168.254.1 ... Open

User Access Verification

Password:
R1#
```

Task 9:

```
R2#show ip nat translations
Pro Inside global      Inside local    Outside local      Outside global
icmp 192.168.254.2:4813 10.2.2.4:4813     192.168.254.1:4813
192.168.254.1:4813
icmp 192.168.254.2:4814 10.2.2.4:4814     192.168.254.1:4814
192.168.254.1:4814
icmp 192.168.254.2:4815 10.2.2.4:4815     192.168.254.1:4815
192.168.254.1:4815
icmp 192.168.254.2:4816 10.2.2.4:4816     192.168.254.1:4816
192.168.254.1:4816
icmp 192.168.254.2:4817 10.2.2.4:4817     192.168.254.1:4817
192.168.254.1:4817
tcp 192.168.254.2:12801 10.2.2.4:12801    192.168.254.1:23
192.168.254.1:23
R2#
R2#show ip nat statistics
Total active translations: 6 (0 static, 6 dynamic; 6 extended)
Outside interfaces:
  Serial0/0
Inside interfaces:
  FastEthernet0/0
Hits: 250  Misses: 40
Expired translations: 32
```

```
Dynamic mappings:
-- Inside Source
[Id: 3] access-list 140 interface Serial0/0 refcount 6
[Id: 4] access-list NAT-ACL pool PAT-POOL refcount 0
 pool PAT-POOL: netmask 255.255.255.248
        start 192.168.254.4 end 192.168.254.4
        type generic, total addresses 1, allocated 0 (0%), misses 0
```

5.0 Infrastructure Maintenance

LAB 49: CONFIGURING PASSWORDS ON CATALYST SWITCHES

Lab Objective:

The objective of this lab exercise is to configure passwords that contain special characters, such as question marks, on switches. By default, the question mark invokes IOS help options for a command.

Lab Purpose:

Advanced password configuration is a fundamental skill. By default, when the question mark (?) is used, the Cisco IOS help menu displays possible options for completing the command being typed. This can become a problem if you want to configure a password such as C?sc0, for example. As a Cisco engineer, as well as in the Cisco CCNA exam, you will be expected to know how to configure passwords with special characters.

Certification Level:

This lab is suitable for CCNA certification exam preparation.

Lab Difficulty:

This lab has a difficulty rating of 4/10.

Readiness Assessment:

When you are ready for your certification exam, you should complete this lab in no more than 10 minutes.

Lab Topology:

Use any single switch to complete this lab.

Task 1:

Configure an enable password or enable secret of C?1sc0 on your Catalyst Switch. If you find that you cannot configure the password, try and remember the keys you need to type in before configuring special characters in a password.

Task 2:

Disable password encryption and verify that your password shows up in the configuration as configured.

LAB 49: CONFIGURATION AND VERIFICATION

Task 1:

```
Sw1#conf t
Enter configuration commands, one per line.  End with CTRL/Z.
Sw1(config)#enable password C?1sc0
Sw1(config)#end
Sw1#
```

NOTE: In order to use a question mark in a password on Cisco devices, you must type in CTRL/Z (the CTRL key followed by the letter Z key) before you type in the question mark. This feature won't work on Packet Tracer.

Task 2:

```
Sw1#conf t
Enter configuration commands, one per line.  End with CTRL/Z.
Sw1(config)#no service password-encryption
Sw1(config)#end
Sw1#
Sw1#show running-config
Building configuration...

Current configuration : 3093 bytes
!
version 12.1
no service pad
no service password-encryption
!
hostname Sw1
!
no logging console
enable password C?1sc0
!
```

LAB 50: PERMITTING TELNET ACCESS TO CATALYST IOS SWITCHES

Lab Objective:
The objective of this lab exercise is for you to learn and understand how to configure a switch to be accessed remotely via Telnet. By default, you can telnet to a switch but cannot log in if no password has been set.

Lab Purpose:
Telnet access configuration is a fundamental skill. More often than not, switches are accessed and configured remotely via Telnet. As a Cisco engineer, as well as in the Cisco CCNA exam, you will be expected to know how to configure a switch to allow an administrator to log in via Telnet.

Certification Level:
This lab is suitable for both CCENT and CCNA certification exam preparation.

Lab Difficulty:
This lab has a difficulty rating of 4/10.

Readiness Assessment:
When you are ready for your certification exam, you should complete this lab in no more than 10 minutes.

Lab Topology:
Please use the following topology to complete this lab exercise:

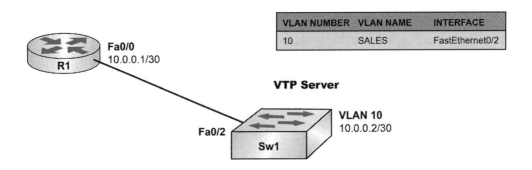

VLAN NUMBER	VLAN NAME	INTERFACE
10	SALES	FastEthernet0/2

Task 1:

Configure hostnames on Sw1 and R1 as illustrated in the topology.

Task 2:

Create VLAN10 on Sw1 and assign port FastEthernet0/2 to this VLAN as an access port.

Task 3:

Configure IP address 10.0.0.1/30 on R1's FastEthernet0/0 interface and IP address 10.0.0.2/30 on Sw1's VLAN10 interface. Verify that R1 can ping Sw1, and vice versa.

Task 4:

Configure Telnet access to Sw1 using the password CISCO. The password is case-sensitive so take that into consideration in your configuration. Verify your configuration by creating a Telnet session from R1.

LAB 50: CONFIGURATION AND VERIFICATION

Task 1:

For reference information on configuring hostnames, please refer to earlier labs.

Task 2:

For reference information on configuring and verifying VLANs, please refer to earlier labs.

Task 3:

For reference information on configuring IP interfaces and SVIs, please refer to earlier labs.

Task 4:

```
Sw1#conf t
Enter configuration commands, one per line.  End with CTRL/Z.
Sw1(config)#line vty 0 15
Sw1(config-line)#password CISCO
Sw1(config-line)#login
Sw1(config-line)#end
Sw1#
```

> **NOTE:** Most people forget the fact that switches typically have 16 VTY lines (numbered 0 to 15), unlike routers, which typically have five VTY lines (numbered 0 to 4). Take care to remember this when configuring switches, as you may leave some lines unsecured if you use `line vty 0` on a router. We have already discussed that GNS3 has more VTY lines.

```
R1#telnet 10.0.0.2
Trying 10.0.0.2 ... Open

User Access Verification

Password:
Sw1#
Sw1#
```

LAB 51: PERMITTING TELNET ACCESS TO CATALYST IOS SWITCHES—LOGIN LOCAL

Lab Objective:
The objective of this lab exercise is for you to learn and understand how to configure a switch to be accessed remotely via Telnet. By default, you can telnet to a switch but cannot log in if no password has been set.

Lab Purpose:
Telnet access configuration is a fundamental skill. More often than not, switches are accessed and configured remotely via Telnet. As a Cisco engineer, as well as in the Cisco CCNA exam, you will be expected to know how to configure a switch to allow an administrator to log in via Telnet.

Certification Level:
This lab is suitable for CCENT certification exam preparation.

Lab Difficulty:
This lab has a difficulty rating of 4/10.

Readiness Assessment:
When you are ready for your certification exam, you should complete this lab in no more than 10 minutes.

Lab Topology:
Please use the following topology to complete this lab exercise:

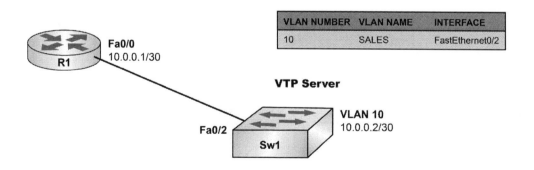

Task 1:

Configure hostnames on Sw1 and R1 as illustrated in the topology.

Task 2:

Create VLAN10 on Sw1 and assign port FastEthernet0/2 to this VLAN as an access port.

Task 3:

Configure IP address 10.0.0.1/30 on R1's FastEthernet0/0 interface and IP address 10.0.0.2/30 on Sw1's VLAN10 interface. Verify that R1 can ping Sw1, and vice versa.

Task 4:

Configure Telnet access to Sw1 using the local username howtonetwork and the password CISCO. The password is case-sensitive so take that into consideration in your configuration. Verify your configuration by creating a Telnet session from R1.

LAB 51: CONFIGURATION AND VERIFICATION

Task 1:

For reference information on configuring hostnames, please refer to earlier labs.

Task 2:

For reference information on configuring and verifying VLANs, please refer to earlier labs.

Task 3:

For reference information on configuring IP interfaces, please refer to earlier labs.

Task 4:

```
Sw1#conf t
Enter configuration commands, one per line.  End with CTRL/Z.

Sw1(config)#username howtonetwork password  CISCO
Sw1(config)#line vty 0 15
Sw1(config-line)#login local
Sw1(config-line)#
```

NOTE: When you specify the `login local` command, the router will check for a username and password combination. If you just specify `login`, then you can reference a password added directly under the vty lines.

```
R1#telnet 10.0.0.2
Trying 10.0.0.2 ...Open

User Access Verification

Username: howtonetwork
Password:
Sw1>
```

LAB 52: PERMITTING CONSOLE ACCESS TO CATALYST IOS SWITCHES—LOGIN LOCAL

Lab Objective:
The objective of this lab exercise is for you to learn and understand how to configure a switch to be secure on the console port.

Lab Purpose:
Console access configuration is a fundamental skill. Switches are always configured first via console access because there is no Telnet access configured. As a Cisco engineer, as well as in the Cisco CCNA exam, you will be expected to know how to configure a switch to allow access via the console.

Certification Level:
This lab is suitable for CCENT certification exam preparation.

Lab Difficulty:
This lab has a difficulty rating of 4/10.

Readiness Assessment:
When you are ready for your certification exam, you should complete this lab in no more than 5 minutes.

Lab Topology:
Please use the following topology to complete this lab exercise:

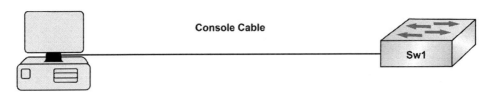

Task 1:
Configure a hostname on Sw1.

Task 2:
Permit console access using the local username howtonetwork and the password CISCO.

Task 3:
Test access if you have a PC and console port.

LAB 52: CONFIGURATION AND VERIFICATION

Task 1:

For reference information on configuring hostnames, please refer to earlier labs.

Task 2:

```
Sw1#conf t
Enter configuration commands, one per line.  End with CTRL/Z.
Sw1(config)#username howtonetwork password CISCO
Sw1(config)#line console 0
Sw1(config-line)#login local
Sw1(config-line)#exit
```

Task 3:

Here is my console connection to the switch (the password won't show when typed):

```
User Access Verification

Username: howtonetwork
Password:

Switch>
```

LAB 53: CONFIGURING AN ENABLE SECRET PASSWORD AND EXEC TIMEOUT ON CATALYST SWITCHES

Lab Objective:

The objective of this lab exercise is for you to learn and understand how to configure a switch to be secure on the console port with a timeout value and protect enable mode with a secret password.

Lab Purpose:

Console access configuration is a fundamental skill. Switches are always configured first via console access because there is no Telnet access configured. As a Cisco engineer, as well as in the Cisco CCNA exam, you will be expected to know how to configure a switch to allow access via the console as well as set a timeout value when the session is idle.

Certification Level:

This lab is suitable for CCENT certification exam preparation.

Lab Difficulty:

This lab has a difficulty rating of 5/10.

Readiness Assessment:

When you are ready for your certification exam, you should complete this lab in no more than 5 minutes.

Lab Topology:

Please use the following topology to complete this lab exercise:

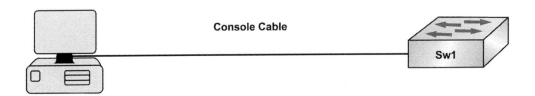

Task 1:

Configure a hostname on Sw1.

Task 2:

Set a password on the console line of HELLO. Set an exec timeout on the console port of 5 minutes and 30 seconds.

Task 3:

Set the enable secret password CISCO. Test the connection if you have console access to your device.

Task 4:

Check the `show run`. The passwords are encrypted by default.

LAB 53: CONFIGURATION AND VERIFICATION

Task 1:

For reference information on configuring hostnames, please refer to earlier labs.

Task 2:

```
Sw1(config)#line console 0
Sw1(config-line)#password HELLO
Sw1(config-line)#exec-timeout ?
  <0-35791>  Timeout in minutes
Sw1(config-line)#exec-timeout 5 ?
  <0-2147483>  Timeout in seconds
  <cr>
Sw1(config-line)#exec-timeout 5 30
```

Task 3:

```
Sw1#conf t
Enter configuration commands, one per line.  End with CTRL/Z.
Sw1(config)#enable secret CISCO
Sw1(config)#
```

Task 4:

```
Sw1#show run

hostname Sw1
!
enable secret 5 $1$mERr$NJdjwh5wX8Ia/X8aC4RIu.
```

LAB 54: CONFIGURING USER PRIVILEGES ON CISCO IOS DEVICES

Lab Objective:

The objective of this lab exercise is for you to learn and understand how to configure user privileges on devices.

Lab Purpose:

Configuring user privilege levels on Cisco IOS devices is a fundamental skill. Users can be configured with certain privilege levels that allow them to execute certain commands. As a Cisco engineer, as well as in the Cisco CCNA exam, you will be expected to know how to configure user privilege levels on Cisco IOS devices.

Certification Level:

This lab is suitable for CCNA certification exam preparation.

Lab Difficulty:

This lab has a difficulty rating of 6/10.

Readiness Assessment:

When you are ready for your certification exam, you should complete this lab in no more than 10 minutes.

Lab Topology:

Please use the following topology to complete this lab:

Task 1:

Configure the hostnames on R1 and R3 as illustrated in the topology.

Task 2:

Configure R1 to provide clocking to R3 at a rate of 2 Mbps. Next, configure the IP addresses on R1 and R3 as illustrated in the network topology.

Task 3:

Configure the VTY lines on R3 to allow users to log into the router based on locally configured usernames and passwords. Also, configure the enable secret of SAFE on R3.

Task 4:

Configure R3 with the following user accounts:

Username	Password	Privilege Level
admin	cisco	15
test	cisco	1

Connect via Telnet from R1 to R3. First, log in with the username admin and check your privilege level and the router prompt after login. Next, log in with the username test and check your privilege level and the router prompt after login. Do you notice any differences?

LAB 54: CONFIGURATION AND VERIFICATION

Task 1:

For reference information on configuring hostnames, please refer to earlier labs.

Task 2:

For reference information on configuring DCE clocking and IP addressing, please refer to earlier labs.

Task 3:

```
R3#conf t
Enter configuration commands, one per line.  End with CTRL/Z.
R3(config)#line vty 0 4
R3(config-line)#login local
R3(config-line)#end
R3#
```

> **NOTE:** The `login local` command specifies that the device should use the local database for user authentication. When configured, you must also configure username and password pairs to be used to gain access to the device.

Task 4:

```
R3#conf t
Enter configuration commands, one per line.  End with CTRL/Z.
R3(config)#username admin privilege 15 password cisco
R3(config)#username test privilege 1 password cisco
R3(config)#end
R3#

R1#telnet 192.168.254.2
Trying 192.168.254.3 ... Open

User Access Verification

Username: admin
Password:
R3#

R1#telnet 192.168.254.2
Trying 192.168.254.3 ... Open

User Access Verification

Username: test
Password:
R3>
```

NOTE: Notice how user admin is automatically in Privileged Exec mode after successful login, as illustrated by the # symbol; however, you can see that user test (who has a privilege level of 1) is automatically put into User Exec mode after successful login, as illustrated by the > symbol.

LAB 55: CONFIGURING COMMAND AND PASSWORD PRIVILEGE LEVELS ON DEVICES

Lab Objective:

The objective of this lab exercise is for you to learn and understand how to configure privilege levels for certain commands and passwords on Cisco IOS devices.

Lab Purpose:

Configuring user privilege levels on Cisco IOS devices is a fundamental skill. Users can be configured with certain privilege levels that allow them to execute certain commands. As a Cisco engineer, as well as in the Cisco CCNA exam, you will be expected to know how to configure user privilege levels on Cisco IOS devices.

Certification Level:

This lab is suitable for CCENT certification exam preparation.

Lab Difficulty:

This lab has a difficulty rating of 6/10.

Readiness Assessment:

When you are ready for your certification exam, you should complete this lab in no more than 10 minutes.

Lab Topology:

Please use any single Cisco IOS router or switch to complete the following lab.

Task 1:

Configure a hostname of your liking on your Cisco IOS router or switch. It may be easier to use a router for this lab.

Task 2:

Configure a level 15 secret of cisco456 on your device.

Task 3:

Issue the `show ip interface brief` command from User Exec mode (i.e., where you see the > symbol after the device name). Verify that this command works and you do see the current interface status.

Task 4:

Configure the `show ip interface brief` command to work only for users with Level 15 access.

Task 5:

If you are connected via the console, type in the command `disable` to return to User Exec mode (i.e., where you see the `>` symbol after the device hostname). Next, issue the `show ip interfaces brief` command. If you have configured your device correctly, this command will no longer work in User Exec mode.

Task 6:

Next, type in enable and type in the Level 15 password cisco456. Attempt to issue the `show ip interface brief` command. If your configuration is correct, this will work.

LAB 55: CONFIGURATION AND VERIFICATION

Task 1:

For reference information on configuring hostnames, please refer to earlier labs.

Task 2:

```
R1#conf t
Enter configuration commands, one per line.  End with CTRL/Z.
R1(config)#enable secret level 15 cisco456
R1(config)#^Z
R1#
```

Task 3:

```
R1>show ip interface brief
Interface      IP-Address   OK? Method Status                Protocol
Ethernet0/0    unassigned   YES manual administratively down down
Serial0/0      unassigned   YES manual administratively down down
Serial0/1      unassigned   YES manual administratively down down
```

Task 4:

```
R1#conf t
Enter configuration commands, one per line.  End with CTRL/Z.
R1(config)#privilege exec level 15 show ip interface brief
R1(config)#end
R1#
```

> **NOTE:** The `privilege exec` command is used to set different privilege levels for commands. By default, the `show ip interfaces brief` command has a privilege level of 1, which means that it can be issued from the User Exec prompt (i.e., the > prompt after the hostname of the device).

Task 5:

```
R1#disable
R1>show ip interface brief
   ^
% Invalid input detected at "^" marker.
```

Task 6:

```
R1>enable
Password:
R1#show ip interface brief
Interface      IP-Address   OK? Method Status                Protocol
Ethernet0/0    unassigned   YES manual administratively down down
Serial0/0      unassigned   YES manual administratively down down
Serial0/1      unassigned   YES manual administratively down down
```

LAB 56: CONFIGURING MOTD BANNERS

Lab Objective:
The objective of this lab exercise is for you to learn and understand how to configure message of the day banners on Cisco IOS devices.

Lab Purpose:
MOTD banner configuration is a fundamental skill. The MOTD banner is displayed on all terminals connected and is useful for sending messages that affect all users. As a Cisco engineer, as well as in the Cisco CCNA exam, you will be expected to know how to configure an MOTD banner.

Certification Level:
This lab is suitable for CCNA certification exam preparation.

Lab Difficulty:
This lab has a difficulty rating of 3/10.

Readiness Assessment:
When you are ready for your certification exam, you should complete this lab in no more than 10 minutes.

Lab Topology:
Please use any Cisco IOS device to complete this lab.

Task 1:
Configure a hostname of your liking on your device.

Task 2:
Configure the device MOTD banner exactly as follows:

```
###############################################

This is a private system. If you have connected to this devicea
ccidentally, please disconnect immediately!

###############################################
```

Task 3:
If you are connected to the device via the console port, issue the quit command to reset the console. Now connect back to the device (hit Enter) and you should see the MOTD banner.

LAB 56: CONFIGURATION AND VERIFICATION

Task 1:

For reference information on configuring hostnames, please refer to earlier labs.

Task 2:

```
R1#conf t
Enter configuration commands, one per line.  End with CTRL/Z.
R1(config)#banner motd %
Enter TEXT message.  End with the character "%".
##############################################################

This is a private system. If you have connected to this device
accidentally, please disconnect immediately!

##############################################################
%
R1(config)#end
R1#
```

> **NOTE:** Be careful not to use the delimiting character in your banner configuration. Most people have a tendency to use the # symbol as a delimiting character, and then forget and use it in their banner configuration, resulting in an incomplete banner on the device. Practice configuring banners with other delimiting characters as well.

Task 3:

```
Press RETURN to get started.


##############################################################

This is a private system. If you have connected to this device
accidentally, please disconnect immediately!

##############################################################

R1>
```

LAB 57: CHANGING THE CONFIGURATION REGISTER ON CISCO IOS DEVICES

Lab Objective:
The objective of this lab exercise is for you to learn and understand how to change the configuration register value on Cisco IOS devices.

Lab Purpose:
Changing the configuration register is a fundamental skill. The configuration register is typically changed when performing a password recovery procedure on a Cisco IOS device. The settings within the configuration register are used to change the default behavior of Cisco IOS devices. As a Cisco engineer, as well as in the Cisco CCNA exam, you will be expected to know how to change and verify the configuration register.

Certification Level:
This lab is suitable for CCENT and CCNA certification exam preparation.

Lab Difficulty:
This lab has a difficulty rating of 2/10.

Readiness Assessment:
When you are ready for your certification exam, you should complete this lab in no more than 5 minutes.

Lab Topology:
Please use any single router or switch to complete this lab.

Task 1:
Configure any desired hostname on your device.

Task 2:
Verify the current setting of the configuration register using the `show version` command. The configuration register will be at the very end of the output from this command.

Task 3:
Change the configuration register value to 102 and save your configuration. Verify that your new configuration register will be used after your device has been rebooted.

LAB 57: CONFIGURATION AND VERIFICATION

Task 1:

For reference information on configuring hostnames, please refer to earlier labs.

Task 2:

```
R1#show version
Cisco Internetwork Operating System Software
IOS (tm) C2600 Software (C2600-IK9O3S3-M), Version 12.3(26), RELEASE
SOFTWARE (fc2)
Technical Support: http://www.cisco.com/techsupport
Copyright (c) 1986-2008 by cisco Systems, Inc.
Compiled Mon 17-Mar-08 15:23 by dchih

ROM: System Bootstrap, Version 11.3(2)XA4, RELEASE SOFTWARE (fc1)

R1 uptime is 2 hours, 12 minutes
System returned to ROM by power-on
System image file is "flash:c2600-ik9o3s3-mz.123-26.bin"

If you require further assistance please contact us by sending email to
export@cisco.com.

cisco 2610 (MPC860) processor (revision 0x203) with 61440K/4096K bytes
of memory.
Processor board ID JAD05090GA8 (596408632)
M860 processor: part number 0, mask 49
Bridging software.
X.25 software, Version 3.0.0.
1 Ethernet/IEEE 802.3 interface(s)
2 Serial network interface(s)
32K bytes of non-volatile configuration memory.
16384K bytes of processor board System flash (Read/Write)

Configuration register is 0x2102

[Output Truncated]
```

Task 3:

```
R1#conf t
Enter configuration commands, one per line.  End with CTRL/Z.
R1(config)#config-register 0x102
R1(config)#end
R1#
R1#show version
Cisco Internetwork Operating System Software
IOS (tm) C2600 Software (C2600-IK9O3S3-M), Version 12.3(26), RELEASE
SOFTWARE (fc2)
Technical Support: http://www.cisco.com/techsupport
```

```
Copyright (c) 1986-2008 by cisco Systems, Inc.
Compiled Mon 17-Mar-08 15:23 by dchih

ROM: System Bootstrap, Version 11.3(2)XA4, RELEASE SOFTWARE (fc1)

R1 uptime is 2 hours, 13 minutes
System returned to ROM by power-on
System image file is "flash:c2600-ik9o3s3-mz.123-26.bin"

cisco 2610 (MPC860) processor (revision 0x203) with 61440K/4096K bytes
of memory.
Processor board ID JAD05090GA8 (596408632)
M860 processor: part number 0, mask 49
Bridging software.
X.25 software, Version 3.0.0.
1 Ethernet/IEEE 802.3 interface(s)
2 Serial network interface(s)
32K bytes of non-volatile configuration memory.
16384K bytes of processor board System flash (Read/Write)

Configuration register is 0x2102 (will be 0x102 at next reload)

[Output Truncated]
```

NOTE: The configuration register is always in hexadecimal format. Therefore, always remember to issue the 0x before specifying the desired configuration register value. This is often forgotten, so ensure that you remember it!

LAB 58: CONFIGURING SSH ACCESS/DISABLE TELNET ACCESS

Lab Objective:

The objective of this lab exercise is for you to learn and understand how to configure a router or switch for SSH access. Your router or switch IOS must support encryption in order for the commands to work. You should see a k9 in the image name as well as a security statement from Cisco saying "This product contains cryptographic features...".

Lab Purpose:

Protecting your Cisco devices by disabling Telnet and enabling SSH-only access is a core security step, as well as a CCNA exam requirement.

Certification Level:

This lab is suitable for CCENT certification exam preparation.

Lab Difficulty:

This lab has a difficulty rating of 7/10.

Readiness Assessment:

When you are ready for your certification exam, you should complete this lab in no more than 5 minutes.

Lab Topology:

Please use any single router or switch to complete this lab so long as it has the correct IOS image.

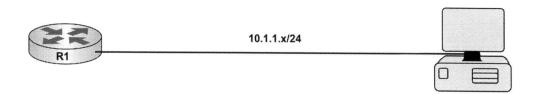

Task 1:

Attach a PC to a router using a switch or crossover cable and add the IP settings above to the devices. Configure any desired hostname on your device.

Task 2:

Configure a username and password on your router. Disable Telnet access on the VTY lines and enable SSH access.

Task 3:

Configure the router to use SSH with the settings below:

- Doman name: howtonetwork.com
- 1024 modulus
- SSH timeout: 60 seconds
- Authentication retries: 2
- SSH version 2

Task 4:

Disable HTTP (Hypertext Transfer Protocol) access to the router. Issue the appropriate show commands to check your SSH settings.

Task 5:

Connect to the router using a PC with SSH.

LAB 58: CONFIGURATION AND VERIFICATION

Task 1:

For reference information on configuring hostnames and IP addresses, please refer to earlier labs.

For the PC (if you are using Packet Tracer):

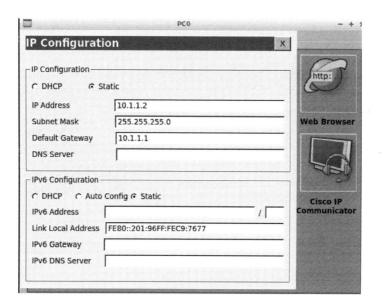

Task 2:

```
R1(config)#username howtonetwork password cisco
R1(config)#line vty 0 15
R1(config-line)#transport input ?
  all     All protocols
  none    No protocols
  ssh     TCP/IP SSH protocol
  telnet  TCP/IP Telnet protocol
R1(config-line)#transport input ssh
```

This command will also disable Telnet.

Task 3:

```
R1(config)#ip domain-name howtonetwork.com
R1(config)#crypto key generate rsa
The name for the keys will be: R1.howtonetwork.com
Choose the size of the key modulus in the range of 360 to 2048 for your
```

General Purpose Keys. Choosing a key modulus greater than 512 may take a few minutes.

How many bits in the modulus [512]: 1024
% Generating 1024 bit RSA keys, keys will be non-exportable...[OK]

R1(config)#ip ssh time-out ?
  <1-120> SSH time-out interval (secs)
R1(config)#ip ssh time-out 60
R1(config)#ip ssh authentication-retries 2
R1(config)#ip ssh version 2

Task 4:

R1(config)#no ip http server

R1#show ip ssh
SSH Enabled - version 2.0
Authentication timeout: 60 secs; Authentication retries: 2
R1#
R1#show crypto key ?
  mypubkey Show public keys associated with this router
R1#show crypto key my
R1#show crypto key mypubkey rsa
% Key pair was generated at: 0:2:58 UTC Mar 1 1993
Key name: R1.howtonetwork.com
 Storage Device: not specified
 Usage: General Purpose Key
 Key is not exportable.
 Key Data:
 6af47136 7dfa1d2d 53435e72 197f4ed8 229d6342 5c5b3b19 601bbae0
 18491391
 7d676c5e 3f4e6cb4 32e2f903 31b53943 40cb31ea 5d2552b3 00160600
 77791266
 51180b5a 4f759502 5df3ea6c 4ffda4fc 4b5351bb 11f16ac4 2374aeb6
 44f60c4e
% Key pair was generated at: 0:2:58 UTC Mar 1 1993
Key name: R1.howtonetwork.com.server
Temporary key
 Usage: Encryption Key
 Key is not exportable.
 Key Data:
 6b8a0260 167f96e7 117d29b7 58907508 704e7231 637db8c1 25a136f0
 5b42e367
 6177d5ee 78e49562 74c2323f 04153930 553fd07b 54dded20 1c5e4cc1
 52a73cda
 142c59d4 4f4145c4 045c761d 54f78bbe 2c669877 04727c1e 4c709e24
 7d7ea3d2

Task 5:
```
PC>ssh -1 paul 10.1.1.1
```

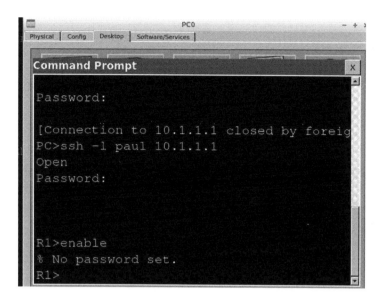

LAB 59: CONFIGURING IOS DEVICE LOGGING TO A SYSLOG SERVER

Lab Objective:

The objective of this lab exercise is for you to learn and understand how to configure Cisco IOS devices to send log messages to a SYSLOG server.

Lab Purpose:

Configuring Cisco IOS devices to send logging information to a SYSLOG server is a fundamental skill. In most networks, a SYSLOG server is present and devices are configured to send log messages to this central repository. Users or groups managing this central repository can therefore see alarms from devices and act accordingly to address the issues. As a Cisco engineer, as well as in the Cisco CCNA exam, you will be expected to know how to configure Cisco IOS devices to send log messages to SYSLOG servers.

Certification Level:

This lab is suitable for CCENT and CCNA certification exam preparation.

Lab Difficulty:

This lab has a difficulty rating of 5/10.

Readiness Assessment:

When you are ready for your certification exam, you should complete this lab in no more than 5 minutes.

> **IMPORTANT NOTE:** The objective of this lab is to simply familiarize you with the steps required to configure a Cisco IOS device to send log messages to a SYSLOG server. Because there will be no real SYSLOG server configured against which to perform testing, the sole objective of this lab is command familiarity.

Lab Topology:

Please use the following topology to complete this lab:

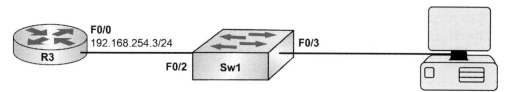

SYSLOG: 192.168.254.254/24

F0/0
192.168.254.3/24

R3

F0/2   Sw1

F0/3

Task 1:

Configure the hostnames on R3 and Sw1 as illustrated in the topology.

Task 2:

At this stage, we know that by default, all interfaces on a Cisco Catalyst Switch are in VLAN1. Therefore, simply enable interfaces FastEthernet0/2 and FastEthernet0/3 on Sw1.

Task 3:

Configure R3 to send SYSLOG messages up to Level 7 to the SYSLOG server 192.168.254.254.

Task 4:

Verify your SYSLOG configuration on R3 using the show logging command.

LAB 59: CONFIGURATION AND VERIFICATION

Task 1:

For reference information on configuring hostnames, please refer to earlier labs.

Task 2:
```
Sw1#config t
Enter configuration commands, one per line.  End with CTRL/Z.
Sw1(config)#interface fastethernet0/2
Sw1(config-if)#no shutdown
Sw1(config-if)#exit
Sw1(config)#interface fastethernet0/3
Sw1(config-if)#no shutdown
Sw1(config-if)#^Z
Sw1#
```

Task 3:
```
R3#conf t
Enter configuration commands, one per line.  End with CTRL/Z.
R3(config)#logging trap debugging
R3(config)#logging host 192.168.254.254
R3(config)#end
R3#
```

NOTE: When configuring logging levels, you can use the number or the keyword for the specific level for which you want to enable logging. You can view the correlation between numbers and keywords by using a question mark after the `logging trap` command as illustrated below:

```
R3(config)#logging trap ?
  <0-7>          Logging severity level
  alerts         Immediate action needed          (severity=1)
  critical       Critical conditions              (severity=2)
  debugging      Debugging messages               (severity=7)
  emergencies    System is unusable               (severity=0)
  errors         Error conditions                 (severity=3)
  informational  Informational messages           (severity=6)
  notifications  Normal but significant conditions (severity=5)
     warnings       Warning conditions               (severity=4)
```

Task 4:
```
R3#show logging
Syslog logging: enabled (0 messages dropped, 1 messages rate-limited, 0
flushes, 0 overruns, xml disabled)
    Console logging: disabled
    Monitor logging: level debugging, 0 messages logged, xml disabled
    Buffer logging: disabled, xml disabled
```

```
Logging Exception size (4096 bytes)
Count and timestamp logging messages: disabled
Trap logging: level debugging, 33 message lines logged
    Logging to 192.168.254.254, 1 message lines logged, xml disabled
```

NOTE: Logging using a level of 7 indicates that the device will send logs for all other levels. If you had a SYSLOG server and performed a configuration task on the router, you would see the log messages on the SYSLOG server.

LAB 60: PERFORMING AN IOS UPGRADE

Lab Objective:
The objective of this lab exercise is for you to learn how to upgrade your Cisco router using TFTP.

Lab Purpose:
Making sure that you know how to upgrade the IOS code in your Cisco device is one of the most important things a network engineer must know. As a Cisco engineer, as well as in the Cisco CCNA exam, you will be expected to know how to upgrade your Cisco IOS router.

You will need another IOS available to replace the current one on your router. If you prefer to use Packet Tracer, then you will need to follow a slightly different process as show in the video.

Certification Level:
This lab is suitable for CCENT and CCNA certification exam preparation.

Lab Difficulty:
This lab has a difficulty rating of 6/10.

Readiness Assessment:
When you are ready for your certification exam, you should complete this lab in no more than 10 minutes.

Lab Topology:
Please use the following topology to complete this lab exercise:

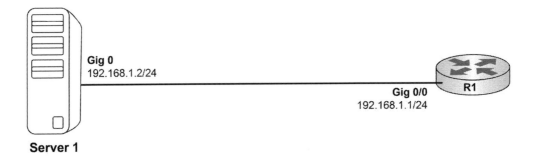

Task 1:

Configure the hostnames on router R1 as illustrated in the topology.

Task 2:

Configure the IP addresses on the Gig0/0 interface of R1 as illustrated in the topology.

Task 3:

Copy the IOS File (.bin image) from Server 1 to R1's flash memory using the TFTP protocol. You can use free TFTP software on the server or use Packet Tracer for this lab, which has it built in.

> **NOTE:** In this lab the IOS code to be uploaded to R1 is c2691-advipservicesk9-mz.124-25d.bin.

Task 4:

Make sure that you set the new image you just uploaded to R1 as the boot image and reboot R1.

LAB 60: CONFIGURATION AND VERIFICATION

Task 1:

For reference information on configuring hostnames, please refer to earlier labs.

Task 2:
```
R1#conf t
Enter configuration commands, one per line.  End with CTRL/Z.
R1(config)#int gig0/0
R1(config-if)#no shutdown
R1(config-if)#ip add 192.168.1.1 255.255.255.0
R1(config-if)#end
R1#
```

Task 3:
```
R1#copy tftp://192.168.1.2/c2691-advipservicesk9-mz.124-25d.bin flash:/
c2691-advipservicesk9-mz.124-25d.bin
```

Task 4:
```
R1#conf t
Enter configuration commands, one per line.  End with CTRL/Z.
R1(config)#boot system flash://c2691-advipservicesk9-mz.124-25d.bin
R1(config)#end
R1#reload
```

When the reboot process ends, the router will be running the new code.

NOTE: In the video solution, I used Packet Tracer, which will only permit the prompts after you type `copy tftp: flash:`, which is another way of updating the IOS. If there is insufficient room for more than one IOS, you will be prompted to erase the current IOS.

LAB 61: PERFORMING AN IOS UPGRADE USING FTP

Lab Objective:

The objective of this lab exercise is for you to learn how to upgrade your Cisco router using FTP.

Lab Purpose:

Making sure that you know how to upgrade the IOS code in your Cisco device is one of the most important things a network engineer must know. As a Cisco engineer, as well as in the Cisco CCNA exam, you will be expected to know how to upgrade your Cisco IOS router.

You will need another IOS available to replace the current one on your router. If you prefer to use Packet Tracer, then you will need to follow a slightly different process as show in the video.

Certification Level:

This lab is suitable for CCENT certification exam preparation.

Lab Difficulty:

This lab has a difficulty rating of 6/10.

Readiness Assessment:

When you are ready for your certification exam, you should complete this lab in no more than 10 minutes.

Lab Topology:

Please use the following topology to complete this lab exercise:

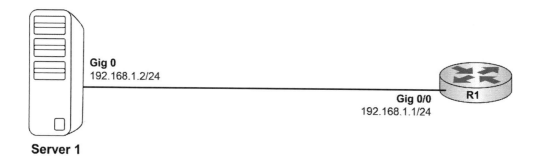

Task 1:

Configure the hostnames on R1 as illustrated in the topology.

Task 2:

Configure the IP addresses on the Gig0/0 interface of R1 as illustrated in the topology.

Task 3:

Copy the IOS File (.bin image) from Server 1 to R1's flash memory using the FTP protocol. You will need to specify a valid FTP username and password in order to access the FTP server.

> **NOTE:** In this lab the IOS code to be uploaded to R1 is c2691-advipservicesk9-mz.124-25d.bin.

Task 4:

Make sure that you set the new image you just uploaded to R1 as the boot image and reboot R1.

LAB 61: CONFIGURATION AND VERIFICATION

Task 1:

For reference information on configuring hostnames, please refer to earlier labs.

Task 2:

For reference information on configuring IP addresses, please refer to earlier labs.

Task 3:
```
R1(config)#ip ftp password cisco
R1(config)#ip ftp username cisco
R1(config)#exit
R1#copy ftp://192.168.1.2/c2691-advipservicesk9-mz.124-25d.bin flash:/
c2691-advipservicesk9-mz.124-25d.bin
```

Task 4:
```
R1#conf t
Enter configuration commands, one per line.  End with CTRL/Z.
R1(config)#boot system flash:c2691-advipservicesk9-mz.124-25d.bin
R1(config)#end
R1#reload
```

When the reboot process ends, the router will be running the new code.

NOTE: In the video solution, I used Packet Tracer, which will only permit the prompts after you type `copy ftp: flash:`, which is another way of updating the IOS. If there is insufficient room for more than one IOS, you will be prompted to erase the current IOS.

LAB 62: PERFORMING PASSWORD RECOVERY

Lab Objective:
The objective of this lab exercise is for you to learn how to perform password recovery on a Cisco IOS router.

Lab Purpose:
Sometimes by mistake you can lose access to your Cisco device for something as simple as forgetting your credentials, so it's important to know how to overcome this specific issue by performing password recovery. As a Cisco engineer, as well as in the Cisco CCNA exam, you will be expected to know how to perform password recovery on your Cisco IOS router.

Certification Level:
This lab is suitable for CCENT certification exam preparation.

Lab Difficulty:
This lab has a difficulty rating of 5/10.

Readiness Assessment:
When you are ready for your certification exam, you should complete this lab in no more than 10 minutes.

Lab Topology:
Please use the following topology to complete this lab exercise:

Task 1:
You are trying to log in to R1 via the console port but keep getting an error when entering your username/password, so you will perform password recovery. Reboot R1.

Task 2:
Press Ctrl+Break as soon as you receive a prompt showing the boot process.

Task 3:

Once you are in ROM monitor mode, instruct the router to bypass the running-configuration bootup by changing the configuration register to 0x2142.

After changing this configuration register, reset the router so you can boot up and finalize password recovery.

Task 4:

Once you are in, copy the startup configuration to the running configuration and make changes to the username and passwords that you are having issues with (Enable, AAA database, etc.).

Task 5:

Finally, change the configuration register to the default of 0x2102, save the configuration, and reboot the router.

> **NOTE:** Your procedure may differ due to platform differences, so Google "Cisco password recovery" for your model. Cisco switches usually follow a different recovery procedure altogether.

LAB 62: CONFIGURATION AND VERIFICATION

Task 1:

Reboot the router manually (i.e., disconnect power from the unit).

Task 2:
```
System Bootstrap, Version 11.3(2)XA4, RELEASE SOFTWARE (fc1)
Copyright (c) 1999 by cisco Systems, Inc.
TAC:Home:SW:IOS:Specials for info
PC = 0xfff0a530, Vector = 0x500, SP = 0x680127c8
C2600 platform with 65536 Kbytes of main memory

program load complete, entry point: 0x80008000, size: 0xf54134
PC = 0xfff0a530, Vector = 0x500, SP = 0x83fffe68
```

Press <Ctrl + Break> as the router boots.

```
monitor: command "boot" aborted due to user interrupt
rommon 1 >
```

Task 3:
```
rommon 1>confreg 0x2142
You must reset or power cycle for new config to take effect
rommon 2>reset
```

Task 4:
```
Router>enable
Router#copy startup-config running-config
Destination filename [running-config]? (hit enter)
Building configuration...
[OK]
R1#configure terminal
R1(config)#enable password cisco
R1(config)#enable secret enter
R1(config)#line console 0
R1(config-line)#password ccna
R1(config-line)#exit
R1(config)#username ccna-labs privilege 15 secret ccna
```

Or you could just use the no enable secret and no username commands.

Task 5:
```
R1#configure terminal
R1(config)#config-register 0x2102
R1(config)#exit
R1#copy running-config startup-config
R1#reload
```

ICND1 Challenge Labs

By now you have completed a number of labs, from simple to complex. These challenge labs consist of two or more of the technologies we have already covered. There is no solution as such but if you get really stuck, you can check out the configurations. There may be more than one way to solve the challenge so if yours differs from mine, don't worry unduly.

If you get stuck, it means that you have found a weak area, so go back to the earlier labs, review your theory guide, and work on the protocol or service.

CHALLENGE LAB 1: STATIC ROUTES AND ACLS

Lab Objective:
The objective of this lab exercise is for you to configure static routes and ACLs on Cisco routers.

Lab Purpose:
These are classic exam subjects you should be very familiar with. Rather than watch a video solution (if you have access to the video course), I have provided show runs and test commands where appropriate.

Certification Level:
This lab is suitable for both CCENT and CCNA certification exam preparation.

Lab Difficulty:
This lab has a difficulty rating of 5/10.

Readiness Assessment:
When you are ready for your certification exam, you should complete this lab in no more than 15 minutes.

Lab Topology:
Please use the following topology to complete this lab exercise:

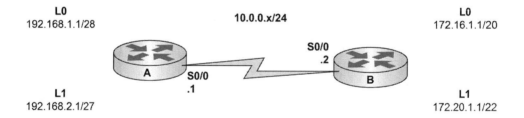

Task 1:
Configure the topology above. You should be able to ping across the Serial interface only because there are no routes from the Loopback networks.

Task 2:
Configure static routes on RouterA with an exit interface of its own Serial interface so it can reach the networks on the Loopbacks for RouterB. On RouterB, configure a default route so all traffic for any networks are sent out of the Serial interface.

Ping all networks to check connectivity.

Task 3:

Add an extended ACL on RouterB to permit Telnet traffic to host 172.16.1.1 from any host or network. All other Telnet traffic should be denied but all other IP traffic permitted. Ensure that you enable Telnet on the router for the VTY lines.

Test your ACL on RouterB by telnetting to RouterB from RouterA. Telnetting to 172.16.1.1 should work but telnetting to the other Loopback or Serial IP addresses should fail.

Task 4:

Add a named ACL on Router A so that only hosts on network 192.168.2.0/27 can be pinged from hosts on network 172.16.1.0/20. All other ICMP traffic should be denied, but all other IP traffic should be permitted. Test your ACL on RouterA by pinging 192.168.2.1 from both Loopbacks on RouterB.

CHALLENGE LAB 1: SOLUTION

Show Runs

RouterA

```
interface Loopback0
 ip address 192.168.1.1 255.255.255.240
!
interface Loopback1
 ip address 192.168.2.1 255.255.255.224
!
interface FastEthernet0/0
 no ip address
 shutdown
 duplex auto
 speed auto
!
interface Serial0/0
 ip address 10.0.0.1 255.255.255.0
 ip access-group stop_ping in
 clock rate 2000000
!
ip route 172.16.0.0 255.255.240.0 Serial0/0
ip route 172.20.0.0 255.255.252.0 Serial0/0
!
no ip http server
no ip http secure-server
!
ip access-list extended stop_ping
 permit icmp 172.16.1.0 0.0.15.255 192.168.2.0 0.0.0.31
 deny icmp any any
 permit ip any any
!
control-plane
!

line con 0
 exec-timeout 0 0
 privilege level 15
 logging synchronous
line aux 0
 exec-timeout 0 0
 privilege level 15
 logging synchronous
line vty 0 4
 login
!
!
end
```

RouterB

```
interface Loopback0
 ip address 172.16.1.1 255.255.240.0
!
interface Loopback1
 ip address 172.20.1.1 255.255.252.0
!
interface FastEthernet0/0
 no ip address
 shutdown
 duplex auto
 speed auto
!
interface Serial0/0
 ip address 10.0.0.2 255.255.255.0
 ip access-group 100 in
 clock rate 2000000
!
interface FastEthernet0/1
 no ip address
 shutdown
 duplex auto
 speed auto
!
ip forward-protocol nd
ip route 0.0.0.0 0.0.0.0 Serial0/0
!
!
no ip http server
no ip http secure-server
!
access-list 100 permit tcp any host 172.16.1.1 eq telnet
access-list 100 deny    tcp any any eq telnet
access-list 100 permit ip any any
!
control-plane
!
line con 0
 exec-timeout 0 0
 privilege level 15
 logging synchronous
line aux 0
 exec-timeout 0 0
 privilege level 15
 logging synchronous
line vty 0 4
 password cisco
 login
line vty 5 903
 password cisco
```

```
  login
  !
  !
  end
```

Test:

```
R1#telnet 172.20.1.1
Trying 172.20.1.1 ...
% Destination unreachable; gateway or host down

R1#telnet 172.16.1.1
Trying 172.16.1.1 ... Open

User Access Verification

Password:
```

Test:

```
R2#ping
Protocol [ip]:
Target IP address: 192.168.2.1
Repeat count [5]:
Datagram size [100]:
Timeout in seconds [2]:
Extended commands [n]: y
Source address or interface: 172.16.1.1
Type of service [0]:
Set DF bit in IP header? [no]:
Validate reply data? [no]:
Data pattern [0xABCD]:
Loose, Strict, Record, Timestamp, Verbose[none]:
Sweep range of sizes [n]:
Type escape sequence to abort.
Sending 5, 100-byte ICMP Echos to 192.168.2.1, timeout is 2 seconds:
Packet sent with a source address of 172.16.1.1
!!!!!
Success rate is 100 percent (5/5), round-trip min/avg/max = 1/5/16 ms

R2#ping
Protocol [ip]:
Target IP address: 192.168.2.1
Repeat count [5]:
Datagram size [100]:
Timeout in seconds [2]:
Extended commands [n]: y
Source address or interface: 172.20.1.1
Type of service [0]:
Set DF bit in IP header? [no]:
Validate reply data? [no]:
Data pattern [0xABCD]:
```

```
Loose, Strict, Record, Timestamp, Verbose[none]:
Sweep range of sizes [n]:
Type escape sequence to abort.
Sending 5, 100-byte ICMP Echos to 192.168.2.1, timeout is 2 seconds:
Packet sent with a source address of 172.20.1.1
U.U.U
Success rate is 0 percent (0/5)
R2#
```

CHALLENGE LAB 2: STATIC ROUTES AND ACLS

Lab Objective:
The objective of this lab exercise is for you to configure static routes and ACLs on Cisco routers.

Lab Purpose:
These are classic exam subjects you should be very familiar with. Rather than watch a video solution, I have provided show runs and test commands where appropriate.

Certification Level:
This lab is suitable for both CCENT and CCNA certification exam preparation.

Lab Difficulty:
This lab has a difficulty rating of 5/10.

Readiness Assessment:
When you are ready for your certification exam, you should complete this lab in no more than 15 minutes.

Lab Topology:
Please use the following topology to complete this lab exercise:

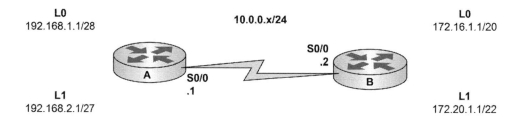

Task 1:
Configure the topology above. You should be able to ping across the Serial interface only because there are no routes from the Loopback networks.

Task 2:
Configure static routes with an exit interface on RouterA so it can reach the networks on the Loopbacks for RouterB. On RouterB, configure a default route so all traffic for any networks are sent out of the Serial interface. Ping all networks to check connectivity.

Task 3:

Add an extended ACL on RouterB to deny all Telnet, HTTP, and DNS traffic incoming. Ensure that you enable Telnet on the router for the VTY lines for testing. Test your ACL on RouterB by telnetting to RouterB from RouterA. Testing the HTTP and DNS will be a little harder without hosts, so just compare your configuration to mine.

Task 4:

Add a named ACL on Router A so that only hosts on network 172.16.1.0 can telnet to hosts on network 192.168.1.0. Ensure that you enable Telnet on the router.

Test your ACL on RouterA by trying to telnet from both Loopbacks on RouterB.

CHALLENGE LAB 2: SOLUTION

Show Runs

RouterA

```
interface Loopback0
 ip address 192.168.1.1 255.255.255.240
!
interface Loopback1
 ip address 192.168.2.1 255.255.255.224
!
interface FastEthernet0/0
 no ip address
 shutdown
 duplex auto
 speed auto
!
interface Serial0/0
 ip address 10.0.0.1 255.255.255.0
 ip access-group block_telnet in
 clock rate 2000000
!
interface FastEthernet0/1
 no ip address
 shutdown
 duplex auto
 speed auto
!
ip forward-protocol nd
ip route 172.16.0.0 255.255.240.0 Serial0/0
ip route 172.20.0.0 255.255.252.0 Serial0/0
!
!
no ip http server
no ip http secure-server
!
ip access-list extended block_telnet
 permit tcp 172.16.0.0 0.0.15.255 192.168.1.0 0.0.0.15 eq telnet
 deny   tcp any any eq telnet
 permit ip any any
!
control-plane
!
line con 0
 exec-timeout 0 0
 privilege level 15
 logging synchronous
line aux 0
 exec-timeout 0 0
```

```
 privilege level 15
 logging synchronous
line vty 0 4
 password cisco
 login
line vty 5 903
 password cisco
 login
 !
end

R1#
```

RouterB

```
interface Loopback0
 ip address 172.16.1.1 255.255.240.0
 !
interface Loopback1
 ip address 172.20.1.1 255.255.252.0
 !
interface FastEthernet0/0
 no ip address
 shutdown
 duplex auto
 speed auto
 !
interface Serial0/0
 ip address 10.0.0.2 255.255.255.0
 ip access-group 100 in
 clock rate 2000000
 !
interface FastEthernet0/1
 no ip address
 shutdown
 duplex auto
 speed auto
 !
ip route 0.0.0.0 0.0.0.0 Serial0/0
 !
no ip http server
no ip http secure-server
 !
access-list 100 deny tcp any any eq telnet
access-list 100 deny tcp any any eq www
access-list 100 deny udp any any eq domain
access-list 100 deny tcp any any eq domain
access-list 100 permit ip any any
 !
control-plane
```

```
!
line con 0
 exec-timeout 0 0
 privilege level 15
 logging synchronous
line aux 0
 exec-timeout 0 0
 privilege level 15
 logging synchronous
line vty 0 4
 password cisco
 login
line vty 5 903
 password cisco
 login
!
!
end
```

Test:

```
RB#telnet 192.168.1.1 /source-interface loopback1
Trying 192.168.1.1 ...
% Destination unreachable; gateway or host down

RB#telnet 192.168.1.1 /source-interface loopback0
Trying 192.168.1.1 ... Open

User Access Verification

Password:
```

NOTE: DNS primarily uses UDP on port number 53 to serve requests. DNS queries consist of a single UDP request from the client followed by a single UDP reply from the server. TCP is used when the response data size exceeds 512 bytes, or for tasks such as zone transfers. Some resolver implementations use TCP for all queries. For more information on DNS, refer to the website below:

http://en.wikipedia.org/wiki/Domain_Name_System

CHALLENGE LAB 3: CDP, BANNER MESSAGES, AND NTP

Lab Objective:
The objective of this lab exercise is for you to configure banner messages, NTP, and CDP on Cisco routers.

Lab Purpose:
None of these subjects are core; however, they are all in the syllabus so they may be the subject of lab or theory questions. Rather than watch a video solution, I have provided show runs and test commands where appropriate.

Certification Level:
This lab is suitable for both CCENT and CCNA certification exam preparation.

Lab Difficulty:
This lab has a difficulty rating of 6/10.

Readiness Assessment:
When you are ready for your certification exam, you should complete this lab in no more than 15 minutes.

Lab Topology:
Please use the following topology to complete this lab exercise:

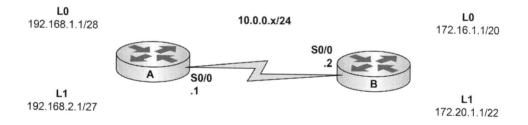

Task 1:
Configure the topology above. You should be able to ping across the Serial interface only because there are no routes from the Loopback networks.

Task 2:

Configure Telnet access on RouterB. Set a banner message on RouterB as follows:

"Warning—this is a secure network."

Task 3:

Set RouterA to get the time from NTP servers 1.1.1.1 primary and 2.2.2.2 secondary.

Task 4:

Use `show` commands to check CDP statistics on neighbor routers. Turn CDP off for interface Loopback0 on RouterA. Turn off CDP for the entire router on RouterB.

CHALLENGE LAB 3: SOLUTION

Show Runs

RouterA

```
R1#show run
Building configuration...

Current configuration : 1340 bytes
!
version 12.4
service timestamps debug datetime msec
service timestamps log datetime msec
no service password-encryption
!
hostname R1
!
boot-start-marker
boot-end-marker
!
!
no aaa new-model
memory-size iomem 5
ip cef
!
no ip domain lookup
ip domain name lab.local
!
multilink bundle-name authenticated
!
archive
 log config
  hidekeys
!
interface Loopback0
 ip address 192.168.1.1 255.255.255.240
 no cdp enable
!
interface Loopback1
 ip address 192.168.2.1 255.255.255.224
!
interface FastEthernet0/0
 no ip address
 shutdown
 duplex auto
 speed auto
!
interface Serial0/0
 ip address 10.0.0.1 255.255.255.0
```

```
 clock rate 2000000
!
interface FastEthernet0/1
 no ip address
 shutdown
 duplex auto
 speed auto
!
ip forward-protocol nd
!
no ip http server
no ip http secure-server
!
control-plane
!
line con 0
 exec-timeout 0 0
 privilege level 15
 logging synchronous
line aux 0
 exec-timeout 0 0
 privilege level 15
 logging synchronous
line vty 0 4
 password cisco
 login
line vty 5 903
 password cisco
 login
!
ntp server 1.1.1.1 prefer
ntp server 2.2.2.2
!
end!
```

RouterB

```
interface Loopback0
 ip address 172.16.1.1 255.255.240.0
!
interface Loopback1
 ip address 172.20.1.1 255.255.252.0
!
interface FastEthernet0/0
 no ip address
 shutdown
 duplex auto
 speed auto
!
interface Serial0/0
```

```
  ip address 10.0.0.2 255.255.255.0
  clock rate 2000000
 !
 interface FastEthernet0/1
  no ip address
  shutdown
  duplex auto
  speed auto
 !
 ip forward-protocol nd
 !
 no ip http server
 no ip http secure-server
 !
 no cdp run
 !
 control-plane
 !
 banner motd ^C
 "Warning - this is a secure network." ^C
 !
 line con 0
  exec-timeout 0 0
  privilege level 15
  logging synchronous
 line aux 0
  exec-timeout 0 0
  privilege level 15
  logging synchronous
 line vty 0 4
  password cisco
  login
 line vty 5 903
  password cisco
  login
 !
 !
 end

 RB#
 !
```

Test:
```
 R1#telnet 10.0.0.2
 Trying 10.0.0.2 ... Open

 "Warning - this is a secure network."
 User Access Verification

 Password:
```

```
R1#show ntp associations
address      ref clock     st  when  poll reach  delay  offset   disp
~1.1.1.1     0.0.0.0       16  -     64   0      0.0    0.00     16000.
~2.2.2.2     0.0.0.0       16  -     64   0      0.0    0.00     16000.
 * master (synced), # master (unsynced), + selected, - candidate, ~
configured
```

CHALLENGE LAB 4: STATIC NAT

Lab Objective:
The objective of this lab exercise is for you to configure static NAT.

Lab Purpose:
NAT is an important exam topic so you can be pretty sure it will crop up. Rather than watch a video solution, I have provided show runs and test commands where appropriate.

Certification Level:
This lab is suitable for both CCENT and CCNA certification exam preparation.

Lab Difficulty:
This lab has a difficulty rating of 5/10.

Readiness Assessment:
When you are ready for your certification exam, you should complete this lab in no more than 15 minutes.

Lab Topology:
Please use the following topology to complete this lab exercise:

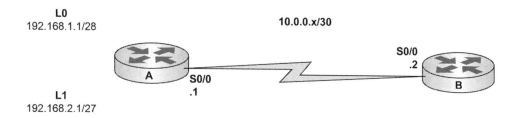

Task 1:
Configure the topology above. You should add a static default route on RouterB to send all traffic out of the Serial interface. Test by pinging the Loopbacks on RouterA. Check that you can ping all interfaces.

Task 2:
Configure static NAT on RouterA. Any traffic coming from 192.168.1.1 should be NATted to 172.16.1.1.

Task 3:

Check your configurations with `show` commands and pings sourced from 192.168.1.1 when you have `debug ip packet` running on RouterB.

CHALLENGE LAB 4: SOLUTION

Show Runs

RouterA

```
interface Loopback0
 ip address 192.168.1.1 255.255.255.240
 ip nat inside
 ip virtual-reassembly
!
interface Loopback1
 ip address 192.168.2.1 255.255.255.224
!
interface FastEthernet0/0
 no ip address
 shutdown
 duplex auto
 speed auto
!
interface Serial0/0
 ip address 10.0.0.1 255.255.255.252
 ip nat outside
 ip virtual-reassembly
 clock rate 2000000
!
interface FastEthernet0/1
 no ip address
 shutdown
 duplex auto
 speed auto
!
ip forward-protocol nd
!
!
no ip http server
no ip http secure-server
ip nat inside source static 192.168.1.1 172.16.1.1
!
!
!
```

RouterB

```
interface Serial0/0
 ip address 10.0.0.2 255.255.255.252
 clock rate 2000000
!
interface FastEthernet0/1
```

```
no ip address
shutdown
duplex auto
speed auto
!
ip forward-protocol nd
ip route 0.0.0.0 0.0.0.0 Serial0/0
```

Test:

```
RA#show ip nat translations
Pro Inside global      Inside local      Outside local    Outside global
--- 172.16.1.1         192.168.1.1          ---               ---
RB#debug ip packet
R1#ping 10.0.0.2 source 192.168.1.1

Type escape sequence to abort.
Sending 5, 100-byte ICMP Echos to 10.0.0.2, timeout is 2 seconds:
Packet sent with a source address of 192.168.1.1
!!!!!
Success rate is 100 percent (5/5), round-trip min/avg/max = 1/6/20 ms
R1#
R2#

*Mar  1 00:14:05.159: IP: tableid=0, s=10.0.0.2 (local), d=172.16.1.1
(Serial0/0), routed via FIB
*Mar  1 00:14:05.159: IP: s=10.0.0.2 (local), d=172.16.1.1 (Serial0/0),
len 100, sending
R2#
```

CHALLENGE LAB 5: NAT POOL

Lab Objective:
The objective of this lab exercise is for you to configure a NAT pool.

Lab Purpose:
NAT is an important exam topic so you can be pretty sure it will crop up. Rather than watch a video solution, I have provided show runs and test commands where appropriate.

Certification Level:
This lab is suitable for both CCENT and CCNA certification exam preparation.

Lab Difficulty:
This lab has a difficulty rating of 5/10.

Readiness Assessment:
When you are ready for your certification exam, you should complete this lab in no more than 15 minutes.

Lab Topology:
Please use the following topology to complete this lab exercise:

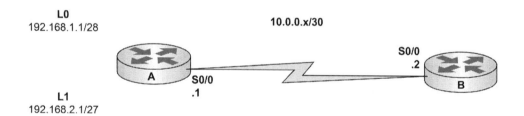

Task 1:
Configure the topology above. You should add a static default route on RouterB to send all traffic out of the Serial interface. Test by pinging the Loopbacks on RouterA. Check that you can ping all interfaces.

Task 2:
Configure a NAT pool on RouterA. The pool is 172.16.1.1 to 172.16.1.20. It should activate if any address from the 192.168.2.0/27 network goes out of the Serial interface. You can add a secondary IP address to the Loopback0 interface to test another address from the pool if you wish.

Task 3:

Check your configurations with show commands and pings sourced from 192.168.1.1 when you have debug ip packet running on RouterB.

CHALLENGE LAB 5: SOLUTION

Show Runs

RouterA

```
interface Loopback0
 ip address 192.168.1.1 255.255.255.240
!
interface Loopback1
 ip address 192.168.2.1 255.255.255.224
 ip address 192.168.2.2 255.255.255.224 secondary
 ip nat inside
 ip virtual-reassembly
!
interface FastEthernet0/0
 no ip address
 shutdown
 duplex auto
 speed auto
!
interface Serial0/0
 ip address 10.0.0.1 255.255.255.252
 ip nat outside
 ip virtual-reassembly
 clock rate 2000000
!
interface FastEthernet0/1
 no ip address
 shutdown
 duplex auto
 speed auto
!
ip forward-protocol nd
!
!
no ip http server
no ip http secure-server
ip nat pool Internet 172.16.1.1 172.16.1.20 netmask 255.255.0.0
ip nat inside source list 1 pool Internet
!
access-list 1 permit 192.168.2.0 0.0.0.31
```

RouterB

```
interface Serial0/0
 ip address 10.0.0.2 255.255.255.252
 clock rate 2000000
!
```

```
interface FastEthernet0/1
 no ip address
 shutdown
 duplex auto
 speed auto
!
ip forward-protocol nd
ip route 0.0.0.0 0.0.0.0 Serial0/0
!
```

Test:

Do an extended ping sourced from 192.168.2.1 (do another one from source 192.168.2.2 also if you wish, but be quick to avoid the NAT entry timing out).

```
Type escape sequence to abort.
Sending 5, 100-byte ICMP Echos to 10.0.0.2, timeout is 2 seconds:
Packet sent with a source address of 192.168.2.1
!!!!!
Success rate is 100 percent (5/5), round-trip min/avg/max = 4/6/12 ms

R1#show ip nat tran
Pro Inside global    Inside local    Outside local    Outside global
icmp 172.16.1.1:4    192.168.2.1:4   10.0.0.2:4       10.0.0.2:4
---  172.16.1.1       192.168.2.1     ---              ---
R1#
```

(Try the same thing again with the secondary IP address if you wish.)

```
R2#debug ip traffic
*Mar  1 00:32:00.639: IP: s=172.16.1.1 (Serial0/0), d=10.0.0.2
(Serial0/0), len 100, rcvd 3
*Mar  1 00:32:00.639: IP: tableid=0, s=10.0.0.2 (local), d=172.16.1.1
(Serial0/0), routed via FIB
*Mar  1 00:32:00.639: IP: s=10.0.0.2 (local), d=172.16.1.1 (Serial0/0),
len 100, sending
R2#
```

CHALLENGE LAB 6: NAT OVERLOAD

Lab Objective:
The objective of this lab exercise is for you to learn and understand how to configure NAT overload.

Lab Purpose:
NAT overload (or PAT) is an important exam topic so you can be pretty sure it will crop up. Rather than watch a video solution, I have provided show runs and test commands where appropriate.

Certification Level:
This lab is suitable for both CCENT and CCNA certification exam preparation.

Lab Difficulty:
This lab has a difficulty rating of 7/10.

Readiness Assessment:
When you are ready for your certification exam, you should complete this lab in no more than 15 minutes.

Lab Topology:
Please use the following topology to complete this lab exercise:

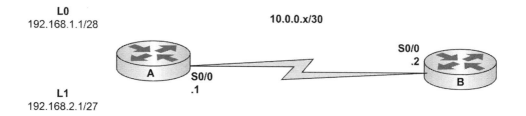

Task 1:
Configure the topology above. You should add a static default route on RouterB to send all traffic out of the Serial interface. Test by pinging the Loopbacks on RouterA. Check that you can ping all interfaces.

Task 2:

Configure a NAT pool on RouterA. The pool should consist of addresses 172.16.1.1 to 20/19 and it should NAT if any hosts from network 192.168.2.0/27 try to reach the Internet. Overload the pool.

Task 3:

Check your configurations with `show` commands and pings sourced from 192.168.1.1 when you have `debug ip packet` running on RouterB.

CHALLENGE LAB 6: SOLUTION

Show Runs

RouterA

```
interface Loopback0
 ip address 192.168.1.1 255.255.255.240
!
interface Loopback1
 ip address 192.168.2.1 255.255.255.224
 ip nat inside
 ip virtual-reassembly
!
interface FastEthernet0/0
 no ip address
 shutdown
 duplex auto
 speed auto
!
interface Serial0/0
 ip address 10.0.0.1 255.255.255.252
 ip nat outside
 ip virtual-reassembly
 clock rate 2000000
!
interface FastEthernet0/1
 no ip address
 shutdown
 duplex auto
 speed auto
!
ip forward-protocol nd
!
!
no ip http server
no ip http secure-server
ip nat pool Internet 172.16.1.1 172.16.1.20 netmask 255.255.224.0
ip nat inside source list 1 pool Internet overload
!
access-list 1 permit 192.168.2.0 0.0.0.31
```

RouterB

```
interface Serial0/0
 ip address 10.0.0.2 255.255.255.252
 clock rate 2000000
!
interface FastEthernet0/1
```

```
 no ip address
 shutdown
 duplex auto
 speed auto
!
ip forward-protocol nd
ip route 0.0.0.0 0.0.0.0 Serial0/0
!
```

Test:

Issue an extended ping to 10.0.0.2 from source 192.168.2.1.

```
Type escape sequence to abort.
Sending 5, 100-byte ICMP Echos to 10.0.0.2, timeout is 2 seconds:
Packet sent with a source address of 192.168.2.1
!!!!!
Success rate is 100 percent (5/5), round-trip min/avg/max = 1/8/24 ms
R1#

R1#show ip nat tran
Pro Inside global    Inside local    Outside local    Outside global
icmp 172.16.1.1:5    192.168.2.1:5   10.0.0.2:5       10.0.0.2:5
R1#
```

Test:

Issue an extended ping to 10.0.0.2 from source 192.168.2.1.

```
Type escape sequence to abort.
Sending 5, 100-byte ICMP Echos to 10.0.0.2, timeout is 2 seconds:
Packet sent with a source address of 192.168.2.1
!!!!!
Success rate is 100 percent (5/5), round-trip min/avg/max = 1/3/8 ms
R1#

R1#show ip nat tran
Pro Inside global    Inside local    Outside local    Outside global
icmp 172.16.1.1:5    192.168.2.1:5   10.0.0.2:5       10.0.0.2:5
icmp 172.16.1.1:6    192.168.2.1:6   10.0.0.2:6       10.0.0.2:6
R1#
```

CHALLENGE LAB 7: STATIC IPV6 ROUTES

Lab Objective:
The objective of this lab exercise is for you to configure IPv6 static routing.

Lab Purpose:
IPv6 static routing is not specifically referred to in the exam syllabus. Static routing is and IPv6 is also, so you might be tested on both together in the exam. Rather than watch a video solution, I have provided show runs and test commands where appropriate.

Certification Level:
This lab is suitable for both CCENT and CCNA certification exam preparation.

Lab Difficulty:
This lab has a difficulty rating of 4/10.

Readiness Assessment:
When you are ready for your certification exam, you should complete this lab in no more than 15 minutes.

Lab Topology:
Please use the following topology to complete this lab exercise:

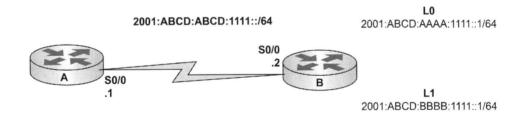

Task 1:
Configure the topology above. You will need to find the link-local next hop address for RouterA to send the traffic for **Task 2**. This will be under the IPv6 interface for RouterB. Don't copy the link-local address I used because it is unique to my router. Check that you can ping across the Serial link.

Task 2:

Configure two static routes on RouterA so it can reach the networks behind RouterB.

Task 3:

Ping the Loopback interfaces on RouterB from RouterA.

CHALLENGE LAB 7: SOLUTION

Show Runs

RouterA

```
ipv6 unicast-routing
!
multilink bundle-name authenticated
!
archive
 log config
  hidekeys
!
interface Serial0/0
 no ip address
 no shut
 ipv6 address 2001:ABCD:ABCD:1111::1/64
 clock rate 2000000
!
ip forward-protocol nd
!
no ip http server
no ip http secure-server
!
ipv6 route 2001:ABCD:AAAA:1111::/64 Serial0/0 FE80::C001:7FF:FE0A:0
ipv6 route 2001:ABCD:BBBB:1111::/64 Serial0/0 FE80::C001:7FF:FE0A:0
!
```

RouterB

```
ipv6 unicast-routing
!
interface Loopback0
 no ip address
 ipv6 address 2001:ABCD:AAAA:1111::1/64
!
interface Loopback1
 no ip address
 ipv6 address 2001:ABCD:BBBB:1111::1/64
!
interface Serial0/0
 no ip address
 ipv6 address 2001:ABCD:ABCD:1111::2/64
 clock rate 2000000
```

Test:

```
RB#ping ipv6 2001:ABCD:ABCD:1111::1
Type escape sequence to abort.
Sending 5, 100-byte ICMP Echos to 2001:ABCD:ABCD:1111::1, timeout is 2
seconds:
!!!!!
Success rate is 100 percent (5/5), round-trip min/avg/max = 0/0/0 ms

RA(config)#ipv6 route 2001:abcd:aaaa:1111::/64 serial 0/0 ?
  <1-254>     Administrative distance
  X:X:X:X::X  IPv6 address of next-hop (get this from R2 s0/0)
  multicast   Route only usable by multicast
  tag         value
  unicast     Route only usable by unicast
  <cr>

RB#show ipv6 int s0/0
Serial0/0 is up, line protocol is up
  IPv6 is enabled, link-local address is FE80::C001:7FF:FE0A:0
  No Virtual link-local address(es):
  Global unicast address(es):
    2001:ABCD:ABCD:1111::2, subnet is 2001:ABCD:ABCD:1111::/64

RA#ping ipv6 2001:abcd:aaaa:1111::1
Type escape sequence to abort.
Sending 5, 100-byte ICMP Echos to 2001:ABCD:AAAA:1111::1, timeout is 2
seconds:
!!!!!
Success rate is 100 percent (5/5), round-trip min/avg/max = 0/3/8 ms

RA#ping ipv6 2001:abcd:bbbb:1111::1
Type escape sequence to abort.
Sending 5, 100-byte ICMP Echos to 2001:ABCD:BBBB:1111::1, timeout is 2
seconds:
!!!!!
Success rate is 100 percent (5/5), round-trip min/avg/max = 0/1/4 ms
R1#
```

CHALLENGE LAB 8: SWITCHPORT SECURITY

Lab Objective:
The objective of this lab exercise is for you to protect a switchport with port security.

Lab Purpose:
Configuring port security on switches is a very important CCNA exam topic. I can almost guarantee that you'll be asked a question or be given a lab on it. Rather than watch a video solution, I have provided show runs and test commands where appropriate.

Certification Level:
This lab is suitable for both CCENT and CCNA certification exam preparation.

Lab Difficulty:
This lab has a difficulty rating of 6/10.

Readiness Assessment:
When you are ready for your certification exam, you should complete this lab in no more than 15 minutes.

Lab Topology:
Please use the following topology to complete this lab exercise:

Task 1:
Connect a PC to a switchport. Configure the port as an access port.

Task 2:
Configure the switchport as an access port and put it into VLAN20. Add IP address 10.0.0.2 to VLAN20 and a default gateway of the PC IP address.

Task 3:

Configure port security on the switchport. Add a command to ensure that the switch adds the learned MAC address to the startup configuration file.

Task 4:

Optional: Change the MAC address on the PC using Packet Tracer or a physical device if you have a home lab. Now check that the port has been shut down.

CHALLENGE LAB 8: SOLUTION

Show Runs

```
Switch#show run
hostname Switch
!
spanning-tree mode pvst
!
interface FastEthernet0/1
 switchport access vlan 20
 switchport mode access
 switchport port-security
 switchport port-security mac-address sticky
 switchport port-security mac-address sticky 0004.9AAA.C6D8 <-this was
                                    learned by the switch, not manually entered.
!
interface FastEthernet0/2
interface Vlan1
 no ip address
 shutdown
!
interface Vlan20
 ip address 10.0.0.2 255.255.255.0
!
ip default-gateway 10.0.0.1
```

Test:
```
Switch#show port-security int f0/1
Port Security               : Enabled
Port Status                 : Secure-up
Violation Mode              : Shutdown
Aging Time                  : 0 mins
Aging Type                  : Absolute
SecureStatic Address Aging  : Disabled
Maximum MAC Addresses       : 1
Total MAC Addresses         : 1
Configured MAC Addresses    : 0
Sticky MAC Addresses        : 1
Last Source Address:Vlan    : 0004.9AAA.C6D8:20
Security Violation Count    : 0
```

After changing the MAC address, you should see the following:

```
%LINK-5-CHANGED: Interface FastEthernet0/1, changed state to
administratively down

Switch#show port-security int f0/1
Port Security               : Enabled
```

```
Port Status                  : Secure-shutdown
Violation Mode               : Shutdown
Aging Time                   : 0 mins
Aging Type                   : Absolute
SecureStatic Address Aging   : Disabled
Maximum MAC Addresses        : 1
Total MAC Addresses          : 1
Configured MAC Addresses     : 0
Sticky MAC Addresses         : 1
Last Source Address:Vlan     : 0004.9AAA.C6D9:20
Security Violation Count     : 1
```

CHALLENGE LAB 9: TRUNKING AND VTP

Lab Objective:
The objective of this lab exercise is for you to configure VTP and trunking settings.

Lab Purpose:
Configuring VTP and securing the trunk link is a vital CCNA-level skill. Rather than watch a video solution, I have provided show runs and test commands where appropriate.

Certification Level:
This lab is suitable for both CCENT and CCNA certification exam preparation.

Lab Difficulty:
This lab has a difficulty rating of 7/10.

Readiness Assessment:
When you are ready for your certification exam, you should complete this lab in no more than 15 minutes.

Lab Topology:
Please use the following topology to complete this lab exercise:

VLAN NUMBER	VLAN NAME
10	Sales
20	Marketing
30	HR

Task 1:
Connect two switches together as shown above. Set the relevant hostnames and the F0/1 interfaces to trunk.

Task 2:
Configure SwitchA as a VTP server with the VTP domain howtonetwork.com and VTP password Cisco. Set SwitchB as a VTP client with the same VTP domain settings.

Task 3:

Configure the three VLANs as per the diagram.

Task 4:

Turn off DTP for the trunk interfaces.

Task 5:

Set the native VLAN on both switches to VLAN888. Shut down VLAN1 on both switches.

Task 6:

Permit only VLANs 10, 20, and 30 to cross the trunk link. I know we haven't covered this yet so feel free to take a peek at the configurations. It's a Layer 2 security step that you will need to know.

Task 7:

Issue relevant show commands to verify your configurations.

CHALLENGE LAB 9: SOLUTION

Many of the Layer 2 settings do not show in the show run (they are held in the VLAN database). All of the commands are in the videos though if you are using these to accompany the book. You have already seen the VTP commands in previous labs. You would permit VLAN888 in the real world but don't worry about that for this lab.

Show Runs

```
hostname SwitchA
!
spanning-tree mode pvst
!
interface FastEthernet0/1
 switchport trunk native vlan888
 switchport trunk allowed vlan10,20,30
 switchport mode trunk
 switchport nonegotiate

hostname SwitchB
!
spanning-tree mode pvst
!
interface FastEthernet0/1
 switchport trunk native vlan888
 switchport trunk allowed vlan10,20,30
 switchport mode trunk
 switchport nonegotiate
```

Test:
```
SwitchB#show vtp status
VTP Version                      : 2
Configuration Revision           : 6
Maximum VLANs supported locally : 255
Number of existing VLANs         : 8
VTP Operating Mode               : Client
VTP Domain Name                  : howtonetwork.com
VTP Pruning Mode                 : Disabled
VTP V2 Mode                      : Disabled
VTP Traps Generation             : Disabled
MD5 digest                       : 0xA7 0x6A 0x55 0x45 0xBB 0x6B 0x23
0x14
Configuration last modified by 0.0.0.0 at 3-1-93 00:19:44

SwitchB#show in trunk
Port       Mode       Encapsulation  Status      Native vlan
Fa0/1      on         802.1q         trunking    888
```

```
Port        Vlans allowed on trunk
Fa0/1       10,20,30

Port        Vlans allowed and active in management domain
Fa0/1       10,20,30

Port        Vlans in spanning tree forwarding state and not pruned
Fa0/1       10,20,30
SwitchB#

SwitchB#show int f0/1 switchport
Name: Fa0/1
Switchport: Enabled
Administrative Mode: trunk
Operational Mode: trunk
Administrative Trunking Encapsulation: dot1q
Operational Trunking Encapsulation: dot1q
Negotiation of Trunking: Off
Access Mode VLAN: 1 (default)
Trunking Native Mode VLAN: 888 (Inactive)


VLAN Name                       Status    Ports
---- -------------------------- --------- -------------------------------
1    default                    active    Fa0/2, Fa0/3, Fa0/4, Fa0/5
                                          Fa0/6, Fa0/7, Fa0/8, Fa0/9
                                          Fa0/10, Fa0/11, Fa0/12, Fa0/13
                                          Fa0/14, Fa0/15, Fa0/16, Fa0/17
                                          Fa0/18, Fa0/19, Fa0/20, Fa0/21
                                          Fa0/22, Fa0/23, Fa0/24, Gig1/1
                                          Gig1/2
10   Sales                      active
20   Marketing                  active
30   HR                         active
1002 fddi-default               active
```

CHALLENGE LAB 10: DHCP, INTER-VLAN ROUTING, AND RIPV2

Lab Objective:
This is a challenge lab designed to test and validate the skills you have acquired throughout this lab guide on DHCP, inter-VLAN routing, and RIP version 2.

Lab Purpose:
The purpose of this lab is to reinforce DHCP, inter-VLAN routing, and RIP version 2 configuration.

Certification Level:
This lab is suitable for CCNA certification exam preparation.

Lab Difficulty:
This lab has a difficulty rating of 8/10.

Readiness Assessment:
When you are ready for your certification exam, you should complete this lab in no more than 20 minutes.

Lab Topology:
Please use the following topology to complete this lab:

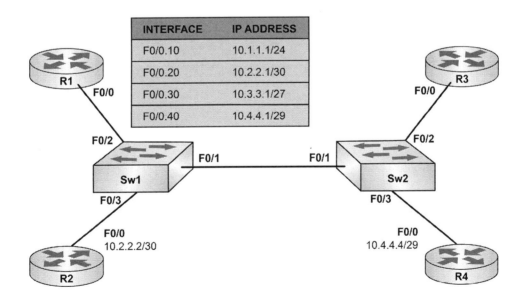

INTERFACE	IP ADDRESS
F0/0.10	10.1.1.1/24
F0/0.20	10.2.2.1/30
F0/0.30	10.3.3.1/27
F0/0.40	10.4.4.1/29

Task 1:

Configure the hostname on all devices as illustrated in the network topology.

Task 2:

Configure Sw1 as a VTP server and Sw2 as a VTP client. Both switches should be in VTP domain CISCO. Configure the F0/1 interfaces on both switches as trunk links. Verify that your trunk link is operational and propagating all VLAN information.

Task 3:

Configure the following VLANs on Sw1:

VLAN Number	VLAN Name
10	VLAN10
20	VLAN20
30	VLAN30
40	VLAN40

Task 4:

Make sure your VLAN information propagates to Sw2. Next, configure Sw1 Fa0/2 as a trunk link and Fa0/3 in VLAN20. Configure Sw2 Fa0/2 in VLAN30 and Fa0/3 in VLAN40.

Task 5:

Configure IP addresses as specified in the topology on R2 and R4. On Sw1 and Sw2, configure interface VLAN10 with an IP address of 10.1.1.2/24 and 10.1.1.3/24, respectively. The default gateway of all switches should be 10.1.1.1.

Task 6:

Configure subinterfaces on R1 as illustrated in the topology. Ensure that Fa0/0.10 is in VLAN10, Fa0/0.20 is in VLAN20, Fa0/0.30 is in VLAN30, and Fa0/0.40 is in VLAN40.

Task 7:

Configure R1 as a Cisco IOS DHCP server for the 10.3.3.0/27 subnet. The domain name should be howtonetwork.com; the default gateway should be 10.3.3.1; the DHCP lease should be for 7 days. Next, configure R3 to receive IP addressing on F0/0 via DHCP. Some of these commands won't work on Packet Tracer.

Task 8:

Configure RIP version 2 on R1, R2, R3, and R4. Make sure that there is no automatic summarization.

Task 9:

If you have configured everything correctly, all routers and all switches should be able to ping each other. Verify this to see if you have completed the lab successfully.

CHALLENGE LAB 10: SOLUTION

Show Runs

```
R1#show run
!
hostname R1
!
ip dhcp pool funpool
 network 10.3.3.0 255.255.255.224
 default-router 10.3.3.1
 domain-name howtonetwork.com
 default-router 10.3.3.1
 lease 7
!
interface FastEthernet0/0
 no ip address
 duplex auto
 speed auto
!
interface FastEthernet0/0.10
 encapsulation dot1Q 10
 ip address 10.1.1.1 255.255.255.0
!
interface FastEthernet0/0.20
 encapsulation dot1Q 20
 ip address 10.2.2.1 255.255.255.252
!
interface FastEthernet0/0.30
 encapsulation dot1Q 30
 ip address 10.3.3.1 255.255.255.224
!
interface FastEthernet0/0.40
 encapsulation dot1Q 40
 ip address 10.4.4.1 255.255.255.248
!
interface Vlan1
 no ip address
 shutdown
!
router rip
 version 2
 network 10.0.0.0
 no auto-summary

R2#show run
Building configuration...
!
hostname R2
!
```

```
interface FastEthernet0/0
 ip address 10.2.2.2 255.255.255.252
 duplex auto
 speed auto
!
router rip
 version 2
 network 10.0.0.0
 no auto-summary
!


R3#show run
Building configuration...
!
hostname R3
!
interface FastEthernet0/0
 ip address dhcp
 duplex auto
 speed auto
!
router rip
 version 2
 network 10.0.0.0
 no auto-summary
!


R4#show run
Building configuration...
!
hostname R4
!
interface FastEthernet0/0
 ip address 10.4.4.4 255.255.255.248
 duplex auto
 speed auto
!
router rip
 version 2
 network 10.0.0.0
 no auto-summary

Sw1#show run
Building configuration...
!
hostname Sw1
!
spanning-tree mode pvst
!
interface FastEthernet0/1
 switchport mode trunk
```

```
!
interface FastEthernet0/2
 switchport mode trunk
!
interface FastEthernet0/3
 switchport access vlan20
 switchport mode access
!
interface Vlan1
 no ip address
 shutdown
!
interface Vlan10
 mac-address 0002.4add.7001
 ip address 10.1.1.2 255.255.255.0
!
ip default-gateway 10.1.1.1

Sw2#show run
Building configuration...
!
hostname Sw2
!
interface FastEthernet0/1
 switchport mode trunk
!
interface FastEthernet0/2
 switchport access vlan30
 switchport mode access
!
interface FastEthernet0/3
 switchport access vlan40
 switchport mode access
!
interface Vlan1
 no ip address
 shutdown
!
interface Vlan10
 mac-address 0001.c700.7c01
 ip address 10.1.1.3 255.255.255.0
!
ip default-gateway 10.1.1.1
```

Test:
```
R2#ping 10.2.2.1

Type escape sequence to abort.
Sending 5, 100-byte ICMP Echos to 10.2.2.1, timeout is 2 seconds:
.!!!!
Success rate is 80 percent (4/5), round-trip min/avg/max = 0/0/0 ms
```

```
R2#show ip route
Codes: C - connected, S - static, I - IGRP, R - RIP, M - mobile,
       B-BGP, D - EIGRP, EX - EIGRP external, O - OSPF,
       IA - OSPF inter area, N1 - OSPF NSSA external type 1,
       N2 - OSPF NSSA external type 2, E1 - OSPF external type 1,
       E2 - OSPF external type 2, E-EGP, i - IS-IS,
       L1 - IS-IS level-1, L2 - IS-IS level-2, ia - IS-IS inter area,
       * - candidate default, U - per-user static route,
       o-ODR, P - periodic downloaded static route

Gateway of last resort is not set

     10.0.0.0/8 is variably subnetted, 4 subnets, 4 masks
R       10.1.1.0/24 [120/1] via 10.2.2.1, 00:00:26, FastEthernet0/0
C       10.2.2.0/30 is directly connected, FastEthernet0/0
R       10.3.3.0/27 [120/1] via 10.2.2.1, 00:00:26, FastEthernet0/0
R       10.4.4.0/29 [120/1] via 10.2.2.1, 00:00:26, FastEthernet0/0

R3#show ip int brief
Interface        IP-Address  OK? Method Status         Protocol
FastEthernet0/0  10.3.3.2    YES DHCP   up             up
R3#

R3#show ip route
Codes: C - connected, S - static, I - IGRP, R - RIP, M - mobile, B
 - BGP
       D - EIGRP, EX - EIGRP external, O - OSPF, IA - OSPF inter area
       N1 - OSPF NSSA external type 1, N2 - OSPF NSSA external type 2
       E1 - OSPF external type 1, E2 - OSPF external type 2, E - EGP
       i - IS-IS, L1 - IS-IS level-1, L2 - IS-IS level-2,
       ia - IS-IS inter area, * - candidate default,
       U - per-user static route, o - ODR
       P - periodic downloaded static route

Gateway of last resort is 10.3.3.1 to network 0.0.0.0

     10.0.0.0/8 is variably subnetted, 4 subnets, 4 masks
R       10.1.1.0/24 [120/1] via 10.3.3.1, 00:00:08, FastEthernet0/0
R       10.2.2.0/30 [120/1] via 10.3.3.1, 00:00:08, FastEthernet0/0
C       10.3.3.0/27 is directly connected, FastEthernet0/0
R       10.4.4.0/29 [120/1] via 10.3.3.1, 00:00:08, FastEthernet0/0
S*    0.0.0.0/0 [254/0] via 10.3.3.1

R3#ping 10.2.2.2

Type escape sequence to abort.
Sending 5, 100-byte ICMP Echos to 10.2.2.2, timeout is 2 seconds:
.!!!!
Success rate is 80 percent (4/5), round-trip min/avg/max = 0/0/0 ms

R3#
```

```
Sw2#show vlan brief

VLAN Name                          Status     Ports
---- ------------------------------ ---------- --------------------------------
1    default                       active     Fa0/4, Fa0/5, Fa0/6, Fa0/7
                                              Fa0/8, Fa0/9, Fa0/10, Fa0/11
                                              Fa0/12, Fa0/13, Fa0/14, Fa0/15
                                              Fa0/16, Fa0/17, Fa0/18, Fa0/19
                                              Fa0/20, Fa0/21, Fa0/22, Fa0/23
                                              Fa0/24, Gig0/1, Gig0/2
10   VLAN-10                       active
20   VLAN-20                       active
30   VLAN-30                       active     Fa0/2
40   VLAN-40                       active     Fa0/3
1002 fddi-default                  active
1003 token-ring-default            active
1004 fddinet-default               active
1005 trnet-default                 active

Sw2#show vtp status
VTP Version                       : 2
Configuration Revision            : 8
Maximum VLANs supported locally   : 255
Number of existing VLANs          : 9
VTP Operating Mode                : Client
VTP Domain Name                   : CISCO
VTP Pruning Mode                  : Disabled
VTP V2 Mode                       : Disabled
VTP Traps Generation              : Disabled
MD5 digest                        : 0xBA 0x39 0x13 0x74 0x56 0x60 0xCF
0xF9
Configuration last modified by 0.0.0.0 at 3-1-93 00:04:45
Sw2#

Sw1#show int trunk
Port         Mode          Encapsulation  Status        Native vlan
Fa0/1        on            802.1q         trunking      1
Fa0/2        on            802.1q         trunking      1

Port         Vlans allowed on trunk
Fa0/1        1-1005
Fa0/2        1-1005

Port         Vlans allowed and active in management domain
Fa0/1        1,10,20,30,40
Fa0/2        1,10,20,30,40

Port         Vlans in spanning tree forwarding state and not pruned
Fa0/1        1,10,20,30,40
Fa0/2        1,10,20,30,40

Sw1#
```

ICND2: 200-105

1.0 LAN Switching Technologies

LAB 63: CONFIGURING EXTENDED VLANS ON CISCO CATALYST SWITCHES

Lab Objective:
The objective of this lab exercise is for you to learn and understand how to configure extended VLANs 1006–4096 on Cisco Catalyst IOS Switches. In addition, you are required to familiarize yourself with the commands available in Cisco IOS to validate and check your configurations.

Lab Purpose:
VLAN configuration is a fundamental skill. VLANs allow you to segment your network into multiple, smaller broadcast domains. As a Cisco engineer, as well as in the Cisco CCNA exam, you will be expected to know how to configure extended VLANs on Cisco switches.

Certification Level:
This lab is suitable for ICND2 and CCNA certification exam preparation.

Lab Difficulty:
This lab has a difficulty rating of 5/10.

Readiness Assessment:
When you are ready for your certification exam, you should complete this lab in no more than 10 minutes.

Lab Topology:

Please use the following topology to complete this lab exercise:

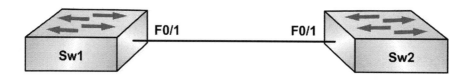

VLAN NUMBER	VLAN NAME	VLAN NAME
2010	SALES	FastEthernet0/5
2020	MANAGERS	FastEthernet0/6
2030	ENGINEERS	FastEthernet0/7
2040	SUPPORT	FastEthernet0/8

Task 1:

In preparation for VLAN configuration, configure a hostname on Sw1 as well as the VLANs depicted in the topology. Keep in mind that extended VLANs can only be configured on a switch in VTP Transparent mode.

Task 2:

Configure ports FastEthernet0/5 to FastEthernet0/8 as access ports and assign them to the VLANs specified.

Task 3:

Verify your VLAN configuration. Feel free to replicate the steps above on Sw2.

LAB 63: CONFIGURATION AND VERIFICATION

Task 1:

NOTE: By default, Cisco switches are VTP servers. Only standard range VLANS 1–1005 are configurable on VTP servers. To configure extended range VLANS (1006–4096), you must configure the switch as a VTP Transparent switch. Otherwise, you will get the following error message:

```
Sw1(config)#vlan2010
Sw1(config-vlan)#end
Extended VLANs not allowed in VTP SERVER mode
Failed to commit extended VLAN(s) changes.
```

NOTE: Configuration files will be kept from previous labs. In order to remove them, you can re-type the commands with the word "no" in front as shown below:

```
Sw1(config)#no vlan2010
```

You may also need to reset the switch back to VTP server mode if appropriate.

```
Switch#config t
Enter configuration commands, one per line.  End with CTRL/Z.
Switch(config)#hostname Sw1
Sw1(config)#vtp mode transparent
Setting device to VTP TRANSPARENT mode.
Sw1(config)#vlan2010
Sw1(config-vlan)#name SALES
Sw1(config-vlan)#exit
Sw1(config)#vlan2020
Sw1(config-vlan)#name MANAGERS
Sw1(config-vlan)#exit
Sw1(config)#vlan2030
Sw1(config-vlan)#name ENGINEERS
Sw1(config-vlan)#exit
Sw1(config)#vlan2040
Sw1(config-vlan)#name SUPPORT
```

Task 2:

```
Sw1#config t
Enter configuration commands, one per line.  End with CTRL/Z.
Sw1(config)#interface fastethernet0/5
Sw1(config-if)#switchport mode access
Sw1(config-if)#switchport access vlan2010
Sw1(config-if)#exit
Sw1(config)#interface fastethernet0/6
Sw1(config-if)#switchport mode access
Sw1(config-if)#switchport access vlan2020
```

```
Sw1(config-if)#exit
Sw1(config-if)#interface fastethernet0/7
Sw1(config-if)#switchport mode access
Sw1(config-if)#switchport access vlan2030
Sw1(config-if)#exit
Sw1(config-if)#interface fastethernet0/8
Sw1(config-if)#switchport mode access
Sw1(config-if)#switchport access vlan2040
```

Task 3:

```
Sw1#show vlan brief

VLAN Name                     Status     Ports
---- -------------------- --------- -------------------------------
1    default               active     Fa0/1, Fa0/2, Fa0/3, Fa0/4
                                       Fa0/9, Fa0/10, Fa0/11, Fa0/12
                                       Fa0/13, Fa0/14, Fa0/15, Fa0/16
                                       Fa0/17, Fa0/18, Fa0/19, Fa0/20
                                       Fa0/21, Fa0/22, Fa0/23, Fa0/24
                                       Gi0/1, Gi0/2
2010 SALES                 active     Fa0/5
2020 MANAGERS              active     Fa0/6
2030 ENGINEERS             active     Fa0/7
2040 SUPPORT               active     Fa0/8

[Output Truncated]
```

LAB 64: CHANGING THE NATIVE VLAN AND SHUTTING DOWN UNUSED PORTS

Lab Objective:
The objective of this lab exercise is for you to learn and understand how to change the native VLAN to one other than VLAN1 and how to shut down unused switchports in order to prevent unauthorized access.

Lab Purpose:
Securing the switch involves knowing how to change the native VLAN as well as shutting down unused ports in case somebody plugs a device into one to try to gain network access.

Certification Level:
This lab is suitable for both ICND2 and CCNA certification exam preparation.

Lab Difficulty:
This lab has a difficulty rating of 4/10.

Readiness Assessment:
When you are ready for your certification exam, you should complete this lab in no more than 5 minutes.

Lab Topology:
Please use the following topology to complete this lab exercise:

Task 1:
Set any interface to trunk and then specify VLAN20 as the native VLAN for the trunk link.

Task 2:
Shut down ports FastEthernet 10 to 15, inclusive.

Task 3:
Issue the relevant show commands to prove your configurations.

LAB 64: CONFIGURATION AND VERIFICATION

Task 1:

```
Sw1#show int fast0/5 switchport
Name: Fa0/5
Switchport: Enabled
Administrative Mode: trunk
Operational Mode: down
Administrative Trunking Encapsulation: dot1q
Operational Trunking Encapsulation: dot1q
Negotiation of Trunking: On
Access Mode VLAN: 1 (default)
Trunking Native Mode VLAN: 1 (default)
Voice VLAN: none

Sw1#conf t
Sw1(config)#vlan20
Sw1(config-vlan)#name SUPPORT
Enter configuration commands, one per line.  End with CTRL/Z.
Sw1(config)#int fast0/5
Sw1(config-if)#switchport mode trunk
Sw1(config-if)#switchport trunk native vlan20
```

Task 2:

```
Sw1#conf t
Enter configuration commands, one per line.  End with CTRL/Z.
Sw1(config)#interface range f0/10 - f0/15
Sw1(config-if-range)#shutdown
```

The interface range command will not work on older switch models (sorry). Some models want you to have a space between the ranges and some don't, so test it for yourself with the ?.

Task 3:

```
Sw1#show int fast0/5 switchport
Name: Fa0/5
Switchport: Enabled
Administrative Mode: trunk
Operational Mode: down
Administrative Trunking Encapsulation: dot1q
Operational Trunking Encapsulation: dot1q
Negotiation of Trunking: On
Access Mode VLAN: 1 (default)
Trunking Native Mode VLAN: 20 (SUPPORT)
```

LAB 65: RESTRICTING EXTENDED VLANS ON TRUNKS AND CHANGING THE VTP VERSION

Lab Objective:

The objective of this lab exercise is for you to learn and understand how to restrict VLANs traversing trunks. By default, all VLANs are allowed to traverse trunks.

Lab Purpose:

VLAN trunk restriction is a fundamental skill. By default, all VLANs traverse trunks. However, in some cases, this may result in unnecessary VLANs being propagated, and this may pose a security risk. As a Cisco engineer, as well as in the Cisco CCNA exam, you will be expected to know how to restrict VLANs from traversing trunks.

Certification Level:

This lab is suitable for CCNA certification exam preparation.

Lab Difficulty:

This lab has a difficulty rating of 6/10.

Readiness Assessment:

When you are ready for your certification exam, you should complete this lab in no more than 15 minutes.

Lab Topology:

Please use the following topology to complete this lab exercise:

VLAN NUMBER	VLAN NAME
2010	SALES
2020	MANAGERS
2030	ENGINEERS
2040	SUPPORT

Task 1:

In preparation for VLAN configuration, configure a hostname on Sw1 and Sw2 as illustrated in the topology.

Task 2:

Configure and verify Sw1 and Sw2 as VTP Transparent switches. Both switches should be in the VTP domain named CISCO. Configure the switches to use legacy VTP version 1. Configure FastEthernet0/1 as a trunk between Sw1 and Sw2.

Task 3:

Configure and verify your VLAN configuration switches Sw1 or Sw2 and ensure that they are identical.

Task 4:

Allow only VLAN2040 to traverse the trunk link on Sw1 and verify your configuration.

LAB 65: CONFIGURATION AND VERIFICATION

Task 1:

For reference information on configuring hostnames, please refer to earlier labs.

Task 2:

```
Sw1#config t
Enter configuration commands, one per line.  End with CTRL/Z.
Sw1(config)#vtp mode transparent
Setting device to VTP TRANSPARENT mode.
Sw1(config)#vtp domain CISCO
Changing VTP domain name from Null to CISCO
Sw1(config)#vtp version 1
Sw1(config)#vlan2010
Sw1(config-vlan)#name SALES
Sw1(config-vlan)#exit
Sw1(config)#vlan2020
Sw1(config-vlan)#name MANAGERS
Sw1(config-vlan)#exit
Sw1(config)#vlan2030
Sw1(config-vlan)#name ENGINEERS
Sw1(config-vlan)#exit
Sw1(config)#vlan2040
Sw1(config-vlan)#name SUPPORT
Sw1(config-vlan)#exit
Sw1(config)#interface fastethernet0/1
Sw1(config-if)#switchport mode trunk

Sw2#config t
Enter configuration commands, one per line.  End with CTRL/Z.
Sw2(config)#vtp mode transparent
Setting device to VTP TRANSPARENT mode.
Sw2(config)#vtp domain CISCO
Changing VTP domain name from Null to CISCO
Sw2(config)#vtp version 1
Sw2(config)#vlan2010
Sw2(config-vlan)#name SALES
Sw2(config-vlan)#exit
Sw2(config)#vlan2020
Sw2(config-vlan)#name MANAGERS
Sw2(config-vlan)#exit
Sw2(config)#vlan2030
Sw2(config-vlan)#name ENGINEERS
Sw2(config-vlan)#exit
Sw2(config)#vlan2040
Sw2(config-vlan)#name SUPPORT
Sw2(config-vlan)#exit
Sw2(config)#interface fastethernet0/1
Sw2(config-if)#switchport mode trunk
```

Task 3:

For reference information on configuring and verifying VLANs, please refer to earlier labs.

Task 4:
```
Sw1#conf t
Enter configuration commands, one per line.  End with CTRL/Z.
Sw1(config)#interface fastethernet0/1
Sw1(config-if)#switchport trunk allowed vlan2040
Sw1(config-if)#^Z
Sw1#
Sw1#show interfaces trunk

Port        Mode        Encapsulation  Status      Native Vlan
Fa0/1       on          802.1q         trunking    1

Port        Vlans allowed on trunk
Fa0/1       2040
```

> **NOTE:** By default, ALL configured VLANs are allowed to traverse ALL configured trunk links. You can restrict certain VLANs to certain trunks by using the `switchport trunk allowed vlan` command. You can test this command, which can also add or remove ranges of VLANs, so please spend some time trying out all the options. Beware that it can remove VLANs you have currently allowed if you don't enter the correct inputs.

LAB 66: VERIFYING SPANNING TREE PORT STATES ON CATALYST SWITCHES

Lab Objective:
The objective of this lab exercise is to verify the different Spanning Tree port states (i.e., Listening, Learning, etc.) and understand the IOS commands that can be used to determine the state of a port at any given time.

Lab Purpose:
Understanding the different Spanning Tree Protocol port states is a fundamental skill. In Spanning Tree operation, ports transition from a Blocking state -> Listening state -> Learning state -> Forwarding state. A switched network is said to be converged when all ports are in the Forwarding or Blocking state. As a Cisco engineer, as well as in the Cisco CCNA exam, you will be expected to know the different Spanning Tree port states.

Certification Level:
This lab is suitable for CCNA certification exam preparation.

Lab Difficulty:
This lab has a difficulty rating of 5/10.

Readiness Assessment:
When you are ready for your certification exam, you should complete this lab in no more than 15 minutes.

Lab Topology:
Please use the following topology to complete this lab exercise:

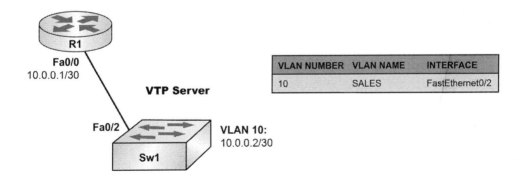

VLAN NUMBER	VLAN NAME	INTERFACE
10	SALES	FastEthernet0/2

Task 1:

In preparation for VLAN configuration, configure a hostname on Sw1 and R1 as illustrated in the topology.

Task 2:

Configure and verify Sw1 as a VTP server in the VTP domain named CISCO. The VTP domain should have the password CISCO.

Task 3:

Configure VLAN10 on Sw1 as illustrated in the topology. Configure FastEthernet0/2 on Sw1 as an access port in VLAN10 and bring up the FastEthernet0/0 interface on router R1.

Configure the IP address on R1's FastEthernet0/0 and configure VLAN10 with the IP address on Sw1 as illustrated in the topology. Verify IP connectivity using pings.

Task 4:

On Sw1, issue a `shutdown` and then a `no shutdown` command on FastEthernet0/2. Verify the transition of the Spanning Tree state of the port to Forwarding. Make sure that you see the interface in at least three different Spanning Tree states.

LAB 66: CONFIGURATION AND VERIFICATION

Task 1:

For reference information on configuring hostnames, please refer to earlier labs.

Task 2:

For reference information on configuring a VTP domain and password, please refer to earlier labs.

Task 3:

For reference information on configuring standard VLANs, please refer to earlier labs. To check the IP address for VLAN10 on the switch, issue the following:

```
Sw1#show ip interface brief
```

> **NOTE:** VLAN1 is the default management interface on Cisco switches. When configuring another interface with an IP address, it is good practice to shut down interface VLAN1 and issue a no shutdown command on the new management interface you are configuring.

Task 4:

```
Sw1#conf t
Enter configuration commands, one per line.  End with CTRL/Z.
Sw1(config)#int fastethernet0/2
Sw1(config-if)#shut
Sw1(config-if)#no shutdown
Sw1(config-if)#end
Sw1#
Sw1#show spanning-tree interface fastethernet0/2
no spanning tree info available for FastEthernet0/2
```

After about 10 to 15 seconds, the port transitions to the Listening state as shown below:

```
Sw1#show spanning-tree interface fastethernet0/2

Vlan            Role Sts Cost      Prio.Nbr Type
---------------- ---- --- --------- -------- --------
VLAN0010        Desg LIS 100       128.2    Shr
```

After about 10 to 15 seconds, the port transitions to the Learning state as shown below:

```
Sw1#show spanning-tree interface fastEthernet0/2

Vlan            Role Sts Cost      Prio.Nbr Type
---------------- ---- --- --------- -------- --------
VLAN0010        Desg LRN 100       128.2    Shr
```

After about 10 to 15 seconds, the port transitions to the Forwarding state as shown below:

```
Sw1#show spanning-tree interface fastethernet0/2

Vlan              Role Sts Cost      Prio.Nbr Type
---------------- ---- --- ---------- -------- --------
VLAN0010          Desg FWD 100        128.2    Shr
```

Possible interface types (according to Cisco) include:

- P2p/Shr—The interface is considered a point-to-point (shared) interface by Spanning Tree.
- Edge—The port is configured as an STP edge port (either globally using the default command or directly on the interface) and no BPDU has been received.
- Network—The port is configured as an STP network port (either globally using the default command or directly on the interface).
- *ROOT_Inc, *LOOP_Inc, *PVID_Inc, *BA_Inc, and *TYPE_Inc—The port is in a broken state (BKN*) for an inconsistency. The broken states are Root Inconsistent, Loopguard Inconsistent, PVID Inconsistent, Bridge Assurance Inconsistent, or Type Inconsistent.

LAB 67: CONFIGURING SPANNING TREE PROTOCOL ROOT BRIDGES MANUALLY

Lab Objective:
The objective of this lab exercise is for you to learn and understand how to manually configure a switch to become the root bridge for a particular VLAN. By default, all VLANs have a priority of 32,768 (plus the VLAN number), which are used to determine the Spanning Tree root bridge.

Lab Purpose:
STP root bridge configuration is a fundamental skill. It is always recommended that the root bridge be manually configured to ensure that the Layer 2 network is deterministic. As a Cisco engineer, as well as in the Cisco CCNA exam, you will be expected to know how to configure a switch as a root bridge.

Certification Level:
This lab is suitable for ICND2 and CCNA certification exam preparation.

Lab Difficulty:
This lab has a difficulty rating of 6/10.

Readiness Assessment:
When you are ready for your certification exam, you should complete this lab in no more than 15 minutes.

Lab Topology:
Please use the following topology to complete this lab exercise:

VLAN NUMBER	VLAN NAME	PORT
2010	SALES	FastEthernet0/5
2020	MANAGERS	FastEthernet0/6
2030	ENGINEERS	FastEthernet0/7
2040	SUPPORT	FastEthernet0/8

Task 1:

Based on the topology above, configure a hostname on Sw1 and Sw2 and configure the VLANs listed.

Task 2:

Configure the switches to support the VLANs listed in the topology. Configure the VLANs and check that they are visible on both switches. Manually set the interface to trunk on one side.

Task 3:

Configure Sw1 as the root bridge for VLANs 2010 and 2030. Configure Sw2 as the root bridge for VLANS 2020 and 2040. Use the second non-zero priority value for root bridges.

Task 4:

Verify your configuration with the appropriate show commands.

LAB 67: CONFIGURATION AND VERIFICATION

Task 1:

For reference information on configuring hostnames, please refer to earlier labs.

Task 2:

> **NOTE:** By default, Cisco switches are VTP servers. However, to configure the extended range of VLANs (i.e., VLANs 1006 and above), you need to configure the switch as a VTP Transparent switch. For reference information on Transparent mode and extended VLANs, please refer to earlier labs.

Task 3:

> **NOTE:** Spanning Tree priority values increment in amounts of 4096. The allowed values are illustrated on the switch if you issue an illegal value:

```
Sw1(config)#spanning-tree vlan2010 priority 4192
% Bridge Priority must be in increments of 4096.
% Allowed values are:
  0    4096  8192  12288 16384 20480 24576 28672
  32768 36864 40960 45056 49152 53248 57344 61440

Sw1(config)#spanning-tree vlan2010 priority 8192
Sw1(config)#spanning-tree vlan2030 priority 8192

Sw2(config)#spanning-tree vlan2020 priority 8192
Sw2(config)#spanning-tree vlan2040 priority 8192
```

Task 4:

> **NOTE:** Verify the same for VLAN2030 on Sw1, as well as for VLANs 2020 and 2040 on Sw2. In addition, you can also issue the show spanning-tree root command (it won't work on Packet Tracer) to view the Spanning Tree root bridge for all VLANs in the domain. This is illustrated below:

```
Sw1#show spanning-tree root

                                 Root Hello Max Fwd
Vlan                Root ID      Cost  Time Age Dly  Root Port
----------------   --------------------  ----- ----- --- ---  ----------
VLAN2010           10202 000d.bd06.4100    0    2   20  15

Sw1#show spanning-tree vlan2010

VLAN2010
  Spanning tree enabled protocol ieee
```

```
Root ID      Priority    10202
             Address     000d.bd06.4100
             This bridge is the root
             Hello Time   2 sec  Max Age 20 sec  Forward Delay 15 sec

Bridge ID    Priority    10202  (priority 8192 sys-id-ext 2010)
             Address     000d.bd06.4100
             Hello Time   2 sec  Max Age 20 sec  Forward Delay 15 sec
             Aging Time 15

Interface        Role Sts Cost       Prio.Nbr Type
---------------- ---- --- ---------- -------- ------------------------
Fa0/1            Desg FWD 100        128.2    Shr
```

LAB 68: CONFIGURING SPANNING TREE PROTOCOL ROOT BRIDGES USING THE IOS MACRO

Lab Objective:

The objective of this lab exercise is to use the macro in Cisco IOS to configure a switch to automatically adjust its Spanning Tree priority for a particular VLAN, or group of VLANs, ensuring that it is the most likely elected root bridge.

Lab Purpose:

VLAN root bridge configuration is a fundamental skill. It is always recommended that the root bridge be manually configured to ensure that the Layer 2 network is deterministic. However, the macro available in Cisco IOS can also be used. As a Cisco engineer, as well as in the Cisco CCNA exam, you will be expected to know how to configure a switch as a root bridge using the macro available in Cisco IOS.

Certification Level:

This lab is suitable for ICND2 and CCNA certification exam preparation.

Lab Difficulty:

This lab has a difficulty rating of 6/10.

Readiness Assessment:

When you are ready for your certification exam, you should complete this lab in no more than 15 minutes.

Lab Topology:

Please use the following topology to complete this lab exercise:

VLAN NUMBER	VLAN NAME	PORT
2010	SALES	FastEthernet0/5
2020	MANAGERS	FastEthernet0/6
2030	ENGINEERS	FastEthernet0/7
2040	SUPPORT	FastEthernet0/8

Task 1:
In preparation for VLAN configuration, configure a hostname on Sw1 and Sw2 and configure the VLANs depicted in the topology above.

Task 2:
Configure the switches to support the VLANs listed in the topology. Configure the VLANs and check that they are visible on both switches. Configure FastEthernet0/1 on both switches as a trunk.

Task 3:
Configure Sw1 as the root bridge for VLANs 2010 and 2030. Configure Sw2 as the root bridge for VLANS 2020 and 2040. Configure the switches to automatically update their priorities as follows:

   a) Sw1 will always be the root bridge for VLANs 2010 and 2030 and Sw2 will always be the backup root bridge for those VLANs.
   b) Sw2 will always be the root bridge for VLANs 2020 and 2040 and Sw1 will always be the backup root bridge for those VLANs.

Task 4:
Verify your configurations with the appropriate commands.

LAB 68: CONFIGURATION AND VERIFICATION

Task 1:

For reference information on configuring hostnames, please refer to earlier labs.

Task 2:

> **NOTE:** By default, Cisco switches are VTP servers. However, to configure the extended range of VLANs (i.e., VLANs 1006 and above), you need to configure the switch as a VTP Transparent switch.

For reference information on Transparent mode, trunks, and extended VLANs, please refer to earlier labs.

Task 3:

> **NOTE:** The `spanning-tree vlan <number> root primary` command is a macro that allows Catalyst Switches to automatically configure a Spanning Tree priority value that ensures that the switch this command is issued on will most likely be elected as root bridge. The `spanning-tree vlan <number> root secondary` is a macro that allows Catalyst Switches to automatically configure a Spanning Tree priority value that ensures that the switch this command is issued on will most likely be elected as backup root bridge.

```
Sw1#conf t
Enter configuration commands, one per line. End with CTRL/Z.
Sw1(config)#spanning-tree vlan2010 root primary
Sw1(config)#spanning-tree vlan2030 root primary
Sw1(config)#spanning-tree vlan2020 root secondary
Sw1(config)#spanning-tree vlan2040 root secondary
Sw1(config)#end
Sw1#

Sw1#conf t
Enter configuration commands, one per line. End with CTRL/Z.
Sw2(config)#spanning-tree vlan2020 root primary
Sw2(config)#spanning-tree vlan2040 root primary
Sw2(config)#spanning-tree vlan2010 root secondary
Sw2(config)#spanning-tree vlan2030 root secondary
Sw2(config)#end
Sw2#
```

Task 4:

> **NOTE:** Verify the same for VLAN 2030 on Sw1, as well as for VLANs 2020 and 2040 on Sw2. In addition, you can also issue the `show spanning-tree root` command to view the Spanning Tree root bridge for all VLANs in the domain. This is illustrated below:

```
Sw1#show spanning-tree root

                                      Root Hello Max Fwd
Vlan                    Root ID       Cost Time Age Dly  Root Port
----------------  --------------------  ------ ----- --- ---  ----------
VLAN2010          26586 000d.bd06.4100      0    2   20  15

Sw1#show spanning-tree vlan2010

VLAN2010
  Spanning tree enabled protocol ieee
  Root ID     Priority    26586
              Address     000d.bd06.4100
              This bridge is the root
              Hello Time   2 sec  Max Age 20 sec  Forward Delay 15 sec

  Bridge ID   Priority    26586  (priority 24576 sys-id-ext 2010)
              Address     000d.bd06.4100
              Hello Time   2 sec  Max Age 20 sec  Forward Delay 15 sec
              Aging Time 300

Interface        Role Sts Cost      Prio.Nbr Type
----------------  ---- --- --------  -------- ------------------------
Fa0/1            Desg FWD 100        128.2    Shr
```

> **NOTE:** Notice the strange priority value. This means that there is no switch in the switched LAN that has a priority that is numerically less than the manually set value of 28672. To test the macro, change the priority of VLAN2010 on switch Sw2 to 20480 and then check the priority on Sw1 again. Try the reverse and change priorities on Sw1. You should see the Sw2 Spanning Tree priority values change.

LAB 69: ASSIGNING MULTIPLE INSTANCES TO A VLAN SIMULTANEOUSLY

Lab Objective:
The objective of this lab exercise is to understand how to configure many interfaces that share the same common configuration at the same time without having to do them one at a time

Lab Purpose:
Configuring multiple interfaces on a switch at the same time is a fundamental skill. Some high-end Cisco Catalyst Switches can have in excess of 500 interfaces that may need to be configured almost identically. In such situations, configuring a single interface at a time would not be acceptable. As a Cisco engineer, as well as in the Cisco CCNA exam, you will be expected to know how to configure multiple switch interfaces at the same time using user-defined macros.

Certification Level:
This lab is suitable for CCNA certification exam preparation.

Lab Difficulty:
This lab has a difficulty rating of 4/10.

Readiness Assessment:
When you are ready for your certification exam, you should complete this lab in no more than 5 minutes.

Lab Topology:
You can use any stand-alone (single) switch to complete this lab. This lab is strictly about configuration syntax.

Task 1:
Configure a hostname of your liking on your lab switch, which should have at least 24 ports.

Task 2:
Configure VLAN10 named SALES on the switch and VLAN20 named TECH on the switch.

Task 3:

To simplify configuration tasks, you should create a macro called VLAN_10_Macro for configuring ports FastEthernet0/1 to FastEthernet0/12 that will be in VLAN10 and a macro called VLAN_20_Macro for configuring ports FastEthernet0/13 to FastEthernet0/24 that will be in VLAN20.

> **NOTE:** Because this lab is for practicing macro configuration, do NOT use the `interface range` command.

Task 4:

Configure interfaces FastEthernet0/1 to 12 and FastEthernet0/13 to 24 in VLAN10 and VLAN20, respectively, using the macro. These ports should be configured as access ports.

Task 5:

Verify your configuration using the appropriate commands in Cisco IOS.

LAB 69: CONFIGURATION AND VERIFICATION

Task 1:

For reference information on configuring hostnames, please refer to earlier labs.

Task 2:

For reference information on configuring standard VLANs, please refer to earlier labs.

Task 3:

```
Sw1#config t
Enter configuration commands, one per line.  End with CTRL/Z.
Sw1(config)#define interface-range VLAN_10_Macro FastEthernet 0/1 - 12
Sw1(config)#define interface-range VLAN_20_Macro FastEthernet 0/13-24
Sw1(config)#^Z
Sw1#
```

Task 4:

```
Sw1#conf t
Enter configuration commands, one per line.  End with CNTL/Z.
Sw1(config)#interface range macro VLAN_10_Macro
Sw1(config-if-range)#switchport mode access
Sw1(config-if-range)#switchport access vlan10
Sw1(config-if-range)#exit
Sw1(config)#interface range macro VLAN_20_Macro
Sw1(config-if-range)#switchport mode access
Sw1(config-if-range)#switchport access vlan20
Sw1(config-if-range)#end
Sw1#
```

Task 5:

```
Sw1#show vlan brief

VLAN Name                             Status     Ports
---- -------------------------------- ---------  -------------------------------
1    default                          active     Gi0/1, Gi0/2
2    VLAN0002                         active
10   SALES                            active     Fa0/1, Fa0/2, Fa0/3, Fa0/4
                                                 Fa0/5, Fa0/6, Fa0/7, Fa0/8
                                                 Fa0/9, Fa0/10, Fa0/11, Fa0/12
20   MANAGERS                         active     Fa0/13, Fa0/14, Fa0/15, Fa0/16
                                                 Fa0/17, Fa0/18, Fa0/19, Fa0/20
                                                 Fa0/21, Fa0/22, Fa0/23, Fa0/24

[Output Truncated]
```

LAB 70: CONFIGURING SPANNING TREE PROTOCOL FOR ACCESS PORTS (PORTFAST)

Lab Objective:
The objective of this lab exercise is to configure access ports to transition immediately to the Forwarding state, instead of going through the typical Spanning Tree states (i.e., Blocking, Listening, Learning, etc.).

Lab Purpose:
Bypassing default Spanning Tree port states is a fundamental skill. By default, it can take up to 60 seconds for a switchport to transition to the Forwarding state and begin forwarding frames. In most cases, this is acceptable; however, on a network with DHCP clients, for example, that need IP addressing information from a DHCP server, this duration may cause these clients to think that the DHCP server is unavailable.

Certification Level:
This lab is suitable for both ICND2 and CCNA certification exam preparation.

Lab Difficulty:
This lab has a difficulty rating of 4/10.

Readiness Assessment:
When you are ready for your certification exam, you should complete this lab in no more than 10 minutes.

Lab Topology:
Please use any single switch for this lab. This lab is strictly about validating command syntax.

Task 1:
Configure a hostname of your liking on your switch, which should have at least 12 ports.

Task 2:
Configure VLAN10 named SALES on the switch.

Task 3:

Configure ports FastEthernet0/1 and FastEthernet0/2 using the `interface range` command so that Spanning Tree Protocol transitions these interfaces into a Forwarding state immediately. These interfaces should also be configured as access ports in VLAN10.

Task 4:

Verify your configuration using the appropriate commands in Cisco IOS.

LAB 70: CONFIGURATION AND VERIFICATION

Task 1:

For reference information on configuring hostnames, please refer to earlier labs.

Task 2:

For reference information on configuring and verifying VLANs, please refer to earlier labs.

Task 3:

```
Sw1#conf t
Enter configuration commands, one per line.  End with CTRL/Z.
Sw1(config)#interface range fastethernet0/1 - 2
Sw1(config-if-range)#switchport mode access
Sw1(config-if-range)#switchport access vlan10
Sw1(config-if-range)#spanning-tree portfast
%Warning: portfast should only be enabled on ports connected to a
single host. Connecting hubs, concentrators, switches, bridges, etc...
to this interface  when portfast is enabled, can cause temporary
bridging loops. Use with CAUTION

%Portfast will be configured in 2 interfaces due to the range command
 but will only have effect when the interfaces are in a non-trunking
mode.
Sw1(config-if-range)#end
Sw1#

Task 4:
Sw1#show spanning-tree interface fastethernet 0/2 detail
 Port 2 (FastEthernet0/2) of VLAN0010 is forwarding
   Port path cost 100, Port priority 128, Port Identifier 128.2.
   Designated root has priority 4106, address 000d.bd06.4100
   Designated bridge has priority 4106, address 000d.bd06.4100
   Designated port id is 128.2, designated path cost 0
   Timers: message age 0, forward delay 0, hold 0
   Number of transitions to forwarding state: 1
   The port is in the portfast mode
   Link type is shared by default
   BPDU: sent 81, received 0
```

The command above won't work on Packet Tracer so use a show run instead if you don't have access to a live switch.

LAB 71: ENABLING RAPID PER-VLAN SPANNING TREE

Lab Objective:
The objective of this lab exercise is for you to learn and understand how to configure RPVST. By default, RPVST converges much faster than traditional STP.

Lab Purpose:
RPVST configuration is a fundamental skill. As a Cisco engineer, as well as in the Cisco CCNA exam, you will be expected to know how to configure RPVST.

Certification Level:
This lab is suitable for both ICND2 and CCNA certification exam preparation.

Lab Difficulty:
This lab has a difficulty rating of 4/10.

Readiness Assessment:
When you are ready for your certification exam, you should complete this lab in no more than 10 minutes.

Lab Topology:
Please use the following topology to complete this lab exercise:

VLAN NUMBER	VLAN NAME	PORT
10	SALES	FastEthernet0/5
20	MANAGERS	FastEthernet0/6
30	ENGINEERS	FastEthernet0/7
40	SUPPORT	FastEthernet0/8

Task 1:

Configure a hostname on Sw1 and Sw2 as illustrated in the topology diagram above.

Task 2:

Configure Sw1 as a VTP server and configure Sw2 as a VTP client. Both switches should be in the VTP domain named CISCO. Secure VTP messages with the password CISCO.

Task 3:

Configure and verify FastEthernet0/1 between Sw1 and Sw2 as an 802.1Q trunk.

Task 4:

Configure and verify VLANs 10, 20, 30, and 40 on Sw1 with the names provided above. Validate that these VLANs are still propagated to Sw2 after VTP has been secured.

Task 5:

Verify that the switches are running in Per-VLAN Spanning Tree mode. This is the default mode for switches.

Task 6:

Update your switch to a Spanning Tree mode that ensures the fastest convergence for the Layer 2 network and verify your configuration.

LAB 71: CONFIGURATION AND VERIFICATION

Task 1:

For reference information on configuring hostnames, please refer to earlier labs.

Task 2:

> **NOTE:** By default, Cisco switches are VTP servers so no configuration is necessary for server mode on Sw1. This can be verified using the show vtp status command. However, you do need to configure the domain.

For reference information on configuring the VTP mode and password, please refer to earlier labs.

Task 3:

For reference information on configuring and verifying trunks, please refer to earlier labs.

Task 4:

For reference information on configuring and verifying VLANs, please refer to earlier labs.

> **NOTE:** Make sure that the MD5 digest at the end of the output of the show vtp status command is the same when VTP passwords have been configured on switches within the same VTP domain.

Task 5:

```
Sw1#show spanning-tree summary
Switch is in pvst mode
Root bridge for: VLAN0010, VLAN0020, VLAN0030, VLAN0040
EtherChannel misconfiguration guard is enabled
Extended system ID      is enabled
Portfast                is disabled by default
PortFast BPDU Guard      is disabled by default
Portfast BPDU Filter  is disabled by default
Loopguard               is disabled by default
UplinkFast              is disabled
BackboneFast            is disabled
Pathcost method used is short
```

Name	Blocking	Listening	Learning	Forwarding	STP Active
VLAN0010	0	0	0	1	1
VLAN0020	0	0	0	1	1
VLAN0030	0	0	0	1	1

VLAN0040	0	0	0	1	1
4 vlans	0	0	0	4	4

Task 6:
```
Sw1#conf t
Enter configuration commands, one per line.  End with CTRL/Z.
Sw1(config)#spanning-tree mode rapid-pvst
Sw1(config)#^Z
Sw1#
Sw1#show spanning-tree summary
```
Switch is in rapid-pvst mode
```
Root bridge for: VLAN0010, VLAN0020, VLAN0030, VLAN0040
EtherChannel misconfiguration guard is enabled
Extended system ID   is enabled
Portfast             is disabled by default
PortFast BPDU Guard  is disabled by default
Portfast BPDU Filter is disabled by default
Loopguard            is disabled by default
UplinkFast           is disabled
BackboneFast         is disabled
Pathcost method used is short
```

Name	Blocking	Listening	Learning	Forwarding	STP Active
VLAN0010	0	0	0	1	1
VLAN0020	0	0	0	1	1
VLAN0030	0	0	0	1	1
VLAN0040	0	0	0	1	1
4 vlans	0	0	0	4	4

NOTE: RPVST enables the fastest convergence of Layer 2 switched networks.

LAB 72: CONFIGURE, VERIFY, AND TROUBLESHOOT ETHERCHANNELS (STATIC/PAGP/LACP)

Lab Objective:
The objective of this lab exercise is for you to learn and understand how to use redundant links between Cisco switches in order to build port channels.

Lab Purpose:
Understanding how to enable the different port-channel protocols on a Layer 2 network is a must for every engineer to know. As a Cisco engineer, as well as in the Cisco CCNA exam, you will be expected to know how to configure port-channels using LACP, PAgP or the ON mechanism.

Certification Level:
This lab is suitable for ICND2 and CCNA certification exam preparation.

Lab Difficulty:
This lab has a difficulty rating of 7/10.

Readiness Assessment:
When you are ready for your certification exam, you should complete this lab in no more than 20 minutes.

Lab Topology:
Please use the following topology to complete this lab exercise:

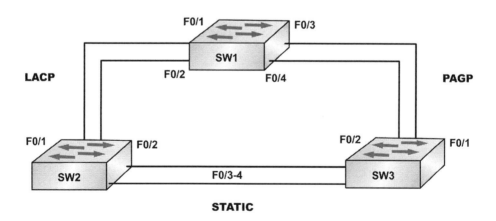

Task 1:
Configure the hostnames on Sw1, Sw2, and Sw3 as illustrated in the topology.

Task 2:
Create two VLANs on every switch as follows:

- VLAN10: Data
- VLAN20: Management

Task 3:
Configure each switchport shown in the diagram as a trunk and make sure all VLANs are allowed.

Task 4:
Start configuring the port channels as follows:

- Links between Sw1 and Sw2: Port channel 1/Protocol LACP
- Links between Sw1 and Sw3: Port channel 2/Protocol PAgP
- Links between Sw2 and Sw3: Port channel 3/Use the ON mode

NOTE: You can select which side is active/passive or desirable/auto.

Task 5:
Make sure each port channel is up and running by issuing the following command on each switch:

- `show etherchannel summary`

LAB 72: CONFIGURATION AND VERIFICATION

Task 1:

For reference information on configuring hostnames, please refer to earlier labs.

Task 2:

For reference information on configuring VLANs, please refer to earlier labs.

Task 3:

```
SW1(config)#int range fa0/1-4
SW1(config-if-range)#switchport mode trunk
SW1(config-if-range)#switchport trunk allow vlan all
SW1(config-if-range)#exit
SW1(config)#

SW2(config)#int range fa0/1-4
SW2(config-if-range)#switchport mode trunk
SW2(config-if-range)#switchport trunk allow vlan all
SW2(config-if-range)#exit
SW2(config)#

SW3(config)#int range fa0/1-4
SW3(config-if-range)#switchport mode trunk
SW3(config-if-range)#switchport trunk allow vlan all
SW3(config-if-range)#exit
SW3(config)#
```

Task 4:

```
SW1(config)#interface range fa0/1-2
SW1(config-if-range)#channel-group 1 mode active
SW1(config-if-range)#exit
SW1(config)#

SW1(config)#interface range fa0/3-4
SW1(config-if-range)#channel-group 2 mode desirable
SW1(config-if-range)#exit
SW1(config)#

SW2(config)#interface range fa0/1-2
SW2(config-if-range)#channel-group 1 mode passive
SW2(config-if-range)#exit
SW2(config)#

SW2(config)#interface range fa0/3-4
SW2(config-if-range)#channel-group 3 mode on
SW2(config-if-range)#exit
SW2(config)#
```

```
SW3(config)#interface range fa0/1-2
SW3(config-if-range)#channel-group 2 mode auto
SW3(config-if-range)#exit
SW3(config)#

SW3(config)#interface range fa0/3-4
SW3(config-if-range)#channel-group 3 mode on
SW3(config-if-range)#exit
SW3(config)#
```

Task 5:

```
SW1#show etherchannel summary
Flags:  D - down        P - in port-channel
        I - stand-alone s - suspended
        H - Hot-standby (LACP only)
        R - Layer3      S - Layer2
        U - in use      f - failed to allocate aggregator
        u - unsuitable for bundling
        w - waiting to be aggregated
        d - default port

Number of channel-groups in use: 2
Number of aggregators: 2

Group  Port-channel  Protocol    Ports
------+-------------+-----------+------------------------------------

1      Po1(SU)          LACP    Fa0/1(P) Fa0/2(P)
2      Po2(SU)          PAgP    Fa0/3(P) Fa0/4(P)

SW2#show etherchannel summary
Flags:  D - down        P - in port-channel
        I - stand-alone s - suspended
        H - Hot-standby (LACP only)
        R - Layer3      S - Layer2
        U - in use      f - failed to allocate aggregator
        u - unsuitable for bundling
        w - waiting to be aggregated
        d - default port

Number of channel-groups in use: 2
Number of aggregators: 2

Group  Port-channel  Protocol    Ports
------+-------------+-----------+------------------------------------

1      Po1(SU)          LACP    Fa0/1(P) Fa0/2(P)
3      Po3(SU)          -       Fa0/3(D) Fa0/4(P)
```

```
SW3#show etherchannel summary
Flags:  D - down          P - in port-channel
        I - stand-alone  s - suspended
        H - Hot-standby (LACP only)
        R - Layer3        S - Layer2
        U - in use        f - failed to allocate aggregator
        u - unsuitable for bundling
        w - waiting to be aggregated
        d - default port

Number of channel-groups in use: 2
Number of aggregators: 2

Group  Port-channel  Protocol    Ports
------+-------------+-----------+------------------------------------

2      Po2(SU)          PAgP     Fa0/1(P) Fa0/2(P)
3      Po3(SU)            -       Fa0/3(D) Fa0/4(P)
```

LAB 73: CONFIGURING 802.1X SECURITY

Lab Objective:
The objective of this lab exercise is for you to learn how to configure 802.1X in your switch infrastructure.

Lab Purpose:
Understanding how to enable and configure 802.1X in your switch infrastructure is a core security topic when you think about security in Layer 2 of your network. As a Cisco engineer, as well as in the Cisco CCNA exam, you will be expected to know how to configure 802.1X.

Certification Level:
This lab is suitable for ICND2 and CCNA certification exam preparation.

Lab Difficulty:
This lab has a difficulty rating of 6/10.

Readiness Assessment:
When you are ready for your certification exam, you should complete this lab in no more than 10 minutes.

Lab Topology:
Please use the following topology to complete this lab exercise. This lab will not work on Packet Tracer, so you will need a live switch that supports 802.1X:

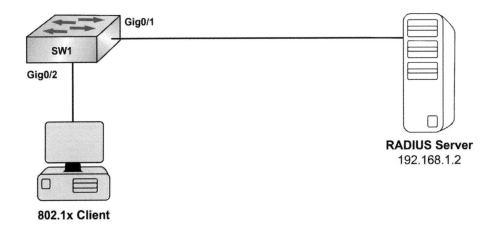

> **NOTE:** We will only focus on the switch side of the configuration (the server and clients are already configured).

Task 1:

Configure the hostnames on Switch1 as illustrated in the topology.

Task 2:

Enable AAA authentication on Sw1 and configure the RADIUS server using 1812 and 1813 for authentication and accounting, respectively (use CCNA as the key between the server and the switch).

Task 3:

Configure AAA authentication for 802.1X using the RADIUS server already defined (use default as the authentication method list).

Task 4:

Enable 8021.X globally, and then make sure that the Gigabit0/2 interface runs EAPoL (802.1X).

Task 5:

Make sure that the configuration is up and working by running the command below after a user connects to the Gigabit0/2 port on Sw1.

- `show dot1x interface gig0/2`

LAB 73: CONFIGURATION AND VERIFICATION

Task 1:

For reference information on configuring hostnames, please refer to earlier labs.

Task 2:

```
SW1(config)#aaa new-model
SW1(config)#radius-server host 192.168.1.2 auth-port 1812 acct-port
1813 key CCNA
SW1(config)#exit
```

Task 3:

```
SW1(config)#aaa authentication dot1x default group radius
```

Task 4:

```
SW1(config)#dot1x system-auth-control
SW1(config)#interface gig0/2
SW1(config-if)#switchport mode access
SW1(config-if)#dot1x port-control auto
```

Task 5:

```
SW1#show dot1x interface gig0/2
Dot1x Info for GigabitEthernet0/2
---------------------------------
PAE = AUTHENTICATOR
PortControl = AUTO
ControlDirection = In
HostMode = SINGLE HOST
ReAuthentication = Disabled
QuietPeriod = 60
ServerTimeout = 30
SuppTimeout = 30
ReAuthPeriod = 3600 (Locally configured)
ReAuthMax = 2
MaxReq = 2
TxPeriod = 30
RateLimitPeriod = 0
```

Your output may differ from mine slightly.

LAB 74: CONFIGURING DHCP SNOOPING

Lab Objective:
The objective of this lab exercise is for you to learn how to implement DHCP snooping in your network to protect your DHCP environment.

Lab Purpose:
DHCP snooping is a feature that enables a network to trust only the required DHCP servers in the network to prevent rogue DHCP servers from providing malicious information. As a Cisco engineer, as well as in the Cisco CCNA exam, you will be expected to know how to configure DHCP snooping in your network.

Certification Level:
This lab is suitable for ICND2 and CCNA certification exam preparation.

Lab Difficulty:
This lab has a difficulty rating of 6/10.

Readiness Assessment:
When you are ready for your certification exam, you should complete this lab in no more than 10 minutes.

Lab Topology:
Please use the following topology to complete this lab exercise (LAN 192.168.1.0/24 belongs to VLAN1):

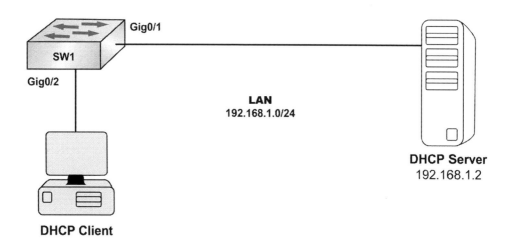

NOTE: We will only focus on the switch side of the configuration (the server and clients are already configured). Packet Tracer will let you enable DHCP (and a pool) on a server and allocate the IP address shown. For the client, you can configure it to use DHCP to obtain IP information.

Task 1:
Configure the hostnames on Sw1 as illustrated in the topology.

Task 2:
Enable DHCP snooping globally and then on the specific VLAN (1).

Task 3:
Make sure that Sw1 trusts the connection to the DHCP server.

Task 4:
Check the DHCP status by running the following commands:

- `show ip dhcp snooping`
- `show ip dhcp snooping binding` (Use this command after a PC requests an address via DHCP.)

LAB 74: CONFIGURATION AND VERIFICATION

Task 1:

For reference information on configuring hostnames, please refer to earlier labs.

Task 2:
```
SW1(config)#ip dhcp snooping
SW1(config)#ip dhcp snooping vlan1
```

Task 3:
```
SW1(config)#interface gigabithethernet0/1
SW1(config-if)#ip dhcp snooping trust
```

Task 4:
```
SW1#show ip dhcp snooping
Switch DHCP snooping is enabled
DHCP snooping is configured on following VLANs: 1
Insertion of option 82 is enabled

Interface           Trusted Rate limit (pps)
------------------  ------- ----------------
Gigabitethernet0/1  yes     unlimited
Gigabitethernet0/2  no      unlimited

SW1#show ip dhcp snooping binding
Option 82 on untrusted port is not allowed
MacAddress       IpAddress      Lease(sec) Type    VLAN    Interface
00:12:34:81:21:9A 192.168.1.10  85545        dynamic  1
Gigabitethernet0/2
```

2.0 Routing Technologies

LAB 75: CONFIGURING OSPF ON POINT-TO-POINT NETWORKS

Lab Objective:
The objective of this lab exercise is for you to learn and understand how to enable Open Shortest Path First (OSPF) on point-to-point network types. These include High-level Data Link Control (HDLC) and point-to-point protocol (PPP).

Lab Purpose:
Enabling OSPF on point-to-point network types is a fundamental skill. OSPF is the most popular Interior Gateway Protocol (IGP) and it is imperative to understand how OSPF adjacencies are established on point-to-point network types. OSPF uses the concept of Areas. In order for two OSPF-enabled routers to establish an adjacency, they must reside in the same OSPF Area. Unlike EIGRP, which uses autonomous system numbers (ASNs), OSPF is enabled using a locally significant process ID. As a Cisco engineer, as well as in the Cisco CCNA exam, you will be expected to know how to enable OSPF on point-to-point network types.

Certification Level:
This lab is suitable for ICND2 and CCNA certification exam preparation.

Lab Difficulty:
This lab has a difficulty rating of 5/10.

Readiness Assessment:
When you are ready for your certification exam, you should complete this lab in no more than 10 minutes.

Lab Topology:

Please use the following topology to complete this lab exercise:

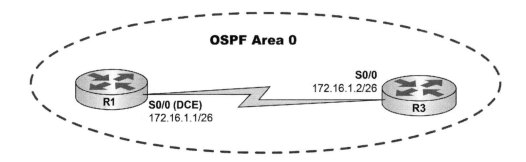

Task 1:

Configure the hostnames on R1 and R3 as illustrated in the topology.

Task 2:

Configure R1 S0/0, which is a DCE, to provide a clock rate of 768 Kbps to R3. Enable PPP on the link between R1 and R3 and configure the IP addresses illustrated in the topology (we will cover this in detail later so just copy my commands for now).

Task 3:

Enable OSPF in area 0 between R1 and R3. For R1, use OSPF process ID 1. For R3 use OSPF process ID 3. Verify that your OSPF adjacency has formed between R1 and R3. Also verify that the default network type for the PPP link between R1 and R3 is point-to-point.

LAB 75: CONFIGURATION AND VERIFICATION

Task 1:

For reference information on configuring hostnames, please refer to earlier labs.

Task 2:

```
R1#conf t
Enter configuration commands, one per line.  End with CTRL/Z.
R1(config)#int s0/0
R1(config-if)#clock rate 768000
R1(config-if)#encapsulation ppp
R1(config-if)#ip address 172.16.1.1 255.255.255.192
R1(config-if)#no shut
R1(config-if)#end
R1#

R3#conf t
Enter configuration commands, one per line.  End with CTRL/Z.
R3(config)#int s0/0
R3(config-if)#ip address 172.16.1.2 255.255.255.192
R3(config-if)#encap ppp
R3(config-if)#no shutdown
R3(config-if)#^Z
R3#

R1#ping 172.16.1.2

Type escape sequence to abort.
Sending 5, 100-byte ICMP Echos to 172.16.1.2, timeout is 2 seconds:
!!!!!
Success rate is 100 percent (5/5), round-trip min/avg/max = 4/4/4 ms
```

Task 3:

> **NOTE:** Unlike EIGRP configuration where wildcard masks following network statements are optional, in OSPF you MUST use a wildcard mask with your network statements. To determine the wildcard mask, you can simply subtract the network mask for the network on which you want to enable OSPF from the broadcast mask. This concept is illustrated in the subtraction table shown below:

Broadcast Mask	255	255	255	255
[minus] Subnet Mask	255	255	255	192
[equals] Wildcard Mask	0	0	0	63

In our example, the subnet mask of the 172.16.1.0/26 subnet is 255.255.255.192. If this is subtracted from the broadcast mask of 255.255.255.255, the result is 0.0.0.63, which is the wildcard mask we used to enable OSPF for this subnet. Take some time to practice configuring wildcard masks for different subnets.

```
R1#conf t
Enter configuration commands, one per line.  End with CTRL/Z.
R1(config)#router ospf 1
R1(config-router)#network 172.16.1.0 0.0.0.63 area 0
R1(config-router)#end
R1#

R3#conf t
Enter configuration commands, one per line.  End with CTRL/Z.
R3(config)#router ospf 3
R3(config-router)#network 172.16.1.0 0.0.0.63 area 0
R3(config-router)#^Z
R3#

R1#show ip ospf neighbor

Neighbor ID     Pri   State       Dead Time   Address        Interface
172.16.1.2        0   FULL/   -   00:00:36    172.16.1.2     Serial0/0

R1#show ip ospf interface serial0/0
Serial0/0 is up, line protocol is up
  Internet Address 172.16.1.1/26, Area 0
  Process ID 1, Router ID 172.16.1.1, Network Type POINT_TO_POINT,
Cost: 64
  Transmit Delay is 1 sec, State POINT_TO_POINT,
  Timer intervals configured, Hello 10, Dead 40, Wait 40, Retransmit 5
    oob-resync timeout 40
    Hello due in 00:00:06
  Index 1/1, flood queue length 0
  Next 0x0(0)/0x0(0)
  Last flood scan length is 1, maximum is 1
  Last flood scan time is 0 msec, maximum is 0 msec
  Neighbor Count is 1, Adjacent neighbor count is 1
    Adjacent with neighbor 172.16.1.2
  Suppress hello for 0 neighbor(s)
```

NOTE: When verifying OSPF adjacencies, always ensure that neighbors are in the FULL state for point-to-point networks. If they are in any other state, you will need to perform some troubleshooting to identify the root cause of the issue. Take a moment to look at the detail contained in the output of the show ip ospf interface serial0/0 command. From this output, we can determine that the OSPF network type is point-to-point (Network Type POINT_TO_POINT), the interface has an OSPF metric, or cost, of 64 (Cost: 64), and at the very bottom, there is one OSPF neighbor with which an OSPF adjacency has been created via this interface (Adjacent with neighbor 172.16.1.2).

LAB 76: CONFIGURING OSPF ON BROADCAST NETWORKS

Lab Objective:
The objective of this lab exercise is for you to learn and understand how to enable OSPF on broadcast network types. These include Ethernet and Token Ring (although you are not likely to encounter Token Ring).

Lab Purpose:
Enabling OSPF on broadcast network types is a fundamental skill. OSPF is the most popular Interior Gateway Protocol (IGP) and it is imperative to understand how OSPF adjacencies are established on broadcast network types. OSPF uses the concept of Areas. In order for two OSPF-enabled routers to establish an adjacency, they must reside in the same OSPF Area. Unlike EIGRP, which uses ASNs, OSPF is enabled using a locally significant process ID. As a Cisco engineer, as well as in the Cisco CCNA exam, you will be expected to know how to enable OSPF on point-to-point network types.

Certification Level:
This lab is suitable for ICND2 and CCNA certification exam preparation.

Lab Difficulty:
This lab has a difficulty rating of 5/10.

Readiness Assessment:
When you are ready for your certification exam, you should complete this lab in no more than 10 minutes.

Lab Topology:
Please use the following topology to complete this lab exercise:

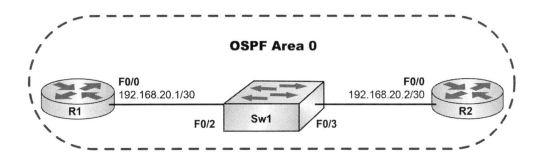

Task 1:

Configure hostnames on R1, R2, and Sw1 as illustrated in the topology.

Task 2:

Configure VLAN4010 on Sw1 and name it OSPF_VLAN. Assign ports FastEthernet0/2 and FastEthernet0/3 to this VLAN as access ports. Configure IP addresses on R1 and R2 FastEthernet0/0 interfaces and enable them.

Task 3:

Enable OSPF in area 0 between R1 and R2. For R1, use OSPF process ID 1, and for R2, use OSPF process ID 2. Verify that your OSPF adjacency has formed between R1 and R3. Also verify that the default network type for the Ethernet link between R1 and R2 is broadcast.

LAB 76: CONFIGURATION AND VERIFICATION

Task 1:

For reference information on configuring hostnames, please refer to earlier labs.

Task 2:

For reference information on configuring IP addressing, transparent switching, and extended VLANs, please refer to earlier labs.

Task 3:

```
R2#conf t
Enter configuration commands, one per line.  End with CTRL/Z.
R2(config)#router ospf 2
R2(config-router)#network 192.168.20.0 0.0.0.3 area 0
R2(config-router)#^Z
R2#

R1#conf t
Enter configuration commands, one per line.  End with CTRL/Z.
R1(config)#router ospf 1
R1(config-router)#network 192.168.20.0 0.0.0.3 area 0
R1(config-router)#end
R1#
Mar  1 01:53:20.828: %OSPF-5-ADJCHG: Process 1, Nbr 192.168.20.2 on
FastEthernet0/0 from LOADING to FULL, Loading Done

R1#show ip ospf neighbor

Neighbor ID    Pri   State       Dead Time   Address         Interface
192.168.20.2    1    FULL/DR     00:00:37    192.168.20.2    Fast 0/0

R1#show ip ospf interface fastethernet 0/0
FastEthernet0/0 is up, line protocol is up
  Internet Address 192.168.20.1/30, Area 0
  Process ID 1, Router ID 192.168.20.1, Network Type BROADCAST, Cost: 1
  Transmit Delay is 1 sec, State BDR, Priority 1
  Designated Router (ID) 192.168.20.2, Interface address 192.168.20.2
  Backup Designated router (ID) 192.168.20.1, Interface address
192.168.20.1
  Timer intervals configured, Hello 10, Dead 40, Wait 40, Retransmit 5
    oob-resync timeout 40
    Hello due in 00:00:04
  Index 1/1, flood queue length 0
  Next 0x0(0)/0x0(0)
  Last flood scan length is 1, maximum is 1
  Last flood scan time is 0 msec, maximum is 0 msec
  Neighbor Count is 1, Adjacent neighbor count is 1
    Adjacent with neighbor 192.168.20.2  (Designated Router)
  Suppress hello for 0 neighbor(s)
```

NOTE: On broadcast and non-broadcast multi-access networks, OSPF elects a designated router and a backup designated router for the subnet. When you are verifying OSPF adjacencies on these network types, make sure that the state is either `FULL/DR`, `FULL/BDR`, or `FULL/DROTHER`. The output of the `show ip ospf interface` command shows that the elected DR is R2, `Designated Router (ID) 192.168.20.2`, and that R1 is the BDR, `Backup Designated router (ID) 192.168.20.1`.

LAB 77: CONFIGURING THE OSPF ROUTER ID MANUALLY

Lab Objective:
The objective of this lab exercise is for you to learn and understand how to manually configure the OSPF router ID.

Lab Purpose:
Manually configuring the OSPF router ID is a fundamental skill. By default, if only physical interfaces are configured on a router, the highest IP address of those interfaces is used as the OSPF router ID. However, if both Loopback and physical interfaces are configured, then the Loopback interfaces are preferred when Cisco IOS selects the router ID for OSPF. However, the recommended method to select an OSPF router ID is to manually configure it. As a Cisco engineer, as well as in the Cisco CCNA exam, you will be expected to know how to manually configure an OSPF router ID.

Certification Level:
This lab is suitable for ICND2 and CCNA certification exam preparation.

Lab Difficulty:
This lab has a difficulty rating of 5/10.

Readiness Assessment:
When you are ready for your certification exam, you should complete this lab in no more than 10 minutes.

Lab Topology:
Please use the following topology to complete this lab exercise:

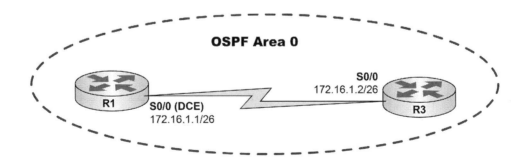

Task 1:

Configure hostnames on R1 and R3 as illustrated in the topology.

Task 2:

Configure R1 S0/0, which is a DCE, to provide a clock rate of 768 Kbps to R3. Configure the IP addresses on the Serial interfaces of R1 and R3 as illustrated in the topology.

Task 3:

Enable OSPF in area 0 between R1 and R3. For R1, use OSPF process ID 1. For R3, use OSPF process ID 3. Verify that your OSPF adjacency has formed between R1 and R3. Make a mental note of the OSPF router ID being used at this time after the adjacency between R1 and R3 has been established.

Task 4:

Manually configure OSPF router ID 1.1.1.1 on R1 and 3.3.3.3 on R3. Reset the OSPF process on R1 and R3 by issuing the `clear ip ospf process` command. Verify that the OSPF adjacency has been re-established between R1 and R3. Verify that the OSPF neighbor IP addresses are now showing as the manually configured router IDs instead of the physical interface IP addresses.

LAB 77: CONFIGURATION AND VERIFICATION

Task 1:

For reference information on configuring hostnames, please refer to earlier labs.

Task 2:

For reference information on configuring IP addressing, please refer to earlier labs.

Task 3:

```
R1#config t
Enter configuration commands, one per line.  End with CTRL/Z.
R1(config)#router ospf 1
R1(config-router)#network 172.16.1.0 0.0.0.63 area 0
R1(config-router)#^Z
R1#

R3#conf t
Enter configuration commands, one per line.  End with CTRL/Z.
R3(config)#router ospf 3
R3(config-router)#network 172.16.1.0 0.0.0.63 area 0
R3(config-router)#end
*Mar  1 01:51:39.406: %OSPF-5-ADJCHG: Process 3, Nbr 192.168.1.1 on
Serial0/0 from LOADING to FULL, Loading Done

R1#show ip ospf neighbor detail
 Neighbor 172.16.3.3, interface address 172.16.1.2
    In the area 0 via interface Serial0/0
    Neighbor priority is 0, State is FULL, 12 state changes
    DR is 0.0.0.0 BDR is 0.0.0.0
    Options is 0x52
    LLS Options is 0x1 (LR)
    Dead timer due in 00:00:35
    Neighbor is up for 00:01:04
    Index 1/1,retransmission queue length 0,number of retransmission 1
    First 0x0(0)/0x0(0) Next 0x0(0)/0x0(0)
    Last retransmission scan length is 1, maximum is 1
    Last retransmission scan time is 0 msec, maximum is 0 msec

R3#show ip ospf neighbor detail
 Neighbor 192.168.1.1, interface address 172.16.1.1
    In the area 0 via interface Serial0/0
    Neighbor priority is 0, State is FULL, 6 state changes
    DR is 0.0.0.0 BDR is 0.0.0.0
    Options is 0x52
    LLS Options is 0x1 (LR)
    Dead timer due in 00:00:39
    Neighbor is up for 00:00:48
    Index 1/1,retransmission queue length 0,number of retransmission 1
```

```
First 0x0(0)/0x0(0) Next 0x0(0)/0x0(0)
Last retransmission scan length is 1, maximum is 1
Last retransmission scan time is 0 msec, maximum is 0 msec
```

> **NOTE:** The `show ip ospf neighbor [detail]` command provides detailed information on OSPF neighbors. It provides the neighbor router ID as well as the interface on which the neighbor was discovered, among other things. In addition, it will also provide the IP address of the routers that are DR and BDR, respectively, on broadcast or NBMA network types. Familiarize yourself with the information provided by this command.

Task 4:
```
R1#conf t
Enter configuration commands, one per line.  End with CTRL/Z.
R1(config)#router ospf 1
R1(config-router)#router-id 1.1.1.1
```
Reload or use "`clear ip ospf process`" **command, for this to take effect**
```
R1(config-router)#end
R1#

R3#conf t
Enter configuration commands, one per line.  End with CTRL/Z.
R3(config)#router ospf 3
R3(config-router)#router-id 3.3.3.3
Reload or use "clear ip ospf process" command, for this to take effect
R3(config-router)#end
R3#
R3#clear ip ospf process
Reset ALL OSPF processes? [no]: yes
*Mar  1 01:58:27.875: %OSPF-5-ADJCHG: Process 3, Nbr 1.1.1.1 on
Serial0/0 from FULL to DOWN, Neighbor Down: Interface down or detached
*Mar  1 01:58:27.959: %OSPF-5-ADJCHG: Process 3, Nbr 1.1.1.1 on
Serial0/0 from LOADING to FULL, Loading Done
```

> **NOTE:** Whenever you manually change the OSPF router ID for an established OSPF adjacency, the change is not immediate and you either have to reboot the router or reset the OSPF process as indicated in the message that is printed on the console when you configured the router ID on R3:

```
Reload or use "clear ip ospf process" command, for this to take effect
```

After resetting the OSPF process, a new adjacency is re-established and both routers use the configured router IDs.

```
R1#show ip ospf neighbor

Neighbor ID     Pri   State         Dead Time   Address        Interface
```

```
3.3.3.3            0   FULL/  -   00:00:37   172.16.1.2     Serial0/0

R3#show ip ospf neighbor

Neighbor ID    Pri  State     Dead Time  Address        Interface
1.1.1.1          0  FULL/  -   00:00:39   172.16.1.1     Serial0/0
```

LAB 78: CONFIGURING THE OSPF PASSIVE INTERFACE MANUALLY

Lab Objective:

The objective of this lab exercise is for you to learn and understand how to manually configure the OSPF passive interface. We will repeat the previous lab but then make one of the interfaces passive. This of course will bring down the OSPF connection.

Lab Purpose:

Manually configuring the OSPF passive interface is a fundamental skill.

Certification Level:

This lab is suitable for CCENT certification exam preparation.

Lab Difficulty:

This lab has a difficulty rating of 5/10.

Readiness Assessment:

When you are ready for your certification exam, you should complete this lab in no more than 10 minutes.

Lab Topology:

Please use the following topology to complete this lab exercise:

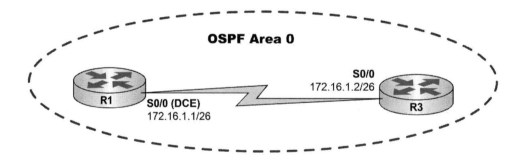

Task 1:

Configure hostnames on routers R1 and R3 as illustrated in the topology.

Task 2:

Configure R1 S0/0, which is a DCE, to provide a clock rate of 768 Kbps to R3. Configure the IP addresses on the Serial interfaces of R1 and R3 as illustrated in the topology.

Task 3:

Enable OSPF in area 0 between R1 and R3. For R1, use OSPF process ID 1. For R3, use OSPF process ID 3. Verify that your OSPF adjacency has formed between R1 and R3. Make a mental note of the OSPF router ID being used at this time after the adjacency between R1 and R3 has been established.

Task 4:

Manually configure OSPF router ID 1.1.1.1 on R1 and 3.3.3.3 on R3. Reset the OSPF process ID on R1 and R3 by issuing the `clear ip ospf process` command. Verify that the OSPF adjacency has been re-established between R1 and R3. Verify that the OSPF neighbor IP addresses are now showing as the manually configured router IDs instead of the physical interface IP addresses.

Task 5:

Set S0/0 on R3 as a passive interface.

LAB 78: CONFIGURATION AND VERIFICATION

Task 1:

See previous lab.

Task 2:

See previous lab.

Task 3:

See previous lab.

Task 4:

See previous lab.

```
R1#show ip ospf neighbor

Neighbor ID     Pri   State        Dead Time    Address        Interface
3.3.3.3           0   FULL/  -     00:00:37     172.16.1.2     Serial0/0

R3#show ip ospf neighbor

Neighbor ID     Pri   State        Dead Time    Address        Interface
1.1.1.1           0   FULL/  -     00:00:39     172.16.1.1     Serial0/0
```

Task 5

```
R3#show ip protocols

Routing Protocol is "ospf 3"
Outgoing update filter list for all interfaces is not set
Incoming update filter list for all interfaces is not set
Router ID 3.3.3.3
Number of areas in this router is 1. 1 normal 0 stub 0 nssa
Maximum path: 4
Routing for Networks:
172.16.1.0 0.0.0.63 area 0
Routing Information Sources:
Gateway Distance Last Update
1.1.1.1 110 00:00:10
3.3.3.3 110 00:00:10
172.16.1.2 110 00:00:35
Distance: (default is 110)

R3#conf t
Enter configuration commands, one per line. End with CTRL/Z.
R3(config)#router ospf 3
R3(config-router)#pass
R3(config-router)#passive-interface s0/0
```

R3(config-router)#
00:04:05: %OSPF-5-ADJCHG: Process 3, Nbr 1.1.1.1 on Serial0/0 from FULL
to DOWN, Neighbor Down: Interface down or detached

R3(config-router)#end

R3#show ip prot

Routing Protocol is "ospf 3"
Outgoing update filter list for all interfaces is not set
Incoming update filter list for all interfaces is not set
Router ID 3.3.3.3
Number of areas in this router is 1. 1 normal 0 stub 0 nssa
Maximum path: 4
Routing for Networks:
172.16.1.0 0.0.0.63 area 0
Passive Interface(s):
Serial0/0
Routing Information Sources:
Gateway Distance Last Update
1.1.1.1 110 00:00:48
3.3.3.3 110 00:00:05
172.16.1.2 110 00:01:13
Distance: (default is 110)

LAB 79: CONFIGURING SINGLE-AREA OSPFV3

Lab Objective:
The objective of this lab exercise is for you to learn and understand how to manually configure OSPFv3, which is a core ICND2 and CCNA topic.

Lab Purpose:
Manually configure IPv6 interface addressing and then configure a Single-Area OSPFv3 connection.

Certification Level:
This lab is suitable for ICND2 and CCNA certification exam preparation.

Lab Difficulty:
This lab has a difficulty rating of 7/10.

Readiness Assessment:
When you are ready for your certification exam, you should complete this lab in no more than 10 minutes.

Lab Topology:
Please use the following topology to complete this lab exercise:

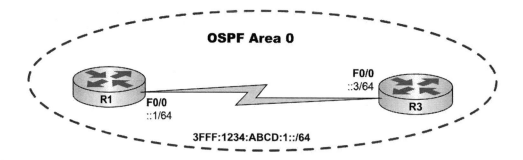

Task 1:
Configure hostnames on routers R1 and R3 as illustrated in the topology.

Task 2:
Configure the IPv6 addresses on the FastEthernet interfaces of R1 and R3 as illustrated in the topology.

Task 3:

Enable OSPF in area 0 between R1 and R3. For R1, use OSPF process ID 1. For R3, use OSPF process ID 3. Configure router ID 1.1.1.1 for R1 and 3.3.3.3 for R3.

Task 4:

Ping across the link and then use the relevant show commands to verify your configurations.

LAB 79: CONFIGURATION AND VERIFICATION

Task 1:

For reference information on configuring hostnames, please refer to earlier labs.

Task 2:
```
R1#conf t
R1(config)#ipv6 unicast-routing
Enter configuration commands, one per line.  End with CTRL/Z.
R1(config)#int f0/0
R1(config-if)#ipv6 address 3fff:1234:abcd:1::1/64

R3#conf t
R3(config)#ipv6 unicast-routing
R3(config-if)#int f0/0
R3(config-if)#ipv6 address 3fff:1234:abcd:1::3/64
```

Task 3:
```
R1(config)#ipv6 router ospf 1
R1(config-rtr)#
*Mar  1 00:05:32.755: %OSPFv3-4-NORTRID: OSPFv3 process 1 could not
pick a router-id,
please configure manually
R1(config-rtr)#router-id 1.1.1.1
R1(config-rtr)#int f0/0
R1(config-if)#ipv6 ospf 1 area 0
R1(config-if)#end

R3(config)#ipv6 router ospf 3
R3(config-rtr)#
*Mar  1 00:06:57.451: %OSPFv3-4-NORTRID: OSPFv3 process 3 could not
pick a router-id,
please configure manually
R3(config-rtr)#router-id 3.3.3.3
R3(config-rtr)#int f0/0
R3(config-if)#ipv6 ospf 3 area 0
R3(config-if)#exit
```

Task 4:
```
R1#ping ipv6 3fff:1234:abcd:1::3

Type escape sequence to abort.
Sending 5, 100-byte ICMP Echos to 3FFF:1234:ABCD:1::3, timeout is 2
seconds:
!!!!!
Success rate is 100 percent (5/5), round-trip min/avg/max = 16/22/36 ms
*Mar  1 00:09:12.183: %OSPFv3-5-ADJCHG: Process 1, Nbr 3.3.3.3 on
FastEthernet0/0 from LOADING to FULL, Loading Done
```

```
R1#show ipv6 ospf nei

Neighbor ID   Pri   State    Dead Time   Interface ID    Interface
3.3.3.3        1    FULL/DR  00:00:39    4               FastEthernet0/0

R1#show ipv6 ospf nei detail
 Neighbor 3.3.3.3
    In the area 0 via interface FastEthernet0/0
    Neighbor: interface-id 4, link-local address FE80::C001:8FF:FE52:0
    Neighbor priority is 1, State is FULL, 6 state changes
    DR is 3.3.3.3 BDR is 1.1.1.1
    Options is 0x674EE6BD
    Dead timer due in 00:00:38
    Neighbor is up for 00:01:01
    Index 1/1,retransmission queue length 0,number of retransmission 0
    First 0x0(0)/0x0(0)/0x0(0) Next 0x0(0)/0x0(0)/0x0(0)
    Last retransmission scan length is 0, maximum is 0
    Last retransmission scan time is 0 msec, maximum is 0 msec

R1#show ipv6 int brie
FastEthernet0/0              [up/up]
    FE80::C000:8FF:FE52:0
    3FFF:1234:ABCD:1::1
```

LAB 80: CONFIGURING MULTI-AREA OSPF

Lab Objective:

The objective of this lab exercise is for you to learn and understand how to enable OSPF using more than one Area.

Lab Purpose:

Enabling Multi-Area OSPF is a fundamental skill. When configuring Multi-Area OSPF, it is imperative to remember that all Areas must be connected to the OSPF backbone area, which is area 0. As a Cisco engineer, as well as in the Cisco CCNA exam, you will be expected to know how to enable Multi-Area OSPF.

Certification Level:

This lab is suitable for ICND2 and CCNA certification exam preparation.

Lab Difficulty:

This lab has a difficulty rating of 8/10.

Readiness Assessment:

When you are ready for your certification exam, you should complete this lab in no more than 30 minutes.

Lab Topology:

Please use the following topology to complete this lab exercise:

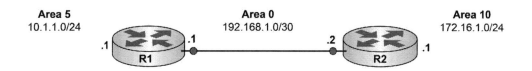

Task 1:

Configure hostnames on R1 and R2 as illustrated in the topology.

Task 2:

Enable the IP addressing scheme as illustrated. The .1 addresses on either end of R1 and R2 are for Loopback0, which makes it easy to test the commands without having to add switches.

Task 3:

Configure area 0 (the backbone area) between R1 and R2 FastEthernet interfaces.

Task 4:

Enable OSPF in area 5 for the network attached to Loopback0 on R1. Enable OSPF in Area 10 for the network attached to Loopback0 attached to R2.

Task 5:

Issue some `show` commands to check that your configurations have worked.

LAB 80: CONFIGURATION AND VERIFICATION

Task 1:

For reference information on configuring hostnames, please refer to earlier labs.

Task 2:

For reference information on configuring IP addresses, please refer to earlier labs.

Task 3:
```
R1(config-if)#router ospf 1
R1(config-router)#network 192.168.1.0 0.0.0.3 area 0

R2(config)#router ospf 1
R2(config-router)#net 192.168.1.0 0.0.0.3 area 0
*Mar  1 00:04:49.211: %OSPF-5-ADJCHG: Process 1, Nbr 10.1.1.1 on
FastEthernet0/0 from LOADING to FULL, Loading Done
```

Task 4:
```
R1(config-router)#router ospf 1
R1(config-router)#net 10.1.1.0 0.0.0.255 area 5

R2(config-router)#router ospf 1
R2(config-router)#network 172.16.1.0 0.0.0.255 area 10
```

Task 5:
```
R1#show ip route ospf
      172.16.0.0/32 is subnetted, 1 subnets
O IA    172.16.1.1 [110/11] via 192.168.1.2, 00:02:09, FastEthernet0/0

R2#show ip route ospf
      10.0.0.0/32 is subnetted, 1 subnets
O IA    10.1.1.1 [110/11] via 192.168.1.1, 00:03:03, FastEthernet0/0

R1#show ip ospf database

            OSPF Router with ID (10.1.1.1) (Process ID 1)

            Router Link States (Area 0)

Link ID         ADV Router       Age       Seq#        Checksum Link
count
10.1.1.1        10.1.1.1         385       0x80000003 0x006DC7 1
172.16.1.1      172.16.1.1       319       0x80000003 0x00547C 1

            Net Link States (Area 0)
```

```
Link ID          ADV Router       Age          Seq#        Checksum
192.168.1.2      172.16.1.1       576          0x80000001 0x00FE47

                 Summary Net Link States (Area 0)

Link ID          ADV Router       Age          Seq#        Checksum
10.1.1.1         10.1.1.1         381          0x80000001 0x0080A1
172.16.1.1       172.16.1.1       315          0x80000001 0x005965

                 Router Link States (Area 5)

Link ID          ADV Router       Age          Seq#           Checksum Link
count
10.1.1.1         10.1.1.1         385          0x80000001 0x004CBD 1

                 Summary Net Link States (Area 5)

Link ID          ADV Router       Age          Seq#        Checksum
172.16.1.1       10.1.1.1         316          0x80000001 0x00ED78
192.168.1.0      10.1.1.1         389          0x80000001 0x00AF0F
R1#
```

NOTE: Understanding the information printed in the OSPF database is key to understanding the operation of OSPF. The `show ip ospf database` command shows the router ID of the router this command is issued on, as well as the locally significant OSPF process ID that has been enabled on the router. It also shows the different types of OSPF LSAs and the routes associated with those LSA types, as well as the OSPF Areas. In addition, each link ID listed in the OSPF database is identified by the originator of the LSA under the column `ADV Router`.

LAB 81: DEBUGGING OSPF ADJACENCIES

Lab Objective:

The objective of this lab exercise is for you to learn and understand how to debug OSPF adjacencies.

Lab Purpose:

Debugging OSPF adjacencies is a fundamental troubleshooting skill. Using debugging, you can identify issues that may be causing OSPF to stop operating. As a Cisco engineer, as well as in the Cisco CCNA exam, you will be expected to know how to decipher OSPF adjacency debugging messages.

Certification Level:

This lab is suitable for ICND2 and CCNA certification exam preparation.

Lab Difficulty:

This lab has a difficulty rating of 7/10.

Readiness Assessment:

When you are ready for your certification exam, you should complete this lab in no more than 10 minutes.

Lab Topology:

Please use the following topology to complete this lab exercise:

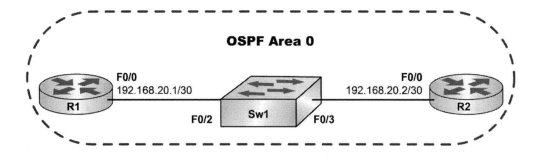

Task 1:

Configure hostnames on R1, R2, and Sw1 as illustrated in the topology.

Task 2:

Configure VLAN4010 on Sw1 and name it OSPF_VLAN. Assign ports FastEthernet0/2 and FastEthernet0/3 to this VLAN as access ports. Configure IP addressing on R1 and R2 FastEthernet0/0 interfaces.

Task 3:

Enable OSPF in area 0 between R1 and R2. For R1, use OSPF process ID 1, and for R2, use OSPF process ID 2. Verify that your OSPF adjacency has formed between R1 and R2. Also verify that the default network type for the Ethernet link between R1 and R2 is broadcast.

Task 4:

Enable OSPF adjacency debugging on R1 using the `debug ip ospf adj` command. Reset the OSPF process on R2. As the OSPF adjacency re-establishes, verify that you can see the different states that OSPF transitions through as it moves to the `FULL` state.

LAB 81: CONFIGURATION AND VERIFICATION

Task 1:

For reference information on configuring hostnames, please refer to earlier labs.

Task 2:

For reference information on configuring VLANs and IP addressing, please refer to earlier labs.

Task 3:

For reference information on configuring OSPF, please refer to earlier labs.

Task 4:

```
R2#debug ip ospf adj
OSPF adjacency events debugging is on
R2#clear ip ospf process
Reset ALL OSPF processes? [no]: yes
*Mar  1 02:13:21.660: OSPF: Elect BDR 0.0.0.0
*Mar  1 02:13:21.660: OSPF: Elect DR 0.0.0.0
*Mar  1 02:13:21.660:         DR: none     BDR: none
*Mar  1 02:13:21.660: OSPF: Remember old DR 192.168.20.1 (id)
*Mar  1 02:13:21.721: OSPF: Interface FastEthernet0/0 going Up
*Mar  1 02:13:21.721: OSPF: i_up : interface is down
*Mar  1 02:13:21.725: OSPF: 2 Way Communication to 192.168.20.1 on
FastEthernet0/0, state 2WAY
*Mar  1 02:13:21.725: OSPF: Backup seen Event before WAIT timer on
FastEthernet0/0
*Mar  1 02:13:21.725: OSPF: DR/BDR election on FastEthernet0/0
*Mar  1 02:13:21.725: OSPF: Elect BDR 10.1.1.2
*Mar  1 02:13:21.729: OSPF: Elect DR 192.168.20.1
*Mar  1 02:13:21.729: OSPF: Elect BDR 10.1.1.2
*Mar  1 02:13:21.729: OSPF: Elect DR 192.168.20.1
*Mar  1 02:13:21.729:         DR: 192.168.20.1 (Id)   BDR: 10.1.1.2 (Id)
*Mar  1 02:13:21.729: OSPF: Send DBD to 192.168.20.1 on FastEthernet0/0
seq 0x1614 opt 0x52 flag 0x7 len 32
*Mar  1 02:13:21.733: OSPF: Rcv DBD from 192.168.20.1 on Ethernet0/0
seq 0xEB3 opt 0x52 flag 0x7 len 32  mtu 1500 state EXSTART
*Mar  1 02:13:21.737: OSPF: NBR Negotiation Done. We are the SLAVE
*Mar  1 02:13:21.737: OSPF: Send DBD to 192.168.20.1 on FastEthernet0/0
seq 0xEB3 opt 0x52 flag 0x0 len 32
*Mar  1 02:13:21.741: OSPF: Rcv DBD from 192.168.20.1 on
FastEthernet0/0 seq 0xEB4 opt 0x52 flag 0x3 len 172  mtu 1500 state
EXCHANGE
*Mar  1 02:13:21.741: OSPF: Send DBD to 192.168.20.1 on FastEthernet0/0
seq 0xEB4 opt 0x52 flag 0x0 len 32
```

```
*Mar  1 02:13:21.749: OSPF: Rcv DBD from 192.168.20.1 on
FastEthernet0/0 seq 0xEB5 opt 0x52 flag 0x1 len 32  mtu 1500 state
EXCHANGE
*Mar  1 02:13:21.749: OSPF: Exchange Done with 192.168.20.1 on
FastEthernet0/0
*Mar  1 02:13:21.749: OSPF: Send LS REQ to 192.168.20.1 length 84 LSA
count 7
*Mar  1 02:13:21.749: OSPF: Send DBD to 192.168.20.1 on FastEthernet0/0
seq 0xEB5 opt 0x52 flag 0x0 len 32
*Mar  1 02:13:21.753: OSPF: Rcv LS UPD from 192.168.20.1 on
FastEthernet0/0 length 332 LSA count 7
*Mar  1 02:13:21.757: OSPF: Synchronized with 192.168.20.1 on
FastEthernet0/0, state FULL
*Mar  1 02:13:21.757: %OSPF-5-ADJCHG: Process 2, Nbr 192.168.20.1 on
FastEthernet0/0 from LOADING to FULL, Loading Done
*Mar  1 02:13:26.544: OSPF: Rcv LS UPD from 192.168.20.1 on
FastEthernet0/0 length 64 LSA count 1
*Mar  1 02:13:27.001: OSPF: Rcv LS UPD from 192.168.20.1 on
FastEthernet0/0 length 64 LSA count 1R2#undebug all
All possible debugging has been turned off
R2#
```

> **NOTE:** From the output above, you can clearly see OSPF transition from the 2WAY state to the EXSTART state to the EXCHANGE state and, finally, to the FULL state. Because this is a broadcast network type, a DR and BDR router are also elected. If this were a point-to-point or point-to-multipoint network type, you would not see the DR and BDR election taking place.

LAB 82: CONFIGURE, VERIFY, AND TROUBLESHOOT SINGLE-AREA AND MULTI-AREA OSPFV3 FOR IPV6

Lab Objective:

The objective of this lab exercise is for you to learn how to configure OSPF running IPv6.

Lab Purpose:

OSPFv3 will allow you to run a link-state routing protocol in your infrastructure when running IPv6. As a Cisco engineer, as well as in the Cisco CCNA exam, you will be expected to know how to implement this OSPFv3 in the IPv6 world.

Certification Level:

This lab is suitable for ICND2 certification exam preparation.

Lab Difficulty:

This lab has a difficulty rating of 7/10.

Readiness Assessment:

When you are ready for your certification exam, you should complete this lab in no more than 20 minutes.

Lab Topology:

Please use the following topology to complete this lab exercise:

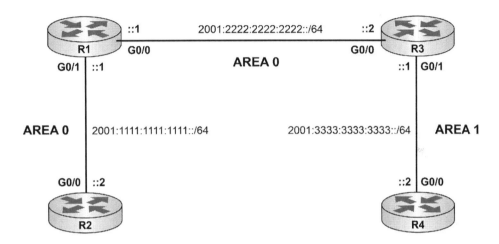

OSPF AS 100

INTERFACE	IPv6 ADDRESS
Loopback 1	2001:AAAA:AAAA:AAAA::1/64
Loopback 2	2001:BBBB:BBBB:CCCC::1/64

INTERFACE	IPv6 ADDRESS
Loopback 1	2001:4444:4444:0001::1/64
Loopback 2	2001:4444:4444:0002::1/64
Loopback 3	2001:4444:4444:0003::1/64

Task 1:

Configure hostnames on R1, R2, R3, and R4 as illustrated in the topology.

Task 2:

Configure each router with its respective IPv6 addresses and Gigabit interfaces, and make sure that your router is ready to route IPv6 traffic.

> **NOTE:** You can select the Gigabit interface you want to use (Gig0/0 or Gig0/1) for any network shown in the diagram.

Task 3:

Configure OSPFv3 for IPv6 in the network as follows:

- All the routers will be inside AS 100;
- There are no IPv4 addresses at all so manually create a router ID for each router (different on each unit); and
- Make sure that you advertise every network shown in the diagram (including Loopbacks) according to their respective Areas.

Task 4:

Make sure that you can ping from R2 Loopbacks to R4 Loopbacks to ensure that there is full connectivity.

Task 5:

To see the OSPF database, provide the following information from R1:

- `show ipv6 ospf neighbors`
- `show ipv6 ospf database`
- `show ipv6 route`

LAB 82: CONFIGURATION AND VERIFICATION

Task 1:

For reference information on configuring hostnames, please refer to earlier labs.

Task 2:

```
R1#conf t
Enter configuration commands, one per line.  End with CTRL/Z.

R1(config)#ipv6 unicast-routing
R1(config)#int gig0/0
R1(config-if)#ipv6 address 2001:2222:2222:2222::1/64
R1(config-if)#no shut
R1(config)#int gig0/1
R1(config-if)#ipv6 address 2001:1111:1111:1111::1/64
R1(config-if)#no shut

R2(config)#ipv6 unicast-routing
R2(config)#int gig0/0
R2(config-if)#ipv6 address 2001:1111:1111:1111::2/64
R2(config-if)#no shut
R2(config)#int loopback1
R2(config-if)#ipv6 address 2001:AAAA:AAAA:AAAA::1/64
R2(config)#int loopback2
R2(config-if)#ipv6 address 2001:BBBB:BBBB:CCCC::1/64

R3(config)#ipv6 unicast-routing
R3(config)#int gig0/0
R3(config-if)#ipv6 address 2001:2222:2222:2222::2/64
R3(config-if)#no shut
R3(config)#int gig0/1
R3(config-if)#ipv6 address 2001:3333:3333:3333::1/64
R3(config-if)#no shut

R4(config)#ipv6 unicast-routing
R4(config)#int gig0/0
R4(config-if)#ipv6 address 2001:3333:3333:3333::2/64
R4(config-if)#no shut
R4(config)#int loopback1
R4(config-if)#ipv6 address 2001:4444:4444:0001::1/64
R4(config)#int loopback2
R4(config-if)#ipv6 address 2001:4444:4444:0002::1/64
R4(config)#int loopback3
R4(config-if)#ipv6 address 2001:4444:4444:0003::1/64
```

Task 3:
```
R1(config)#ipv6 router ospf 100
R1(config-rtr)#router-id 1.1.1.1
R1(config)#int gig0/0
R1(config-if)#ipv6 ospf 100 area 0
R1(config)#int gig0/1
R1(config-if)#ipv6 ospf 100 area 0

R2(config)#ipv6 router ospf 100
R2(config-rtr)#router-id 2.2.2.2
R2(config)#int gig0/0
R2(config-if)#ipv6 ospf 100 area 0
R2(config)#int loop1
R2(config-if)#ipv6 ospf 100 area 0
R2(config)#int loop2
R2(config-if)#ipv6 ospf 100 area 0

R3(config)#ipv6 router ospf 100
R3(config-rtr)#router-id 3.3.3.3
R3(config)#int gig0/0
R3(config-if)#ipv6 ospf 100 area 0
R3(config)#int gig0/1
R3(config-if)#ipv6 ospf 100 area 1

R4(config)#ipv6 router ospf 100
R4(config-rtr)#router-id 4.4.4.4
R4(config)#int gig0/0
R4(config-if)#ipv6 ospf 100 area 1
R4(config)#int loop1
R4(config-if)#ipv6 ospf 100 area 1
R4(config)#int loop2
R4(config-if)#ipv6 ospf 100 area 1
R4(config)#int loop3
R4(config-if)#ipv6 ospf 100 area 1
```

Task 4:
```
R2#ping 2001:4444:4444:0002::1 source 2001:BBBB:BBBB:CCCC::1

Type escape sequence to abort.
Sending 5, 100-byte ICMP Echos to 2001:4444:4444:2::1, timeout is 2
seconds:
Packet sent with a source address of 2001:BBBB:BBBB:CCCC::1
!!!!!
Success rate is 100 percent (5/5), round-trip min/avg/max = 28/57/72 ms
```

This command won't work on Packet Tracer so you will have to use an extended ping on that.

```
R4#ping 2001:AAAA:AAAA:AAAA::1 source 2001:4444:4444:0001::1

Type escape sequence to abort.
Sending 5, 100-byte ICMP Echos to 2001:AAAA:AAAA:AAAA::1, timeout is 2
seconds:
Packet sent with a source address of 2001:4444:4444:1::1
!!!!!
Success rate is 100 percent (5/5), round-trip min/avg/max = 24/31/44 ms
Distance: external 20 internal 200 local 200
```

Task 5:

```
R1#sh ipv6 ospf neighbor

Neighbor ID     Pri  State     Dead Time  Interface ID    Interface
3.3.3.3           1  FULL/DR   00:00:37   4               G0/0
2.2.2.2           1  FULL/DR   00:00:30   4               G0/1


R1#show ipv6 ospf database

            OSPFv3 Router with ID (1.1.1.1) (Process ID 100)

    Router Link States (Area 0)

ADV Router      Age        Seq#          Fragment ID  Link count  Bits
1.1.1.1         53         0x80000008    0            2           None
2.2.2.2         76         0x80000005    0            1           B
3.3.3.3         46         0x80000005    0            1           None

    Net Link States (Area 0)

ADV Router      Age        Seq#          Link ID   Rtr count
2.2.2.2         87         0x80000001    4         2
3.3.3.3         62         0x80000001    4         2

    Inter Area Prefix Link States (Area 0)

ADV Router      Age        Seq#        Prefix
2.2.2.2         111        0x80000001  2001:3333:3333:3333::/64
2.2.2.2         32         0x80000001  2001:4444:4444:3::1/128
2.2.2.2         22         0x80000001  2001:4444:4444:1::1/128
2.2.2.2         22         0x80000001  2001:4444:4444:2::1/128

    Link (Type-8) Link States (Area 0)

ADV Router      Age        Seq#          Link ID   Interface
1.1.1.1         142        0x80000001    5         G0/1
3.3.3.3         104        0x80000001    4         G0/0
```

```
1.1.1.1          144        0x80000001  4            G0/0
2.2.2.2          128        0x80000001  4            G0/1

    Intra Area Prefix Link States (Area 0)

ADV Router       Age        Seq#        Link ID      Ref-lstype   Ref-LSID
2.2.2.2          89         0x80000001  4096         0x2002       4
3.3.3.3          64         0x80000003  0            0x2001       0
3.3.3.3          64         0x80000001  4096         0x2002       4

R1#show ipv6 route
IPv6 Routing Table - 11 entries
Codes: C - Connected, L - Local, S - Static, R - RIP, B—BGP,
       U - Per-user Static route, M - MIPv6,
       I1 - ISIS L1, I2 - ISIS L2, IA - ISIS interarea, IS - ISIS
summary,
       O - OSPF intra, OI - OSPF inter, OE1 - OSPF ext 1,
       OE2 - OSPF ext 2, ON1 - OSPF NSSA ext 1, ON2 - OSPF NSSA ext 2,
       D - EIGRP, EX - EIGRP external

C    2001:1111:1111:1111::/64 [0/0]
      via ::, G0/1
L    2001:1111:1111:1111::1/128 [0/0]
      via ::, G0/1
C    2001:2222:2222:2222::/64 [0/0]
      via ::, G0/0
L    2001:2222:2222:2222::1/128 [0/0]
      via ::, G0/0
OI   2001:3333:3333:3333::/64 [110/20]
      via FE80::C007:51FF:FE93:0, G0/0
OI   2001:4444:4444:1::1/128 [110/20]
      via FE80::C007:51FF:FE93:0, G0/0
OI   2001:4444:4444:2::1/128 [110/20]
      via FE80::C007:51FF:FE93:0, G0/0
OI   2001:4444:4444:3::1/128 [110/20]
      via FE80::C007:51FF:FE93:0, G0/0
O    2001:AAAA:AAAA:AAAA::1/128 [110/10]
      via FE80::C006:51FF:FE92:0, G0/1
O    2001:BBBB:BBBB:CCCC::1/128 [110/10]
      via FE80::C006:51FF:FE92:0, G0/1
L    FF00::/8 [0/0]
      via ::, Null0
```

LAB 83: CONFIGURING BASIC EIGRP ROUTING

Lab Objective:
The objective of this lab exercise is for you to learn and understand how to enable basic EIGRP routing using a single autonomous system.

Lab Purpose:
Enabling basic EIGRP routing is a fundamental skill. EIGRP is an advanced distance vector routing protocol. It is also a Cisco proprietary protocol (but now also an open standard) that runs over IP protocol number 88. As a Cisco engineer, as well as in the Cisco CCNA exam, you will be expected to know how to enable basic EIGRP routing.

Certification Level:
This lab is suitable for ICND2 and CCNA certification exam preparation.

Lab Difficulty:
This lab has a difficulty rating of 4/10.

Readiness Assessment:
When you are ready for your certification exam, you should complete this lab in no more than 10 minutes.

Lab Topology:
Please use the following topology to complete this lab exercise:

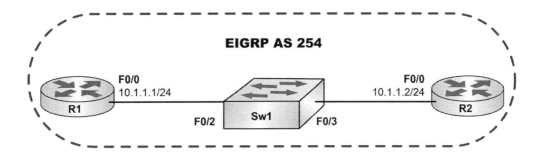

Task 1:
Configure hostnames on R1, R2, and Sw1 as illustrated in the topology.

Task 2:

Configure VLAN10 named EIGRP_VLAN on Sw1. Keep in mind that, by default, Sw1 will be a VTP server so you can simply create the VLAN and assign it the name provided. Next, assign ports FastEthernet0/2 and FastEthernet0/3 on Sw1 to VLAN10 as access ports and enable those ports.

Task 3:

Configure the F0/0 interfaces on R1 and R2 with the IP addresses in the topology and bring up the interfaces. Perform a ping from R1 to R2, and vice versa, and ensure that the routers can ping each other.

Task 4:

Enable EIGRP on R1 and R2 for the subnet configured on their F0/0 interfaces. Make sure that EIGRP uses ASN 254 as illustrated in the topology.

Task 5:

Verify that an EIGRP adjacency has formed between R1 and R2 using appropriate commands.

LAB 83: CONFIGURATION AND VERIFICATION

Task 1:

For reference information on configuring hostnames, please refer to earlier labs.

Task 2:

For reference information on configuring and verifying VLANs, please refer to earlier labs.

Task 3:

For reference information on configuring and verifying IP addressing, please refer to earlier labs.

Task 4:

```
R1#conf t
Enter configuration commands, one per line.  End with CTRL/Z.
R1(config)#router eigrp 254
R1(config-router)#network 10.0.0.0
R1(config-router)#end
R1#

R2#conf t
Enter configuration commands, one per line.  End with CTRL/Z.
R2(config)#router eigrp 254
R2(config-router)#network 10.0.0.0
R2(config-router)#end
R2#
*Mar  1 00:11:46.782: %DUAL-5-NBRCHANGE: IP-EIGRP(0) 254: Neighbor
10.1.1.1 (FastEthernet0/0) is up: new adjacency
R2#
```

NOTE: When configuring EIGRP, you must use an ASN. This can be any number from 1 through 65535. This is configured as follows:

```
R1(config)#router eigrp ?
  <1-65535>  Autonomous system number
```

In addition, when you configure EIGRP, you will see an adjacency form if EIGRP has been configured correctly. This will be indicated by the log message printed on the console:

```
*Mar  1 00:11:46.782: %DUAL-5-NBRCHANGE: IP-EIGRP(0) 254: Neighbor
10.1.1.1 (FastEthernet0/0) is up: new adjacency
```

Task 5:

```
R1#show ip eigrp neighbors
IP-EIGRP neighbors for process 254

H    Address      Interface    Hold Uptime     SRTT   RTO   Q  Seq
                                (sec)          (ms)         Cnt Num
0    10.1.1.2     Fa0/0          13 00:07:40     1   4500   0  1
R1#


R2#show ip eigrp neighbors
IP-EIGRP neighbors for process 254
H    Address          Interface         Hold Uptime     SRTT   RTO   Q  Seq
                                        (sec)          (ms)         Cnt Num
0    10.1.1.1          Fa0/0             13 00:04:56   862   5000   0  1
R2#
```

LAB 84: CONFIGURING EIGRP ROUTING USING WILDCARD MASKS

Lab Objective:
The objective of this lab exercise is for you to learn and understand how to enable EIGRP routing using a single autonomous system while using a wildcard mask for EIGRP network statements.

Lab Purpose:
Enabling basic EIGRP routing using wildcard masks is a fundamental skill. As a Cisco engineer, as well as in the Cisco CCNA exam, you will be expected to know how to enable basic EIGRP routing while using wildcard masks.

Certification Level:
This lab is suitable for CCNA certification exam preparation.

Lab Difficulty:
This lab has a difficulty rating of 7/10.

Readiness Assessment:
When you are ready for your certification exam, you should complete this lab in no more than 20 minutes.

Lab Topology:
Please use the following topology to complete this lab exercise:

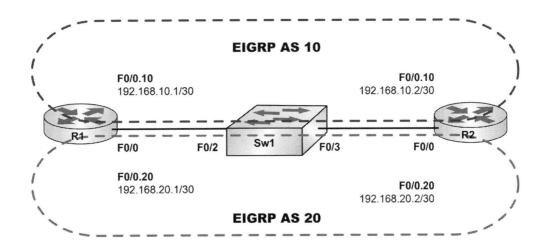

Task 1:

Configure hostnames on R1, R2, and Sw1 as illustrated in the topology.

Task 2:

Configure VLAN10 named EIGRP_10 and VLAN20 named EIGRP_20 on Sw1. Next, configure Sw1 F0/2 and F0/3 as trunks. These should be connected to R1 and R2 F0/0 interfaces, respectively.

Task 3:

Configure subinterfaces Fa0/0.10 and F0/0.20 on R1 and R2, respectively. Subinterface Fa0/0.10 on either router should be associated with VLAN10 and subinterface Fa0/0.20 on either router should be associated with VLAN20. Configure IP addresses on both the subinterfaces as illustrated in the topology.

Task 4:

Ping between R1 and R2 on subinterface Fa0/0.10 and Fa0/0.20 to verify IP connectivity.

Task 5:

Enable EIGRP using ASN 10 between R1 and R2 F0/0.10 subinterfaces. EIGRP using ASN 10 should only be enabled for these interfaces. Use a wildcard mask to achieve this.

Task 6:

Enable EIGRP using ASN 20 between R1 and R2 F0/0.20 subinterfaces. EIGRP using ASN 20 should only be enabled for these interfaces. Use a wildcard mask to achieve this.

Task 7:

Verify that you have two EIGRP adjacencies on R1 and R2. One adjacency should be for EIGRP using ASN 10 and the other for EIGRP using ASN 20.

LAB 84: CONFIGURATION AND VERIFICATION

Task 1:

For reference information on configuring hostnames, please refer to earlier labs.

Task 2:

```
Sw1#conf t
Enter configuration commands, one per line.  End with CTRL/Z.
Sw1(config)#vlan10
Sw1(config-vlan)#name EIGRP_10
Sw1(config-vlan)#exit
Sw1(config)#vlan20
Sw1(config-vlan)#name EIGRP_20
Sw1(config-vlan)#exit
Sw1(config)#int f0/2
Sw1(config-if)#switchport mode trunk
Sw1(config-if)#no shut
Sw1(config-if)#exit
Sw1(config)#int f0/3
Sw1(config-if)#switchport mode trunk
Sw1(config-if)#no shut
Sw1(config-if)#^Z

Sw1#show interfaces trunk

Port        Mode          Encapsulation  Status      Native vlan
Fa0/2       on            802.1q         trunking    1
Fa0/3       on            802.1q         trunking    1

Port        Vlans allowed on trunk
Fa0/2       1-4094
Fa0/3       1-4094

Port        Vlans allowed and active in management domain
Fa0/2       1,10,20
Fa0/3       1,10,20

Port        Vlans in spanning tree forwarding state and not pruned
Fa0/2       1,10,20
Fa0/3       1,10,20

Sw1#show vlan id 10

VLAN Name                             Status    Ports
---- -------------------------------- --------- -----------------------
10   EIGRP_10                         active    Fa0/2, Fa0/3

Sw1#show vlan id 20
```

```
VLAN Name                              Status    Ports
---- --------------------------------- --------- ----------------------
20   EIGRP_20                          active    Fa0/2, Fa0/3
```

Task 3:
```
R1#conf t
Enter configuration commands, one per line.  End with CTRL/Z.
R1(config)#int fa0/0
R1(config-if)#no shutdown
R1(config-if)#int fa0/0.10
R1(config-subif)#encapsulation dot1q 10
R1(config-subif)#ip address 192.168.10.1 255.255.255.252
R1(config-subif)#exit
R1(config)#int fa0/0.20
R1(config-subif)#encapsulation dot1q 20
R1(config-subif)#ip address 192.168.20.1 255.255.255.252
R1(config-subif)#end
R1#show ip int bri
Interface       IP-Address    OK? Method Status          Protocol
Fast0/0         unassigned    YES manual up              up
Fast0/0.10      192.168.10.1  YES manual up              up
Fast0/0.20      192.168.20.1  YES manual up              up

R2#conf t
Enter configuration commands, one per line.  End with CTRL/Z.
R2(config)#int fa0/0
R2(config-if)#no shutdown
R2(config-if)#int fa0/0.10
R2(config-subif)#encapsulation dot1q 10
R2(config-subif)#ip address 192.168.10.2 255.255.255.252
R2(config-subif)#exit
R2(config)#int fa0/0.20
R2(config-subif)#encapsulation dot1q 20
R2(config-subif)#ip address 192.168.20.2 255.255.255.252
R2(config-subif)#end
R2#
R2#show ip interface brief
Int             IP-Address    OK? Method Status          Protocol
Fast0/0         unassigned    YES manual up              up
Fast0/0.10      192.168.10.2  YES manual up              up
Fast0/0.20      192.168.20.2  YES manual up              up
```

Task 4:
```
R1#ping 192.168.10.2

Type escape sequence to abort.
Sending 5, 100-byte ICMP Echos to 192.168.10.2, timeout is 2 seconds:
.!!!!
Success rate is 80 percent (4/5), round-trip min/avg/max = 1/3/4 ms
```

```
R1#ping 192.168.20.2

Type escape sequence to abort.
Sending 5, 100-byte ICMP Echos to 192.168.20.2, timeout is 2 seconds:
.!!!!
Success rate is 80 percent (4/5), round-trip min/avg/max = 1/3/4 ms
```

Task 5:
```
R1#conf t
Enter configuration commands, one per line.  End with CTRL/Z.
R1(config)#router eigrp 10
R1(config-router)#network 192.168.10.0 0.0.0.3
R1(config-router)#end
R1#

R2#conf t
Enter configuration commands, one per line.  End with CTRL/Z.
R2(config)#router eigrp 10
R2(config-router)#network 192.168.10.0 0.0.0.3
R2(config-router)#^Z
*Mar  1 00:52:23.436: %DUAL-5-NBRCHANGE: IP-EIGRP(0) 10: Neighbor
192.168.10.1 (FastEthernet0/0.10) is up: new adjacency
R2#
```

Task 6:
```
R1#config t
Enter configuration commands, one per line.  End with CTRL/Z.
R1(config)#router eigrp 20
R1(config-router)#net 192.168.20.0 0.0.0.3
R1(config-router)#end
R1#

R2#conf t
Enter configuration commands, one per line.  End with CTRL/Z.
R2(config)#router eigrp 20
R2(config-router)#network 192.168.20.0 0.0.0.3
R2(config-router)#^Z
*Mar  1 01:08:55.887: %DUAL-5-NBRCHANGE: IP-EIGRP(0) 20: Neighbor
192.168.20.1 (FastEthernet0/0.20) is up: new adjacency
R2#
```

Task 7:
```
R1#show ip eigrp neighbors
IP-EIGRP neighbors for process 10
H   Address           Interface        Hold Uptime   SRTT   RTO  Q  Seq
                                       (sec)         (ms)       Cnt Num
0   192.168.10.2      Fa0/0.10          12 00:18:51    1   4500  0  1
IP-EIGRP neighbors for process 20
H   Address           Interface        Hold Uptime   SRTT   RTO  Q  Seq
                                       (sec)         (ms)       Cnt Num
```

```
0    192.168.20.2      Fa0/0.20           12 00:02:20    1  4500  0  1

R2#show ip eigrp neighbors
IP-EIGRP neighbors for process 10
H    Address           Interface      Hold Uptime    SRTT    RTO  Q   Seq
                                      (sec)          (ms)         Cnt Num
0    192.168.10.1      Fa0/0.10        10 00:17:58 1907    5000  0   1
IP-EIGRP neighbors for process 20
H    Address           Interface      Hold Uptime    SRTT    RTO  Q   Seq
                                      (sec)          (ms)         Cnt Num
0    192.168.20.1      Fa0/0.20        11 00:01:26  452    2712  0   1
```

LAB 85: EIGRP AUTOMATIC SUMMARIZATION

Lab Objective:
The objective of this lab exercise is for you to learn and understand how EIGRP performs automatic summarization at classful network boundaries.

Lab Purpose:
Dealing with EIGRP automatic summarization is a fundamental skill. EIGRP is an advanced distance vector routing protocol. Cisco changed the rule for automatic summarization in IOS 15.X so you can issue a `show ip protocols` command to establish whether you have it on already or you need to enable it. Look for the line below to see if it is turned on:

```
Automatic network summarization is in effect
```

Or is not turned on:

```
Automatic network summarization is not in effect
```

Certification Level:
This lab is suitable for ICND2 and CCNA certification exam preparation.

Lab Difficulty:
This lab has a difficulty rating of 5/10.

Readiness Assessment:
When you are ready for your certification exam, you should complete this lab in no more than 15 minutes.

Lab Topology:
Please use the following topology to complete this lab exercise:

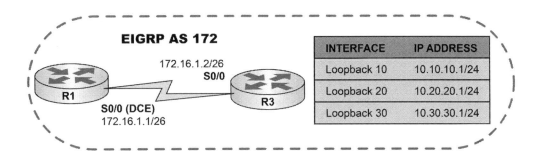

Task 1:

Configure hostnames on R1 and R3 as illustrated in the topology. Since R1 S0/0 is the DCE end of the back-to-back Serial connection, configure R1 to send R3 clocking information at a rate of 256 Kbps. Configure the IP addresses for R1 and R3 S0/0 interfaces as specified in the topology and ping between the routers to verify connectivity based on your configurations.

Task 2:

Configure the Loopback interfaces on R3 as illustrated in the topology.

Task 3:

Enable EIGRP using ASN 172 on both R1 and R3 and configure EIGRP network statements for R1 and R3 S0/0 interfaces and for the Loopback interfaces on R3.

Task 4:

On R1, verify the EIGRP routes you are receiving from R3. You should notice that you only have one route, which is 10.0.0.0/8, for the three Loopback interfaces configured on R3.

Task 5:

Configure R3 so that it does not perform automatic summarization at classful boundaries, and clear the IP routing table on R3 and R1 using the `clear ip route *` command (or let the EIGRP process run again).

Task 6:

On R1, verify the EIGRP routes you are receiving from R3. You should now have three routes for the 10.x.x.x/24 Loopback interfaces configured on R3 and advertised by EIGRP. Ping these IP addresses to verify connectivity.

LAB 85: CONFIGURATION AND VERIFICATION

Task 1:

For reference information on configuring hostnames and IP addressing, please refer to earlier labs.

```
R1#ping 172.16.1.2

Type escape sequence to abort.
Sending 5, 100-byte ICMP Echos to 172.16.1.2, timeout is 2 seconds:
!!!!!
Success rate is 100 percent (5/5), round-trip min/avg/max = 4/6/8 ms
```

Task 2:

For reference information on configuring hostnames and IP addressing, please refer to earlier labs.

Task 3:

```
R1#conf terminal
Enter configuration commands, one per line.  End with CTRL/Z.
R1(config)#router eigrp 172
R1(config-router)#network 172.16.1.0
R1(config-router)#end
R1#

R3#conf t
Enter configuration commands, one per line.  End with CTRL/Z.
R3(config)#router eigrp 172
R3(config-router)#network 10.0.0.0
R3(config-router)#network 172.16.1.0
R3(config-router)#^Z
*Mar  1 01:52:35.842: %DUAL-5-NBRCHANGE: IP-EIGRP(0) 172: Neighbor
172.16.1.1 (Serial0/0) is up: new adjacency
```

Task 4:

```
R1#show ip route
Codes: C - connected, S - static, R - RIP, M - mobile, B—BGP,
       D - EIGRP, EX - EIGRP external, O - OSPF, IA - OSPF inter area,
       N1 - OSPF NSSA external type 1, N2 - OSPF NSSA external type 2,
       E1 - OSPF external type 1, E2 - OSPF external type 2,
       i - IS-IS, su - IS-IS summary, L1 - IS-IS level-1,
       L2 - IS-IS level-2, ia - IS-IS inter area,
       * - candidate default, U - per-user static route, o - ODR,
       P - periodic downloaded static route

Gateway of last resort is not set
```

```
       172.16.0.0/16 is variably subnetted, 2 subnets, 2 masks
C         172.16.1.0/26 is directly connected, Serial0/0
C         172.16.3.0/25 is directly connected, FastEthernet0/0
D      10.0.0.0/8 [90/2297856] via 172.16.1.3, 00:04:24, Serial0/0
```

> **NOTE:** Pay attention to the routing protocol keywords. Notice that internal EIGRP routes are labeled with a D. A code type of D EX would be for external EIGRP routes.

Task 5:
```
R3#conf t
Enter configuration commands, one per line.  End with CTRL/Z.
R3(config)#router eigrp 172
R3(config-router)#no auto-summary
R3(config-router)#end
*Mar  1 02:01:30.535: %DUAL-5-NBRCHANGE: IP-EIGRP(0) 172: Neighbor
172.16.1.1 (Serial0/0) is down: summary configured
*Mar  1 02:01:30.599: %DUAL-5-NBRCHANGE: IP-EIGRP(0) 172: Neighbor
172.16.1.1 (Serial0/0) is up: new adjacency
```

> **NOTE:** By default, in a manner similar to RIP, EIGRP will perform automatic summarization at classful boundaries. It is considered good practice to disable this default feature. When you disable automatic summarization, the EIGRP adjacencies are reset, so be careful when performing this, especially in a production network environment. This is printed on the console as follows:

```
*Mar  1 02:01:30.535: %DUAL-5-NBRCHANGE: IP-EIGRP(0) 172: Neighbor
172.16.1.1 (Serial0/0) is down: summary configured
*Mar  1 02:01:30.599: %DUAL-5-NBRCHANGE: IP-EIGRP(0) 172: Neighbor
172.16.1.1 (Serial0/0) is up: new adjacency
```

Task 6:
```
R1#show ip route
Codes: C - connected, S - static, R - RIP, M - mobile, B—BGP,
       D - EIGRP, EX - EIGRP external, O - OSPF, IA - OSPF inter area,
       N1 - OSPF NSSA external type 1, N2 - OSPF NSSA external type 2,
       E1 - OSPF external type 1, E2 - OSPF external type 2,
       i - IS-IS, su - IS-IS summary, L1 - IS-IS level-1,
       L2 - IS-IS level-2, ia - IS-IS inter area, o - ODR,
       * - candidate default, U - per-user static route,
       P - periodic downloaded static route

Gateway of last resort is not set

       172.16.0.0/16 is variably subnetted, 2 subnets, 2 masks
C         172.16.1.0/26 is directly connected, Serial0/0
C         172.16.3.0/25 is directly connected, FastEthernet0/0
       10.0.0.0/24 is subnetted, 3 subnets
D         10.30.30.0 [90/2297856] via 172.16.1.3, 00:05:37, Serial0/0
```

```
D        10.20.20.0 [90/2297856] via 172.16.1.3, 00:05:37, Serial0/0
D        10.10.10.0 [90/2297856] via 172.16.1.3, 00:05:37, Serial0/0

R1#ping 10.10.10.1

Type escape sequence to abort.
Sending 5, 100-byte ICMP Echos to 10.10.10.1, timeout is 2 seconds:
!!!!!
Success rate is 100 percent (5/5), round-trip min/avg/max = 4/5/8 ms

R1#ping 10.20.20.1

Type escape sequence to abort.
Sending 5, 100-byte ICMP Echos to 10.20.20.1, timeout is 2 seconds:
!!!!!
Success rate is 100 percent (5/5), round-trip min/avg/max = 4/6/8 ms

R1#ping 10.30.30.1

Type escape sequence to abort.
Sending 5, 100-byte ICMP Echos to 10.30.30.1, timeout is 2 seconds:
!!!!!
Success rate is 100 percent (5/5), round-trip min/avg/max = 4/5/8 ms
```

LAB 86: PASSIVE INTERFACES FOR EIGRP UPDATES

Lab Objective:

The objective of this lab exercise is for you to learn and understand how to prevent EIGRP from sending unnecessary updates by using passive interfaces.

Lab Purpose:

Preventing unnecessary EIGRP updates using passive interfaces is a fundamental skill. By default, EIGRP sends updates via multicast on all interfaces for which EIGRP has been enabled. This means that EIGRP adjacencies will form on all interfaces for which EIGRP has been enabled. In some cases, this may not be desirable and should be prevented. As a Cisco engineer, as well as in the Cisco CCNA exam, you will be expected to know how to prevent EIGRP from sending unnecessary updates.

Certification Level:

This lab is suitable for CCNA certification exam preparation.

Lab Difficulty:

This lab has a difficulty rating of 6/10.

Readiness Assessment:

When you are ready for your certification exam, you should complete this lab in no more than 10 minutes.

Lab Topology:

Please use the following topology to complete this lab exercise:

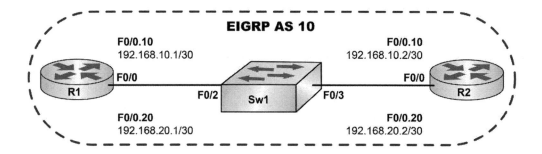

Task 1:
Configure hostnames on R1, R2, and Sw1 as illustrated in the topology.

Task 2:
Configure VLAN10 named EIGRP_10 and VLAN20 named EIGRP_20 on Sw1. Next, configure Sw1 F0/2 and F0/3 as trunks. These should be connected to R1 and R2 F0/0 interfaces, respectively.

Task 3:
Configure subinterfaces Fa0/0.10 and F0/0.20 on R1 and R2. Subinterface Fa0/0.10 on either router should be associated with VLAN10 and subinterface Fa0/0.20 on either router should be associated with VLAN20. Configure IP addresses on both the subinterfaces as illustrated in the topology.

Task 4:
Ping between R1 and R2 on subinterface Fa0/0.10 and Fa0/0.20 to verify IP connectivity.

Task 5:
Enable EIGRP using ASN 10 on R1 and R2 F0/0.10 and F0/0.20 subinterfaces, respectively, and verify that you have two EIGRP neighbor adjacencies on R1 and R2, one through the F0/0.10 subinterface and the other through the Fa0/0.20 subinterface. On either R1 or R2, verify that you have two EIGRP adjacencies to your peer router.

Task 6:
Prevent EIGRP from forming an adjacency via Fa0/0.20 on R1 and R2. Verify that you now have only one EIGRP neighbor adjacency on R1 and R2, only through each F0/0.10 subinterface.

LAB 86: CONFIGURATION AND VERIFICATION

Task 1:

For reference information on configuring hostnames, please refer to earlier labs.

Task 2:

For reference information on configuring VLANs, please refer to earlier labs.

Task 3:

For reference information on configuring router subinterfaces, please refer to earlier labs.

Task 4:
```
R1#ping 192.168.10.2

Type escape sequence to abort.
Sending 5, 100-byte ICMP Echos to 192.168.10.2, timeout is 2 seconds:
.!!!!
Success rate is 80 percent (4/5), round-trip min/avg/max = 1/3/4 ms
```

Task 5:

For reference information on configuring EIGRP, please refer to earlier labs.

```
R2#show ip eigrp neighbors
IP-EIGRP neighbors for process 10
H   Address          Interface      Hold Uptime   SRTT   RTO  Q  Seq
                                    (sec)         (ms)        Cnt Num
1   192.168.20.1     Fa0/0.20       11 00:02:31   1779   5000 0  2
0   192.168.10.1     Fa0/0.10       12 00:02:34   809    4854 0  1
```

Task 6:
```
R2(config)#router eigrp 10
R2(config-router)#passive-interface e0/0.20
*Mar  1 01:34:53.925: %DUAL-5-NBRCHANGE: IP-EIGRP(0) 10: Neighbor
192.168.20.1 (FastEthernet0/0.20) is down: interface passive
R2(config-router)#end
R2#
R2#show ip eigrp neighbors
IP-EIGRP neighbors for process 10
H   Address          Interface      Hold Uptime   SRTT   RTO  Q  Seq
                                    (sec)         (ms)        Cnt Num
0   192.168.10.1     Fa0/0.10       11 00:04:46   647    3882 0  3
```

NOTE: When configuring passive interfaces under EIGRP, it is important to know that they need to be applied to only one side of the adjacency to prevent routing updates on that interface. In our example, specifying FastEthernet0/0.20 in R2 as passive dropped the adjacency on R1 and R2 FastEthernet0/0.20. Remember that you can issue the show ip protocols command to see which interfaces are currently passive.

LAB 87: SUMMARIZING ROUTES WITH EIGRP

Lab Objective:
The objective of this lab exercise is for you to learn and understand how to summarize routes with EIGRP. Route summarization allows the size of routing tables to be reduced by advertising a summary route for a range of multiple specific routes.

Lab Purpose:
Route summarization is a fundamental skill for network engineers. With the subnetted networks of today, routing tables can grow very large due to the sheer number of network entries. In order to reduce the burden of extremely large routing tables on routers, route summarization can be used. This topic is actually outside the exam (according to the syllabus) so feel free to skip it, but we felt that you need to know this for the real world.

Certification Level:
This lab is suitable for CCNA certification exam preparation.

Lab Difficulty:
This lab has a difficulty rating of 8/10.

Readiness Assessment:
When you are ready for your certification exam, you should complete this lab in no more than 10 minutes.

Lab Topology:
Please use the following topology to complete this lab exercise:

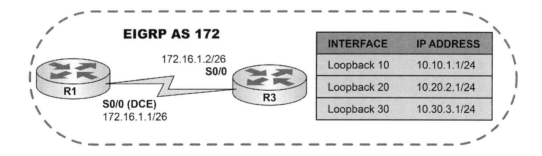

Task 1:

Configure hostnames on R1 and R3 as illustrated in the topology. Since R1 S0/0 is the DCE end of the back-to-back Serial connection, configure R1 to send R3 clocking information at a rate of 256 Kbps. Configure the IP addresses for R1 and R3 S0/0 interfaces as specified in the topology and ping between the routers to verify connectivity based on your configurations.

Task 2:

Configure the Loopback interfaces on R3 as illustrated in the topology.

Task 3:

Enable EIGRP using ASN 172 on both R1 and R3, and configure EIGRP network statements for R1 and R3 S0/0 interfaces and for the Loopback interfaces on R3. Ensure that EIGRP does not perform automatic summarization at classful network boundaries.

Task 4:

On R1, verify the EIGRP routes you are receiving from R3. You should have three routes for the 10.x.x.x/24 Loopback interfaces configured on R3 and advertised by EIGRP. Ping these IP addresses to verify connectivity.

Task 5:

Configure R3 to send a summarized route for the 10.x.x.x/24 Loopback interfaces to R1.

Task 6:

Verify the EIGRP routes you are receiving from R3 on R1. You should now have one route for the 10.x.x.x/24 Loopback interfaces configured on R3 and advertised by EIGRP. Ping these IP addresses to verify connectivity.

LAB 87: CONFIGURATION AND VERIFICATION

Task 1:

For reference information on configuring hostnames, please refer to earlier labs.

Task 2:

For reference information on configuring Loopback interfaces, please refer to earlier labs.

Task 3:

For reference information on enabling EIGRP and disabling auto summarization, please refer to earlier labs.

Task 4:

```
R1#show ip route eigrp
     10.0.0.0/24 is subnetted, 3 subnets
D       10.30.3.0 [90/2297856] via 172.16.1.2, 00:00:33, Serial0/0
D       10.20.2.0 [90/2297856] via 172.16.1.2, 00:00:34, Serial0/0
D       10.10.1.0 [90/2297856] via 172.16.1.2, 00:00:34, Serial0/0

R1#ping 10.10.1.1

Type escape sequence to abort.
Sending 5, 100-byte ICMP Echos to 10.10.1.1, timeout is 2 seconds:
!!!!!
Success rate is 100 percent (5/5), round-trip min/avg/max = 4/6/8 ms

R1#ping 10.20.2.1

Type escape sequence to abort.
Sending 5, 100-byte ICMP Echos to 10.20.2.1, timeout is 2 seconds:
!!!!!
Success rate is 100 percent (5/5), round-trip min/avg/max = 4/6/8 ms

R1#ping 10.30.3.1

Type escape sequence to abort.
Sending 5, 100-byte ICMP Echos to 10.30.3.1, timeout is 2 seconds:
!!!!!
Success rate is 100 percent (5/5), round-trip min/avg/max = 4/6/8 ms
```

Task 5:

The second octet in binary notation for the three Loopback interface subnets on R3 would be written as follows:

128	64	32	16	8	4	2	1
0	0	0	0	1	0	1	0
0	0	0	1	0	1	0	0
0	0	0	0	0	0	1	0
0	0	0	1	1	1	1	0

The last value under which all four bits are the same is 32. Therefore, to determine the summary address, insert a value of 1 all the way through the column with the 4 in it and add those bits up. The answer will be the decimal value, which you will use to create the summary address subnet mask. This is illustrated as follows:

128	64	32	16	8	4	2	1
1	1	1	0	0	0	0	0

The subnet mask for your summarized network would be 128 + 64 + 32, which equals 224. The summary address would then be written as 10.0.0.0 255.255.224.0 or 10.0.0.0/11. To configure EIGRP to send this summary address instead of the three 10.x.x.x/24 network entries, use the ip summary-address eigrp <as-number> command under the interface EIGRP uses to send updates to other RIPv2 routers as illustrated below. Do not forget to add the ASN when configuring EIGRP route summarization.

```
R3#conf t
Enter configuration commands, one per line.  End with CTRL/Z.
R3(config)#int s0/0
R3(config-if)#ip summ
R3(config-if)#ip summary-address eigrp 172 10.0.0.0 255.224.0.0
R3(config-if)#end
*Mar  1 02:39:48.125: %DUAL-5-NBRCHANGE: IP-EIGRP(0) 172: Neighbor
172.16.1.1 (Serial0/0) is down: summary configured
*Mar  1 02:39:50.305: %DUAL-5-NBRCHANGE: IP-EIGRP(0) 172: Neighbor
172.16.1.1 (Serial0/0) is up: new adjacency
R3#
R3#show running-config interface s0/0
Building configuration...

Current configuration : 134 bytes
!
interface Serial0/0
 ip address 172.16.1.2 255.255.255.192
```

```
    ip summary-address eigrp 172 10.0.0.0 255.224.0.0 5
    no fair-queue
    end
```

> **NOTE:** As can be seen in the output above, when an EIGRP summary address is configured, the EIGRP neighbor adjacencies via that interface are reset. Be careful when doing this in a production network environment. Because of this, there is no need to issue the `clear ip route *` command. Also notice that under the interface configuration, even though we issued the command `ip summary-address eigrp 172 10.0.0.0 255.224.0.0`, there is an additional 5 at the end. This is because EIGRP summary routes have a default administrative distance of 5. This can be viewed on the router performing the summarization as follows:

```
R2#show ip route 10.30.3.1 255.224.0.0
Routing entry for 10.0.0.0/11
  Known via "eigrp 172", distance 5, metric 128256, type internal
  Redistributing via eigrp 172
  Routing Descriptor Blocks:
  * directly connected, via Null0
      Route metric is 128256, traffic share count is 1
      Total delay is 5000 microseconds, minimum bandwidth is 10000000
Kbit
      Reliability 255/255, minimum MTU 1514 bytes
      Loading 1/255, Hops 0
```

Summary routes in EIGRP will always point to the Null0 interface, which is simply a logical black-hole interface in Cisco IOS routers. Detailed knowledge of Null0 is beyond the scope of this course, so don't worry too much about it; however, be familiar with the fact that EIGRP summary routes will be automatically created and use Null0.

Task 6:

```
R1#show ip route eigrp
      10.0.0.0/11 is subnetted, 1 subnets
D        10.0.0.0 [90/2297856] via 172.16.1.2, 00:03:20, Serial0/0

R1#ping 10.10.1.1

Type escape sequence to abort.
Sending 5, 100-byte ICMP Echos to 10.10.10.1, timeout is 2 seconds:
!!!!!
Success rate is 100 percent (5/5), round-trip min/avg/max = 4/6/8 ms

R1#ping 10.20.2.1

Type escape sequence to abort.
Sending 5, 100-byte ICMP Echos to 10.20.20.1, timeout is 2 seconds:
!!!!!
```

Success rate is 100 percent (5/5), round-trip min/avg/max = 4/5/8 ms

R1#ping 10.30.3.1

Type escape sequence to abort.
Sending 5, 100-byte ICMP Echos to 10.30.30.1, timeout is 2 seconds:
!!!!!
Success rate is 100 percent (5/5), round-trip min/avg/max = 4/6/8 ms

LAB 88: VERIFYING THE EIGRP DATABASE

Lab Objective:
The objective of this lab exercise is for you to learn and understand how to verify the EIGRP database using the appropriate Cisco IOS commands.

Lab Purpose:
Verifying the EIGRP database is a fundamental skill. EIGRP is an advanced distance vector protocol that incorporates features from both distance vector and link-state routing protocols. The EIGRP database is a feature of link-state routing protocols. As a Cisco engineer, as well as in the Cisco CCNA exam, you will be expected to know how to verify routes in the EIGRP database.

Certification Level:
This lab is suitable for CCNA certification exam preparation.

Lab Difficulty:
This lab has a difficulty rating of 6/10.

Readiness Assessment:
When you are ready for your certification exam, you should complete this lab in no more than 10 minutes.

Lab Topology:
Please use the following topology to complete this lab exercise:

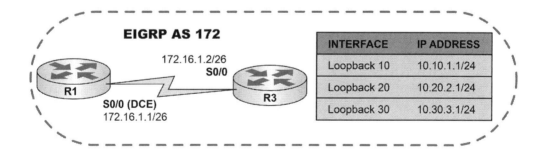

Task 1:

Configure hostnames on R1 and R3 as illustrated in the topology. Since R1 S0/0 is the DCE end of the back-to-back Serial connection, configure R1 to send R3 clocking information at a rate of 256 Kbps. Configure the IP addresses for R1 and R3 S0/0 interfaces as specified in the topology and ping between the routers to verify connectivity based on your configuration.

Task 2:

Configure the Loopback interfaces on R3 as illustrated in the topology.

Task 3:

Enable EIGRP using ASN 172 on both R1 and R3 and configure EIGRP network statements for R1 and R3 S0/0 interfaces and for the Loopback interfaces on R3. Ensure that EIGRP does not perform automatic summarization at classful network boundaries.

Task 4:

On R1, verify the state of the received routes in the EIGRP database using the appropriate show commands. To take a more detailed look, also verify the EIGRP database information of the 10.20.20.0/24 subnet.

LAB 88: CONFIGURATION AND VERIFICATION

Task 1:

For reference information on configuring hostnames, please refer to earlier labs.

Task 2:

For reference information on configuring Loopback interfaces, please refer to earlier labs.

Task 3:

For reference information on enabling EIGRP, please refer to earlier labs.

Task 4:

```
R1#show ip route eigrp
        10.0.0.0/24 is subnetted, 3 subnets
D       10.30.30.0 [90/2297856] via 172.16.1.2, 00:00:33, Serial0/0
D       10.20.20.0 [90/2297856] via 172.16.1.2, 00:00:34, Serial0/0
D       10.10.10.0 [90/2297856] via 172.16.1.2, 00:00:34, Serial0/0

R1#ping 10.10.1.1

Type escape sequence to abort.
Sending 5, 100-byte ICMP Echos to 10.10.10.1, timeout is 2 seconds:
!!!!!
Success rate is 100 percent (5/5), round-trip min/avg/max = 4/6/8 ms

R1#ping 10.20.2.1

Type escape sequence to abort.
Sending 5, 100-byte ICMP Echos to 10.20.20.1, timeout is 2 seconds:
!!!!!
Success rate is 100 percent (5/5), round-trip min/avg/max = 4/6/8 ms

R1#ping 10.30.3.1

Type escape sequence to abort.
Sending 5, 100-byte ICMP Echos to 10.30.30.1, timeout is 2 seconds:
!!!!!
Success rate is 100 percent (5/5), round-trip min/avg/max = 4/6/8 ms

R1#show ip eigrp topology
IP-EIGRP Topology Table for AS(172)/ID(17.16.1.1)

Codes: P - Passive, A - Active, U - Update, Q - Query, R - Reply,
       r - reply Status, s - sia Status

P 10.30.30.0/24, 1 successors, FD is 2297856
```

```
           via 172.16.1.2 (2297856/128256), Serial0/0
P 10.20.20.0/24, 1 successors, FD is 2297856
           via 172.16.1.2 (2297856/128256), Serial0/0
P 10.10.10.0/24, 1 successors, FD is 2297856
           via 172.16.1.2 (2297856/128256), Serial0/0
P 172.16.1.0/26, 1 successors, FD is 2169856
           via Connected, Serial0/0
```

NOTE: The output of the `show ip eigrp topology` command will show you the EIGRP router ID of the local router, the route metric, Feasible Distance, Successors, and Feasible Successors (if applicable). These are core EIGRP components that you are expected to know. Take some time to familiarize yourself with the information contained in the output of this command. It should be explained in more detail in your theory guide.

```
R1#show ip eigrp topology 10.20.2.0 255.255.255.0
IP-EIGRP (AS 172): Topology entry for 10.20.2.0/24
  State is Passive, Query origin flag is 1, 1 Successor(s), FD is
2297856
  Routing Descriptor Blocks:
  172.16.1.2 (Serial0/0), from 172.16.1.2, Send flag is 0x0
      Composite metric is (2297856/128256), Route is Internal
      Vector metric:
        Minimum bandwidth is 1544 Kbit
        Total delay is 25000 microseconds
        Reliability is 255/255
        Load is 1/255
        Minimum MTU is 1500
        Hop count is 1
```

NOTE: The output of the `show ip eigrp topology [network] [mask]` command will show you where the route is from, the composite metric of the route, and the components included in the calculation of the metric, such as bandwidth, delay, reliability, load, and MTU. It also includes the hop count of the route. Again, these are core EIGRP components that you are expected to know. Therefore, take some time to familiarize yourself with the information contained in the output of this command.

LAB 89: EIGRP SPLIT HORIZON

Lab Objective:
The objective of this lab exercise is for you to learn and understand the effects of split horizon in a typical hub-and-spoke topology. Feel free to skip this lab because it's unlikely to come up in the exam. Just note the command to disable split horizon below.

Lab Purpose:
Configuring and troubleshooting split horizon is a fundamental skill. EIGRP is an advanced distance vector protocol and as such uses split horizon to prevent routing loops. Split horizon mandates that EIGRP will not send updates back out of the interface on which they were received. While this default feature is generally a good thing, it can have a disastrous effect on traditional hub-and-spoke topologies. As a Cisco engineer, as well as in the Cisco CCNA exam, you will be expected to know how to address split horizon issues in EIGRP.

Certification Level:
This lab is suitable for ICND2 and CCNA certification exam preparation.

Lab Difficulty:
This lab has a difficulty rating of 8/10.

Readiness Assessment:
When you are ready for your certification exam, you should complete this lab in no more than 20 minutes.

> **IMPORTANT NOTE:** In order to configure frame relay between two routers in your lab, you will need THREE routers! The first two routers will be regular routers, and the third will need to be configured as a frame relay switch. This can be any Cisco router that has at least two Serial interfaces. Please refer to Appendix B: Cabling and Configuring a Frame Relay Switch For Three Routers for the appropriate configuration to issue on the frame relay switch.

Lab Topology:

Please use the following topology to complete this lab exercise:

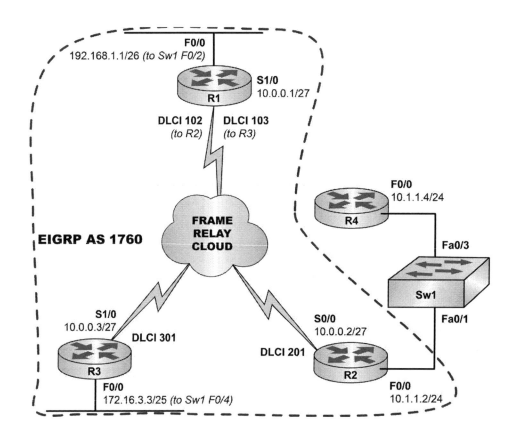

Task 1:

This lab will only be performed on R1, R2, and R3. Configure hostnames on R1, R2, and R3 as shown above.

Task 2:

Configure the switch in the topology with the hostname Sw1. Enable F0/1, F0/2, and F0/4 on Sw1 so that when you bring up the router interfaces connected to those switchports they can come up.

Task 3:

Configure IP addresses on the Fa0/0 interfaces on R1, R2, and R3. Make sure that you enable these interfaces and they are up.

Task 4:

Configure frame relay on R1, R2, and R3. Use the IP addresses in the topology for their respective Serial interfaces. Use the default frame relay encapsulation of Cisco. Configure static frame relay maps between R1, R2, and R3, so that each router has a static frame relay map to the other two routers on the frame relay network.

Task 5:

Enable EIGRP in ASN 1760 on R1, R2, and R3 for all the subnets configured on those respective routers. Be sure to prevent EIGRP from automatically summarizing at classful network boundaries.

Task 6:

If you have configured everything as requested, you will not be able to see the 10.1.1.0/24 route via EIGRP on R3, nor will you be able to see the 172.16.3.0/25 route via EIGRP on R2. However, R1 will have both routes. Verify that this is the case using the appropriate commands.

Task 7:

Based on your studies, you know that the reason you are not seeing the 10.1.1.0/24 route via EIGRP on R3 and the 172.16.3.0/25 route via EIGRP on R2 is because these routes are both sent to R1 via EIGRP, but since distance vector protocols do not send routing information back out of the same interface they received it, R1 will not send the routing information for 10.1.1.0/24 to R3 or the routing information for 172.16.3.0/25 since the routing information was received on the same interface. To prevent this from happening, disable this default feature.

Task 8:

Now verify that you can see the 10.1.1.0/24 route via EIGRP on R3 and the 172.16.3.0/25 route via EIGRP on R2. Ping 10.1.1.1 from R3 and 172.16.3.3 from R2 to verify network connectivity.

LAB 89: CONFIGURATION AND VERIFICATION

Task 1:

For reference information on configuring hostnames, please refer to earlier labs.

Task 2:

For reference information on configuring opening (no shutting) switch interfaces, please refer to earlier labs.

Task 3:

For reference information on configuring IP addresses, please refer to earlier labs.

Task 4:

For reference information on verifying frame relay mapping, please refer to earlier labs.

```
R1#show frame-relay map
Serial1/0(up): ip 10.0.0.2 dlci 102(0x66,0x1860), static,
            broadcast,
            CISCO, status defined, active
Serial1/0 (up): ip 10.0.0.3 dlci 103(0x67,0x1870), static,
            broadcast,
            CISCO, status defined, active

R2#show frame-relay map
Serial0/0 (up): ip 10.0.0.1 dlci 201(0xC9,0x3090), static,
            broadcast,
            CISCO, status defined, active
Serial0/0 (up): ip 10.0.0.3 dlci 201(0xC9,0x3090), static,
            broadcast,
            CISCO, status defined, active

R3#show frame-relay map
Serial1/0 (up): ip 10.0.0.1 dlci 301(0x12D,0x48D0), static,
            broadcast,
            CISCO, status defined, active
Serial1/0 (up): ip 10.0.0.2 dlci 301(0x12D,0x48D0), static,
            broadcast,
            CISCO, status defined, active
```

Task 5:

```
R1#conf t
Enter configuration commands, one per line.  End with CTRL/Z.
R1(config)#router eigrp 1760
R1(config-router)#no auto-summary
R1(config-router)#net 10.0.0.0
R1(config-router)#network 192.168.1.0
R1(config-router)#end
```

```
R1#

R2#config t
Enter configuration commands, one per line.  End with CTRL/Z.
R2(config)#router eigrp 1760
R2(config-router)#no auto-summary
R2(config-router)#network 10.0.0.0
R2(config-router)#network 10.1.1.0
R2(config-router)#^Z
R2#

R3#config t
Enter configuration commands, one per line.  End with CTRL/Z.
R3(config)#router eigrp 1760
R3(config-router)#no auto-summary
R3(config-router)#network 10.0.0.0
R3(config-router)#network 172.16.3.0
R3(config-router)#^Z
R3#

R1#show ip eigrp neighbors
IP-EIGRP neighbors for process 1760
H   Address           Interface       Hold Uptime    SRTT   RTO  Q  Seq
                                      (sec)          (ms)        Cnt Num
1   10.0.0.2          Se1/0           165 00:01:07    24    200  0  2
0   10.0.0.3          Se1/0           153 00:01:25   124    744  0  2

R2#show ip eigrp neighbors
IP-EIGRP neighbors for process 1760
H   Address           Interface       Hold Uptime    SRTT   RTO  Q  Seq
                                      (sec)          (ms)        Cnt Num
0   10.0.0.1          Se0/0           128 00:00:53   911   5000  0  4

R3#show ip eigrp neighbors
IP-EIGRP neighbors for process 1760
H   Address           Interface       Hold Uptime    SRTT   RTO  Q  Seq
                                      (sec)          (ms)        Cnt Num
0   10.0.0.1          Se1/0           156 00:02:20     8    200  0  4
```

Task 6:

```
R3#show ip route eigrp
     192.168.1.0/26 is subnetted, 1 subnets
D       192.168.1.0 [90/2195456] via 10.0.0.1, 00:10:53, Serial1/0

R2#show ip route eigrp
     192.168.1.0/26 is subnetted, 1 subnets
D       192.168.1.0 [90/2195456] via 10.0.0.1, 00:10:55, Serial0/0

R1#show ip route eigrp
     172.16.0.0/25 is subnetted, 1 subnets
```

```
D        172.16.3.0 [90/2195456] via 10.0.0.3, 00:12:23, Serial1/0
         10.0.0.0/8 is variably subnetted, 2 subnets, 2 masks
D        10.1.1.0/24 [90/2195456] via 10.0.0.2, 00:12:04, Serial1/0
```

Task 7:
```
R1#conf t
Enter configuration commands, one per line.  End with CTRL/Z.
R1(config)#int s1/0
R1(config-if)#no ip split-horizon eigrp 1760
R1(config-if)#end
R1#
*Mar  1 01:20:39.104: %DUAL-5-NBRCHANGE: IP-EIGRP(0) 1760: Neighbor
10.0.0.2 (Serial1/0) is down: split horizon changed
*Mar  1 01:20:39.108: %DUAL-5-NBRCHANGE: IP-EIGRP(0) 1760: Neighbor
10.0.0.3 (Serial1/0) is down: split horizon changed
*Mar  1 01:20:39.677: %DUAL-5-NBRCHANGE: IP-EIGRP(0) 1760: Neighbor
10.0.0.3 (Serial1/0) is up: new adjacency
*Mar  1 01:21:34.122: %DUAL-5-NBRCHANGE: IP-EIGRP(0) 1760: Neighbor
10.0.0.2 (Serial1/0) is up: new adjacency
```

NOTE: When you disable (or re-enable) split horizon on an interface, all EIGRP adjacencies that have been established via that interface are reset as indicated in the output above. You can verify that the neighbors have been re-established successfully using the show ip eigrp neighbors command as illustrated in the following output:

```
R1#show ip eigrp neighbors
IP-EIGRP neighbors for process 1760
H   Address          Interface        Hold Uptime   SRTT   RTO  Q  Seq
                                       (sec)         (ms)        Cnt Num
1   10.0.0.2         Se1/0            131 00:00:50 1512   5000  0  4
0   10.0.0.3         Se1/0            131 00:01:44   13    200  0  5
```

Task 8:
```
R2#show ip route eigrp
      172.16.0.0/25 is subnetted, 1 subnets
D        172.16.3.0 [90/2707456] via 10.0.0.1, 00:00:05, Serial0/0
      192.168.1.0/26 is subnetted, 1 subnets
D        192.168.1.0 [90/2195456] via 10.0.0.1, 00:00:05, Serial0/0

R2#ping 172.16.3.3

Type escape sequence to abort.
Sending 5, 100-byte ICMP Echos to 172.16.3.3, timeout is 2 seconds:
!!!!!
Success rate is 100 percent (5/5), round-trip min/avg/max = 28/32/40 ms

R3#show ip route eigrp
      10.0.0.0/8 is variably subnetted, 2 subnets, 2 masks
D        10.1.1.0/24 [90/2707456] via 10.0.0.1, 00:00:47, Serial1/0
```

```
      192.168.1.0/26 is subnetted, 1 subnets
D        192.168.1.0 [90/2195456] via 10.0.0.1, 00:00:47, Serial1/0

R3#ping 10.1.1.2

Type escape sequence to abort.
Sending 5, 100-byte ICMP Echos to 10.1.1.2, timeout is 2 seconds:
!!!!!
Success rate is 100 percent (5/5), round-trip min/avg/max = 24/27/32 ms
```

LAB 90: CONFIGURING EIGRP FOR IPV6

Lab Objective

The objective of this lab exercise is for you to learn how to configure EIGRP running IPv6.

Lab Purpose:

EIGRP for IPv6 will allow you to run a distance vector routing protocol in your infrastructure when running IPv6. As a Cisco engineer, as well as in the Cisco CCNA exam, you will be expected to know how to implement EIGRP on an IPv6-enabled network.

Certification Level:

This lab is suitable for ICND2 certification exam preparation.

Lab Difficulty:

This lab has a difficulty rating of 7/10.

Readiness Assessment:

When you are ready for your certification exam, you should complete this lab in no more than 20 minutes.

Lab Topology:

Please use the following topology to complete this lab exercise:

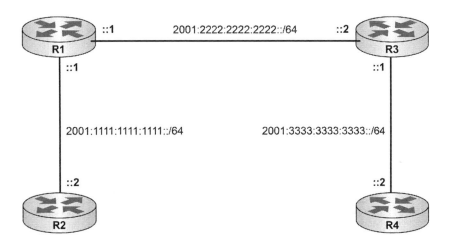

EIGRP AS 100

INTERFACE	IPv6 ADDRESS
Loopback 1	2001:AAAA:AAAA:AAAA::1/64
Loopback 2	2001:BBBB:BBBB:CCCC::1/64

INTERFACE	IPv6 ADDRESS
Loopback 1	2001:4444:4444:0001::1/64
Loopback 2	2001:4444:4444:0002::1/64
Loopback 3	2001:4444:4444:0003::1/64

Task 1:

Configure hostnames on R1, R2, R3, and R4 as illustrated in the topology.

Task 2:

Configure each router with its respective IPv6 addresses and Gigabit interfaces, and make sure that your router is ready to route IPv6 traffic.

> **NOTE:** You can select the Gigabit interface you want to use (Gig0/0 or Gig0/1) for any network shown in the diagram.

Task 3:

Configure EIGRP for IPv6 in the network as follows:

- All the routers will be inside ASN 100;
- There are no IPv4 addresses at all so manually create a router ID for each router (different on each unit); and
- Make sure that you advertise every network shown in the diagram (including Loopbacks).

Task 4:

Make sure that you can ping from R2 Loopbacks to R4 Loopbacks to ensure that there is full connectivity.

Task 5:

To see the EIGRP database, provide the following information from R1:

- `show ipv6 eigrp neighbhors`
- `show ipv6 eigrp topology`
- `show ipv6 route`

LAB 90: CONFIGURATION AND VERIFICATION

Task 1:

For reference information on configuring hostnames, please refer to earlier labs.

Task 2:

For reference information on configuring IPv6 and IPv6 interfaces, please refer to earlier labs.

Task 3:

```
R1#config t
Enter configuration commands, one per line.  End with CTRL/Z.
R1(config)#ipv6 router eigrp 100
R1(config-rtr)#router-id 1.1.1.1
R1(config-rtr)#no shut
R1(config)#int gig0/0
R1(config-if)#ipv6 eigrp 100
R1(config)#int gig0/1
R1(config-if)#ipv6 eigrp 100

R2#config t
Enter configuration commands, one per line.  End with CTRL/Z.
R2(config)#ipv6 router eigrp 100
R2(config-rtr)#router-id 2.2.2.2
R2(config-rtr)#no shut
R2(config)#int gig0/0
R2(config-if)#ipv6 eigrp 100
R2(config)#int loop1
R2(config-if)#ipv6 eigrp 100
R2(config)#int loop2
R2(config-if)#ipv6 eigrp 100

R3#config t
Enter configuration commands, one per line.  End with CTRL/Z.
R3(config)#ipv6 router eigrp 100
R3(config-rtr)#router-id 3.3.3.3
R3(config-rtr)#no shut
R3(config)#int gig0/0
R3(config-if)#ipv6 eigrp 100
R3(config)#int gig0/1
R3(config-if)#ipv6 eigrp 100

R4#config t
Enter configuration commands, one per line.  End with CTRL/Z.
R4(config)#ipv6 router eigrp 100
R4(config-rtr)#router-id 4.4.4.4
R4(config-rtr)#no shut
```

```
R4(config)#int gig0/0
R4(config-if)#ipv6 eigrp 100
R4(config)#int loop1
R4(config-if)#ipv6 eigrp 100
R4(config)#int loop2
R4(config-if)#ipv6 eigrp 100
R4(config)#int loop3
R4(config-if)#ipv6 eigrp 100
```

Task 4:

```
R2#ping 2001:4444:4444:0002::1 source 2001:BBBB:BBBB:CCCC::1

Type escape sequence to abort.
Sending 5, 100-byte ICMP Echos to 2001:4444:4444:2::1, timeout is 2
seconds:
Packet sent with a source address of 2001:BBBB:BBBB:CCCC::1
!!!!!
Success rate is 100 percent (5/5), round-trip min/avg/max = 28/57/72 ms

R4#ping 2001:AAAA:AAAA:AAAA::1 source 2001:4444:4444:0001::1

Type escape sequence to abort.
Sending 5, 100-byte ICMP Echos to 2001:AAAA:AAAA:AAAA::1, timeout is 2
seconds:
Packet sent with a source address of 2001:4444:4444:1::1
!!!!!
Success rate is 100 percent (5/5), round-trip min/avg/max = 24/31/44 ms
Distance: external 20 internal 200 local 200
```

Task 5:

```
R1#show ipv6 eigrp neighbors
IPv6-EIGRP neighbors for process 100
H    Address              Interface       Hold Uptime    SRTT   RTO   Q  Seq
                                          (sec)          (ms)       Cnt Num
1    Link-local address:G0/0              11 00:00:08 1032   5000  0  17
     FE80::C007:51FF:FE93:0
0    Link-local address:G0/1              12 00:09:30  31    200   0  6
     FE80::C006:51FF:FE92:0

R1#show ipv6 eigrp topology
IPv6-EIGRP Topology Table for AS(100)/ID(1.1.1.1)

Codes: P - Passive, A - Active, U - Update, Q - Query, R - Reply,
       r - reply Status, s - sia Status

P 2001:4444:4444:1::/64, 1 successors, FD is 435200
      via FE80::C007:51FF:FE93:0 (435200/409600), G0/0
P 2001:4444:4444:3::/64, 1 successors, FD is 435200
      via FE80::C007:51FF:FE93:0 (435200/409600), G0/0
P 2001:4444:4444:2::/64, 1 successors, FD is 435200
```

```
        via FE80::C007:51FF:FE93:0 (435200/409600), G0/0
P 2001:1111:1111:1111::/64, 1 successors, FD is 281600
        via Connected, G0/1
P 2001:2222:2222:2222::/64, 1 successors, FD is 281600
        via Connected, G0/0
P 2001:3333:3333:3333::/64, 1 successors, FD is 307200
        via FE80::C007:51FF:FE93:0 (307200/281600), G0/0
P 2001:AAAA:AAAA:AAAA::/64, 1 successors, FD is 409600
        via FE80::C006:51FF:FE92:0 (409600/128256), G0/0
P 2001:BBBB:BBBB:CCCC::/64, 1 successors, FD is 409600
        via FE80::C006:51FF:FE92:0 (409600/128256), G0/0


R1#show ipv6 route
IPv6 Routing Table - 11 entries
Codes: C - Connected, L - Local, S - Static, R - RIP, B-BGP,
       U - Per-user Static route, M - MIPv6,
       I1 - ISIS L1, I2 - ISIS L2, IA - ISIS interarea, IS - ISIS
summary,
       O - OSPF intra, OI - OSPF inter, OE1 - OSPF ext 1,
       OE2 - OSPF ext 2, ON1 - OSPF NSSA ext 1, ON2 - OSPF NSSA ext 2,
       D - EIGRP, EX - EIGRP external

C   2001:1111:1111:1111::/64 [0/0]
     via ::, G0/1
L   2001:1111:1111:1111::1/128 [0/0]
     via ::, G0/1
C   2001:2222:2222:2222::/64 [0/0]
     via ::, G0/0
L   2001:2222:2222:2222::1/128 [0/0]
     via ::, G0/0
D   2001:3333:3333:3333::/64 [90/307200]
     via FE80::C007:51FF:FE93:0, G0/0
D   2001:4444:4444:1::/64 [90/435200]
     via FE80::C007:51FF:FE93:0, G0/0
D   2001:4444:4444:2::/64 [90/435200]
     via FE80::C007:51FF:FE93:0, G0/0
D   2001:4444:4444:3::/64 [90/435200]
     via FE80::C007:51FF:FE93:0, G0/0
D   2001:AAAA:AAAA:AAAA::/64 [90/409600]
     via FE80::C006:51FF:FE92:0, G0/1
D   2001:BBBB:BBBB:CCCC::/64 [90/409600]
     via FE80::C006:51FF:FE92:0, G0/1
L   FF00::/8 [0/0]
     via ::, Null0
```

3.0 WAN Technologies

LAB 91: CONFIGURING BACK-TO-BACK SERIAL CONNECTIONS

Lab Objective:
The objective of this lab exercise is to configure back-to-back Serial interfaces between two Cisco routers. By default, router Serial interfaces receive their clocking information from an external device such as a CSU/DSU.

Lab Purpose:
Back-to-back Serial interface configuration is a fundamental skill. Because routers typically receive clocking from an external device such as a CSU/DSU, it is imperative to understand how to bring up a back-to-back Serial connection between two routers to set up your home lab, for example. As a Cisco engineer, as well as in the Cisco CCNA exam, you will be expected to know how to configure back-to-back Serial connections.

Certification Level:
This lab is suitable for both CCENT and CCNA certification exam preparation.

Lab Difficulty:
This lab has a difficulty rating of 3/10.

Readiness Assessment:
When you are ready for your certification exam, you should complete this lab in no more than 10 minutes.

Lab Topology:

Please use the following topology to complete this lab exercise:

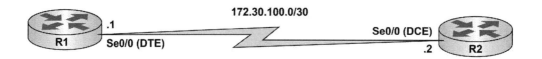

Task 1:

Configure hostnames on R1 and R2 as illustrated in the topology.

Task 2:

Enable Serial interfaces on R1 and R2. The Serial0/0 interface on R2 is identified as the DCE in the topology. Use the appropriate show command to verify that this interface is indeed the DCE.

Task 3:

Configure the DCE interface on R2 to provide clocking to R1. The clock speed should be 256 Kbps. Remember that 1 Kbps = 1000 bps. Verify that R1 receives clocking information from R2.

Task 4:

Configure IP addressing on R1 and R2 Serial0/0 interfaces as illustrated in the topology.

Task 5:

Verify your interface status and ping between R1 and R2 to validate connectivity.

LAB 91: CONFIGURATION AND VERIFICATION

Task 1:

For reference information on configuring hostnames, please refer to earlier labs.

Task 2:

```
R1(config)#interface serial0/0
R1(config-if)#no shut
*Mar  1 00:36:47.282: %LINK-3-UPDOWN: Interface Serial0/0, changed
state to down
R1(config-if)#end
R1#

R2(config)#interface serial0/0
R2(config-if)#no shut
*Mar  1 00:36:47.282: %LINK-3-UPDOWN: Interface Serial0/0, changed
state to down
R2(config-if)#end
R2#show controllers serial 0/0
Interface Serial0/0
Hardware is PowerQUICC MPC860
DCE V.35, no clock
```

NOTE: The `show controllers` command will tell you whether the interface is the DCE side (which provides the clocking) or the DTE side (which receives the clocking) on a particular router interface. Note that GNS3 doesn't use actual cables so there is no need to configure clocking.

Task 3:

```
R2#conf t
Enter configuration commands, one per line.  End with CTRL/Z.
R2(config)#interface serial0/0
R2(config-if)#clock rate 256000
R2(config-if)#end
R2#show controllers serial0/0
Interface Serial0/0
Hardware is PowerQUICC MPC860
DCE V.35, clock rate 256000

R1#show controllers serial0/2
Interface Serial0/0
Hardware is PowerQUICC MPC860
DTE V.35 TX and RX clocks detected.
```

Task 4:

For reference information on configuring IP addressing, please refer to earlier labs.

Task 5:

```
R1#show ip interface brief
Interface     IP-Address     OK? Method Status          Protocol
Serial0/0     172.30.100.1   YES manual up              up

R1#ping 172.30.100.2

Type escape sequence to abort.
Sending 5, 100-byte ICMP Echos to 172.30.100.2, timeout is 2 seconds:
!!!!!
Success rate is 100 percent (5/5), round-trip min/avg/max = 8/8/12 ms

R2#show  ip interface brief
Interface   IP-Address     OK? Method Status          Protocol
Serial0/0   172.30.100.2    YES manual up              up

R2#ping 172.30.100.1

Type escape sequence to abort.
Sending 5, 100-byte ICMP Echos to 172.30.100.1, timeout is 2 seconds:
!!!!!
Success rate is 100 percent (5/5), round-trip min/avg/max = 8/8/12 ms
```

LAB 92: VERIFYING CISCO HDLC ENCAPSULATION

Lab Objective:
The objective of this lab exercise is to verify Cisco HDLC encapsulation, which is the default encapsulation method for WAN interfaces on Cisco IOS routers.

Lab Purpose:
Cisco HDLC verification is a fundamental skill. Cisco HDLC encapsulation is the default encapsulation on all Cisco router Serial interfaces. As a Cisco engineer, as well as in the Cisco CCNA exam, you will be expected to know how to verify Cisco HDLC encapsulation.

Certification Level:
This lab is suitable for both CCENT and CCNA certification exam preparation.

Lab Difficulty:
This lab has a difficulty rating of 2/10.

Readiness Assessment:
When you are ready for your certification exam, you should complete this lab in no more than 10 minutes.

Lab Topology:
Please use the following topology to complete this lab exercise:

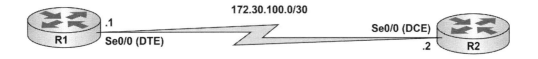

Task 1:
Configure hostnames on R1 and R2 as illustrated in the topology.

Task 2:
Enable Serial interfaces on R1 and R2. The Serial0/0 interface on R2 is identified as the DCE in the topology. Configure the DCE interface on R2 to provide clocking to R1. The clock speed should be 256 Kbps. Remember that 1 Kbps = 1000 bps. Verify that R2 is sending clocking information and that R1 receives this information from R2.

Task 3:

Configure IP addressing on R1 and R2 Serial0/0 interfaces as illustrated in the topology. Verify your interface encapsulation, which should be HDLC by default.

Task 4:

Enable debugging on the Cisco router to validate that HDLC keepalive messages are being sent between the two routers. Ensure that you disable debugging when you are finished. Verify that HDLC messages are sent in the keepalive interval that is listed under the interface, which should be approximately every 10 seconds.

LAB 92: CONFIGURATION AND VERIFICATION

Task 1:

For reference information on configuring hostnames, please refer to earlier labs.

Task 2:

```
R1(config)#interface serial0/0
R1(config-if)#no shut
*Mar  1 00:36:47.282: %LINK-3-UPDOWN: Interface Serial0/0, changed
state to down
R1(config-if)#end
R1#

R2(config)#interface serial0/0
R2(config-if)#no shut
*Mar  1 00:36:47.282: %LINK-3-UPDOWN: Interface Serial0/0, changed
state to down
R2(config-if)#end
R2#show controllers serial0/0
Interface Serial0/0
Hardware is PowerQUICC MPC860
DCE V.35, no clock
```

NOTE: The show controllers command will tell you whether the interface is the DCE side (which provides the clocking) or the DTE side (which receives the clocking) on a particular router interface.

```
R2#conf t
Enter configuration commands, one per line.  End with CTRL/Z.
R2(config)#interface serial0/0
R2(config-if)#clock rate 256000
R2(config-if)#end
R2#
R2#show controllers serial0/0
Interface Serial0/0
Hardware is PowerQUICC MPC860
DCE V.35, clock rate 256000

R1#show controllers serial0/2
Interface Serial0/0
Hardware is PowerQUICC MPC860
DTE V.35 TX and RX clocks detected.
```

Task 3:

For reference information on configuring IP addressing, please refer to earlier labs.

```
R1#show interfaces serial0/0
Serial0/0 is up, line protocol is up
   Hardware is PowerQUICC Serial
   Internet address is 172.30.100.1/30
   MTU 1500 bytes, BW 1544 Kbit, DLY 20000 usec,
       reliability 255/255, txload 1/255, rxload 1/255
   Encapsulation HDLC, loopback not set
   Keepalive set (10 sec)

R2#show interfaces serial0/0
Serial0/0 is up, line protocol is up
   Hardware is PowerQUICC Serial
   Internet address is 172.30.100.2/30
   MTU 1500 bytes, BW 1544 Kbit, DLY 20000 usec,
       reliability 255/255, txload 1/255, rxload 1/255
   Encapsulation HDLC, loopback not set
   Keepalive set (10 sec)
```

Task 4:

```
R1#debug serial interface
Serial network interface debugging is on
*Mar  1 01:17:34.686: Serial0/0: HDLC myseq 232, mineseen 232*,
yourseen 230, line up
*Mar  1 01:17:44.686: Serial0/0: HDLC myseq 233, mineseen 233*,
yourseen 231, line up
*Mar  1 01:17:54.687: Serial0/0: HDLC myseq 234, mineseen 234*,
yourseen 232, line up
R1#
R1#
R1#undebug all
All possible debugging has been turned off
```

LAB 93: CONFIGURING PPP ENCAPSULATION

Lab Objective:

The objective of this lab exercise is to enable PPP encapsulation on Cisco router Serial interfaces and verify the state of the PPP-encapsulated interfaces. This lab also covers debugging PPP links to see the different states of PPP negotiation

Lab Purpose:

PPP configuration and verification is a fundamental skill. PPP is one of the most popular Layer 2 protocols used on WANs. As a Cisco engineer, as well as in the Cisco CCNA exam, you will be expected to know how to configure and verify PPP encapsulation.

Certification Level:

This lab is suitable for both ICND2 and CCNA certification exam preparation.

Lab Difficulty:

This lab has a difficulty rating of 4/10.

Readiness Assessment:

When you are ready for your certification exam, you should complete this lab in no more than 10 minutes.

Lab Topology:

Please use the following topology to complete this lab exercise:

Task 1:

Configure hostnames on R1 and R2 as illustrated in the topology.

Task 2:

Enable Serial interfaces on R1 and R2. The Serial0/0 interface on R2 is identified as the DCE in the topology. Use the appropriate show command to verify that this interface is indeed the DCE. Configure the DCE interface on R2 to provide clocking to R1. The clock speed should be 512 Kbps. Verify that R1 receives clocking information from R2.

Task 3:

Enable PPP encapsulation on R1 and R2 Seriaol0/0 interfaces. Configure IP addressing on R1 and R2 Serial0/0 interfaces as illustrated in the topology. Verify your interface encapsulation, which should now be PPP. Test connectivity between R1 and R2 by pinging between the routers over the PPP link.

Task 4:

Enable PPP link negotiation debugging on R1. Next, issue the `shutdown` command, followed by the `no shutdown` command on Serial0/0. As the interface goes down and comes back up, you should see the different phases of PPP link negotiation. Disable debugging when you are done.

LAB 93: CONFIGURATION AND VERIFICATION

Task 1:

For reference information on configuring hostnames, please refer to earlier labs.

Task 2:

For reference information on verifying DTE/DCE status, please refer to earlier labs.

Task 3:

```
R1#conf t
Enter configuration commands, one per line.  End with CTRL/Z.
R1(config)#int s0/2
R1(config-if)#encapsulation ppp
R1(config-if)#ip address 10.0.254.1 255.255.255.240
R1(config-if)#^Z
R1#

R2#conf t
Enter configuration commands, one per line.  End with CTRL/Z.
R2(config)#interface s0/0
R2(config-if)#encapsulation ppp
R2(config-if)#ip add 10.0.254.2 255.255.255.240
R2(config-if)#end
R2#

R1#show interfaces s0/0
Serial0/0 is up, line protocol is up
  Hardware is PowerQUICC Serial
  Internet address is 10.0.254.1/28
  MTU 1500 bytes, BW 1544 Kbit, DLY 20000 usec,
     reliability 255/255, txload 1/255, rxload 1/255
  Encapsulation PPP, LCP Open
  Open: IPCP, CDPCP, loopback not set
  Keepalive set (10 sec)

R1#ping 10.0.254.2

Type escape sequence to abort.
Sending 5, 100-byte ICMP Echos to 10.0.254.2, timeout is 2 seconds:
!!!!!
Success rate is 100 percent (5/5), round-trip min/avg/max = 4/5/8 ms
```

Task 4:

```
R1#debug ppp negotiation
PPP protocol negotiation debugging is on
R1#conf ter
Enter configuration commands, one per line.  End with CNTL/Z.
R1(config)#int s0/0
R1(config-if)#shut
*Mar  1 02:00:08.949: %LINK-5-CHANGED: Interface Serial0/0, changed
state to administratively down
```

```
*Mar  1 02:00:08.949: Se0/0 PPP: Sending Acct Event[Down] id[4]
*Mar  1 02:00:08.949: Se0/0 CDPCP: State is Closed
*Mar  1 02:00:08.949: Se0/0 IPCP: State is Closed
*Mar  1 02:00:08.953: Se0/0 PPP: Phase is TERMINATING
*Mar  1 02:00:08.953: Se0/0 LCP: State is Closed
*Mar  1 02:00:08.953: Se0/0 PPP: Phase is DOWN
*Mar  1 02:00:08.953: Se0/0 IPCP: Remove route to 10.0.254.2
*Mar  1 02:00:09.951: %LINEPROTO-5-UPDOWN: Line protocol on Interface
Serial0/0, changed state to down

R1(config-if)#no shut
*Mar  1 02:00:14.746: Se0/0 PPP: Outbound cdp packet dropped
*Mar  1 02:00:16.746: %LINK-3-UPDOWN: Interface Serial0/0, changed
state to up
*Mar  1 02:00:16.746: Se0/0 PPP: Using default call direction
*Mar  1 02:00:16.746: Se0/0 PPP: Treating connection as a dedicated
line
*Mar  1 02:00:16.746: Se0/0 PPP: Session handle[A7000001] Session id[2]
*Mar  1 02:00:16.746: Se0/0 PPP: Phase is ESTABLISHING, Active Open
*Mar  1 02:00:16.750: Se0/0 LCP: O CONFREQ [Closed] id 22 len 10
*Mar  1 02:00:16.750: Se0/0 LCP:    MagicNumber 0x05CC8E89
(0x050605CC8E89)
*Mar  1 02:00:16.750: Se0/0 LCP: I CONFREQ [REQsent] id 2 len 10
*Mar  1 02:00:16.750: Se0/0 LCP:    MagicNumber 0x052E783E
(0x0506052E783E)
*Mar  1 02:00:16.754: Se0/0 LCP: O CONFACK [REQsent] id 2 len 10
*Mar  1 02:00:16.754: Se0/0 LCP:    MagicNumber 0x052E783E
(0x0506052E783E)
*Mar  1 02:00:16.754: Se0/0 LCP: I CONFACK [ACKsent] id 22 len 10
*Mar  1 02:00:16.754: Se0/0 LCP:    MagicNumber 0x05CC8E89
(0x050605CC8E89)
*Mar  1 02:00:16.754: Se0/0 LCP: State is Open
*Mar  1 02:00:16.758: Se0/0 PPP: Phase is FORWARDING, Attempting
Forward
*Mar  1 02:00:16.758: Se0/0 PPP: Queue IPCP code[1] id[1]
*Mar  1 02:00:16.758: Se0/0 PPP: Discarded CDPCP code[1] id[1]
*Mar  1 02:00:16.762: Se0/0 PPP: Phase is ESTABLISHING, Finish LCP
*Mar  1 02:00:16.762: Se0/0 PPP: Phase is UP
*Mar  1 02:00:16.762: Se0/0 IPCP: O CONFREQ [Closed] id 1 len 10
*Mar  1 02:00:16.762: Se0/0 IPCP:    Address 10.0.254.1
*Mar  1 02:00:16.774: Se0/0 IPCP: State is Open
*Mar  1 02:00:16.778: Se0/0 IPCP: Install route to 10.0.254.2
*Mar  1 02:00:17.763: %LINEPROTO-5-UPDOWN: Line protocol on Interface
Serial0/0, changed state to up
*Mar  1 02:00:18.741: Se0/0 CDPCP: I CONFREQ [ACKrcvd] id 2 len 4
*Mar  1 02:00:18.741: Se0/0 CDPCP: O CONFACK [ACKrcvd] id 2 len 4
*Mar  1 02:00:18.741: Se0/0 CDPCP: State is Open
R1(config-if)#end
*Mar  1 02:00:25.777: %SYS-5-CONFIG_I: Configured from console by
console
R1#undebug all
All possible debugging has been turned off
```

LAB 94: PPP AUTHENTICATION USING PAP

Lab Objective:
The objective of this lab exercise is to configure two routers sharing a back-to-back Serial link encapsulated by PPP to authenticate each other using Password Authentication Protocol (PAP). By default, PPP connections are not authenticated or secured.

Lab Purpose:
PPP PAP authentication configuration is a fundamental skill. One of the main reasons that PPP is so popular is because it has the capability to be secured and devices communicating using PPP can be authenticated. PAP authentication is the least preferred method to secure PPP as it sends usernames and passwords in clear text. However, as a Cisco engineer, as well as in the Cisco CCNA exam, you will be expected to know how to configure PPP PAP authentication.

Certification Level:
This lab is suitable for ICND2 and CCNA certification exam preparation.

Lab Difficulty:
This lab has a difficulty rating of 4/10.

Readiness Assessment:
When you are ready for your certification exam, you should complete this lab in no more than 15 minutes.

Lab Topology:
Please use the following topology to complete this lab exercise:

Task 1:
Configure hostnames on R1 and R2 as illustrated in the topology.

Task 2:
Enable Serial interfaces on R1 and R2. The Serial0/0 interface on R2 is identified as the DCE in the topology. Use the appropriate commands to verify that this interface is indeed

the DCE. Configure the DCE interface on R2 to provide clocking to R1. The clock speed should be 768 Kbps. Again, remember that 1 Kbps = 1000 bps. Verify that R1 receives clocking information from R2.

Task 3:

Enable PPP encapsulation on R1 and R2 Seriaol0/0 interfaces. Configure IP addressing on R1 and R2 Serial0/0 interfaces as illustrated in the topology.

Task 4:

Verify your interface encapsulation, which should now be PPP. Test connectivity between R1 and R2 by pinging between the routers.

Task 5:

Configure a username on R1 and R2. The user account should be the hostname of the remote router that will be authenticating with the local device. For example, on R1 the user account that will be used to authenticate router R2 will be R2. The password on both routers should be PAP.

Task 6:

Configure the Serial0/0 interfaces of R1 and R2 for PPP Authentication via PAP. Each router should send its configured hostname as the PAP username, and the configured password PAP should be used for PAP authentication between the routers.

Task 7:

Enable PPP authentication debugging on R1. Next, perform a `shutdown` command, followed by a `no shutdown` command, on Serial0/0. Verify that you see the two routers authenticating each other via PPP PAP. Disable debugging when you are done.

LAB 94: CONFIGURATION AND VERIFICATION

Task 1:
For reference information on configuring hostnames, please refer to earlier labs.

Task 2:
For reference information on verifying DTE/DCE status, please refer to earlier labs.

Task 3:
For reference information on enabling PPP and IP addressing, please refer to earlier labs.

Task 4:
For reference information on verifying Serial encapsulation, please refer to earlier labs.

Task 5:
```
R1#conf t
Enter configuration commands, one per line.  End with CTRL/Z.
R1(config)#username R2 password PAP
R1(config)#end
R1#

R2#conf t
Enter configuration commands, one per line.  End with CTRL/Z.
R2(config)#username R1 password PAP
R2(config)#^Z
R2#
```

Task 6:
```
R1#conf t
Enter configuration commands, one per line.  End with CTRL/Z.
R1(config)#int s0/0
R1(config-if)#ppp authentication pap
R1(config-if)#ppp pap sent-username R1 password PAP
R1(config-if)#^Z
R1#

R2#conf t
Enter configuration commands, one per line.  End with CTRL/Z.
R2(config)#interface serial0/0
R2(config-if)#ppp authentication pap
R2(config-if)#ppp pap sent-username R2 password PAP
R2(config-if)#end
R2#
```

Task 7:

```
R1#debug ppp authentication
PPP authentication debugging is on
R1#conf t
Enter configuration commands, one per line.  End with CTRL/Z.
R1(config)#int s0/0
R1(config-if)#shut
R1(config-if)#
*Mar  1 02:24:04.158: %LINK-5-CHANGED: Interface Serial0/0, changed
state to administratively down
*Mar  1 02:24:05.159: %LINEPROTO-5-UPDOWN: Line protocol on Interface
Serial0/0, changed state to down
R1(config-if)#no shut
R1(config-if)#
*Mar  1 02:24:14.943: %LINK-3-UPDOWN: Interface Serial0/0, changed
state to up
*Mar  1 02:24:14.943: Se0/0 PPP: Using default call direction
*Mar  1 02:24:14.943: Se0/0 PPP: Treating connection as a dedicated line
*Mar  1 02:24:14.943: Se0/0 PPP: Session handle[BC000002] Session id[4]
*Mar  1 02:24:14.943: Se0/0 PPP: Authorization required
*Mar  1 02:24:14.951: Se0/0 PAP: Using hostname from interface PAP
*Mar  1 02:24:14.951: Se0/0 PAP: Using password from interface PAP
*Mar  1 02:24:14.951: Se0/0 PAP: O AUTH-REQ id 2 len 11 from "R1"
*Mar  1 02:24:14.951: Se0/0 PAP: I AUTH-REQ id 2 len 11 from "R2"
*Mar  1 02:24:14.951: Se0/0 PAP: Authenticating peer R2
*Mar  1 02:24:14.955: Se0/0 PPP: Sent PAP LOGIN Request
*Mar  1 02:24:14.955: Se0/0 PPP: Received LOGIN Response PASS
*Mar  1 02:24:14.959: Se0/0 PPP: Sent LCP AUTHOR Request
*Mar  1 02:24:14.959: Se0/0 PPP: Sent IPCP AUTHOR Request
*Mar  1 02:24:14.963: Se0/0 PAP: I AUTH-ACK id 2 len 5
*Mar  1 02:24:14.963: Se0/0 LCP: Received AAA AUTHOR Response PASS
*Mar  1 02:24:14.963: Se0/0 IPCP: Received AAA AUTHOR Response PASS
*Mar  1 02:24:14.967: Se0/0 PAP: O AUTH-ACK id 2 len 5
*Mar  1 02:24:14.967: Se0/0 PPP: Sent CDPCP AUTHOR Request
*Mar  1 02:24:14.971: Se0/0 PPP: Sent IPCP AUTHOR Request
*Mar  1 02:24:14.975: Se0/0 CDPCP: Received AAA AUTHOR Response PASS
*Mar  1 02:24:15.969: %LINEPROTO-5-UPDOWN: Line protocol on Interface
Serial0/0, changed state to up
R1(config-if)#end
*Mar  1 02:24:22.339: %SYS-5-CONFIG_I: Configured from console by
console
R1#
R1#undebug all
All possible debugging has been turned off
```

NOTE: By default, PAP sends usernames and passwords in clear text and is generally not considered a secure authentication means for PPP. The recommended and most common means to secure and authenticate via PPP is to use the Challenge Handshake Authentication Protocol (CHAP). In the debug output above, while the password is not shown, you can see the usernames "R1" and "R2" printed.

LAB 95: PPP AUTHENTICATION USING CHAP (METHOD #1)

Lab Objective:
The objective of this lab exercise is to configure two routers sharing a back-to-back Serial link encapsulated by PPP to authenticate each other using default CHAP parameters on Cisco IOS. By default, PPP connections are not authenticated or secured.

Lab Purpose:
PPP CHAP authentication configuration is a fundamental skill. One of the main reasons that PPP is so popular is because it has the capability to be secured and devices communicating using PPP can be authenticated. CHAP authentication is the most preferred method to secure PPP as it does not send usernames and passwords in clear text. As a Cisco engineer, as well as in the Cisco CCNA exam, you will be expected to know how to configure PPP CHAP authentication.

Certification Level:
This lab is suitable for CCNA certification exam preparation.

Lab Difficulty:
This lab has a difficulty rating of 4/10.

Readiness Assessment:
When you are ready for your certification exam, you should complete this lab in no more than 15 minutes.

Lab Topology:
Please use the following topology to complete this lab exercise:

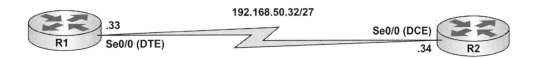

Task 1:
Configure hostnames on R1 and R2 as illustrated in the topology.

Task 2:

Enable Serial interfaces on R1 and R2. The Serial0/0 interface on R2 is identified as the DCE in the topology. Use the appropriate command to verify that this interface is indeed the DCE. Configure the DCE interface on R2 to provide clocking to R1. The clock speed should be 768 Kbps. Verify that R1 receives clocking information from R2.

Task 3:

Enable PPP encapsulation on R1 and R2 Serial0/0 interfaces. Configure IP addressing on R1 and R2 Serial0/0 interfaces as illustrated in the topology.

Task 4:

Verify your interface encapsulation, which should now be PPP. Test connectivity between R1 and R2 by pinging between the routers.

Task 5:

Configure the Serial0/0 interfaces of R1 and R2 for PPP authentication via CHAP. Both R1 and R2 should authenticate using their hostnames and the password CHAP.

Task 6:

Enable PPP authentication debugging on R2. Next, perform a `shutdown` command, followed by a `no shutdown` command, on Serial0/0. Verify that you see the two routers authenticating each other via PPP CHAP. Disable debugging when you are done.

LAB 95: CONFIGURATION AND VERIFICATION

Task 1:

For reference information on configuring hostnames, please refer to earlier labs.

Task 2:

For reference information on configuring clock rates, please refer to earlier labs.

Task 3:

For reference information on configuring PPP and IP addressing, please refer to earlier labs.

Task 4:

For reference information on verifying Serial encapsulation, please refer to earlier labs.

```
R1#ping 192.168.50.34

Type escape sequence to abort.
Sending 5, 100-byte ICMP Echos to 192.168.50.34, timeout is 2 seconds:
!!!!!
Success rate is 100 percent (5/5), round-trip min/avg/max = 4/4/8 ms
```

Task 5:

```
R1#conf t
Enter configuration commands, one per line.  End with CTRL/Z.
R1(config)#username R2 password CHAP
R1(config)#int s0/0
R1(config-if)#ppp authentication chap
R1(config-if)#end
R1#

R2#conf t
Enter configuration commands, one per line.  End with CTRL/Z.
R2(config)#username R1 password CHAP
R2(config)#int s0/0
R2(config-if)#ppp authentication chap
R2(config-if)# ^Z
R2#
```

NOTE: By default, there is no need to configure a hostname to be used for CHAP authentication on Cisco IOS routers as they will use the hostname configured on the router. There is also no need to define a password to be used for authentication since CHAP does not send the passwords across the link like PAP does. Therefore, a hash will be created using the configured passwords in the username command. These passwords must be identical on both routers, otherwise authentication will fail!

Task 6:
```
R1#debug ppp authentication
PPP authentication debugging is on
R1#conf t
Enter configuration commands, one per line.  End with CTRL/Z.
R1(config)#interface serial0/0
R1(config-if)#shutdown
*Mar  1 03:04:40.496: %LINK-5-CHANGED: Interface Serial0/0, changed
state to administratively down
*Mar  1 03:04:41.497: %LINEPROTO-5-UPDOWN: Line protocol on Interface
Serial0/0, changed state to down
R1(config-if)#no shutdown
*Mar  1 03:04:48.292: %LINK-3-UPDOWN: Interface Serial0/0, changed
state to up
*Mar  1 03:04:48.292: Se0/0 PPP: Using default call direction
*Mar  1 03:04:48.292: Se0/0 PPP: Treating connection as a dedicated
line
*Mar  1 03:04:48.292: Se0/0 PPP: Session handle[A3000003] Session id[5]
*Mar  1 03:04:48.292: Se0/0 PPP: Authorization required
*Mar  1 03:04:48.300: Se0/0 CHAP: O CHALLENGE id 1 len 23 from "R1"
*Mar  1 03:04:48.300: Se0/0 CHAP: I CHALLENGE id 1 len 23 from "R2"
*Mar  1 03:04:48.304: Se0/0 CHAP: Using hostname from unknown source
*Mar  1 03:04:48.304: Se0/0 CHAP: Using password from AAA
*Mar  1 03:04:48.304: Se0/0 CHAP: O RESPONSE id 1 len 23 from "R1"
*Mar  1 03:04:48.308: Se0/0 CHAP: I RESPONSE id 1 len 23 from "R2"
*Mar  1 03:04:48.308: Se0/0 PPP: Sent CHAP LOGIN Request
*Mar  1 03:04:48.312: Se0/0 PPP: Received LOGIN Response PASS
*Mar  1 03:04:48.312: Se0/0 PPP: Sent LCP AUTHOR Request
*Mar  1 03:04:48.316: Se0/0 PPP: Sent IPCP AUTHOR Request
*Mar  1 03:04:48.316: Se0/0 CHAP: I SUCCESS id 1 len 4
*Mar  1 03:04:48.316: Se0/0 LCP: Received AAA AUTHOR Response PASS
*Mar  1 03:04:48.320: Se0/0 IPCP: Received AAA AUTHOR Response PASS
*Mar  1 03:04:48.320: Se0/0 CHAP: O SUCCESS id 1 len 4
*Mar  1 03:04:48.324: Se0/0 PPP: Sent CDPCP AUTHOR Request
*Mar  1 03:04:48.324: Se0/0 PPP: Sent IPCP AUTHOR Request
*Mar  1 03:04:48.328: Se0/0 CDPCP: Received AAA AUTHOR Response PASS
*Mar  1 03:04:49.322: %LINEPROTO-5-UPDOWN: Line protocol on Interface
Serial0/0, changed state to up
R1(config-if)#end
*Mar  1 03:04:55.308: %SYS-5-CONFIG_I: Configured from console by
console
R1#undebug all
All possible debugging has been turned off
```

LAB 96: PPP AUTHENTICATION USING CHAP (METHOD #2)

Lab Objective:
The objective of this lab exercise is to configure two routers sharing a back-to-back Serial link encapsulated by PPP to authenticate each other using default CHAP parameters on Cisco IOS. By default, PPP connections are not authenticated or secured.

Lab Purpose:
PPP CHAP authentication configuration is a fundamental skill. One of the main reasons that PPP is so popular is because it has the capability to be secured and devices communicating using PPP can be authenticated. CHAP authentication is the most preferred method to secure PPP as it does not send usernames and passwords in clear text. As a Cisco engineer, as well as in the Cisco CCNA exam, you will be expected to know how to configure PPP CHAP authentication.

Certification Level:
This lab is suitable for CCNA certification exam preparation.

Lab Difficulty:
This lab has a difficulty rating of 6/10.

Readiness Assessment:
When you are ready for your certification exam, you should complete this lab in no more than 15 minutes.

Lab Topology:
Please use the following topology to complete this lab exercise:

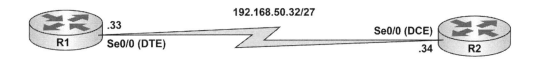

Task 1:
Configure the hostnames on R1 and R2 as illustrated in the topology.

Task 2:

Enable the Serial interfaces on R1 and R2. The Serial0/0 interface on R2 is identified as the DCE in the topology. Use the appropriate `show` command to verify that this interface is indeed the DCE. Configure the DCE interface on R2 to provide clocking to R1. The clock speed should be 768 Kbps. Verify that R1 receives clocking information from R2.

Task 3:

Enable PPP encapsulation on R1 and R2 Serial0/0 interfaces. Configure IP addressing on R1 and R2 Serial0/0 interfaces as illustrated in the topology.

Task 4:

Verify your interface encapsulation, which should be PPP by default. Test connectivity between R1 and R2 by pinging between the routers.

Task 5:

Configure PPP CHAP authentication on R1 and R2. Configure R1 to use the CHAP username Router1 with the password MyPass. Configure R2 to use the CHAP username Router2 with the password MyPass.

Task 6:

Enable PPP authentication debugging on R1. Next, perform a `shutdown` command followed by a `no shutdown` command on Serial0/0. Verify that you see the two routers authenticating each other via PPP CHAP. Disable debugging when you are done.

LAB 96: CONFIGURATION AND VERIFICATION

Task 1:

For reference information on configuring hostnames, please refer to earlier labs.

Task 2:

For reference information on verifying DTE/DCE status, please refer to earlier labs.

Task 3:

For reference information on enabling PPP encapsulation, please refer to earlier labs.

Task 4:

For reference information on verifying Serial encapsulation, please refer to earlier labs.

```
R1#ping 192.168.50.34

Type escape sequence to abort.
Sending 5, 100-byte ICMP Echos to 192.168.50.34, timeout is 2 seconds:
!!!!!
Success rate is 100 percent (5/5), round-trip min/avg/max = 4/4/8 ms

R2#ping 192.168.50.33

Type escape sequence to abort.
Sending 5, 100-byte ICMP Echos to 192.168.50.33, timeout is 2 seconds:
!!!!!
Success rate is 100 percent (5/5), round-trip min/avg/max = 4/4/8 ms
```

Task 5:

```
R1#conf t
Enter configuration commands, one per line.  End with CTRL/Z.
R1(config)#int s0/0
R1(config-if)#ppp authentication chap
R1(config-if)#ppp chap ?
  hostname  Set alternate CHAP hostname
  password  Set default CHAP password
  refuse    Refuse to authenticate using CHAP
  wait      Wait for caller to authenticate first
R1(config-if)#ppp chap hostname Router1
R1(config-if)#ppp chap password MyPass
R1(config-if)#exit
R1(config)#username Router2 password MyPass
R1(config)#end
R1#

R2#configure ter
Enter configuration commands, one per line.  End with CTRL/Z.
```

```
R2(config)#interf ser0/0
R2(config-if)#ppp authentication chap
R2(config-if)#ppp chap hostname Router2
R2(config-if)#ppp chap password MyPass
R2(config-if)#exit
R2(config)#username Router1 password MyPass
R2(config)#end
R2#
```

NOTE: By default, there is no need to configure a hostname to be used for CHAP authentication on Cisco IOS routers as they will use the hostname configured on the router. However, to use a different hostname, CHAP must be configured for that. This is performed using the ppp chap hostname and ppp chap password commands on the PPP interface used for CHAP authentication.

Task 6:

```
R2#debug ppp authentication
PPP authentication debugging is on.
R2#config t
Enter configuration commands, one per line.  End with CTRL/Z.
R2(config)#int s0/0
R2(config-if)#shut
*Mar  1 03:54:08.805: %LINK-5-CHANGED: Interface Serial0/0, changed
state to administratively down
*Mar  1 03:54:09.807: %LINEPROTO-5-UPDOWN: Line protocol on Interface
Serial0/0, changed state to down
R2(config-if)#no shut
*Mar  1 03:54:15.861: %LINK-3-UPDOWN: Interface Serial0/0, changed
state to up
*Mar  1 03:54:15.861: Se0/0 PPP: Using default call direction
*Mar  1 03:54:15.861: Se0/0 PPP: Treating connection as a dedicated
line
*Mar  1 03:54:15.861: Se0/0 PPP: Session handle[D50000E3] Session
id[229]
*Mar  1 03:54:15.861: Se0/0 PPP: Authorization required
*Mar  1 03:54:15.869: Se0/0 CHAP: O CHALLENGE id 181 len 28 from
"Router2"
*Mar  1 03:54:15.869: Se0/0 CHAP: I CHALLENGE id 181 len 28 from
"Router1"
*Mar  1 03:54:15.873: Se0/0 CHAP: Using hostname from interface CHAP
*Mar  1 03:54:15.877: Se0/0 CHAP: Using password from AAA
*Mar  1 03:54:15.877: Se0/0 CHAP: O RESPONSE id 181 len 28 from
"Router2"
*Mar  1 03:54:15.877: Se0/0 CHAP: I RESPONSE id 181 len 28 from
"Router1"
*Mar  1 03:54:15.881: Se0/0 PPP: Sent CHAP LOGIN Request
*Mar  1 03:54:15.881: Se0/0 PPP: Received LOGIN Response PASS
*Mar  1 03:54:15.885: Se0/0 PPP: Sent LCP AUTHOR Request
*Mar  1 03:54:15.885: Se0/0 PPP: Sent IPCP AUTHOR Request
```

```
*Mar  1 03:54:15.885: Se0/0 CHAP: I SUCCESS id 181 len 4
*Mar  1 03:54:15.889: Se0/0 LCP: Received AAA AUTHOR Response PASS
*Mar  1 03:54:15.889: Se0/0 IPCP: Received AAA AUTHOR Response PASS
*Mar  1 03:54:15.889: Se0/0 CHAP: O SUCCESS id 181 len 4
*Mar  1 03:54:15.893: Se0/0 PPP: Sent CDPCP AUTHOR Request
*Mar  1 03:54:15.897: Se0/0 PPP: Sent IPCP AUTHOR Request
*Mar  1 03:54:15.897: Se0/0 CDPCP: Received AAA AUTHOR Response PASS
*Mar  1 03:54:16.895: %LINEPROTO-5-UPDOWN: Line protocol on Interface
Serial0/0, changed state to up
R2(config-if)#end
R2#
*Mar  1 03:54:21.114: %SYS-5-CONFIG_I: Configured from console by
console
R2#undebug ppp authentication
PPP authentication debugging is off
R2#
```

LAB 97: CONFIGURING MULTILINK PPP (MLPPP)

Lab Objective

The objective of this lab exercise is for you to learn how to configure a Multilink PPP connection.

Lab Purpose:

MLPPP is a feature that will allow you to provide redundancy and some sort of load balancing by using two links (interfaces) and the benefits of the encapsulation protocol of PPP. As a Cisco engineer, as well as in the Cisco CCNA exam, you will be expected to know how to implement MLPPP functionality.

Certification Level:

This lab is suitable for ICND2 and CCNA certification exam preparation.

Lab Difficulty:

This lab has a difficulty rating of 7/10.

Readiness Assessment:

When you are ready for your certification exam, you should complete this lab in no more than 10 minutes.

Lab Topology:

Please use the following topology to complete this lab exercise:

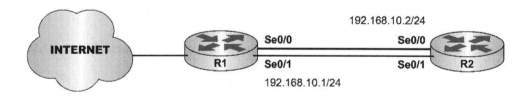

Task 1:

Configure hostnames on R1 and R2 as illustrated in the topology.

Task 2:

Create a Multilink interface on R1 and R2 with the following settings:

- Multilink group: 1
- Encapsulation type: PPP
- IP address: As in the diagram

Task 3:

Configure both Serial interfaces on R1 and R2 to join Multilink group 1.

Task 4:

Make sure that there is reachability between R1 and R2 via the MLPPP interface and that the interface is up and running.

LAB 97: CONFIGURATION AND VERIFICATION

Task 1:

For reference information on configuring hostnames, please refer to earlier labs.

Task 2:

```
R1#conf t
Enter configuration commands, one per line.  End with CTRL/Z.
R1(config)#int multilink 1
R1(config-if)#encapsulation ppp
R1(config-if)#ppp multilink group 1
R1(config-if)#no shutdown
R1(config-if)#ip add 192.168.10.1 255.255.255.252
R1(config-if)#end

R2(config)#int multilink 1
R2(config-if)#encapsulation ppp
R2(config-if)#ppp multilink group 1
R2(config-if)#no shutdown
R2(config-if)#ip add 192.168.10.2 255.255.255.252
R2(config-if)#end
```

Task 3:

```
R1#config t
Enter configuration commands, one per line.  End with CTRL/Z.
R1(config)#int serial0/0
R1(config-if)#encapsulation ppp
R1(config-if)#ppp multilink group 1
R1(config-if)#no shutdown
R1(config-if)#exit

R1(config)#int serial0/1
R1(config-if)#encapsulation ppp
R1(config-if)#ppp multilink group 1
R1(config-if)#no shutdown
R1(config-if)#exit

R2(config)#int serial0/0
R2(config-if)#encapsulation ppp
R2(config-if)#ppp multilink group 1
R2(config-if)#no shutdown
R2(config-if)#exit

R2(config)#int serial0/1
R2(config-if)#encapsulation ppp
R2(config-if)#ppp multilink group 1
R2(config-if)#no shutdown
R2(config-if)#exit
```

Task 4:

```
R1#sh ip int brief
Interface    IP-Address    OK?   Method    Status    Protocol
Serial0/0    unassigned    YES   unset     up        up
Serial0/1    unassigned    YES   unset     up        up
Multilink1   192.168.10.1  YES   manual    up        up

R2#sh ip int brief
Interface    IP-Address    OK?   Method    Status    Protocol
Serial0/0    unassigned    YES   unset     up        up
Serial0/1    unassigned    YES   unset     up        up
Multilink1   192.168.10.2  YES   manual    up        up

R1#ping 192.168.10.2

Type escape sequence to abort.
Sending 5, 100-byte ICMP Echos to 192.168.10.2, timeout is 2 seconds:
!!!!!
Success rate is 100 percent (5/5), round-trip min/avg/max = 56/67/96 ms
```

LAB 98: CONFIGURING PPPOE

Lab Objective

The objective of this lab exercise is for you to learn how to configure PPP over an Ethernet link.

Lab Purpose:

PPP over Ethernet (PPPoE) emulates a point-to-point link across a shared medium such as DSL, but in this case, we will run it over Ethernet. This is normally used in connections from SoHo network to the ISP. As a Cisco engineer, as well as in the Cisco CCNA exam, you will be expected to know how to implement PPPoE functionality.

Certification Level:

This lab is suitable for ICND2 and CCNA certification exam preparation.

Lab Difficulty:

This lab has a difficulty rating of 8/10.

Readiness Assessment:

When you are ready for your certification exam, you should complete this lab in no more than 20 minutes.

Lab Topology:

Please use the following topology to complete this lab exercise:

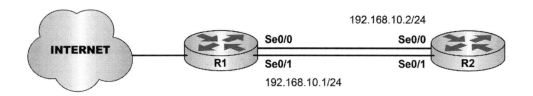

Task 1:

Configure hostnames on R1 and R2 as illustrated in the topology.

Task 2:

Configure R1 as a PPPoE server with the following settings:

- The broadband aggregation group will be named MyPPPoEGroup;
- A virtual-template interface number 1 must be created and assigned with an IP address of 192.168.10.1/24;
- Create an IP pool named PPPoE for the same 192.168.10.0/24 subnet; and
- Assign the interface Gig0/0 to this PPPoE group.

Task 3:

Configure R2 as a PPPoE client with the following settings:

- Create a dialer interface numbered 1;
- The encapsulation protocol must be PPP;
- It should obtain an IP address dynamically; and
- The MTU of the interface must be 1492 to avoid unneeded fragmentation.

Task 4:

Issue the appropriate show commands to check that the interface is up. Ping across the link and issue appropriate PPPoE show commands.

LAB 98: CONFIGURATION AND VERIFICATION

Task 1:

For reference information on configuring hostnames, please refer to earlier labs.

Task 2:

```
R1#conf t
Enter configuration commands, one per line.  End with CTRL/Z.
R1(config)#bba-group pppoe MyPPPoEGroup
R1(config-bba-group)#virtual-template 1
R1(config-bba-group)#exit
R1(config)#int virtual-template 1
R1(config-if)#ip address 192.168.10.1 255.255.255.0
R1(config-if)#peer default ip address pool PPPoE

R1(config)#ip local pool PPPoE 192.168.10.2 192.168.10.254
R1(config)#int g0/0
R1(config-if)#no ip address
R1(config-if)#pppoe enable group MyPPPoEGroup
R1(config-if)#no shut
```

Task 3:

```
R2#config t
Enter configuration commands, one per line.  End with CTRL/Z.
R2(config)#interface dialer 1
R2(config-if)#dialer pool 1
R2(config-if)#encapsulation ppp
R2(config-if)#ip address negotiated
R2(config-if)#mtu 1492
R2(config-if)#interface g0/0
R2(config-if)#pppoe-client dial-pool-number 1
R2(config-if)#no shut
```

Task 4:

```
R2#sh ip int brief | exclude unassigned
Interface IP-Address      OK? Method Status     Protocol
Dialer1    192.168.10.2    YES IPCP   up         up
R2#

R2#ping 192.168.10.1

Type escape sequence to abort.
Sending 5, 100-byte ICMP Echos to 192.168.10.1, timeout is 2 seconds:
!!!!!
Success rate is 100 percent (5/5), round-trip min/avg/max = 40/56/68 ms
```

LAB 99: CONFIGURING EBGP ADVANCED

Lab Objective
The objective of this lab exercise is for you to learn how to configure eBGP and some of its advanced features.

Lab Purpose:
Border Gateway Protocol (BGP) is the routing protocol used to exchange information on the Internet; in this lab, we will configure some of the advanced features of the exterior BGP relationships. As a Cisco engineer, as well as in the Cisco CCNA exam, you will be expected to know how to implement eBGP (external BGP) features in your network.

Certification Level:
This lab is suitable for ICND2 and CCNA certification exam preparation.

Lab Difficulty:
This lab has a difficulty rating of 9/10.

Readiness Assessment:
When you are ready for your certification exam, you should complete this lab in no more than 20 minutes.

Lab Topology:
Please use the following topology to complete this lab exercise:

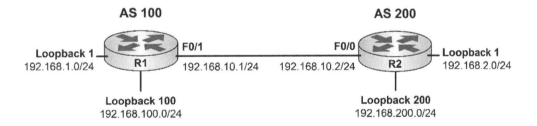

Task 1:
Configure hostnames on R1 and R2 as illustrated in the topology.

Task 2:
Configure each router with its respective IPv4 addresses in both the Loopback and GigabitEthernet interfaces.

Task 3:

Configure an eBGP session between R1 and R2 with the following requirements:

- R1 will be inside ASN 100 and R2 will be inside ASN 200;
- R1 should use Loopback100 as the peer source address and R2 should do the same;
- Make sure that if at some point R2 learns an IP prefix from another BGP router and then sends it to R1, the next hop address will remain as the R2 IP address (increase the TTL to 2);
- Hellos will be sent every 5 seconds, with a hold timer of 15 seconds;
- Authentication will be done with the password CCNA (unencrypted); and
- Make sure that they advertise their Loopback1 network address and the Gigabit interface via BGP.

Task 4:

Confirm that eBGP is working properly by running the following commands:

- `show ip protocols`
- `show ip bgp summary`
- `show ip route bgp`
- Ping 192.168.2.1 source Loopback1 (from R1)
- Ping 192.168.1.1 source Loopback1 (from R2)

LAB 99: CONFIGURATION AND VERIFICATION

Task 1:

For reference information on configuring hostnames, please refer to earlier labs.

Task 2:

```
R1#conf t
Enter configuration commands, one per line.  End with CTRL/Z.
R1(config)#int fa0/0
R1(config-if)#ip address 192.168.10.1 255.255.255.0
R1(config-if)#no shut
R1(config)#int loopback1
R1(config-if)#ip address 192.168.1.1 255.255.255.0
R1(config)#int loopback100
R1(config-if)#ip address 192.168.100.1 255.255.255.0
R1(config)#ip route 192.168.200.0 255.255.255.0 192.168.10.2

R2(config)#int fa0/0
R2(config-if)#ip address 192.168.10.2 255.255.255.0
R2(config-if)#no shut
R2(config)#int loopback1
R2(config-if)#ip address 192.168.2.1 255.255.255.0
R2(config)#int loopback200
R2(config-if)#ip address 192.168.200.1 255.255.255.0
R2(config)#ip route 192.168.100.0 255.255.255.0 192.168.10.1
```

Task 3:

```
R1#config t
Enter configuration commands, one per line.  End with CTRL/Z.
R1(config)#router bgp 100
R1(config-router)#neighbor 192.168.200.1 remote-as 200
R1(config-router)#neighbor 192.168.200.1 update-source loopback100
R1(config-router)#neighbor 192.168.200.1 ebgp-multihop 2
R1(config-router)#neighbor 192.168.200.1 timers 5 15
R1(config-router)#neighbor 192.168.200.1 password CCNA
R1(config-router)#network 192.168.10.0 mask 255.255.255.0
R1(config-router)#network 192.168.1.0 mask 255.255.255.0

R2#config t
Enter configuration commands, one per line.  End with CTRL/Z.
R2(config)#router bgp 200
R2(config-router)#neighbor 192.168.100.1 remote-as 100
R2(config-router)#neighbor 192.168.100.1 update-source loopback200
R2(config-router)#neighbor 192.168.100.1 ebgp-multihop 2
R2(config-router)#neighbor 192.168.100.1 next-hop-self
R2(config-router)#neighbor 192.168.100.1 timers 5 15
R2(config-router)#neighbor 192.168.100.1 password CCNA
R2(config-router)#network 192.168.10.0 mask 255.255.255.0
R2(config-router)#network 192.168.2.0 mask 255.255.255.0
```

Task 4:

```
R1#sh ip bgp summary
BGP router identifier 192.168.100.1, local AS number 100
BGP table version is 4, main routing table version 4
3 network entries using 351 bytes of memory
4 path entries using 208 bytes of memory
3/2 BGP path/bestpath attribute entries using 372 bytes of memory
0 BGP route-map cache entries using 0 bytes of memory
0 BGP filter-list cache entries using 0 bytes of memory
BGP using 931 total bytes of memory
BGP activity 3/0 prefixes, 4/0 paths, scan interval 60 secs

Neighbor       V  AS MsgRcvd MsgSent   TblVer   InQ OutQ Up/Down   State/
PfxRcd
192.168.200.1 4 200      37        37        4    0    0 00:33:15          2

R1#show ip protocols
Routing Protocol is "bgp 100"
  Outgoing update filter list for all interfaces is not set
  Incoming update filter list for all interfaces is not set
  IGP synchronization is disabled
  Automatic route summarization is disabled
  Neighbor(s):
    Address        FiltIn FiltOut DistIn DistOut Weight RouteMap
    192.168.200.1
  Maximum path: 1
  Routing Information Sources:
    Gateway        Distance      Last Update
    192.168.200.1        20      00:32:56
  Distance: external 20 internal 200 local 200

R1#sh ip route bgp
B    192.168.2.0/24 [20/0] via 192.168.100.1, 00:32:59

R1#ping 192.168.2.1 source loopback 1

Type escape sequence to abort.
Sending 5, 100-byte ICMP Echos to 192.168.2.1, timeout is 2 seconds:
Packet sent with a source address of 192.168.1.1
!!!!!
Success rate is 100 percent (5/5), round-trip min/avg/max = 8/14/20 ms

R2#sh ip bgp summary
BGP router identifier 192.168.100.1, local AS number 200
BGP table version is 4, main routing table version 4
3 network entries using 351 bytes of memory
4 path entries using 208 bytes of memory
3/2 BGP path/bestpath attribute entries using 372 bytes of memory
0 BGP route-map cache entries using 0 bytes of memory
0 BGP filter-list cache entries using 0 bytes of memory
```

```
BGP using 931 total bytes of memory
BGP activity 3/0 prefixes, 4/0 paths, scan interval 60 secs

Neighbor     V  AS MsgRcvd MsgSent    TblVer   InQ OutQ Up/Down   State/
PfxRcd
192.168.100.1 4 100     39      39        4     0    0 00:35:19        2

R2#show ip protocols
Routing Protocol is "bgp 200"
  Outgoing update filter list for all interfaces is not set
  Incoming update filter list for all interfaces is not set
  IGP synchronization is disabled
  Automatic route summarization is disabled
  Neighbor(s):
    Address          FiltIn FiltOut DistIn DistOut Weight RouteMap
    192.168.100.1
  Maximum path: 1
  Routing Information Sources:
    Gateway         Distance      Last Update
    192.168.100.1        20       00:34:52
  Distance: external 20 internal 200 local 200

R2#show ip route bgp
B    192.168.1.0/24 [20/0] via 192.168.100.1, 00:34:56


R2#ping 192.168.1.1 source loopback1
Type escape sequence to abort.
Sending 5, 100-byte ICMP Echos to 192.168.1.1, timeout is 2 seconds:
Packet sent with a source address of 192.168.2.1
!!!!!
Success rate is 100 percent (5/5), round-trip min/avg/max = 8/13/24 ms
```

LAB 100: CONFIGURING GRE POINT-TO-POINT TUNNELS

Lab Objective

The objective of this lab exercise is for you to learn how to configure point-to-point GRE tunnels.

Lab Purpose:

Generic Routing Encapsulation (GRE) is IP protocol number 47; its main purpose is to encapsulate any network layer protocol. As a Cisco engineer, as well as in the Cisco CCNA exam, you will be expected to know how to implement GRE tunnels.

Certification Level:

This lab is suitable for ICND2 and CCNA certification exam preparation.

Lab Difficulty:

This lab has a difficulty rating of 7/10.

Readiness Assessment:

When you are ready for your certification exam, you should complete this lab in no more than 20 minutes.

Lab Topology:

Please use the following topology to complete this lab exercise:

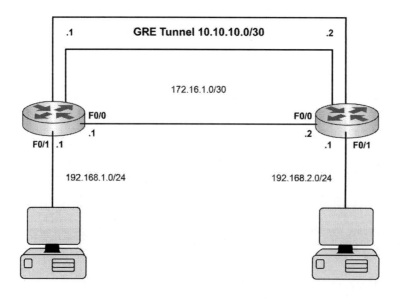

Task 1:
Configure hostnames on R1 and R2 as illustrated in the topology (R1 is on the left).

Task 2:
Configure each router with its respective IPv4 addresses on both of their FastEthernet interfaces.

Task 3:
Configure a GRE tunnel (numbered 1) on each router with the respective IPv4 address (10.10.10.0/30) as per the diagram and add the following settings:

- Tunnel source is interface f0/0;
- Tunnel destination is the other router's interface f0/0; and
- Set the tunnel mode to GRE.

Task 4:
Configure a static route on R1 to 192.168.2.0/24 via the Tunnel 1 interface, and configure a static route on R2 to 192.168.1.0/24 via the Tunnel 1 interface.

Task5:
Check the status of the interface tunnel and make sure that traffic is flowing through the tunnel as expected.

LAB 100: CONFIGURATION AND VERIFICATION

Task 1:

For reference information on configuring hostnames, please refer to earlier labs.

Task 2:

For reference information on configuring IP addressing, please refer to earlier labs.

Task 3:
```
R1#config t
Enter configuration commands, one per line.  End with CTRL/Z.
R1(config)#int Tunnel 1
R1(config-if)#ip address 10.10.10.1 255.255.255.252
R1(config-if)#tunnel source f0/0
R1(config-if)#tunnel destination 172.16.1.2
R1(config-if)#tunnel mode gre ip

R2(config)#int Tunnel 1
R2(config-if)#ip address 10.10.10.2 255.255.255.252
R2(config-if)#tunnel source f0/0
R2(config-if)#tunnel destination 172.16.1.1
R2(config-if)#tunnel mode gre ip
```

Task 4:
```
R1(config)#ip route 192.168.2.0 255.255.255.0 tunnel 1

R2(config)#ip route 192.168.1.0 255.255.255.0 tunnel 1
```

Task 5:
```
R1#sh ip interface brief
Interface       IP-Address      OK? Method Status      Protocol
FastEthernet0/0 172.16.1.1      YES manual up          up
FastEthernet0/1 192.168.1.1     YES manual up          up
Tunnel1         10.10.10.1      YES manual up          up

R2#sh ip int brief
Interface       IP-Address      OK? Method Status      Protocol
FastEthernet0/0 172.16.1.2      YES manual up          up
FastEthernet0/1 192.168.2.1     YES manual up          up
Tunnel1         10.10.10.2      YES manual up          up

R1#show interface tunnel 1
Tunnel1 is up, line protocol is up
  Hardware is Tunnel
  Internet address is 10.10.10.1/30
  MTU 1514 bytes, BW 9 Kbit/sec, DLY 500000 usec,
     reliability 255/255, txload 1/255, rxload 1/255
  Encapsulation TUNNEL, loopback not set
```

```
  Keepalive not set
  Tunnel source 172.16.1.1 (FastEthernet0/0), destination 172.16.1.2
  Tunnel protocol/transport GRE/IP

R2#show interface tunnel 1
Tunnel1 is up, line protocol is up
  Hardware is Tunnel
  Internet address is 10.10.10.2/30
  MTU 1514 bytes, BW 9 Kbit/sec, DLY 500000 usec,
      reliability 255/255, txload 1/255, rxload 1/255
  Encapsulation TUNNEL, loopback not set
  Keepalive not set
  Tunnel source 172.16.1.2 (FastEthernet0/0), destination 172.16.1.1
  Tunnel protocol/transport GRE/IP
```

4.0 Infrastructure Services

LAB 101: CONFIGURING IPV6 TRAFFIC FILTERS

Lab Objective:
The objective of this lab exercise is for you to learn how to configure IPv6 access filters in your network.

Lab Purpose:
At this point, you should already be aware of how access control lists work in an IPv4 environment, but in this lab, we are going to show you how to do the same for IPv6. As a Cisco engineer, as well as in the Cisco CCNA exam, you will be expected to know how to implement IPv6 traffic filters in your network.

Certification Level:
This lab is suitable for ICND2 and CCNA certification exam preparation.

Lab Difficulty:
This lab has a difficulty rating of 7/10.

Readiness Assessment:
When you are ready for your certification exam, you should complete this lab in no more than 20 minutes.

Lab Topology:

Please use the following topology to complete this lab exercise:

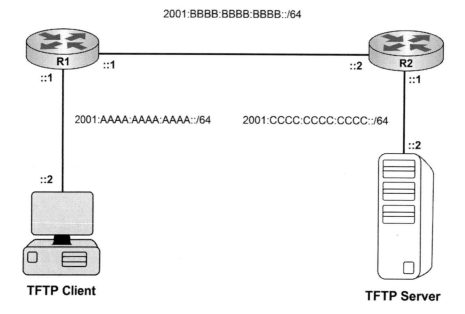

2001:BBBB:BBBB:BBBB::/64

R1 ::1   ::2 R2
::1   ::1

2001:AAAA:AAAA:AAAA::/64   2001:CCCC:CCCC:CCCC::/64

::2

::2

TFTP Client   **TFTP Server**

Interfaces' IP assignment:

    R1 Gig0/0 = 2001:BBBB:BBBB:BBBB::1/64
    R1 Gig0/1 = 2001:AAAA:AAAA:AAAA::1/64
    R2 Gig0/0 = 2001:BBBB:BBBB:BBBB::2/64
    R2 Gig0/1 = 2001:CCCC:CCCC:CCCC::1/64

Or use FastEthernet interfaces if you wish.

Task 1:

Configure hostnames on R1 and R2 as illustrated in the topology.

Task 2:

Configure each router with its respective IPv6 addresses in both of their Gigabit interfaces.

Task 3:

Configure on each IPv6 router an IPv6 route to the non-directly connected networks.

Task 4:

Configure R2 with a traffic filter named Inbound_ACL ,allowing only TFTP traffic from the TFTP client to the TFTP server. Make sure you apply this ACL to Gig0/0 on R2.

Testing the ACL can be a little tricky but there is a traffic generator in Packet Tracer, or you can try to telnet to the remote TFTP server using the following router command:

```
R1#telnet 2001:cccc:cccc:cccc::2 69
```

LAB 101: CONFIGURATION AND VERIFICATION

Task 1:

For reference information on configuring hostnames, please refer to earlier labs.

Task 2:

For reference information on configuring IP addressing, please refer to earlier labs.

Task 3:
```
R1(config)#ipv6 route 2001:CCCC:CCCC:CCCC::/64 2001:BBBB:BBBB:BBBB::2
R2(config)#ipv6 route 2001:AAAA:AAAA:AAAA::/64 2001:BBBB:BBBB:BBBB::1
```

Task 4:
```
R2(config)#ipv6 access-list Inbound_ACL
R2(config-ipv6-acl)#permit udp 2001:AAAA:AAAA:AAAA::2/64
2001:CCCC:CCCC:CCCC::2/64 eq tftp

R2(config)#int gig 0/0
R1(config-if)#ipv6 traffic-filter Inbound_ACL in
```

Testing this ACL can be a bit tricky. In Packet Tracer, you can use a traffic generator on the PC to send TFTP traffic, which will be allowed, and then ping (for example) to see if it's blocked. On live equipment, you can copy `tftp` from a router acting as a host to the remote device. You can specify a port to telnet on and a source interface, but I haven't tested this yet with a sniffer to see what is actually sent. Try it for yourself:

```
R1#telnet 2001:CCCC:CCCC:CCCC::2 69 /source-interface loopback0
```

LAB 102: IMPLEMENTING HSRP

Lab Objective:
The objective of this lab exercise is for you to learn how to implement HSRP in the Core level of your network.

Lab Purpose:
Hot Standby Router Protocol (HSRP) is a protocol that allows you to have redundancy at the Core level by having two routers acting as a default gateway. By configuring a priority level on the router interfaces, you will determine which one acts as primary and which one as secondary. As a Cisco engineer, as well as in the Cisco CCNA exam, you will be expected to know how to implement HSRP functionality.

Certification Level:
This lab is suitable for ICND2 and CCNA certification exam preparation.

Lab Difficulty:
This lab has a difficulty rating of 8/10.

Readiness Assessment:
When you are ready for your certification exam, you should complete this lab in no more than 20 minutes.

Lab Topology:

Please use the following topology to complete this lab exercise:

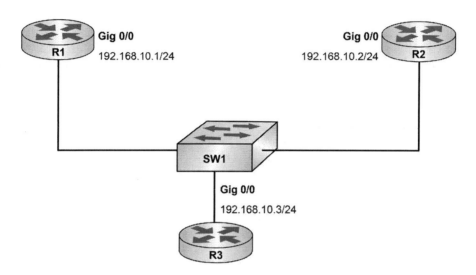

HSRP 100 Virtual IP
192.168.10.254/24

NOTE: R1 and R2 both connect to the Internet.

Task 1:

Configure hostnames on R1, R2, and R3 as illustrated in the topology.

Task 2:

Configure the IP addresses on the Gig0/0 interfaces of R1, R2, and R3 as illustrated in the topology.

NOTE: 192.168.10.254 will be the HSRP address shared between R1 and R2.

Task 3:

Configure HSRP on R1 and R2 as follows:

- HSRP group number: 100
- HSRP virtual IP address: 192.168.10.254
- R1: primary gateway (HSRP Priority 100)
- R2: secondary gateway (HSRP Priority 90)

- HSRP routers should send Hellos every second and detect a failure of a router in 3 seconds
- HSRP routers should authenticate their communication using the key "CCNA".

Task 4:

Configure R3 to use 192.168.10.254 (HSRP virtual IP) as its default gateway.

Task 5:

Check the status of HSRP on R1 and R2 running the following commands:

- `show standby`
- `show standby brief`

LAB 102: CONFIGURATION AND VERIFICATION

Task 1:

For reference information on configuring hostnames, please refer to earlier labs.

Task 2:

For reference information on configuring IP addressing, please refer to earlier labs.

Task 3:
```
R1#config t
R1(config)#int gig0/0
R1(config-if)#standby 100 ip 192.168.10.254
R1(config-if)#standby 100 priority 100
R1(config-if)#standby 100 authentication CCNA
R1(config-if)#standby 100 timers 1 3

R2(config)#int gig0/0
R2(config-if)#standby 100 ip 192.168.10.254
R2(config-if)#standby 100 priority 90
R2(config-if)#standby 100 authentication CCNA
R2(config-if)#standby 100 timers 1 3
```

NOTE: The authentication commands will not work on Packet Tracer.

Task 4:
```
R3(config)#ip route 0.0.0.0 0.0.0.0 192.168.10.254
```

With this configuration, if R3 wants to communicate on the Internet, it will send the IP packets to the HSRP Active Router and if that router fails the other will take over (redundancy at its maximum level).

Task 5:
```
R1#show standby
FastEthernet0/0 - Group 100
  State is Active
    2 state changes, last state change 00:22:01
  Virtual IP address is 192.168.10.254
  Active virtual MAC address is 0000.0c07.ac64
    Local virtual MAC address is 0000.0c07.ac64 (v1 default)
  Hello time 1 sec, hold time 3 sec
    Next hello sent in 0.816 secs
  Authentication text, string "CCNA"
  Preemption disabled
  Active router is local
  Standby router is 192.168.10.2, priority 90 (expires in 2.688 sec)
  Priority 100 (default 100)
  IP redundancy name is "hsrp-Fa0/0-100" (default)
```

```
R2#show standby
FastEthernet0/0 - Group 100
  State is Standby
    1 state change, last state change 00:20:30
  Virtual IP address is 192.168.10.254
  Active virtual MAC address is 0000.0c07.ac64
    Local virtual MAC address is 0000.0c07.ac64 (v1 default)
  Hello time 1 sec, hold time 3 sec
    Next hello sent in 0.648 secs
  Authentication text, string "CCNA"
  Preemption disabled
  Active router is 192.168.10.1, priority 100 (expires in 2.804 sec)
  Standby router is local
  Priority 90 (configured 90)
  IP redundancy name is "hsrp-Fa0/0-100" (default)

R1#sh standby brief
                     P indicates configured to preempt.
                     |
Interface   Grp Prio P State    Active     Standby       Virtual IP
Fa0/0       100 100    Active   local      192.168.10.2  192.168.10.254

R2#show standby brief
                     P indicates configured to preempt.
                     |
Interface   Grp Prio P State    Active        Standby  Virtual IP
Fa0/0       100 90     Standby  192.168.10.1  local    192.168.10.254
```

5.0 Infrastructure Maintenance

LAB 103: CONFIGURING IP SLA

Lab Objective

The objective of this lab exercise is for you to learn how to implement IP SLA functionality on a Cisco router.

Lab Purpose:

Configuring and applying the IP SLA (Service Level Agreement) protocol is a fundamental skill for any network administrator in order to monitor reachability of objects and based on that reachability perform changes in the routing table of the router. As a Cisco engineer, as well as in the Cisco CCNA exam, you will be expected to know how to implement IP SLA functionality.

Certification Level:

This lab is suitable for CCNA and ICND2 certification exam preparation.

Lab Difficulty:

This lab has a difficulty rating of 8/10.

Readiness Assessment:

When you are ready for your certification exam, you should complete this lab in no more than 10 minutes.

Lab Topology:

Please use the following topology to complete this lab exercise:

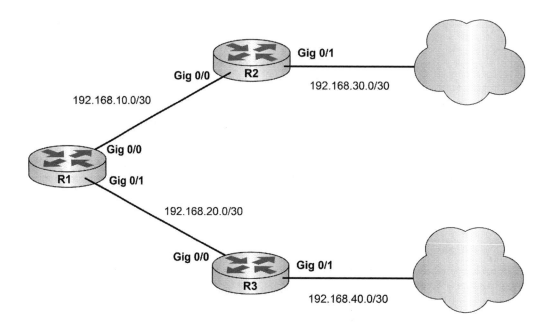

Task 1:

Configure hostnames on R1, R2, and R3 as illustrated in the topology.

Task 2:

Configure IP addresses on the Gig0/0 and Gig0/1 interfaces of R1, R2, and R3 as illustrated in the topology.

> **NOTE:** R1 will always have the .1 IP in each of its Gig interfaces.

> **NOTE:** R2 and R3 will have the .1 IP in its Gig0/1 interfaces.

Task 3:

Configure two default static routes on R1:

- The first one (primary one) will go to R2 with an administrative distance of 1; and
- The secondary one will go to R3 with an administrative distance of 254.

Based on this, all traffic going to an unknown destination will be sent via R2.

Task 4:

Create an IP SLA monitor process numbered 17, and make sure that you ping the Internet host of 4.2.2.2 to perform the monitoring. Also, make sure that the IP SLA starts running now and that it will run forever.

> **NOTE:** In Cisco IOS software versions 12.3(14)T, 12.4, 12.4(2)T, and 12.2(33)SXH, IP SLA is configured using the `ip sla monitor [operation number]` global configuration command. In Cisco IOS 12.4(4)T and later, IP SLA is configured using the `ip sla [operation number]` global configuration command.

Task 5:

Create a track object that makes reference to this IP SLA process and attach it to the primary default route to monitor the state of this link (make sure that you only have the primary tracked route and the secondary route in your routing table).

Task 6:

Check the state of the IP SLA by running the following commands:

- `show ip sla monitor statistics`
- `show ip sla monitor operational-state`
- `show ip route`

> **Note:** You should see the secondary default route as the route being used because IP SLA is failing, as 4.2.2.2 is not responding to the ICMP packets.

Let's create a Loopback interface numbered 1 in R2 with an IP of 4.2.2.2/24 to change this:

```
R2(config)#interface loopback1
R2(config-if)ip address 4.2.2.2 255.255.255.0
```

Run the same `show` commands and check how the results change as now 4.2.2.2 exists and it's reachable.

LAB 103: CONFIGURATION AND VERIFICATION

Task 1:

For reference information on configuring hostnames, please refer to earlier labs.

Task 2:
```
R1#conf t
Enter configuration commands, one per line.  End with CTRL/Z.
R1(config)#int gig0/0
R1(config-if)#no shutdown
R1(config-if)#ip add 192.168.10.1 255.255.255.252
R1(config-if)#end
R1(config)#int gig0/1
R1(config-if)#no shutdown
R1(config-if)#ip add 192.168.20.1 255.255.255.252
R1(config-if)#end
R1#

R2(config)#int gig0/0
R2(config-if)#no shutdown
R2(config-if)#ip add 192.168.10.2 255.255.255.252
R2(config-if)#end
R2(config)#int gig0/1
R2(config-if)#no shutdown
R2(config-if)#ip add 192.168.30.1 255.255.255.252
R2(config-if)#end
R2#

R3(config)#int gig0/0
R3(config-if)#no shutdown
R3(config-if)#ip add 192.168.20.2 255.255.255.252
R3(config-if)#end
R3(config)#int gig0/1
R3(config-if)#no shutdown
R3(config-if)#ip add 192.168.40.1 255.255.255.252
R3(config-if)#end
R3#
```

Task 3:
```
R1(config)#ip route 0.0.0.0 0.0.0.0 192.168.10.2
R1(config)#ip route 0.0.0.0 0.0.0.0 192.168.20.2 254
```

Task 4:
```
R1(config)#ip sla monitor 17
R1(config)#type echo protocol ipIcmpEcho 4.2.2.2
R1(config)#ip sla monitor schedule 17 life forever start-time now
```

Task 5:

```
R1(config)#track 10 rtr 17 reachability
R1(config)#no ip route 0.0.0.0 0.0.0.0 192.168.10.2
R1(config)#ip route 0.0.0.0 0.0.0.0 192.168.10.2 track 10
```

Task 6:

```
R1#sh ip sla monitor statistics
Round trip time (RTT)    Index 17
    Latest RTT: NoConnection/Busy/Timeout
Latest operation start time: *00:26:03.323 UTC Fri Mar 1 2002
Latest operation return code: No connection
Number of successes: 0
Number of failures: 2
Operation time to live: Forever

R1#sh ip sla monitor operational-state
Entry number: 17
Modification time: *00:06:03.319 UTC Fri Mar 1 2002
Number of Octets Used by this Entry: 2224
Number of operations attempted: 2
Number of operations skipped: 0
Current seconds left in Life: Forever
Operational state of entry: Active
Last time this entry was reset: Never
Connection loss occurred: TRUE
Timeout occurred: FALSE
Over thresholds occurred: FALSE
Latest RTT (milliseconds): NoConnection/Busy/Timeout
Latest operation start time: *00:26:03.323 UTC Fri Mar 1 2002
Latest operation return code: No connection
RTT Values:
RTTAvg: 0 RTTMin: 0     RTTMax: 0
NumOfRTT: 0        RTTSum: 0     RTTSum2: 0


R1#show ip route
Codes: C - connected, S - static, R - RIP, M - mobile, B—BGP,
       D - EIGRP, EX - EIGRP external, O - OSPF, IA - OSPF inter area,
       N1 - OSPF NSSA external type 1, N2 - OSPF NSSA external type 2,
       E1 - OSPF external type 1, E2 - OSPF external type 2,
       i - IS-IS, su - IS-IS summary, L1 - IS-IS level-1,
       L2 - IS-IS level-2, ia - IS-IS inter area,
       * - candidate default, U - per-user static route, o - ODR,
       P - periodic downloaded static route

Gateway of last resort is 192.168.20.2 to network 0.0.0.0

     192.168.10.0/30 is subnetted, 1 subnets
C       192.168.10.0 is directly connected, FastEthernet0/0
     192.168.20.0/30 is subnetted, 1 subnets
C       192.168.20.0 is directly connected, FastEthernet0/1
S*    0.0.0.0/0 [254/0] via 192.168.20.2
```

Let's make IP SLA work by having 4.2.2.2 respond to the probes as the lab indicates:

```
R2#conf t
Enter configuration commands, one per line.  End with CTRL/Z.
R2(config)#int loop 1
R2(config-if)#ip address 4.2.2.2 255.255.255.0
```

Then let's wait for a couple of seconds and run the same show commands:

```
R1#sh ip sla monitor statistics
Round trip time (RTT)    Index 17
    Latest RTT: 16 ms
Latest operation start time: *01:10:54.727 UTC Fri Mar 1 2002
Latest operation return code: OK
Number of successes: 4
Number of failures: 2
Operation time to live: Forever

R1#sh ip sla monitor operational-state
Entry number: 17
Modification time: *01:09:54.727 UTC Fri Mar 1 2002
Number of Octets Used by this Entry: 2224
Number of operations attempted: 4
Number of operations skipped: 0
Current seconds left in Life: Forever
Operational state of entry: Active
Last time this entry was reset: Never
Connection loss occurred: FALSE
Timeout occurred: FALSE
Over thresholds occurred: FALSE
Latest RTT (milliseconds): 16
Latest operation start time: *01:10:54.727 UTC Fri Mar 1 2002
Latest operation return code: OK
RTT Values:
RTTAvg: 16 RTTMin: 16    RTTMax: 16
NumOfRTT: 1        RTTSum: 16    RTTSum2: 256

R1#sh ip route
Codes: C - connected, S - static, R - RIP, M - mobile, B—BGP,
       D - EIGRP, EX - EIGRP external, O - OSPF, IA - OSPF inter area,
       N1 - OSPF NSSA external type 1, N2 - OSPF NSSA external type ,2
       E1 - OSPF external type 1, E2 - OSPF external type 2,
       i - IS-IS, su - IS-IS summary, L1 - IS-IS level-1,
       L2 - IS-IS level-2, ia - IS-IS inter area,
       * - candidate default, U - per-user static route,
       o - ODR, P - periodic downloaded static route

Gateway of last resort is 192.168.10.2 to network 0.0.0.0

      192.168.10.0/30 is subnetted, 1 subnets
```

```
C       192.168.10.0 is directly connected, FastEthernet0/0
        192.168.20.0/30 is subnetted, 1 subnets
C       192.168.20.0 is directly connected, FastEthernet0/1
S*      0.0.0.0/0 [1/0] via 192.168.10.2
```

LAB 104: CONFIGURING SNMPV3

Lab Objective:

The objective of this lab exercise is for you to learn how to implement the SNMP protocol using v3.

Lab Purpose:

Configuring and applying the Simple Network Management Protocol (SNMP) is a fundamental skill for any network administrator in order to monitor and gather information about your Cisco device. As a Cisco engineer, as well as in the Cisco CCNA exam, you will be expected to know how to implement SNMP.

Certification Level:

This lab is suitable for ICND2 and CCNA certification exam preparation.

Lab Difficulty:

This lab has a difficulty rating of 7/10.

Readiness Assessment:

When you are ready for your certification exam, you should complete this lab in no more than 10 minutes.

Lab Topology:

Please use the following topology to complete this lab exercise:

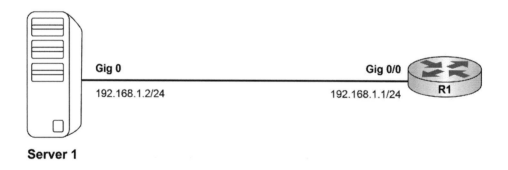

Task 1:

Configure hostnames on R1 as illustrated in the topology.

Task 2:

Configure IP addresses on the Gig0/0 interface of R1 as illustrated in the topology.

Task 3:

Create an SNMPv3 group that uses authentication and encryption named Read-Access to provide full Read permissions (make sure only the 192.168.1.2 server can access this SNMPv3 group).

Task 4:

Create an SNMPv3 user named CCNA-Admin; it will belong to the SNMPv3 group Read-Access and it will use SHA as the authentication mechanism, with the password set as Cisco and Cisco123 as the Des-256 encryption key.

Task 5:

Run the `show snmp user` and `show snmp group` commands and, finally, make sure that the right user and group settings are created.

LAB 104: CONFIGURATION AND VERIFICATION

Task 1:

For reference information on configuring hostnames, please refer to earlier labs.

Task 2:

For reference information on configuring IP addressing, please refer to earlier labs.

Task 3:
```
R1(config)#access-list 10 permit 192.168.1.2
R1(config)#snmp-server group Read-Access v3 priv access 10
```

Task 4:
```
R1(config)#snmp-server user CCNA-Admin Read-Access v3 auth sha Cisco
priv des256 Cisco123
```

Task 5:
```
R1#sh snmp user

User name: CCNA-Admin
Engine ID: 800000090300C00117120000
storage-type: nonvolatile         active
Authentication Protocol: SHA
Privacy Protocol: DES
Group-name: Read-Access

R1#sh snmp group

groupname: Read-Access                    security model:v3 priv
readview : v1default                      writeview: <no writeview
specified>
notifyview: <no notifyview specified>
row status: active        access-list: 10
```

LAB 105: CONFIGURING SNMPV2

Lab Objective:
The objective of this lab exercise is for you to learn how to implement the SNMP protocol using v2.

Lab Purpose:
Configuring and applying the SNMP protocol is a fundamental skill for any network administrator in order to monitor and gather information about your Cisco device. As a Cisco engineer, as well as in the Cisco CCNA exam, you will be expected to know how to implement SNMP.

Certification Level:
This lab is suitable for ICND2 certification exam preparation.

Lab Difficulty:
This lab has a difficulty rating of 5/10.

Readiness Assessment:
When you are ready for your certification exam, you should complete this lab in no more than 10 minutes.

Lab Topology:
Please use the following topology to complete this lab exercise:

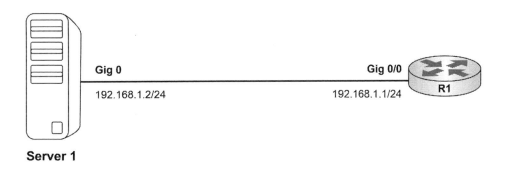

Server 1

Task 1:
Configure hostnames on R1 as illustrated in the topology.

Task 2:

Configure IP addresses on the Gig interface of R1 as illustrated in the topology.

Task 3:

Configure an SNMP Read-Only community called Public. Configure an SNMP Read-Write community called Private.

Task 4:

Configure a standard ACL numbered 10 and add it to the SNMP Private community to allow SNMP access from server 1 only.

Task 5:

Run the `show snmp community` command and make sure that the right communities are created, and that ACL 10 is being used in the appropriate community.

LAB 105: CONFIGURATION AND VERIFICATION

Task 1:

For reference information on configuring hostnames, please refer to earlier labs.

Task 2:

For reference information on configuring IP addressing, please refer to earlier labs.

Task 3:

```
R1(config)#snmp-server community Public RO
R1(config)#snmp-server community Private RW
```

Task 4:

```
R1(config)#access-list 10 permit 192.168.1.2
R1(config)#snmp-server community Private RW 10
```

Task 5:

```
R1#sh snmp  community

Community name: ILMI
Community Index: cisco0
Community SecurityName: ILMI
storage-type: read-only active

Community name: Public
Community Index: cisco2
Community SecurityName: Public
storage-type: nonvolatile active

Community name: Private
Community Index: cisco4
Community SecurityName: Private
storage-type: nonvolatile active          access-list: 10
```

ICND2 Challenge Labs

CHALLENGE LAB 11: CHAP WITH PAP FALLBACK

Lab Objective:
The objective of this lab exercise is for you to configure PAP fallback. This is not covered in earlier labs or in the CCNA syllabus; however, it might come up in the exam!

Lab Purpose:
PAP fallback is a useful feature if your CHAP authentication fails. Rather than watch a video solution, I have provided show runs and test commands where appropriate.

Certification Level:
This lab is suitable for both ICND2 and CCNA certification exam preparation.

Lab Difficulty:
This lab has a difficulty rating of 7/10.

Readiness Assessment:
When you are ready for your certification exam, you should complete this lab in no more than 15 minutes.

Lab Topology:
Please use the following topology to complete this lab exercise:

Task 1:
Configure the topology above. Test by pinging from RouterA to RouterB.

Task 2:

Configure a CHAP with PAP fallback on both routers. Ensure that the encapsulation is set to PPP on both routers.

Task 3:

Check your configurations with `show` commands (just `show run` in this case).

CHALLENGE LAB 11: SOLUTION

Show Runs

RouterA

```
hostname RA
!
username RB password 0 cisco
archive
 log config
  hidekeys
!
interface Serial0/0
 ip address 10.0.0.1 255.255.255.252
 encapsulation ppp
 clock rate 2000000
 ppp authentication chap pap
!
```

RouterB

```
hostname RB
!
username RA password 0 cisco
archive
 log config
  hidekeys
!
interface Serial0/0
 ip address 10.0.0.2 255.255.255.252
 encapsulation ppp
 clock rate 2000000
 ppp authentication chap pap
```

Test:

N/A

CHALLENGE LAB 12: SET STP ROOT BRIDGE MANUALLY

Lab Objective:
The objective of this lab exercise is for you to configure the root bridge manually. One switch you will use for the priority command and the other for the macro.

Lab Purpose:
It is important to know how to manually set your root bridge so that you can ensure optimal routing. Rather than watch a video solution, I have provided show runs and test commands where appropriate.

Certification Level:
This lab is suitable for both ICND and CCNA certification exam preparation.

Lab Difficulty:
This lab has a difficulty rating of 7/10.

Readiness Assessment:
When you are ready for your certification exam, you should complete this lab in no more than 15 minutes.

Lab Topology:
Please use the following topology to complete this lab exercise:

Task 1:
Configure the topology above. Set the interfaces to trunk.

Task 2:
Configure VLANs 10 and 20 on both switches.

Task 3:
On SwitchA, set the priority to ensure that it becomes the root bridge for VLAN10.

Task 4:
On SwitchB, use the IOS macro to ensure that it is the root bridge for VLAN20.

CHALLENGE LAB 12: SOLUTION

Show Runs

SwitchA

```
hostname SwitchA
!
spanning-tree mode pvst
spanning-tree vlan10 priority 0
!
interface FastEthernet0/1
 switchport mode trunk
!
interface FastEthernet0/2
!
  --More—
```

RouterB

```
hostname SwitchB
!
spanning-tree mode pvst
spanning-tree vlan20 root primary
!
interface FastEthernet0/1
 switchport mode trunk
!
```

Tests:
```
SwitchA#show span vlan10

SwitchB#show span vlan20
```

CHALLENGE LAB 13: ENABLE RSTP+

Lab Objective:
The objective of this lab exercise is for you to configure a switch to use the Rapid Spanning Tree Protocol.

Lab Purpose:
RSTP is used in preference to STP. Rather than watch a video solution, I have provided show runs and test commands where appropriate.

Certification Level:
This lab is suitable for both ICND and CCNA certification exam preparation.

Lab Difficulty:
This lab has a difficulty rating of 3/10.

Readiness Assessment:
When you are ready for your certification exam, you should complete this lab in no more than 15 minutes.

Lab Topology:
Please use the following topology to complete this lab exercise:

Task 1:
Configure the topology above. Set the interfaces to trunk.

Task 2:
Configure VLANs 10 and 20 on both switches.

Task 3:
On both switches set RSTP as the protocol.

CHALLENGE LAB 13: SOLUTION

Show Runs

SwitchA

REFER TO THE TESTS!

SwitchB

REFER TO THE TESTS!

Tests:
```
SwitchA#show spanning-tree summary
Switch is in pvst mode

SwitchB#show span summary
Switch is in rapid-pvst mode
```

CHALLENGE LAB 14: EASY EIGRP

Lab Objective:
The objective of this lab exercise is for you to configure EIGRP using two ASNs. One ASN will run between RouterA and RouterB and the other between RouterB and RouterC.

Lab Purpose:
EIGRP is a fundamental CCNA topic. I have provided show runs and test commands where appropriate.

Certification Level:
This lab is suitable for both ICND and CCNA certification exam preparation.

Lab Difficulty:
This lab has a difficulty rating of 7/10.

Readiness Assessment:
When you are ready for your certification exam, you should complete this lab in no more than 15 minutes.

Lab Topology:
Please use the following topology to complete this lab exercise:

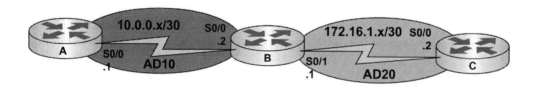

Task 1:
Configure the topology above. Test by pinging from RouterA to RouterB, then RouterB to RouterC. You will not be able to ping from A to C until you have configured EIGRP.

Task 2:
Configure EIGRP between all routers with each interface/subnet and with the correct ASN.

Task 3:
Check your configurations with show commands.

CHALLENGE LAB 14: SOLUTION

I cheated a bit here so you may have struggled. ASN 10 will not speak to ASN 20 without you adding another command not covered in the CCNA exam. But, I do know that Cisco can be sneaky and I've seen other stuff not in the syllabus put into the exam, leaving the test-taker confused and angry! I can't say I blame them.

Just have a play with the `redistribute` command and then re-do the lab, but just put everything into ASN 10 and it will work fine. I just wanted to give you an extra command to learn just in case.

Show Runs

RouterA

```
hostname RouterA
!
interface Serial0/0
 ip address 10.0.0.1 255.255.255.252
 clock rate 2000000
!
router eigrp 10
 network 10.0.0.0 0.0.0.3
 no auto-summary
```

RouterB

```
hostname RouterB
!
interface Serial0/0
 ip address 10.0.0.2 255.255.255.252
 clock rate 2000000
!
interface Serial0/1
 ip address 172.16.1.1 255.255.255.252
 clock rate 2000000
!
router eigrp 10
 redistribute eigrp 20
 network 10.0.0.0 0.0.0.3
 no auto-summary
!
router eigrp 20
 redistribute eigrp 10
 network 172.16.1.0 0.0.0.3
 no auto-summary
```

RouterC

```
hostname RouterC
!
interface Serial0/0
 ip address 172.16.1.2 255.255.255.252
 clock rate 2000000
!
router eigrp 20
 network 172.16.1.0 0.0.0.3
 no auto-summary
```

Test:

```
RouterA#show ip route
Codes: C - connected, S - static, R - RIP, M - mobile, B—BGP,
       D - EIGRP, EX - EIGRP external, O - OSPF, IA - OSPF inter area,
       N1 - OSPF NSSA external type 1, N2 - OSPF NSSA external type 2,
       E1 - OSPF external type 1, E2 - OSPF external type 2,
       i - IS-IS, su - IS-IS summary, L1 - IS-IS level-1,
       L2 - IS-IS level-2, ia - IS-IS inter area,
       * - candidate default, U - per-user static route,
       o - ODR, P - periodic downloaded static route

Gateway of last resort is not set

      172.16.0.0/30 is subnetted, 1 subnets
D EX    172.16.1.0 [170/2681856] via 10.0.0.2, 00:05:33, Serial0/0
      10.0.0.0/30 is subnetted, 1 subnets
C       10.0.0.0 is directly connected, Serial0/0

RouterC#show ip route
Codes: C - connected, S - static, R - RIP, M - mobile, B—BGP,
       D - EIGRP, EX - EIGRP external, O - OSPF, IA - OSPF inter area,
       N1 - OSPF NSSA external type 1, N2 - OSPF NSSA external type 2,
       E1 - OSPF external type 1, E2 - OSPF external type 2,
       i - IS-IS, su - IS-IS summary, L1 - IS-IS level-1,
       L2 - IS-IS level-2, ia - IS-IS inter area,
       * - candidate default, U - per-user static route,
       o - ODR, P - periodic downloaded static route

Gateway of last resort is not set

      172.16.0.0/30 is subnetted, 1 subnets
C       172.16.1.0 is directly connected, Serial0/0
      10.0.0.0/30 is subnetted, 1 subnets
D EX    10.0.0.0 [170/2681856] via 172.16.1.1, 00:06:42, Serial0/0
```

CHALLENGE LAB 15: OSPF PASSIVE INTERFACES

Lab Objective:
The objective of this lab exercise is for you to configure Single-Area OSPF on Cisco routers.

Lab Purpose:
Single-Area OSPF is a core ICND/CCNA exam topic so learn it well. Rather than watch a video solution, I have provided show runs and test commands where appropriate.

Certification Level:
This lab is suitable for both CCENT and CCNA certification exam preparation.

Lab Difficulty:
This lab has a difficulty rating of 5/10.

Readiness Assessment:
When you are ready for your certification exam, you should complete this lab in no more than 15 minutes.

Lab Topology:
Please use the following topology to complete this lab exercise:

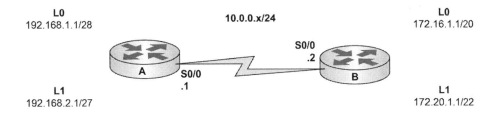

Task 1:
Configure the topology above. You should be able to ping across the Serial interface only because there are no routes from the Loopback networks.

Task 2:
Configure Single-Area OSPF on both routers. Put all networks into area 0. Set the router ID for RouterA to 1.1.1.1 and RouterB to 2.2.2.2. Ping all networks to check connectivity and check the routing tables.

Task 3:
Set Loopback0 on both routers to be a passive interface.

CHALLENGE LAB 15: SOLUTION

Show Runs

RouterA

```
interface Loopback0
ip address 192.168.1.1 255.255.255.240
!
interface Loopback1
ip address 192.168.2.1 255.255.255.224
!
interface Serial0/0
ip address 10.0.0.1 255.255.255.0
clock rate 2000000
!
router ospf 1
router-id 1.1.1.1
log-adjacency-changes
passive-interface Loopback0
network 10.0.0.0 0.0.0.255 area 0
network 192.168.1.0 0.0.0.15 area 0
network 192.168.2.0 0.0.0.31 area 0
!
```

RouterB

```
interface Loopback0
ip address 172.16.1.1 255.255.240.0
!
interface Loopback1
ip address 172.20.1.1 255.255.252.0
!
interface Serial0/0
ip address 10.0.0.2 255.255.255.0
clock rate 2000000
!
router ospf 2
router-id 2.2.2.2
log-adjacency-changes
passive-interface Loopback0
network 10.0.0.0 0.0.0.255 area 0
network 172.16.0.0 0.0.15.255 area 0
network 172.20.0.0 0.0.7.255 area 0
!
```

Test:

```
R1#show ip route
Codes: C - connected, S - static, R - RIP, M - mobile, B—BGP,
       D - EIGRP, EX - EIGRP external, O - OSPF, IA - OSPF inter area,
       N1 - OSPF NSSA external type 1, N2 - OSPF NSSA external type 2,
       E1 - OSPF external type 1, E2 - OSPF external type 2,
       i - IS-IS, su - IS-IS summary, L1 - IS-IS level-1,
       L2 - IS-IS level-2, ia - IS-IS inter area,
       * - candidate default, U - per-user static route,
       o - ODR, P - periodic downloaded static route

Gateway of last resort is not set

       172.16.0.0/32 is subnetted, 1 subnets
O 172.16.1.1 [110/65] via 10.0.0.2, 00:04:50, Serial0/0
       172.20.0.0/32 is subnetted, 1 subnets
O 172.20.1.1 [110/65] via 10.0.0.2, 00:04:50, Serial0/0
       10.0.0.0/24 is subnetted, 1 subnets
C 10.0.0.0 is directly connected, Serial0/0
       192.168.1.0/28 is subnetted, 1 subnets
C 192.168.1.0 is directly connected, Loopback0
       192.168.2.0/27 is subnetted, 1 subnets
C 192.168.2.0 is directly connected, Loopback1


R1#show ip protocols
Routing Protocol is "ospf 1"
Outgoing update filter list for all interfaces is not set
Incoming update filter list for all interfaces is not set
Router ID 1.1.1.1
Number of areas in this router is 1. 1 normal 0 stub 0 nssa
Maximum path: 4
Routing for Networks:
10.0.0.0 0.0.0.255 area 0
192.168.1.0 0.0.0.15 area 0
192.168.2.0 0.0.0.31 area 0
Reference bandwidth unit is 100 mbps
```
Passive Interface(s):
Loopback0
```
Routing Information Sources:
Gateway Distance Last Update
2.2.2.2 110 00:05:12
1.1.1.1 110 00:06:29
192.168.2.1 110 00:06:44
Distance: (default is 110)


R1#show ip ospf nei
Neighbor ID Pri State Dead Time Address Interface
2.2.2.2 0 FULL/ - 00:00:36 10.0.0.2 Serial0/0


R2#show ip route
```

```
Codes: C - connected, S - static, R - RIP, M - mobile, B—BGP,
       D - EIGRP, EX - EIGRP external, O - OSPF, IA - OSPF inter area,
       N1 - OSPF NSSA external type 1, N2 - OSPF NSSA external type 2,
       E1 - OSPF external type 1, E2 - OSPF external type 2,
       i - IS-IS, su - IS-IS summary, L1 - IS-IS level-1,
       L2 - IS-IS level-2, ia - IS-IS inter area,
       * - candidate default, U - per-user static route,
       o - ODR, P - periodic downloaded static route

Gateway of last resort is not set

       172.16.0.0/20 is subnetted, 1 subnets
C 172.16.0.0 is directly connected, Loopback0
       172.20.0.0/22 is subnetted, 1 subnets
C 172.20.0.0 is directly connected, Loopback1
       10.0.0.0/24 is subnetted, 1 subnets
C 10.0.0.0 is directly connected, Serial0/0
       192.168.1.0/32 is subnetted, 1 subnets
O 192.168.1.1 [110/65] via 10.0.0.1, 00:01:11, Serial0/0
       192.168.2.0/32 is subnetted, 1 subnets
O 192.168.2.1 [110/65] via 10.0.0.1, 00:01:11, Serial0/0

R2#show ip prot
Routing Protocol is "ospf 2"
Outgoing update filter list for all interfaces is not set
Incoming update filter list for all interfaces is not set
Router ID 2.2.2.2
Number of areas in this router is 1. 1 normal 0 stub 0 nssa
Maximum path: 4
Routing for Networks:
10.0.0.0 0.0.0.255 area 0
172.16.0.0 0.0.15.255 area 0
172.20.0.0 0.0.7.255 area 0
Reference bandwidth unit is 100 mbps
Passive Interface(s):
Loopback0
Routing Information Sources:
Gateway Distance Last Update
1.1.1.1 110 00:01:48
2.2.2.2 110 00:01:48
Distance: (default is 110)

R2#show ip ospf nei
Neighbor ID Pri State Dead Time Address Interface
1.1.1.1 0 FULL/ - 00:00:35 10.0.0.1 Serial0/0
R2#
```

CHALLENGE LAB 16: MULTI-AREA OSPF

Lab Objective:
The objective of this lab exercise is for you to configure OSPF on three routers using more than one area.

Lab Purpose:
Multi-Area OSPF is a core ICND2 topic. I have provided show runs and test commands where appropriate.

Certification Level:
This lab is suitable for both ICND2 and CCNA certification exam preparation.

Lab Difficulty:
This lab has a difficulty rating of 7/10.

Readiness Assessment:
When you are ready for your certification exam, you should complete this lab in no more than 15 minutes.

Lab Topology:
Please use the following topology to complete this lab exercise:

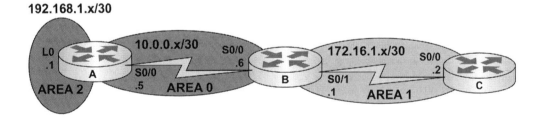

Task 1:
Configure the topology above. Test by pinging from RouterA to RouterB, then RouterB to RouterC. You will not be able to ping from A to C until you have configured OSPF.

Task 2:
Configure OSPF between all routers with each interface/subnet in the correct area.

Task 3:
Check your configurations with show commands.

CHALLENGE LAB 16: SOLUTION

There is a sneaky gotcha in this lab. I hope you spotted it.

The 10.0.0.0 network is not in the first subnet (the zero subnet), so putting the configuration below in for the OSPF network won't work:

```
network 10.0.0.0 0.0.0.3 Area 0
```

The reason is that this would advertise hosts .1 and .2, so if you want to advertise the hosts in the 10.0.0.4 network, which are .5 and .6, you need to enter:

```
network 10.0.0.4 0.0.0.3 Area 0
```

Show Runs

RouterA

```
hostname RouterA
!
interface Loopback0
 ip address 192.168.1.1 255.255.255.252
!
interface Serial0/0
 ip address 10.0.0.5 255.255.255.252
 clock rate 2000000
!
router ospf 1
 log-adjacency-changes
 network 10.0.0.4 0.0.0.3 area 0
 network 192.168.1.0 0.0.0.3 area 2
```

RouterB

```
hostname RouterB
!
interface Serial0/0
 ip address 10.0.0.6 255.255.255.252
 clock rate 2000000
!

interface Serial0/1
 ip address 172.16.1.1 255.255.255.252
 clock rate 2000000
!
router ospf 1
 log-adjacency-changes
 network 10.0.0.4 0.0.0.3 area 0
 network 172.16.1.0 0.0.0.3 area 1
```

RouterC

```
hostname RouterC
!
interface Serial0/0
 ip address 172.16.1.2 255.255.255.252
 clock rate 2000000
!
router ospf 1
 log-adjacency-changes
 network 172.16.1.0 0.0.0.3 area 1
```

Test:

```
RouterA#show ip route
Codes: C - connected, S - static, R - RIP, M - mobile, B—BGP,
       D - EIGRP, EX - EIGRP external, O - OSPF, IA - OSPF inter area,
       N1 - OSPF NSSA external type 1, N2 - OSPF NSSA external type 2,
       E1 - OSPF external type 1, E2 - OSPF external type 2,
       i - IS-IS, su - IS-IS summary, L1 - IS-IS level-1,
       L2 - IS-IS level-2, ia - IS-IS inter area,
       * - candidate default, U - per-user static route,
       o - ODR, P - periodic downloaded static route

Gateway of last resort is not set

     172.16.0.0/30 is subnetted, 1 subnets
O IA    172.16.1.0 [110/128] via 10.0.0.6, 00:06:32, Serial0/0
     10.0.0.0/30 is subnetted, 1 subnets
C       10.0.0.4 is directly connected, Serial0/0
     192.168.1.0/30 is subnetted, 1 subnets
C       192.168.1.0 is directly connected, Loopback0

RouterA#show ip ospf neighbor

Neighbor ID     Pri   State       Dead Time   Address       Interface
172.16.1.1        0   FULL/  -    00:00:30    10.0.0.6      Serial0/0

RouterA#show ip protocols
Routing Protocol is "ospf 1"
  Outgoing update filter list for all interfaces is not set
  Incoming update filter list for all interfaces is not set
  Router ID 192.168.1.1
  It is an area border router
  Number of areas in this router is 2. 2 normal 0 stub 0 nssa
  Maximum path: 4
  Routing for Networks:
    10.0.0.4 0.0.0.3 area 0
    192.168.1.0 0.0.0.3 area 2
  Reference bandwidth unit is 100 mbps
  Routing Information Sources:
```

```
     Gateway        Distance      Last Update
     192.168.1.1         110      00:08:43
     172.16.1.1          110      00:07:11
   Distance: (default is 110)

RouterC#show ip route
Codes: C - connected, S - static, R - RIP, M - mobile, B—BGP,
       D - EIGRP, EX - EIGRP external, O - OSPF, IA - OSPF inter area,
       N1 - OSPF NSSA external type 1, N2 - OSPF NSSA external type 2,
       E1 - OSPF external type 1, E2 - OSPF external type 2,
       i - IS-IS, su - IS-IS summary, L1 - IS-IS level-1,
       L2 - IS-IS level-2, ia - IS-IS inter area,
       * - candidate default, U - per-user static route,
       o - ODR, P - periodic downloaded static route

Gateway of last resort is not set

     172.16.0.0/30 is subnetted, 1 subnets
C       172.16.1.0 is directly connected, Serial0/0
     10.0.0.0/30 is subnetted, 1 subnets
O IA    10.0.0.4 [110/128] via 172.16.1.1, 00:00:15, Serial0/0
     192.168.1.0/32 is subnetted, 1 subnets
O IA    192.168.1.1 [110/129] via 172.16.1.1, 00:00:15, Serial0/0

RouterC#ping 192.168.1.1

Type escape sequence to abort.
Sending 5, 100-byte ICMP Echos to 192.168.1.1, timeout is 2 seconds:
!!!!!
```

CHALLENGE LAB 17: MULTI-AREA OSPF WITH PASSIVE INTERFACES

Lab Objective:

The objective of this lab exercise is for you to configure OSPF on three routers using more than one area. You will then use the `passive-interface default` command to turn off Hellos on all interfaces for RouterA and then enable them on the Serial interface on that router.

Lab Purpose:

Multi-Area OSPF is a core ICND2 topic and you must understand how to use the `passive interface` command. I have provided show runs and test commands where appropriate.

Certification Level:

This lab is suitable for both ICND2 and CCNA certification exam preparation.

Lab Difficulty:

This lab has a difficulty rating of 7/10.

Readiness Assessment:

When you are ready for your certification exam, you should complete this lab in no more than 15 minutes.

Lab Topology:

Please use the following topology to complete this lab exercise:

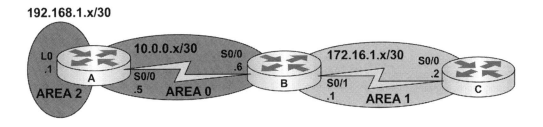

Task 1:

Configure the topology above. Test by pinging from RouterA to RouterB, then RouterB to RouterC. You will not be able to ping from A to C until you have configured OSPF.

Task 2:

Configure OSPF between all routers with each interface/subnet in the correct area.

Task 3:

Make all interfaces on RouterA passive and then enable Serial0/0.

Test 4:

Check your configurations.

CHALLENGE LAB 17: SOLUTION

The `passive-interface` command produces different results for different protocols. The interface for OSPF will no longer send Hellos and so an adjacency will not form on this link. LSAs will be sent however. In this lab, I've set all OSPF interfaces to be passive but then enabled the Serial interface.

Show Runs

RouterA

```
hostname RouterA
!
interface Loopback0
 ip address 192.168.1.1 255.255.255.252
!
interface Serial0/0
 ip address 10.0.0.5 255.255.255.252
 clock rate 2000000
!
router ospf 1
 log-adjacency-changes
 passive-interface default
 no passive-interface Serial0/0
 network 10.0.0.4 0.0.0.3 area 0
 network 192.168.1.0 0.0.0.3 area 2
```

RouterB

```
hostname RouterB
!
interface Serial0/0
 ip address 10.0.0.6 255.255.255.252
 clock rate 2000000
!

interface Serial0/1
 ip address 172.16.1.1 255.255.255.252
 clock rate 2000000
!
router ospf 1
 log-adjacency-changes
 network 10.0.0.4 0.0.0.3 area 0
 network 172.16.1.0 0.0.0.3 area 1
```

RouterC

```
!
hostname RouterC
!
interface Serial0/0
 ip address 172.16.1.2 255.255.255.252
 clock rate 2000000
!
interface FastEthernet0/1
 no ip address
 shutdown
 duplex auto
 speed auto
!
router ospf 1
 log-adjacency-changes
 network 172.16.1.0 0.0.0.3 area 1
```

Test:

```
RouterA#show ip prot
Routing Protocol is "ospf 1"
  Outgoing update filter list for all interfaces is not set
  Incoming update filter list for all interfaces is not set
  Router ID 192.168.1.1
  It is an area border router
  Number of areas in this router is 2. 2 normal 0 stub 0 nssa
  Maximum path: 4
  Routing for Networks:
    10.0.0.4 0.0.0.3 area 0
    192.168.1.0 0.0.0.3 area 2
 Reference bandwidth unit is 100 mbps
  Passive Interface(s):
    FastEthernet0/0
    FastEthernet0/1
    Loopback0
  Routing Information Sources:
    Gateway          Distance      Last Update
    10.0.0.6              110      00:00:04
    192.168.1.1          110      00:05:54
  Distance: (default is 110)
```

CHALLENGE LAB 18: OSPFV3

Lab Objective:
The objective of this lab exercise is for you to configure OSPFv3 static routing.

Lab Purpose:
Configuring OSPFv3 is a CCENT exam subject so you can expect to find it in the exam. I have provided show runs and test commands where appropriate.

Certification Level:
This lab is suitable for both CCENT and CCNA certification exam preparation.

Lab Difficulty:
This lab has a difficulty rating of 6/10.

Readiness Assessment:
When you are ready for your certification exam, you should complete this lab in no more than 15 minutes.

Lab Topology:
Please use the following topology to complete this lab exercise:

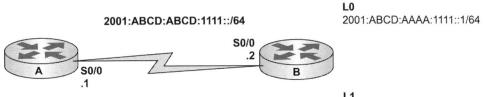

Task 1:
Configure the topology above. Check that you can ping across the Serial link.

Task 2:
Configure OSPFv3 on both routers. Put all networks into area 0. Make the router ID for RouterA 1.1.1.1 and RouterB 2.2.2.2.

Task 3:
Check your IPv6 routing table. Ping the Loopback interfaces on RouterB from RouterA.

CHALLENGE LAB 18: SOLUTION

Show Runs

RouterA

```
ipv6 unicast-routing
!
interface Serial0/0
 no ip address
 ipv6 address 2001:ABCD:ABCD:1111::1/64
 ipv6 ospf 1 area 0
 clock rate 2000000
!
ipv6 router ospf 1
 router-id 1.1.1.1
 log-adjacency-changes
```

RouterB

```
ipv6 unicast-routing
!
interface Loopback0
 no ip address
 ipv6 address 2001:ABCD:AAAA:1111::1/64
 ipv6 ospf 2 area 0
!
interface Loopback1
 no ip address
 ipv6 address 2001:ABCD:BBBB:1111::1/64
 ipv6 ospf 2 area 0
!
interface Serial0/0
 no ip address
 ipv6 address 2001:ABCD:ABCD:1111::2/64
 ipv6 ospf 2 area 0
 clock rate 2000000
!
ip forward-protocol nd
!
ipv6 router ospf 2
 router-id 2.2.2.2
 log-adjacency-changes
!
```

Test:

```
R1#show ipv6 route
IPv6 Routing Table - 5 entries
Codes: C - Connected, L - Local, S - Static, R - RIP, B—BGP,
       U - Per-user Static route, M - MIPv6,
       I1 - ISIS L1, I2 - ISIS L2, IA - ISIS interarea, IS - ISIS
summary,
       O - OSPF intra, OI - OSPF inter, OE1 - OSPF ext 1,
       OE2 - OSPF ext 2, ON1 - OSPF NSSA ext 1, ON2 - OSPF NSSA ext 2,
       D - EIGRP, EX - EIGRP external
O   2001:ABCD:AAAA:1111::1/128 [110/64]
     via FE80::C001:7FF:FE0A:0, Serial0/0
C   2001:ABCD:ABCD:1111::/64 [0/0]
     via ::, Serial0/0
L   2001:ABCD:ABCD:1111::1/128 [0/0]
     via ::, Serial0/0
O   2001:ABCD:BBBB:1111::1/128 [110/64]
     via FE80::C001:7FF:FE0A:0, Serial0/0
L   FF00::/8 [0/0]
     via ::, Null0

R1#ping ipv6 2001:ABCD:AAAA:1111::1

Type escape sequence to abort.
Sending 5, 100-byte ICMP Echos to 2001:ABCD:AAAA:1111::1, timeout is 2
seconds:
!!!!!
Success rate is 100 percent (5/5), round-trip min/avg/max = 0/2/4 ms

R1#ping ipv6 2001:ABCD:BBBB:1111::1

Type escape sequence to abort.
Sending 5, 100-byte ICMP Echos to 2001:ABCD:BBBB:1111::1, timeout is 2
seconds:
!!!!!
Success rate is 100 percent (5/5), round-trip min/avg/max = 0/1/8 ms
R1#
```

CHALLENGE LAB 19: MULTI-AREA OSPFV3

Lab Objective:
The objective of this lab exercise is for you to configure OSPFv3 on three routers using more than one area.

Lab Purpose:
Multi-Area OSPFv3 is a core ICND2 topic. I have provided show runs and test commands where appropriate.

Certification Level:
This lab is suitable for both ICND2 and CCNA certification exam preparation.

Lab Difficulty:
This lab has a difficulty rating of 8/10.

Readiness Assessment:
When you are ready for your certification exam, you should complete this lab in no more than 15 minutes.

Lab Topology:
Please use the following topology to complete this lab exercise:

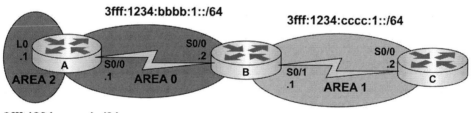

Task 1:
Configure the topology above. Test by pinging from RouterA to RouterB, then RouterB to RouterC. You will not be able to ping from A to C until you have configured OSPFv3.

Task 2:
Configure OSPFv3 between all routers with each interface/subnet in the correct area. Add the router ID manually.

Task 3:
Check your configurations.

CHALLENGE LAB 19: SOLUTION

OSPFv3 is a core CCNA topic, and because it's one of the new additions, you can expect it to be featured in the exam.

Show Runs

RouterA

```
hostname RouterA
!
ipv6 unicast-routing
!
interface Loopback0
 no ip address
 ipv6 address 3FFF:1234:AAAA:1::1/64
 ipv6 ospf 1 area 2
!
interface Serial0/0
 no ip address
 ipv6 address 3FFF:1234:BBBB:1::1/64
 ipv6 ospf 1 area 0
 clock rate 2000000
!
ipv6 router ospf 1
 router-id 1.1.1.1
```

RouterB

```
hostname RouterB
!
ipv6 unicast-routing
!
interface Serial0/0
 no ip address
 ipv6 address 3FFF:1234:BBBB:1::2/64
 ipv6 ospf 1 area 0
 clock rate 2000000
!
interface Serial0/1
 no ip address
 ipv6 address 3FFF:1234:CCCC:1::1/64
 ipv6 ospf 1 area 1
 clock rate 2000000
!
ipv6 router ospf 1
 router-id 2.2.2.2
```

RouterC

```
hostname RouterC
!
ipv6 unicast-routing
!
interface Serial0/0
 no ip address
 ipv6 address 3FFF:1234:CCCC:1::2/64
 ipv6 ospf 1 area 1
 clock rate 2000000
!
ipv6 router ospf 1
router-id 3.3.3.3
```

Test:

```
RouterA#show ipv6 route
IPv6 Routing Table - 6 entries
Codes: C - Connected, L - Local, S - Static, R - RIP, B—BGP,
       U - Per-user Static route, M - MIPv6, I1 - ISIS L1,
       I2 - ISIS L2, IA - ISIS interarea, IS - ISIS summary
       O - OSPF intra, OI - OSPF inter, OE1 - OSPF ext 1,
       OE2 - OSPF ext 2, ON1 - OSPF NSSA ext 1, ON2 - OSPF NSSA ext 2,
       D - EIGRP, EX - EIGRP external
C   3FFF:1234:AAAA:1::/64 [0/0]
     via ::, Loopback0
L   3FFF:1234:AAAA:1::1/128 [0/0]
     via ::, Loopback0
C   3FFF:1234:BBBB:1::/64 [0/0]
     via ::, Serial0/0
L   3FFF:1234:BBBB:1::1/128 [0/0]
     via ::, Serial0/0
OI  3FFF:1234:CCCC:1::/64 [110/128]
     via FE80::C001:7FF:FE17:0, Serial0/0
L   FF00::/8 [0/0]
     via ::, Null0
RouterA#

RouterA#show ipv6 ospf nei

Neighbor ID    Pri  State      Dead Time   Interface ID    Interface
2.2.2.2          1  FULL/  -   00:00:31    6               Serial0/0
RouterA#

RouterA#show ipv6 protocols
IPv6 Routing Protocol is "connected"
IPv6 Routing Protocol is "static"
IPv6 Routing Protocol is "ospf 1"
  Interfaces (Area 0):
    Serial0/0
```

```
   Interfaces (Area 2):
     Loopback0
   Redistribution:
     None
RouterA#
```

CHALLENGE LAB 20: MULTI-AREA OSPFV3 WITH PPP AND LOGGING

Lab Objective:
The objective of this lab exercise is for you to configure OSPFv3 on three routers using more than one area. It's a repeat of the previous lab but with PPP and logging added to make it a little trickier.

Lab Purpose:
Multi-Area OSPFv3, as well as PPP and logging, is a core ICND2 topic. I have provided show runs and test commands where appropriate.

Certification Level:
This lab is suitable for both ICND2 and CCNA certification exam preparation.

Lab Difficulty:
This lab has a difficulty rating of 9/10.

Readiness Assessment:
When you are ready for your certification exam, you should complete this lab in no more than 15 minutes.

Lab Topology:
Please use the following topology to complete this lab exercise:

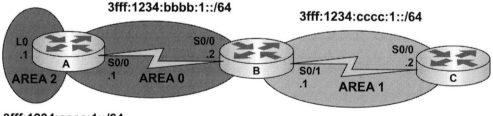

Task 1:
Configure the topology above but change all Serial links to use PPP with CHAP. Use the password cisco and device hostnames. Test by pinging from RouterA to RouterB, then RouterB to RouterC. You will not be able to ping from A to C until you have configured OSPFv3.

Task 2:

Configure OSPFv3 between all routers with each interface/subnet in the correct area. Add the router ID manually.

Task 3:

Set RouterA to log to server 3fff:1234:aaaa:1::2/64 and the severity level should be "emergencies."

Task 4:

Check your configurations with relevant show commands.

CHALLENGE LAB 20: SOLUTION

OSPFv3 is a core CCNA topic, and because it's one of the new additions, you can expect it to be featured in the exam. You can expect the same for logging and PPP.

Show Runs

RouterA

```
hostname RouterA
!
ipv6 unicast-routing
!
username RouterB password 0 cisco
!
interface Loopback0
 no ip address
 ipv6 address 3FFF:1234:AAAA:1::1/64
 ipv6 ospf 1 area 2
!
interface Serial0/0
 no ip address
 encapsulation ppp
 ipv6 address 3FFF:1234:BBBB:1::1/64
 ipv6 ospf 1 area 0
 clock rate 2000000
 ppp authentication chap
!
logging trap emergencies
logging host ipv6 3FFF:1234:AAAA:1::2
ipv6 router ospf 1
 router-id 1.1.1.1
 log-adjacency-changes
!
```

RouterB

```
hostname RouterB
!
ipv6 unicast-routing
!
username RouterA password 0 cisco
username RouterC password 0 cisco
!
interface Serial0/0
 no ip address
 encapsulation ppp
 ipv6 address 3FFF:1234:BBBB:1::2/64
 ipv6 ospf 1 area 0
```

```
 clock rate 2000000
 ppp authentication chap
!
interface Serial0/1
 no ip address
 encapsulation ppp
 ipv6 address 3FFF:1234:CCCC:1::1/64
 ipv6 ospf 1 area 1
 clock rate 2000000
 ppp authentication chap
!
ipv6 router ospf 1
 router-id 2.2.2.2
 log-adjacency-changes
!

RouterB#
```

RouterC

```
hostname RouterC
!
ipv6 unicast-routing
!
username RouterB password 0 cisco
!
interface Serial0/0
 no ip address
 encapsulation ppp
 ipv6 address 3FFF:1234:CCCC:1::2/64
 ipv6 ospf 1 area 1
 clock rate 2000000
 ppp authentication chap
!
ipv6 router ospf 1
 router-id 3.3.3.3
 log-adjacency-changes
!
RouterC#
```

Test:

```
RouterA#show logging

    Trap logging: level emergencies, 35 message lines logged
        Logging to 3FFF:1234:AAAA:1::2 (udp port 514, audit disabled,
            authentication disabled, encryption disabled, link down),
            0 message lines logged,
            0 message lines rate-limited,
            0 message lines dropped-by-MD,
            xml disabled, sequence number disabled
```

```
            filtering disabled

RouterA#show ipv6 route
IPv6 Routing Table - 6 entries
Codes: C - Connected, L - Local, S - Static, R - RIP, B—BGP,
       U - Per-user Static route, M - MIPv6, I1 - ISIS L1,
       I2 - ISIS L2, IA - ISIS interarea, IS - ISIS summary,
       O - OSPF intra, OI - OSPF inter, OE1 - OSPF ext 1,
       OE2 - OSPF ext 2, ON1 - OSPF NSSA ext 1, ON2 - OSPF NSSA ext 2,
       D - EIGRP, EX - EIGRP external
C   3FFF:1234:AAAA:1::/64 [0/0]
     via ::, Loopback0
L   3FFF:1234:AAAA:1::1/128 [0/0]
     via ::, Loopback0
C   3FFF:1234:BBBB:1::/64 [0/0]
     via ::, Serial0/0
L   3FFF:1234:BBBB:1::1/128 [0/0]
     via ::, Serial0/0
OI  3FFF:1234:CCCC:1::/64 [110/128]
     via FE80::C001:7FF:FE17:0, Serial0/0
L   FF00::/8 [0/0]
     via ::, Null0
RouterA#
```

BONUS LABS

LAB A: CONFIGURING AND APPLYING EXTENDED NAMED ACLS OUTBOUND

Lab Objective:

The objective of this lab exercise is for you to learn and understand how to create and apply extended numbered access control lists.

Lab Purpose:

Configuring and applying extended ACLs is a fundamental skill. Extended ACLs filter based on source and destination address, as well as Layer 4 protocols TCP and UDP. Extended ACLs should be applied as close to the source as possible. As a Cisco engineer, as well as in the Cisco CCNA exam, you will be expected to know how to create and apply extended ACLs in the outbound direction.

Certification Level:

This lab is suitable for CCNA certification exam preparation.

Lab Difficulty:

This lab has a difficulty rating of 8/10.

Readiness Assessment:

When you are ready for your certification exam, you should complete this lab in no more than 20 minutes.

Lab Topology:

Please use the following topology to complete this lab exercise:

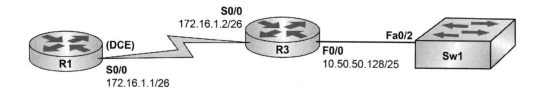

Task 1:

Configure hostnames on R1, R3, and Sw1 as illustrated in the topology.

Task 2:

Configure R1 S0/0, which is a DCE, to provide a clock rate of 768 Kbps to R3. Configure IP addresses on the Serial interfaces of R1 and R3 as illustrated in the topology.

Task 3:

Configure a static default route on R1 pointing to R3 over the Serial connection between the two routers. Also, configure a static default route on R3 pointing to R1 via the Serial connection between the two routers.

Task 4:

Configure VLAN50 on Sw1 and assign it the name ACL-VLAN. Assign port FastEthernet0/2 to this VLAN. Configure interface VLAN50 with the IP address 10.50.50.130/25 and configure a default gateway on the switch to 10.50.50.129. Also, configure interface F0/0 on R3 with the IP address 10.50.50.129 and enable this interface.

Task 5:

Create an extended named ACL called SWITCH-ACL on R3. This ACL should:

- Permit all ICMP traffic from 10.50.50.128/25 to the interface address of R1 S0/0 (172.16.1.1);
- Deny all www traffic from 10.50.50.128/25 to the 172.16.1.0/26 subnet;
- Permit all Telnet traffic from the interface address of Sw1 (10.50.50.130) to the interface address of R1 S0/0;
- Permit all IP traffic from 10.50.50.128/25 to the interface address of R1 S0/0; and
- Deny all IP traffic from the interface address of Sw1 to the 172.16.1.0/26 subnet.

Apply this ACL outbound on R3 S0/0.

Task 6:

Test your ACL configurations by performing ping and telnet exercises as we have done in previous labs, and verify matches against your ACL using the `show ip access-list SWITCH-ACL` command.

LAB A: CONFIGURATION AND VERIFICATION

Task 1:

For reference information on configuring hostnames, please refer to earlier labs.

Task 2:

For reference information on configuring DCE clocking, please refer to earlier labs.

Task 3:

For reference information on configuring static routes, please refer to earlier labs.

Task 4:

For reference information on configuring IP addressing and verifying VLANs, please refer to earlier labs.

Task 5:
```
R3#conf t
Enter configuration commands, one per line.  End with CTRL/Z.
R3(config)#ip access-list extended SWITCH-ACL
R3(config-ext-nacl)#permit icmp 10.50.50.128 0.0.0.127 host 172.16.1.1
R3(config-ext-nacl)#deny tcp 10.50.50.128 0.0.0.127 172.16.1.0 0.0.0.63
eq www
R3(config-ext-nacl)#permit tcp host 10.50.50.130 host 172.16.1.1 eq
telnet
R3(config-ext-nacl)#permit ip 10.50.50.128 0.0.0.127 host 172.16.1.1
R3(config-ext-nacl)#deny ip host 10.50.50.130 172.16.1.0 0.0.0.63
R3(config-ext-nacl)#exit
R3(config)#int s0/0
R3(config-if)#ip access-group SWITCH-ACL out
R3(config-if)#end
R3#
```

Task 6:
```
R3#show ip access-lists SWITCH-ACL
Extended IP access list SWITCH-ACL
    10 permit icmp 10.50.50.128 0.0.0.127 host 172.16.1.1 (15 matches)
    20 deny tcp 10.50.50.128 0.0.0.127 172.16.1.0 0.0.0.63 eq www (2
matches)
    30 permit tcp host 10.50.50.130 host 172.16.1.1 eq telnet (75
matches)
    40 permit ip 10.50.50.128 0.0.0.127 host 172.16.1.1 (30 matches)
    50 deny ip host 10.50.50.130 172.16.1.0 0.0.0.63 (5 matches)
```

Now please test the ACL.

LAB B: RESTRICTING OUTBOUND TELNET ACCESS USING EXTENDED ACLS

Lab Objective:
The objective of this lab exercise is for you to learn and understand how to create and apply extended access control lists to restrict Telnet access from a router or switch.

Lab Purpose:
Configuring and applying extended ACLs to restrict Telnet access is a fundamental skill. Extended ACLs filter based on source and destination address, as well as Layer 4 protocols TCP and UDP. Telnet traffic sourced from the router or switch cannot be filtered using outbound interface ACLs. Instead, because VTY lines are used, this is where the ACL restrictions should be applied. As a Cisco engineer, as well as in the Cisco CCNA exam, you will be expected to know how to create and apply extended numbered ACLs.

Certification Level:
This lab is suitable for CCNA certification exam preparation.

Lab Difficulty:
This lab has a difficulty rating of 8/10.

Readiness Assessment:
When you are ready for your certification exam, you should complete this lab in no more than 20 minutes.

Lab Topology:
Please use the following topology to complete this lab exercise:

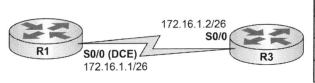

INTERFACE	IP ADDRESS
Loopback10	10.10.10.3/25
Loopback20	10.20.20.3/28
Loopback30	10.30.30.3/31

Task 1:
Configure hostnames on R1 and R3 as illustrated in the topology.

Task 2:

Configure R1 S0/0, which is a DCE, to provide a clock rate of 768 Kbps to R3. Configure IP addresses on the Serial interfaces of R1 and R3 as illustrated in the topology.

Task 3:

Configure a static default route on R1 pointing to R3 over the Serial connection between the two routers. Configure the Loopback interfaces specified in the diagram on R3. Configure R3 to allow Telnet sessions. Use the password CISCO for Telnet login.

Task 4:

To test connectivity, telnet from R1 to R3 Loopback10, Loopback20, and Loopback30 interfaces.

Task 5:

Create an extended named ACL called TELNET-OUT on R1. This ACL should deny all Telnet traffic to 10.10.10.0/25; permit Telnet traffic to 10.20.20.0/28; and deny Telnet traffic to 10.30.30.0/29. Apply this ACL to the Telnet lines on R1 for outbound Telnet traffic originated from the router.

Task 6:

To test your ACL configurations, telnet from R1 from R3 Loopback10, Loopback20, and Loopback30 interfaces. If your ACL configurations are correct, only telnetting from R3 Loopback20 should work.

LAB B: CONFIGURATION AND VERIFICATION

Task 1:

For reference information on configuring hostnames, please refer to earlier labs.

Task 2:

For reference information on configuring IP addressing, please refer to earlier labs.

Task 3:

```
R1#config t
Enter configuration commands, one per line.  End with CTRL/Z.
R1(config)#ip route 0.0.0.0 0.0.0.0 serial0/0 172.16.1.2
R1(config)#line vty 0 4
R1(config-line)#password CISCO
R1(config-line)#login
R1(config-line)#end
R1#

R3#conf t
Enter configuration commands, one per line.  End with CTRL/Z.
R3(config)#int loop10
R3(config-if)#ip address 10.10.10.3 255.255.255.128
R3(config-if)#exit
R3(config)#int loop20
R3(config-if)#ip address 10.20.20.3 255.255.255.240
R3(config-if)#exit
R3(config)#int loop30
R3(config-if)#ip address 10.30.30.3 255.255.255.248
R3(config-if)#exit
R3(config)#line vty 0 4
R3(config-line)#password CISCO
R3(config-line)#login
R3(config-line)#end
R3#
```

Task 4:

```
R1>telnet 10.10.10.3
Trying 10.10.10.3 ... Open

User Access Verification

Password:
R3#

R1>telnet 10.20.20.3
Trying 10.20.20.3 ... Open

User Access Verification
```

```
Password:
R3#

R1>telnet 10.30.30.3
Trying 10.30.30.3 ... Open

User Access Verification

Password:
R3#
```

Task 5:

```
R1#conf t
Enter configuration commands, one per line.  End with CTRL/Z.
R1(config)#ip access-list extended TELNET-OUT
R1(config-ext-nacl)#remark "Deny Traffic To 10.10.10.0/25"
R1(config-ext-nacl)#deny ip any 10.10.10.0 0.0.0.127
R1(config-ext-nacl)#remark "Permit Traffic To 10.20.20.0/28"
R1(config-ext-nacl)#permit ip any 10.20.20.0 0.0.0.15
R1(config-ext-nacl)#remark "Deny Traffic To 10.30.30.0/29"
R1(config-ext-nacl)#deny ip any 10.30.30.0 0.0.0.7
R1(config-ext-nacl)#exit
R1(config)#line vty 0 4
R1(config-line)#access-class TELNET-OUT out
R1(config-line)#end
R1#
```

Task 6:

For reference information on completing Task 6, please use the `telnet` command from R1.

LAB C: CONFIGURING IOS DHCP CLIENTS

Lab Objective:
The objective of this lab exercise is for you to learn and understand how to configure Cisco IOS DHCP clients.

Lab Purpose:
Configuring the Cisco IOS DHCP client feature is a fundamental skill. DHCP provides dynamic addressing information to hosts on a network. Typically, physical DHCP servers (such as Microsoft Windows servers) are used to provide addressing information to DHCP clients (which are devices that request configuration via DHCP). In most cases, DHCP clients are typically computers and other such devices; however, it is also possible to configure Cisco IOS devices to act as DHCP clients and automatically receive configuration information from a DHCP server. As a Cisco engineer, as well as in the Cisco CCNA exam, you will be expected to know how to configure the Cisco IOS DHCP client feature.

Certification Level:
This lab is suitable for CCNA certification exam preparation.

Lab Difficulty:
This lab has a difficulty rating of 5/10.

Readiness Assessment:
When you are ready for your certification exam, you should complete this lab in no more than 10 minutes.

> **IMPORTANT NOTE:** In order to test DHCP functionality, you will need a DHCP server configured and be ready to provide IP addressing information. However, this may not be possible unless you have access to live equipment or Packet Tracer, so the purpose of this lab exercise is to be able to configure the IOS DHCP client feature. The solution will provide information on what you would look for if this was a real network with a functioning DHCP server.

Lab Topology:

Please use the following topology to complete this lab exercise:

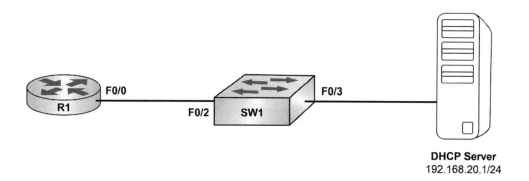

DHCP Server
192.168.20.1/24

Task 1:

Configure hostnames on R1 and Sw1 as illustrated in the topology.

Task 2:

Configure VLAN100 on Sw1 and name it DHCP_VLAN. Assign port Fa0/2 and Fa0/3 to this VLAN. To prevent DHCP request timeouts, enable the ports to automatically transition to the Spanning Tree Forwarding state.

Task 3:

Assuming that the DHCP server is correctly configured, configure R1 F0/0 to receive IP addressing via DHCP. Verify that R1 has received automatic configuration information via DHCP. You can easily configure DHCP settings on a router or Packet Tracer server, which we covered earlier.

LAB C: CONFIGURATION AND VERIFICATION

Task 1:

For reference information on configuring hostnames, please refer to earlier labs.

Task 2:

```
Sw1#config t
Enter configuration commands, one per line.  End with CTRL/Z.
Sw1(config)#vlan100
Sw1(config-vlan)#name DHCP_VLAN
Sw1(config-vlan)#exit
Sw1(config)#interface range fastethernet0/2—3
Sw1(config-if-range)#switchport mode access
Sw1(config-if-range)switchport access vlan100
Sw1(config-if-range)#spanning-tree portfast
%Warning: portfast should only be enabled on ports connected to a
single host. Connecting hubs, concentrators, switches, bridges, etc...
to this interface when portfast is enabled, can cause temporary
bridging loops. Use with CAUTION

%Portfast will be configured in 2 interfaces due to the range command
 but will only have effect when the interfaces are in a non-trunking
mode.

Sw1(config-if-range)#no shutdown
Sw1(config-if-range)#end
Sw1#
```

Task 3:

```
R1#conf t
Enter configuration commands, one per line.  End with CTRL/Z.
R1(config)#int fa0/0
R1(config-if)#ip address dhcp
R1(config-if)#no shutdown
R1(config-if)#end
*Mar  1 02:25:29.029: %LINK-3-UPDOWN: Interface FastEthernet0/0,
changed state to up
*Mar  1 02:25:30.030: %LINEPROTO-5-UPDOWN: Line protocol on Interface
FastEthernet0/0, changed state to up
*Mar  1 02:25:33.164: %DHCP-6-ADDRESS_ASSIGN: Interface FastEthernet0/0
assigned DHCP address 192.168.20.3, mask 255.255.255.0, hostname R1
R1#
```

NOTE: When you see the log message %DHCP-6-ADDRESS_ASSIGN: you know that your device has been assigned an IP address via DHCP. Verify that the interface specified is the one you configured for DHCP.

```
R1#show ip interface fastethernet0/0
FastEthernet0/0 is up, line protocol is up
  Internet address is 192.168.20.3/24
  Broadcast address is 255.255.255.255
  Address determined by DHCP

R1#show dhcp server
  DHCP server: ANY (255.255.255.255)
  Leases:   2
  Offers:   2      Requests: 2     Acks: 2      Naks: 0
  Declines: 0      Releases: 3     Bad:  0
  DNS0:   172.16.1.254,   DNS1:   172.16.2.254
  NBNS0:  10.1.1.254,   NBNS1: 10.2.2.254
  Subnet: 255.255.255.0   DNS Domain: howtonetwork.com
```

NOTE: From the output above, you can see that the DHCP server provided two DNS servers as specified by the line DNS0:   172.16.1.254,   DNS1:   172.16.2.254, as well as two WINS servers, as specified by the line NBNS0:   10.1.1.254,   NBNS1: 10.2.2.254. The subnet mask is /24 and the DNS domain provided is howtonetwork. com. If a workstation, such as a Windows-based computer, were provided IP addressing information from the same DHCP server and you issued ipconfig /all at the command prompt, you would see:

```
Ethernet adapter Local Area Connection 2:

        Connection-specific DNS Suffix  . : howtonetwork.net
        Description . . . . . . . . . . . : Broadcom NetXtreme 57xx Gigabit Cont
roller
        Physical Address. . . . . . . . . : 00-1D-09-D4-02-38
        Dhcp Enabled. . . . . . . . . . . : Yes
        Autoconfiguration Enabled . . . . : Yes
        IP Address. . . . . . . . . . . . : 192.168.20.4
        Subnet Mask . . . . . . . . . . . : 255.255.255.0
        Default Gateway . . . . . . . . . : 192.168.20.1
        DHCP Server . . . . . . . . . . . : 192.168.20.1
        DNS Servers . . . . . . . . . . . : 172.16.1.254
                                            172.16.2.254
        Primary WINS Server . . . . . . . : 10.1.1.254
        Secondary WINS Server . . . . . . : 10.2.2.254
        Lease Obtained. . . . . . . . . . : Sunday, April 19, 2009 8:50:36 PM
        Lease Expires . . . . . . . . . . : Sunday, April 26, 2009 8:50:36 PM
Ethernet adapter Local Area Connection:

        Media State . . . . . . . . . . . : Media disconnected
        Description . . . . . . . . . . . : Bluetooth Personal Area Network
        Physical Address. . . . . . . . . : 00-21-86-42-0A-8A
```

LAB D: CONFIGURING COMMAND ALIASES ON IOS DEVICES

Lab Objective:
The objective of this lab exercise is for you to learn and understand how to configure and use aliases within the Cisco IOS.

Lab Purpose:
Configuring and using aliases is a fundamental skill. Aliases are customized names assigned to Cisco IOS commands that can be used in place of long commands. As a Cisco engineer, as well as in the Cisco CCNA exam, you will be expected to know how to configure and use aliases on Cisco IOS devices.

Certification Level:
This lab is suitable for CCNA certification exam preparation.

Lab Difficulty:
This lab has a difficulty rating of 3/10.

Readiness Assessment:
When you are ready for your certification exam, you should complete this lab in no more than 10 minutes.

Lab Topology:
Please use any single router or switch to complete this lab.

Task 1:
Configure a hostname on your router or switch.

Task 2:
Configure the following aliases on your device:

ALIAS:	REAL Cisco IOS COMMAND
int:	`show ip interfaces brief`
save:	`copy running-config startup-config`
proc:	`show processes cpu`

Task 3:
Verify your configured aliases. Now test your aliases and validate that they operate as expected.

LAB D: CONFIGURATION AND VERIFICATION

Task 1:

For reference information on configuring hostnames, please refer to earlier labs.

Task 2:

```
R1#conf t
Enter configuration commands, one per line.  End with CTRL/Z.
R1(config)#alias exec int show ip interface brief
R1(config)#alias exec save copy running-config startup-config
R1(config)#alias exec proc show processes cpu
R1(config)#end
R1#
```

Task 3:

```
R1#show aliases
Exec mode aliases:
  h                     help
  lo                    logout
  p                     ping
  r                     resume
  s                     show
  u                     undebug
  un                    undebug
  w                     where
  int                   show ip interface brief
  save                  copy running-config startup-config
  proc                  show processes cpu

R1#int
Interface       IP-Address  OK? Method Status                Protocol
FastEthernet0/0 unassigned  YES manual administratively down down
Serial0/0       unassigned  YES NVRAM  administratively down down
Serial0/1       unassigned  YES manual administratively down down

R1#save
Destination filename [startup-config]?
Building configuration...
[OK]

R1#proc
CPU utilization for five seconds: 0%/0%; one minute: 4%; five minutes:
1%
 PID Runtime(ms)   Invoked   uSecs   5Sec   1Min   5Min TTY Process
   1          0         2       0  0.00%  0.00%  0.00%   0 Chunk Manager
   2          0       110       0  0.00%  0.00%  0.00%   0 Load Meter

[output truncated for brevity]
```

LAB E: CONFIGURING LOCAL NAME RESOLUTION ON CISCO IOS DEVICES

Lab Objective:
The objective of this lab exercise is for you to learn and understand how to configure name resolution on Cisco IOS devices.

Lab Purpose:
Configuring name resolution on Cisco IOS devices is a fundamental skill. Name resolution can be used to provide hostnames to Layer 3 address mapping instead of DNS services. It is typically used in small networks with a few internetwork devices. As a Cisco engineer, as well as in the Cisco CCNA exam, you will be expected to know how to configure name resolution on Cisco IOS devices.

Certification Level:
This lab is suitable for CCNA certification exam preparation.

Lab Difficulty:
This lab has a difficulty rating of 5/10.

Readiness Assessment:
When you are ready for your certification exam, you should complete this lab in no more than 10 minutes.

Lab Topology:
Please use the following topology to complete this lab:

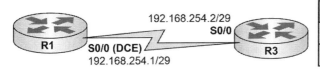

INTERFACE	IP ADDRESS
Loopback0	10.0.0.3/24
Loopback1	10.1.1.3/24

Task 1:
Configure a hostname on your router.

Task 2:
Configure R1 to provide clocking to R3 at rate of 256 Kbps. Next, configure the IP addresses on R1 and R3 as illustrated in the network topology.

Task 3:

Configure R1 with a static default route pointing to R3. Next, configure the two Loopback interfaces on R2 as illustrated in the network topology.

Task 4:

Configure local host name resolution on R1 for R3 Loopback0 and Loopback1. Use the IP addresses of the Loopback interfaces and the hostnames R3-LOOP0 and R3-LOOP1, respectively, on R1.

Task 5:

Test your configurations by pinging R3-LOOP0 and R3-LOOP1. These hostnames should be resolved to the IP addresses of the Loopback0 and Loopback1 interfaces on R3, respectively.

LAB E: CONFIGURATION AND VERIFICATION

Task 1:

For reference information on configuring hostnames, please refer to earlier labs.

Task 2:

For reference information on configuring DCE clocking, please refer to earlier labs.

Task 3:

```
R1#conf t
Enter configuration commands, one per line.  End with CTRL/Z.
R1(config)#ip route 0.0.0.0 0.0.0.0 serial 0/0 192.168.254.2
R1(config)#end
R1#

R3#conf t
Enter configuration commands, one per line.  End with CTRL/Z.
R3(config)#int lo0
R3(config-if)#ip add 10.0.0.3 255.255.255.0
R3(config-if)#exit
R3(config)#int lo1
R3(config-if)#ip add 10.1.1.3 255.255.255.0
R3(config-if)#exit
R3(config)#end
R3#
```

Task 4:

```
R1#conf t
Enter configuration commands, one per line.  End with CTRL/Z.
R1(config)#ip host R3-LOOP0 10.0.0.3
R1(config)#ip host R3-LOOP1 10.1.1.3
R1(config)#end
R1#
R1#show host
Default domain is not set
Name/address lookup uses domain service
Name servers are 255.255.255.255

Codes: UN - unknown, EX - expired, OK - OK, ??—revalidate,
       temp - temporary, perm—permanent,
       NA - Not Applicable None - Not defined

Host                     Port  Flags      Age Type  Address(es)
R3-LOOP0                 None  (perm, OK)  0   IP    10.0.0.3
R3-LOOP1                 None  (perm, OK)  0   IP    10.1.1.3
```

Task 5:

```
R1#ping R3-LOOP0

Type escape sequence to abort.
Sending 5, 100-byte ICMP Echos to 10.0.0.3, timeout is 2 seconds:
!!!!!
Success rate is 100 percent (5/5), round-trip min/avg/max = 8/10/16 ms

R1#ping R3-LOOP1

Type escape sequence to abort.
Sending 5, 100-byte ICMP Echos to 10.1.1.3, timeout is 2 seconds:
!!!!!
Success rate is 100 percent (5/5), round-trip min/avg/max = 8/11/12 ms
```

LAB F: CONFIGURING DOMAIN NAME RESOLUTION ON CISCO IOS DEVICES

Lab Objective:

The objective of this lab exercise is for you to learn and understand how to configure DNS on Cisco IOS devices.

Lab Purpose:

Configuring DNS on Cisco IOS devices is a fundamental skill. DNS provides hostnames to Layer 3 address resolution. DNS servers are typically used in large networks with many hosts and internetworking devices. As a Cisco engineer, as well as in the Cisco CCNA exam, you will be expected to know how to configure DNS on Cisco IOS devices.

Certification Level:

This lab is suitable for CCENT and CCNA certification exam preparation.

Lab Difficulty:

This lab has a difficulty rating of 3/10.

Readiness Assessment:

When you are ready for your certification exam, you should complete this lab in no more than 5 minutes.

> **IMPORTANT NOTE:** The objective of this lab is to simply familiarize you with the steps required to configure a Cisco IOS device to communicate with a DNS server. Because there will be no real DNS server configured against which to perform testing, the sole objective of this lab is command familiarity.

Lab Topology:

Please use any single router or switch to complete this lab.

Task 1:

Configure a hostname on your router or switch.

Task 2:

Configure your router or switch as part of the howtonetwork.com domain. For name resolution, your device should forward traffic to DNS servers 172.16.1.254 or 172.17.1.254.

LAB F: CONFIGURATION AND VERIFICATION

Task 1:

For reference information on configuring hostnames, please refer to earlier labs.

Task 2:

```
R1#conf t
Enter configuration commands, one per line.  End with CTRL/Z.
R1(config)#ip domain-name howtonetwork.com
R1(config)#ip name-server 172.16.1.254 172.17.1.254
R1(config)#ip domain-lookup
R1(config)#end
R1#
```

> **NOTE:** If an actual DNS server was available and was providing name resolution, you could ping or connect to devices based on their hostnames as illustrated below:

```
R1#ping R3

Translating "R3.howtonetwork.com"...domain server (172.16.1.254) [OK]

Type escape sequence to abort.
Sending 5, 100-byte ICMP Echos to 192.168.254.3, timeout is 2 seconds:
!!!!!
Success rate is 100 percent (5/5), round-trip min/avg/max = 8/11/16 ms

R1#telnet R3
Translating "R3"...domain server (172.16.1.254) [OK]
Trying R3.howtonetwork.com (192.168.254.3)... Open

User Access Verification

Password:
R3#
```

LAB G: CONFIGURING COMMAND AND PASSWORD PRIVILEGE LEVELS ON DEVICES

Lab Objective:
The objective of this lab exercise is for you to learn and understand how to configure privilege levels for certain commands and passwords on Cisco IOS devices.

Lab Purpose:
Configuring user privilege levels on Cisco IOS devices is a fundamental skill. Users can be configured with certain privilege levels that allow them to execute certain commands. As a Cisco engineer, as well as in the Cisco CCNA exam, you will be expected to know how to configure user privilege levels on Cisco IOS devices.

Certification Level:
This lab is suitable for CCNA certification exam preparation.

Lab Difficulty:
This lab has a difficulty rating of 6/10.

Readiness Assessment:
When you are ready for your certification exam, you should complete this lab in no more than 10 minutes.

Lab Topology:
Please use any single Cisco IOS router or switch to complete the following lab.

Task 1:
Configure a hostname of your liking on your Cisco IOS router or switch. It may be easier to use a router for this lab.

Task 2:
Configure the secret level 15 password cisco456 on your device.

Task 3:
Issue the `show ip interface brief` command from User Exec mode (i.e., where you see the `>` symbol after the device name). Verify that this command works and you do see the current interface status.

Task 4:

Configure the `show ip interface brief` command to work only for users with Level 15 access.

Task 5:

If you are connected via the console, type in the `disable` command to return to User Exec mode (i.e., where you see the > symbol after the device hostname). Next, issue the `show ip interfaces brief` command. If you have configured your device correctly, this command will no longer work in User Exec mode.

Task 6:

Next, type in enable and type in the Level 15 password cisco456. Attempt to issue the `show ip interface` brief command. If your configuration is correct, this will work.

LAB G: CONFIGURATION AND VERIFICATION

Task 1:

For reference information on configuring hostnames, please refer to earlier labs.

Task 2:

```
R1#conf t
Enter configuration commands, one per line.  End with CTRL/Z.
R1(config)#enable secret level 15 cisco456
R1(config)#^Z
R1#
```

Task 3:

```
R1>show ip interface brief
Interface      IP-Address      OK? Method Status                     Protocol
Ethernet0/0    unassigned      YES manual administratively down down
Serial0/0      unassigned      YES manual administratively down down
Serial0/1      unassigned      YES manual administratively down down
```

Task 4:

```
R1#conf t
Enter configuration commands, one per line.  End with CTRL/Z.
R1(config)#privilege exec level 15 show ip interface brief
R1(config)#end
R1#
```

NOTE: The `privilege exec` command is used to set different privilege levels for commands. By default, the `show ip interfaces brief` command has a privilege level of 1, which means that it can be issued from the User Exec prompt (i.e., the `>` prompt after the hostname of the device).

Task 5:

```
R1#disable
R1>show ip interface brief
    ^
% Invalid input detected at "^" marker.
```

Task 6:

```
R1>enable
Password:
R1#show ip interface brief
Interface      IP-Address      OK? Method Status                     Protocol
Ethernet0/0    unassigned      YES manual administratively down down
Serial0/0      unassigned      YES manual administratively down down
Serial0/1      unassigned      YES manual administratively down down
```

LAB H: ENABLING HTTP ACCESS TO CISCO IOS DEVICES

Lab Objective:
The objective of this lab exercise is for you to learn and understand how to enable HTTP access to devices.

Lab Purpose:
HTTP access to Cisco IOS devices is a fundamental skill. Using HTTP, it is possible to view information on a Cisco IOS device as well as perform basic configuration tasks. Keep in mind, however, that this is not SDM configuration but a legacy means of HTTP access that pre-dates SDM. As a Cisco engineer, as well as in the Cisco CCNA exam, you will be expected to know how to configure HTTP access to legacy Cisco IOS devices.

SDM (Security Device Manager) it was a graphical method of configuring Cisco routers. It has been replaced by Cisco Configuration Professional (CCP), which isn't tested in the CCNA exam.

Certification Level:
This lab is suitable for CCNA certification exam preparation.

Lab Difficulty:
This lab has a difficulty rating of 6/10.

Readiness Assessment:
When you are ready for your certification exam, you should complete this lab in no more than 10 minutes.

> **IMPORTANT NOTE:** The objective of this lab is to simply familiarize you with the steps required to configure a Cisco IOS device to allow HTTP access. You may not have a PC connected to the device to test this configuration; however, the solution will provide relevant screenshots on what you would expect to see when you access a device via HTTP.

Lab Topology:

Please use the following topology to complete this lab:

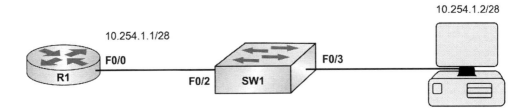

Task 1:

Configure hostnames on R1 and Sw1 as illustrated in the topology.

Task 2:

Configure VLAN20 on Sw1 and assign it the name HTTP_VLAN. Next, configure ports FastEthernet0/2 and FastEthernet0/3 on Sw1 as access ports within this VLAN.

Task 3:

Configure the IP address of your router and PC as illustrated in the topology.

Task 4:

Configure R1 to allow HTTP access. HTTP users should authenticate locally on the router using the username ADMIN and the password CISCO. Ensure that the user has the highest privilege level in Cisco IOS. Using the Web browser on the PC, HTTP to the IP address 10.254.1.1 and verify that you logged in successfully.

LAB H: CONFIGURATION AND VERIFICATION

Task 1:

For reference information on configuring hostnames, please refer to earlier labs.

Task 2:

For reference information on configuring and verifying VLANs, please refer to earlier labs.

Task 3:

For reference information on configuring IP interfaces, please refer to earlier labs.

Task 4:
```
R1#config te
Enter configuration commands, one per line.  End with CTRL/Z.
R1(config)#ip http server
R1(config)#ip http authentication local
R1(config)#username ADMIN privilege 15 password CISCO
R1(config)#end
```

NOTE: Because you will be accessing the device via HTTP, ensure that you set the privilege level of the HTTP administrator to 15. This is a commonly forgotten task. Remember it.

NOTE: If you had access to the device via a PC in your lab, expect to see something similar to the following when you connect to it via HTTP:

Cisco Systems

Accessing Cisco 2610 "R1"

Show diagnostic log - display the diagnostic log.
Monitor the router - HTML access to the command line interface at level 0,1,2,3,4,5,6,7,8,9,10,11,12,13,14,15
Connectivity test - ping the nameserver.

Show tech-support - display information commonly needed by tech support.
Extended Ping - Send extended ping commands.

VPN Device Manager (VDM) - Configure and monitor Virtual Private Networks (VPNs) through the web interface.

Help resources

1. CCO at www.cisco.com - Cisco Connection Online, including the Technical Assistance Center (TAC).
2. tac@cisco.com - e-mail the TAC.
3. **1-800-553-2447 or +1-408-526-7209** - phone the TAC.
4. cs-html@cisco.com - e-mail the HTML interface development group.

You could then navigate using the browser and perform basic configurations as well as basic diagnostic testing on the device.

APPENDICES

APPENDIX A: CABLING AND CONFIGURING A FRAME RELAY SWITCH FOR TWO ROUTERS

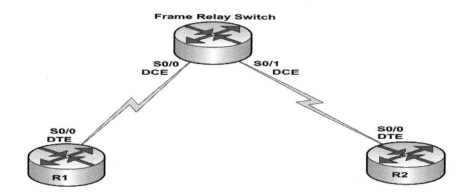

Figure 1: Frame relay physical lab cabling

Frame relay switch configuration:

```
hostname FR-SWITCH
!
frame-relay switching
!
interface serial0/0
description "Connected to R1 Serial0/0"
encapsulation frame-relay
frame-relay intf-type dce
frame-relay route 111 interface serial0/1 222
clock rate 256000
no shutdown
!
interface serial0/1
description "Connected to R2 Serial0/0"
encapsulation frame-relay
frame-relay intf-type dce
frame-relay route 222 interface serial0/0 111
clock rate 256000
no shutdown
!
end
```

NOTE: This frame relay switch configuration is based on the configuration of a Cisco 2610 IOS router with two Serial interfaces. The router is running a basic Enterprise IOS image.

APPENDIX B: CABLING AND CONFIGURING A FRAME RELAY SWITCH FOR THREE ROUTERS

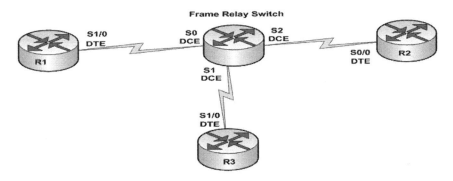

Figure 1: Frame relay physical lab cabling

Frame relay switch configuration:

```
hostname FR-SWITCH
!
frame-relay switching
interface serial0
description "Connected to R1 Serial1/0"
encapsulation frame-relay
frame-relay intf-type dce
frame-relay route 103 interface serial1 301
frame-relay route 102 interface serial2 201
clock rate 800000
no shutdown
!
interface serial1
description "Connected to R3 Serial1/0"
encapsulation frame-relay
frame-relay intf-type dce
frame-relay route 301 interface serial0 103
clock rate 800000
no shutdown
!
serial2
description "Connected to R2 Serial0/0"
encapsulation frame-relay
frame-relay intf-type dce
frame-relay route 201 interface serial0 102
clock rate 115200
no shutdown
!
end
```

NOTE: This frame relay switch configuration is based on the configuration of a Cisco 2521 IOS router with four Serial interfaces. The router is running a basic Enterprise IOS image.

Made in the USA
Middletown, DE
27 May 2019